EASTERN EDGES: NORTH

Burbage, Millstone and Beyond

BMC
thebmc.co.uk

Volume Editor: David Simmonite
Series Editor: Niall Grimes
Researched and compiled by a team of
guidebook volunteers

EASTERN EDGES: NORTH —
Burbage, Millstone and Beyond
The definitive guide —
All the routes, all the bouldering

Copyright © 2005 British Mountaineering Council

Published by:
British Mountaineering Council,
177–179 Burton Road,
Manchester M20 2BB.

First printed 2005
ISBN 0-903908-77-8

Cover photo: James Pearson on Sentinel, Burbage North (page 92).
Photo: David Simmonite.

Produced and typeset by Niall Grimes /
British Mountaineering Council
based on original designs by
Vertebrate Graphics, Sheffield,
www.v-graphics.co.uk
Printed in Slovenia by Compass Press

BMC Participation Statement

Important note

Table of Contents

A climber battling his way up the ferocious crack on Billy Whiz, one of the best E2s in the area (page 129). Photo: Simon Jacques.

Introduction

Prior to editing this guidebook I had the good fortune to climb on all the crags in the guide, be it the popular edges such as Millstone and Bamford or scratching around in the undergrowth at less fashionable venues such as Wyming Brook and Ladybower Quarry, even venturing to Stannington Ruffs twice albeit with a gap of 18 years. With this knowledge of the area it seemed a logical progression to take on the job as editor.

From the outset a complete rewrite was in order and with it a chance to realign the grades in the guide. Some of the crags had gained a very stiff reputation, notably Wharncliffe, as well as keeping the character that each crag holds. As Sheffield is deemed by many as the centre of the climbing universe so the guide needed handling with the utmost care and respect. To complete such a task it was vitally important to recruit a team that I could trust and share my vision and I can't thank them enough for the help and encouragement that they have provided. It's been a long road made easier by working with fantastic people.

Having completed the last guide in the 'old style' it is great to be carrying on the impressive strides made recently with the 'new style' Staffordshire guide and on this I must thank BMC man Niall Grimes for his effort, including layout work, photodiagrams and preparing the whole caboodle for print. It proves that with the right spirit we can evolve and meet the challenge head on of the commercial guidebook producers who well and truly rattled the cage and made everyone roll up their sleeves for the better. It points to a healthy future for the traditional volunteer guidebook ethos and hopefully silences a few critics. Long may it continue.

Cramming so much into this book, including adding comprehensive bouldering and extra crags in Millstone and Lawrencefield has led to a delay in its production but I feel that the wait was worthwhile and has given everyone a bumper guide. It is something I'm immensely proud to have completed.

Being a Sheffielder born and bred I cut my teeth on the gritstone crags on my doorstep, following in the footsteps of countless famous climbers, many of whom I've since had the opportunity to meet and climb with. Sat here with a beer writing this it brought some memories to the fore. In the early days I couldn't drive let alone afford a car, so it was either blag a lift or more often catch the 272 bus to Fox House or the Surprise View, or the 51 to Lodge Moor (ah, the days of cheap public transport) and walk (the horror!) to the crag of choice. Even in the depths of winter and no matter what the weather we would head out. I remember doing a new route at Lawrencefield called The Big Red Jacket after my duvet jacket that I'd picked up second-hand and was two sizes too big. I may have looked silly but I was snug and warmer than anyone else. We even reverted to using hand warmers in our chalk bags just to keep climbing. It's amazing how soft we've all become with the advent of climbing walls.

It got me thinking which crag I'd climbed on most? Only one answer, the small but perfectly formed Burbage North. Ideal for those much needed after work sessions due to its close proximity to Sheffield. My first VS, my first Extreme, they all taken place on these edges and no matter where I've climbed in the world I still can't get enough of them. It's where the heart is and I hope it grabs yours. Enjoy.

David Simmonite, Sheffield, November 2005

Photo: Adam Long

Climbers on Curving Crack, VS 4c, Bamford Edge (page 246), one of the finest crags in the guide.
Photo: Niall Grimes.

Acknowledgements

A debt of gratitude is due to everyone who made this guidebook possible. The most humble apologies to anyone who belongs on this list and does not appear.

Crag writers (and everything else)
Percy Bishton, Stephen Coughlan, Niall Grimes, Paul Harrison, Frank Horsman, Simon Jacques, Martin Kocsis, David Law, Dave Musgrove, David Simmonite, Mike Snell, Graham Sutton, Sarah Whitehouse, Tony Whitehouse.

Photographers who supplied their images free of charge to make this guide such a visual feast (and cheers to all those who have posed for shots).
Stuart Brooks, John Coefield, Brian Cropper, Alex Ekins, Niall Grimes, Simon Jacques, Adam Long, Alex Messenger, Pete O'Donovan, Ian Parnell, Dave Parry, David Simmonite, Ian Smith, Nick Smith, Graham Sutton. Thanks to Alex Messenger and Berie Stott for additional scanning. All crag photography, illustrations and uncredited photographs: Niall Grimes.

BMC Guidebook Committee
Dave Garnett, Niall Grimes, Martin Kocsis, Dave Turnbull, Ken Vickers, Ken Wilson.

All the people who made general input by contributing written sections, route checking and offering advice and other support
John Allen, Roy Bennett (deceased), Mick Carr, Steve Clarke, Chris Craggs, Nigel Edley, Al Evans, Henry Folkard, Jon Fullwood, Mark Goodwin, John Horscroft, Mark Hundleby, Alan Jacques, Nik Jennings, Adam Long, Bunny McCullough, Ian Mount, Dave Parry, James Pearson, Peter Robins, Lynn Robinson, 'Sandy' Sanderson, Tony Sawbridge, Sarah Smart, Simon Triger, John Welford, Richard Wheeldon, Allen Williams.

The access team who do invaluable work to keep the crags open for you to enjoy.
Henry Folkard, Bunny McCullough.

Script checking and proof reading
All the crag writers, Les Ainsworth, John Coefield, Rae Cowie, Ross Cowie, Dave Gregory, Peter Harrison, Paul Mitchell, Darren Pallett, Ian Smith.

And enormous gratitude for all the past guidebook writers, editors, artists and photographers without whom we simply wouldn't have such detailed definitive guides. The climbing community is forever in your debt.

Climbing Notes

Routes and bouldering
This is a guide to routes and boulder problems. To differentiate, routes are identified with a blue circle ●, boulder problems are identified with a red ●. When a route or problem occurs that is not worthy of an individual entry, a pale blue ● or red ● circle will appear before it to indicate it.

Route grades
The system of grading for routes in this volume is the traditional British style, a combination of adjectival and technical grades, and assumes the leader has a normal rack, including standard camming devices, nuts, slings, quickdraws etc. The adjectival grade is the first part of the grade, and attempts to give a sense of the overall difficulty of a climb. This will be influenced by many aspects, including seriousness, sustainedness, technical difficulty, exposure, strenuousness, rock quality, and any other less tangible aspects which lend difficulty to a pitch. It is an open-ended system, and currently runs from Easy to E10. Along the way, and in ascending order, are Moderate (Mod.), Difficult (D), Hard Difficult (HD), Very Difficult (VD), Hard Very Difficult (HVD), Severe (S), Hard Severe (HS), Very Severe (VS), Hard Very Severe (HVS) and Extremely Severe, the last category being split into E1, E2, E3 etc.

The second part of the grade, the technical grade, is there to give an indication of the hardest move to be found on the route, irrespective of how many of them there might be, how strenuous it is, or how frightened you are when you do it. They come onto the scale somewhere around 4a, a savage example of elitism that must have 3c merchants foaming at the mouth, and currently run thus; 4a, 4b, 4c, 5a, 5b, 5c, 6a, 6b, 6c, 7a, 7b. By the time you get to E10 7b, you should start to have an idea of how the system works.

Stars and daggers
For those who need them, stars (none, one, two or three) have been used in this guide to indicate quality. However, on most of these crags, every route is worth doing. Where this is not true it will be clearly stated in the text. An un-starred route is by no means a bad route, and can give as good an experience as a three-star route. Route descriptions also point out the best features of any climb. Read through these and see what appeals to you. Try not to be too guided by stars alone.

Certain routes will have a dagger † symbol by them. This indicates a route where the guidebook team may have doubt about some aspect of the route, such as being unsure of the line, or having an unconfirmed grade due to insufficient repeats. It is not meant to cast doubt on a first ascent.

Ethics and style
The two most basic rules here are be honest, and don't damage the rock. Beyond that, it's entirely up to you, although in terms of style, some ascents are considered better than others. The best is still the on-sight flash, climbing the route first try with no falls and no helpful information. Few hard routes are done in this fashion, many higher grade routes being completed after some form of top-rope practise. However, this is currently acceptable, as long as the final result is a clean lead of the route, ideally placing protection *en route*. Many routes have also become established with side runners for protection. Where this is so, it will be mentioned in the text, and the grade will reflect this fact. And finally, on a happier note, aid points and rest points have now disappeared from the areas covered in this book, and it is unlikely that a new route containing either would be seen as acceptable.

Fixed protection
Fixed protection – bolts, pegs, threads or hammered wires – is considered unacceptable on natural grit. Never, ever, think about placing any, be it on a new route or any subsequent ascent. Historically, it has been tolerated in the quarries, although placing any for a first ascent is still to be avoided if possible, and is considered unacceptable on an established route. Where it occurs, treat with care.

New routes, first ascents etc.
Details of first ascents, including name, grade, individuals involved, date and style of ascent, as well as contact details, should be sent to: guides@thebmc.co.uk. Another first ascent resource can be found at www.ukclimbing.com.

Gritstone – this precious rock
Climb the rock as it is. Do not be tempted to shape it to suit your inadequate skills or to gouge out protection placements where none exist, so leave your wire brush and chisel at home. Brushing with anything other than a toothbrush to remove excess chalk is rarely necessary. Even on new routes brushing should be only done with a nylon brush to remove lichen, moss and algae only (and only on crucial holds) and should never go so far as to expose pink new rock. Once the hard exterior layer is removed, the softer sandy interior erodes very rapidly. If you cannot do a route or problem in its existing state, go away and train harder or accept that you aren't good enough – yet! If new routeing please remember these ethics and in addition do not garden or remove vegetation.

Bouldering notes

Compiling these problems has been quite a task. Traditionally, guides have recorded a select few – the bigger and the more famous. Allen Williams's classic book *Peak Bouldering* and his Rockfax *Peak Bouldering*, and Jason Myers's *Peak Bouldering Plus* guides were a major new step in British climbing guides, and the first to document the major circuits in the area. The authors acknowledge the help that Allen's and Jason's work has been. This new guide covers all these circuits, and a good many more besides, and on top of that, all the problems dotted along crags and odd bits of rock throughout the area.

Bouldering grades
The V system is used in this guide, with problems running from V0-, V0, V0+, V1, V2, V3… V11. This has been used over the other popular system, the Fontainebleau system for several reasons: the Fontainebleau system is more easily confused with the English technical grades that are used in this guide, adding further distractions to the already crowded grade market; few climbers are familiar with the Fontainebleau system below 6a, and grades for easier problems become meaningless; the V system was used in the last guide. At the end of the day, a grade is there to indicate the relative difficulty of a problem. In this respect, the V grade works perfectly. In other words, most people will find a V3 harder than most V2s, and easier than most V4s. There, what more could you ask for. In addition, English technical grades are given in brackets after the V grade. This is more to help differentiate in the lower grades, and to help lower grade climbers who are unused to bouldering grades, and becomes more theoretical as technical grades exceed 6b. That being said, however, there is still a significant body who see the English technical grade as ideal for isolating single moves. For help, see the grade comparrison table inside the back cover.

Highballs
If a boulder problem occurs with a full grade in brackets as opposed to just the technical grade, this means it is a highball problem, with aspects of a route about it. That is, you might not want to fall off! The definition between problems and routes has been who is most likely to do the climb. If it is a group of boulderers out with pads and spotters, a climb will probably be recorded as a boulder problem. If it is traditional climbers with a rope and rack, it will be recorded as a route. Use your sense.

Names and stars
Many of the problems in this guide have been given names. These names are in no way an attempt to 'claim' these problems, just a way of identifying them. A few first ascents have been recorded, but in general, trying to get first ascent information for problems would seem like more trouble than it is worth, and in a way, not in keeping with the spirit of the sport. Due to the subjective nature of quality, stars have not been used for boulder problems. A clear indication of how good an area is will be given in that area's introduction. As for individual problems, if it appeals, climb it.

Bouldering mats
The growing use of pads for bouldering has many positive benefits, protecting both boulderers and the environment. As such, their use is a welcome trend.

They are also commonly used to take the sting out of bolder routes. This is entirely your choice, and in many ways a rational one, but remember the effect their use will have on the grade of a climb. It makes them easier.

Environmental considerations for boulderers

All climbing has an environmental impact. However, boulderers may wish to bear some special points in mind. In a session, a problem can be climbed many more times than a route. This leads to an erosion rate greater than that seen on longer climbs. Try to do all you can to minimise the erosion. Brushing is the most obvious issue. Wire brushes can easily remove the tough outer skin of the rock, leaving the soft unprotected rock beneath to wear away. If you must brush, use a soft, nylon-bristled brush. Always clean your feet before climbing, and climb well to avoid scratching about on the surface. Use as little chalk as possible. Never use Fontainebleau style resin or 'pof'. It ruins problems. Never ever attempt to alter the rock in any way. Don't apply ugly tick marks to the rock. Use a bouldering mat if possible. Try to visit different areas. Generally, always be a good ninja.

Previous Editions of this Guide

1934 – Wharncliffe Crags by Carl Brunning and the Sheffield University Mountaineering Club
1951 – Climbs on Gritstone Volume 2: Sheffield Area, edited by Eric Byne
1956 – Climbs on Gritstone Volume 2: Revised Edition, Sheffield Area, edited by Eric Byne
1957 – Climbs on Gritstone Volume 4: Further Developments in the Peak District, edited by Eric Byne and Wilfred White
1964 – Rock Climbs in the Peak, Second Series, Volume 1, The Sheffield-Stanage Area, edited by Eric Byne
1965 – Rock Climbs in the Peak, Volume 3, The Sheffield-Froggatt Area, edited by Eric Byne
1976 – Rock Climbs in the Peak, Third Series, Volume 1, The Stanage Area, edited by Dave Gregory
1978 – Rock Climbs in the Peak, Volume 3, The Froggatt Area, edited by Dave Gregory
1983 – Peak District Climbs, Fourth Series, Volume 1, Stanage Millstone, edited by Geoff Milburn
1989 – Peak District Climbs, Fifth Series, Volume 1, Stanage, edited by Graham Hoey
1989 – Peak District Climbs, Fifth Series, Volume 3, Froggatt, edited by Geoff Milburn and Keith Sharples

Kim Leyland on the classic Burbage highball, Life in a Radioactive Dustbin, V5 (page 8).
Photo: John Coefield.

Access and Conservation

This guide covers crags in widely different locations. In general there are no access problems on moorland crags where access is now guaranteed under the Countryside and Rights of Way (2000) Act (CRoW), conversely there are quite a lot of access problems in disused quarries and urban fringe locations not mapped as open access. But all is not quite that simple.

Huge swathes of moorland are owned by Sheffield City Council (Burbage, Millstone, Houndkirk) and the National Trust (Longshaw). All moorland is farmed, and most of it is nationally important for ground nesting birds and has been designated a Site of Special Scientific Interest (SSSI). CRoW mapping is not complete in areas covered by the guide outside the Peak National Park. and boundaries of open country are not, therefore,defined as this guide

Fin the Dog – a boulderer, of course. Photo: Richard the Human

goes to press. Whatever our access rights, we all retain responsibility to respect other peoples' property, their usage of it and the wildlife and vegetation.

CRoW does permit landowners to close open access land for different periods of time for a variety of reasons, and where this happens temporary signs will be erected at key access points and notified to the Open Access Contact Centre on 0845 100 3298 or the land managers section of www.countryside-access.gov.uk. You must always respect such signs. Four things are particularly sensitive:

Fire
If you see a moorland fire that is not a controlled burning (normally late winter or early spring) notify the emergency services at once. But you can also help prevent the cause of fire, be it the embered remains of someone's camp fire (which should never have been lit in the first place) or a smouldering cigarette stub someone thought they had rubbed out in the peat two days ago. If you see a group behaving badly, it's not someone else's problem, it's yours. Say your piece.

Ground nesting birds
The key period is the nesting season, during approximately mid-March to the end of June, with some variation from season to season and species to species. But even after leaving the nest, fledglings will remain in the area for some months. It is good practice to keep to established paths and avoid disturbance in untrammeled places. The BMC may agree voluntary restrictions for a minimum period to protect a specific nest. These will be discretely indicated on site and if you come across one - sorry, but be disappointed: your preferred choice of route for the day is not an option. The Wildlife and Countryside (1981) Act, plus various amendments to it, provide for harsh penalties for anyone who disturbs a wild bird or damages any wild bird's nest.

Dogs
This is a huge problem for farmers and land managers and one that is getting worse. And, of course,

it's not actually your well-trained and well-behaved hound that is the issue, but someone else's. herefore, it is a good idea to keep dogs on a lead, especially during the nesting period from the end of March to the end of June. A free running dog is not an issue in November when there are no sheep, no lambs and no birds about, but it is a very major issue in spring and summer – and again there are possible legal penalties. Play your part; if someone else's dog – not even a climber's – is causing trouble to live-stock or wildlife, tell them to get it on the lead or get it off the moor fast. Never mind what you may be called for your pains. CRoW allows for special regulation in respect of grouse moors, where all dogs may be banned at all times for periods of five years.

Vegetation
Gardening on crags and routes can lead to problems as it is a criminal offence under the 1981 Act. Please act responsibly. In your everyday activities, please be careful of the little plants, lichens, mosses, liverworts, as you are of vascular plants.

Old quarries and urban fringe crags
These are not included in open access agreements. Most are in private ownership and for many there are no formal access agreements. You have no right to enter or climb in them. So be tactful and be discreet. The BMC has negotiated access with individual owners for major sites like Rivelin with some difficulty and you neglect the letter of the simple access notes given under each crag at your peril – and everyone else's too. A major and justified concern for many land owners is insurance liability rather than an anti-climber bias per se, but there are also wildlife and vegetation issues on many sites. If you do have difficulty anywhere, the best advice is to withdraw quietly and give the BMC (tel: 0870 0104878) a ring or an email (access@thebmc.co.uk) with details of your experience.

Bunny McCullough

Mountain Rescue and First Aid

Dial 999 and ask for Police – Mountain Rescue. Briefly describe the nature of the incident and give the crag name and OS map reference as listed at the start of each crag section.

The Police will co-ordinate the Mountain Rescue team and, if appropriate, the air ambulance that is available for evacuations from the crag. The local team is based in Edale. Although they should not be contacted directly for call-outs, they are very happy to hear from anyone wishing to support their vol-untary efforts:
Edale Mountain Rescue Team,
PO Box 6490
Bakewell
DE45 1XR
info@edalemountainrescue.co.uk

FIRST AID in case of ACCIDENT
1. **If spinal injuries** or **head injuries** are suspected **do not move the patient** without skilled help, ex-cept to maintain breathing and circulation.
2. **If breathing has stopped**, clear airways and commence **CPR** (cardio-pulmonary resuscitation). **Do not stop** until expert opinion diagnoses death.
3. **Stop bleeding** by applying direct pressure.
4. **Summon help**.

These are the basic principles of first aid. If you climb at all regularly, you should seriously consider taking a first aid course.

Visitor's Information

Accommodation
There are several camp sites in the Hope Valley all of which are no more than a 20-minute car journey from most of the crags described in this guide, the exception being the Wharncliffe Crags that lie to the east on the other side of Sheffield.

The most popular climbers' camp site is **North Lees**, situated a few minutes drive from Hathersage (01433 650838). The camp site is run by the Peak Park and is fully equipped with toilets, showers etc. In the summer and particularly at weekends you will need to book in advance – discount rates are available for people who have travelled by public transport but some form of proof (i.e. a ticket) will be required.

Another popular spot is the **Eric Byne Memorial Camp Site** (01246 582277). This offers fairly basic facilities but has the advantage of being a short walk/stagger from the Robin Hood pub on the main Chesterfield to Baslow road. At the other end of the scale **Laneside Camp Site** (01433 620215) in Hope offers very well-equipped facilities (although at the time of writing no single sex groups are allowed).

Also popular with climbers are camping barns which can be booked through the **Camping Barns Reservation Service** on 01200 420102. Many clubs have huts in the area; information regarding these can be obtained from the BMC.

Hotels and B&Bs are commonplace throughout the area – **Bakewell Tourist Information** (01629 813227) will be able to provide the visiting climber with any further information they may require.

Cafes
Having arrived in the Peak anticipating a full day's climbing, breakfast may be a necessary ingredient to start the day. The following cafes are popular with climbers and offer a wide range of meals:

Outside Café: Hathersage (01433 651 936)
Outside Café: Calver (01433 639 571)
Grindleford Station Café: (01433 631 920)

Gear suppliers
There are several good climbing shops in the area where every conceivable bit of climbing gear you could ever dream of can be obtained (the most important of these being midge repellent, absolutely essential in the summer months) they are as follows:

Outside: Hathersage (01433 651 936)
Nevisport: Hathersage (01433 659 666)
Hitch 'n Hike: Bamford (01433 651 013)

Other services
There are several general stores situated in the area, most now open seven days a week and most, open till around 10pm. In addition to the general stores there is a good pharmacy in Hathersage and a couple of banks, both with cash dispensers.

Pubs
There are many pubs in the area; the ones of most interest to climbers are the **Millstone Inn**, **The Scotsman's Pack** and **The Little John** all in Hathersage, **The Anglers Rest**, **Ye Derwent** and the **Yorkshire Bridge** in Bamford and **The Ladybower** and **The New Norfolk** situated on the A57 between Sheffield and the Ladybower reservoir.
For those sampling the delights of Wharncliffe Crags the **Wortley Arms Hotel** comes highly recommended, this is situated in the village of Wortley about 2km from the crag (see Wharncliffe Crags chapter).

Climbing walls
If on arriving at your chosen crag the weather, or in the summer the midges, conspire to make the thought of climbing outside too much to contemplate the following information may be of some use. Although there are no climbing walls situated in the Peak District National Park itself all are within a 30-minute drive.
The Edge: Sheffield (0114 275 8899)
The Foundry: Sheffield (0114 279 6331)
Glossop Leisure Centre: Glossop (01457 863 223)

Richard Wheeldon

History

by Niall Grimes

'Wharncliffe Crags – immortalised in the legend of that incredible monster – "The Dragon of Wantley" – possesses an even greater distinction for the gritstone climber, for here, JW Puttrell of Sheffield began climbing in 1885, thus making the edge the birthplace of gritstone climbing and "JWP" an independent pioneer of British climbing.'
Eric Byne and R A Brown, 1976 *Stanage Area* Guide

Wharncliffe Crags, that long, dark edge running along the crest of the Don Valley, overlooking sooty industrialism, the garbage-choked engine of early mechanical progress that is the River Don, long marches of electricity pylons that make the very air buzz, and not far from that great symbol of concrete progress, the M1 – holds a special place in the history of gritstone climbing. In the middle years of the 19th century, Britain was a leading player in the world of Alpinism. The gentleman classes of Oxford and Cambridge looked to the snowy summits of Zermatt and Chamonix for their inspiration. When this wasn't possible, they would travel to Wasdale Head or the Pen-y-Gwryd, and grapple with gullies in the name of preparation for their icy aspirations. Thus was the way! Yet amid this staid hegemony, there appeared a small, powerfully built youngster who, in his individual pursuit of his own interests, was to be a forerunner of what gritstone would stand for for over a hundred years.

James 'JWP' Puttrell began to explore the Peak when only 13 years old, performing such feats as a solo crossing of Kinder Scout on New Year's Day in the early 1880s. Soon after, no doubt inspired by reading of the exploits of British climbers in grander playgrounds, he discovered that climbing was available in his own backyard, and began to explore and climb on Wharncliffe. Beginning around 1885, JWP started to develop an exacting circuit of climbs and problems. His small stocky frame was ideally suited to what was known as the 'Grip and Pull' style of climbing, a style which Wharncliffe – with its blocky, angular structure – is ideally suited to. Initially climbing alone, JWP added dozens

of problems, routes a million miles away from the gully struggles of the 'greats', and a style that was to become what gritstone climbing was to become renowned for the world over – short, fierce and technical moves in risky situations on great rock.

Puttrell was later joined by a friend, WJ Watson, and together they went on to fully develop Wharncliffe, turning it into a veritable gymnasium, not just of climbing problems, but of monkey jumps, inverted monkey jumps, sliding stones, imaginary boulders and nerve testing leaps. These two were founder members of the famous Kyndwr Club, that was to range so wide across the moors, crags and caves of Peakland, and a meet was held at Wharncliffe in 1900, showing that by that time, the circuit had achieved quite a repute. When an article on the crag was published in The Climbers' Club Journal of 1910, there numbered 110 climbs. Quite impressive!

Puttrell, along with Watson and other members of the Kyndwr Club, accounted for the first climbing explorations of many of the great crags of the Peak – have a look at first ascents lists – and in many ways, set the ball rolling on Peak gritstone. Interestingly, however, after the primary role played by Wharncliffe in the birth of grit, this and the rest of the crags covered in this book, were to lie virtually untouched for the next thirty years. Only a handful of routes were recorded anywhere, as attention swung away to Stanage, the Roaches and other crags on the high moors.

In 1928, the crash on Wall Street sent the world into economic depression, and the industrial towns of Northern England soon began to feel the full weight of this. Workers were put on short time, or laid off altogether. The dole queues swelled, and the men were left with little money and lots of time. As a response to this, small clubs began to spring up based around sport and physical activities, both as a diversion from the grim situation, and as a means of burning off the excess energy amassed by these unemployed manual workers. Running clubs, weightlifting clubs and boxing clubs sprang up – small and locally-based, with members paying a subscription to buy equipment. Walking clubs began to take off, and the masses moved out on the ubiquitous railway lines to explore the Peakland, much to the disgust of the landed class, and their often heavy-handed gamekeepers.

At that time too, a fresh wave of climbers ventured onto the crags that had stood deserted for so long. From the towns of Sheffield and Nottingham they came. The climbers included Frank Elliot, Harry Dover, Gilbert Ellis, Harry Scarlett, Eric Byne, Nancy Middleton, Byron Connolly, Bert Smith and Clifford Moyer. Right away, these climbers began to add their new routes, learning as they went, and making do with what equipment and transport they could garner. Scarlett famously trawled up to Rivelin, clothes line in hand, and added the crag's first recorded routes. Byne and Moyer began their account on Dovestones Tor, and also on the nearby Bamford Edge. Most significantly of all, in terms of difficulty at least, was The Dover and Ellis Chimney in the esoteric Burbage Quarries, which nowadays weighs in at a hefty E1. Amazingly, both the north and south edges of Burbage had been entirely untouched until this point, and this group began to add many of the climbs that would go on to be some of the crag's easier classics, most notable among them being The Knight's Move and Amazon Crack. The development spurred on the production of a guide to the Burbage Valley, appearing, as was the way at the time, in the 1934 *Mountaineering Journal*, recording 45 climbs. These, apart from a couple of exceptions, were lines fairly below the top standard of the day, but ones that would go on to be the great low grade classics of today. As such, many were recorded without any first ascent details, revealing the sense that you just climbed these things, as it was generally only harder routes that would have first ascent details recorded.

After the war, in the early years of the 1950s, activity got under way again. The post-war years were characterised by a social revolution, and, despite rationing, there was a spirit of revolution. The working classes were not to be kept away from the outdoors any longer. Strict keepering had always been enforced by the privileged land-owning classes up to that point, making any venture onto wild land an act of trespass, likely to result in confrontation. With the formation of the Peak District as the first National Park in April 1951, access was assured for the dwellers of Sheffield, Manchester and the other great cities.

> '**Most significantly of all, in terms of difficulty at least, was The Dover and Ellis Chimney in the esoteric Burbage Quarries, which nowadays weighs in at a hefty E1.**'

Rivelin Edge became a favourite venue for a group of Sheffielders, with Dick Brown, Frank Fitzgerald and Donald Wooller adding many fine climbs to the edge, as well as to Bamford. These climbs were not the hardest about, but stood out as fine routes nonetheless. However, over at Burbage, muscles were being flexed in the powerful form of the legendary Valkyrie Club (later, in 1956, reformed as the Rock and Ice Club). With the two great performers, Joe Brown, with the powerful Slim Sorrell as his second man, and Don Whillans, levels soon began to rise. Characterised by ferocious crack climbs up the steepest of rock, the clubs brought things up to date, culminating in the epoch-defining ascent of The Rasp in 1956.

Besides this group, it was obvious that ever greater numbers of climbers were taking to the Peak. First ascent details of the time reveal a broader range of activists than had previously been in the area. Once again these other performers lagged behind the greats somewhat in terms of the difficulty of their additions, but a tremendous sense of enthusiasm comes across, an enthusiasm that produced a great number of still great climbs. This group included Dave Gregory, Ron Townsend, Andrew Brodie, Alan Clarke and George Kitchin among others, and they accounted for such delights as The Grogan, The Chant, The Reamer, Saul, Keep Crack, Evening Wall, Dowel Crack and Long Tall Sally.

Another notable occurrence in this post-war era was the development of the quarries. Millstone was virtually unexplored – at the time, climbers were not mentally or physically prepared for the steepness and height of these mighty and still somewhat unconsolidated walls. They were deemed, in many respects, unclimbable. Lawrencefield was somewhat more approachable. Members of the Peak Climbing Club and the Sheffield University Mountaineering Club in the form of Bert Shutt, Reg Pillinger, Harry Hartley, Dick Brown and others began to explore Lawrencefield, and a few pleasant routes were added. This development gathered pace, until two notable characters were invited to visit.

Legend has it that a young Peter Biven was hitch-hiking around the Peak one day when a huge Rolls Royce pulled up to offer a lift. At the wheel was Trevor Peck, 30 years his senior, the proprietor of a hosiery factory in the Midlands. Together they went on to form a strong partnership, becoming most renowned in the Peak District for their pegging activities. They visited Lawrencefield in 1955 and added the fine Excalibur, and in the summer of the next year, really made their mark with first ascents of High Street, Boulevard, Suspense and Great Peter, all heavily reliant on piton-work. Many of these covered very steep terrain.

Perhaps more significantly, at the same time the pair moved across the road and began applying their craft to Millstone Edge. A few aid routes existed there already, but the zeal with which the pair applied themselves to steep virgin walls was breathtaking. Weekend after weekend saw them hammering away, summer and winter. While it is easy to see their activities as destructive, one must remember that different eras have different attitudes, and it must be remembered that in the mid-50s, there was a feeling that these walls were not free-climbable, and, as quarries, were,

James Pearson on Time for Tea, E3 5c (page 113), one of the many cracks pegged out at Millstone during the 1950s.
Photo: David Simmonite.

in some way, fair game. The other point is that without their 'whack and dangle' attitude, many of the area's best climbs would never have been 'created'. During this period the cracks of Regent Street, Jermyn Street, Coventry Street and London Wall were all opened out by Biven and Peck alone, today providing some of the best climbs in the area. Add to that the hammer-work done by others on such climbs as Twikker, Knightsbridge, Embankment Route 4, Supra-Direct, and it is obvious that today we are benefiting greatly from their misdemeanours.

Interestingly, the frantic period of full-bore aid climbing that Millstone and Lawrencefield experienced ended almost overnight in 1957 with the visit to Millstone of Harold Drasdo and more importantly, Joe Brown. Brown had been critical of the amount of aid being used, and, putting his money where his mouth was, free climbed Great North Road, The Mall, and added his own Plexity, while Drasdo added Dexterity. With these ascents, it was proven that the super-steep and terrifying walls of these old quarries were now open for the superior business of free climbing.

> Legend has it that a young Peter Biven was hitch-hiking around the Peak one day, when a vast Rolls Royce pulled up to offer a lift. At the wheel was Trevor Peck, 30 years his senior, the proprietor of a hosiery factory in the Midlands.

After the activity of the 1960s, where crags such as Burbage and Millstone steadily gave a procession of quality, but by no means ground-breaking routes, gritstone was ready for some fresh activity. Limestone had been the medium of choice for most of the 1960s, and with routes such as Tom Proctor's Stoney masterpiece Our Father, standards had exceeded what was being achieved on grit. The time was ripe for a new era, and this most certainly came along in the 1970s. The legendary 'Gritstone Renaissance' of the 1970s is perhaps the greatest period in the history of the rock, a period so major that it blew away all that had gone before, and laid the ground for development in the sport that is still being followed today. Technical performance was thrust forward to a wholly new degree, a degree which allowed almost all the great lines to be climbed within a space of a few years, and to leave only a comparatively minor

number of such lines for future generations. This renaissance, characterised by the pushing forward of the technical boundaries in any situation, dangerous or safe, appeared around the same time in Yorkshire and Staffordshire, but it was in the Peak District that it was most felt, led on by a group of seriously talented youngsters, and featured one of the most gifted and visionary activists ever to climb in this country.

John Allen is one of those rare climbers – perhaps along with Joe Brown and Johnny Dawes – whose climbing contemporaries universally speak of with respect. While there were a significant number of others in the 'pack', Allen was obviously at least half a grade ahead of them all, and combined this talent with a keenness. However, despite this keenness and edge over his contemporaries, it is also noted that Allen didn't really have to try too hard to stay ahead, the mark of a true great. In his own way, he accounted for more new routes on the edges than anyone else, by far. But again, it is not just the number of routes that he added that mark him out as special, but the quality of these routes. It's probably fair to say that if the crags were discovered today, virgin, then the most outstanding lines to try will, in most cases, turn out to be John Allen routes. John's sizzling technical ability matched the mood of the day perfectly, as the equipment and fitness developed in the previous decade on the hostile limestone crags, allowed climbers to move away from the security of the cracks onto bold, blank walls.

Having said all that, however, the 'pack' was an incredibly talented bunch themselves. Tom Proctor, the man who had revolutionised limestone climbing over the previous few years, was chief among them, and applied his legendary power to the fiercer, if less subtle lines, often freeing aid climbs on Millstone and Lawrencefield. Steve Bancroft, Allen's regular partner, was in a similar league to Allen, albeit slightly further down. His climbs carry the same technical trademark, and, while not quite adding as

Ron Fawcett, one of the great legends of world climbing, cranking his way along the equally classy London Wall, E5 6a (page 116), John Allen's masterpiece of free climbing from 1975. Photo: Ian Smith.

many, certainly made his efforts count. Further out on the leftfield was the poet/climber/performance artist Edwin Ward-Drummond making his own mark with Flute of Hope and, despite its diminutive stature, with Banana Finger, his description of which was almost longer than the route. Others such as Mick Fowler, Bill Briggs, Andy Parkin and Terry Hirst must be added to the already strong group of climbers operating near the standard of the day. What must be remembered about this period in the 1970s is that there has seldom been as strong a group snapping at the heels of the top climbers.

Inevitably, after such a swell in activity, there followed a lull in gritstone climbing around the 1980s. Limestone climbing became the fashion, and the Dales became the venue of choice for the great and the good. The new routes books that had previously swollen from the records of activity on the edges, now became full of limestone climbs. Fashion had swung once more. Training had allowed new levels of fitness necessary to attack the steep fingery walls, and, especially with the continued acceptance of the placing of protection bolts, more and more of the walls were being climbed. So much so, in fact, that for a good time there was a genuine fear for the sanctity of the British climbing tradition. Bolts, power, lycra tights – sport climbing was sexy, compared to the traditional bearded bumbly shuffling up a wide crack at Stanage.

This is not to say that nothing was happening on grit, however. A dedicated team of pioneers, obsessives and superstars were adding gritstone testpieces aplenty to the edges. The early years of the 1980s saw a strong team in the form of Paul Mitchell and Andy Barker, often revelling in the obscure, regularly adding climbs up to E5. While some of these may have been obscure, others, such as Nosferatu, have gone on to 3-star status, with Burbage South especially feeling their force. Johnny Dawes began to emerge, adding some new routes that hinted at what was to follow (more of him later), whilst another of Britain's finest, Jerry Moffatt, added Messiah. As befitting someone of Jerry's talent, Messiah

was miles ahead – in terms of powerful climbing – of anything else in the area, and even today, sees off a fair few aspirants. Last, but not least, the great Ron Fawcett swooped in on his native gritstone to account for Scritto's Republic, Clock People and Master's Edge, the latter being the all time classic hard route on grit.

In the midst of this, a new character arrived on the scene in the compact shape of Johnny Dawes, a five- foot dynamo who was to set grit climbing on fire in the area. Johnny's unique style, unparalleled boldness and an enigmatic charisma led him to great favour by the climbing media, putting forward a new hero, championing the traditional British values of fair play, and flying in the face of the new French style, which seemed, by comparison to be glorified gymnastics. While there were other superb talents operating on grit – most notably Simon Nadin and Nick Dixon in Staffordshire, and John Dunne in Yorkshire – Johnny had the effect of bringing a new style to grit at a time when the values he stood for were under threat. While, in this guide, there are not very many of his routes from this era – Braille Trail stands out as his finest contribution – the power of this effect cannot be underestimated.

> Allen was obviously at least half a grade ahead of the pack, and it is also noted that he didn't really have to try too hard to stay ahead – the mark of a true great.

In the years immediately after Johnny's reign, which culminated in 1986, the rest of the climbing world played catch-up. However, the single most significant event of the post-Dawes years, was John Dunne's ascent of Parthian Shot. The route, previously known as The Prow on Burbage South, was top-roped by Dawes on a wet day for the TV programme Stone Monkey. A chance remark on Johnny's narration declared himself two years from leading the climb, more to contextualise the route's difficulty than as an assessment of his intentions. Whatever his intentions, however, less than 6 months later, the Big Man from Yorkshire steamed in and led the route. Dunne's ascent started one of the most celebrated furores in recent climbing history. The Sheffield 'Mafia' declared him a liar, a declaration based on nothing more than bitter jealousy, circumstantial evidence, and Dunne's already healthy and widespread reputation for pork pies. The episode stands more as an illustration of the healthy passions and larger than life characters of our top climbers. What is sure, however, is that Parthian Shot remains as far and away the outstanding hard route of the area, with treacherously bold and technical climbing, and possible only to the most determined or insane climbers.

Another event worth noting from the 1980s was the return to grit of the great John Allen. Having done all the best lines in the 1970s, Allen returned to hoover up many of the most technical boulder problems and micro-routes on the edges. Routes such as The Sphinx, Moolah and New Mediterranean are obvious classic examples, although no route shows his vision and talent more than West Side Story. This was the first route claimed at 7a in the area and took many visits to complete. Even today it is still a true benchmark in any serious boulderer's career. With the increased use of mats, many of Allen's additions from that period are starting to get the attention that they deserve.

The 1990s will be remembered as the years of Hard Grit. Up until the mid 90s, hard grit, by which is meant grit E6 and above, was the preserve of a small and dedicated few. With the release of the film of the same name in 1996, centering on Seb Grieve's ascent of Parthian Shot, the climbing world was allowed a unique glimpse into this arcane world. The film showed the multiple top-roped workings that preceeded ascents, and almost overnight, this became common practice. Hard Grit became democratic, open to all, thanks to top-roping. Simultaneously ascents began to lose their value, as with a moderate amount of talent, ascents of E6, E7 and even E8 became common, and no longer raised much of an eyebrow. Amazingly, in the grade-rush that followed, where young weasels would hurl themselves at E whatever with the wildest of abandon, no climber was ever seriously hurt, despite the most sickening of falls in the most horrendous of locations. One thing was for sure, however. Gritstone had moved firmly back in the place of limestone as the medium of choice for the discerning crag rat, and the period from the late 1990s to the early years of the new millennium saw the repeats of all the desperates from previous generations.

New routes, also, continued to arrive, but these became ever more rare, and generally totally desperate. Sean Myles's Captain Invincible, an early one from 1991, continued on what Parthian Shot had started, by putting the highest standards of physical climbing onto gritstone routes. If anything, Captain Invincible is technically harder than Parthian, albeit a lot safer. To date, despite being one of the great routes in the area, it has only had one repeat, a fact that stands as testimony to its difficulty. On Millstone, Adrian Berry led the fierce and bold

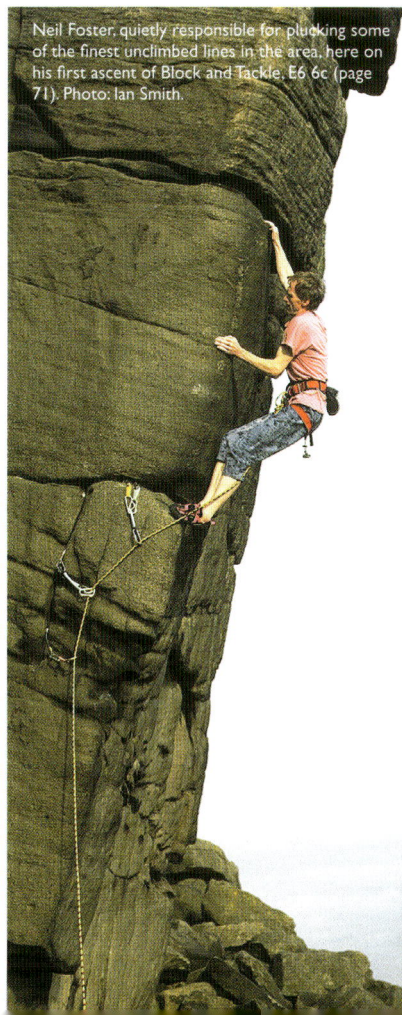

Neil Foster, quietly responsible for plucking some of the finest unclimbed lines in the area, here on his first ascent of Block and Tackle, E6 6c (page 71). Photo: Ian Smith.

slab climb of Elm Street. This had been claimed in 1986, but the claim had been generally disregarded. It stands as one of the hardest slabs in the area, and again, has probably only had one repeat. Miles Gibson brought high levels of bouldering power to the area and tidied up what were probably the two best remaining gaps on Burbage with Superstition and Fagus Sylvatica. Despite getting E8, these routes are a mile away from the E8s typical of the 1980s inasmuch as while they are both still bold, the power needed to do them puts them far beyond the reach of those simply willing to risk their neck. Toby Benham and Simon Moore tidied up Burbage South with Simba's Pride and French Kiss respectively, the latter giving Burbage South Quarries an incredible tally of 3 E8s. Finally, on the fiercely obscure Rivelin Quarries, Nik Jennings ran his way up That's My Lot, a phenomenally pure line with no holds, and despite being unprotected, sits above a fairly good landing. The last word on routes in the area should, of course, go to Neil Bentley's Equilibrium, grit's first E10.

Finally, no history of the climbing in this area would be complete without mentioning bouldering. Certainly the Rock and Ice Club bouldered quite intensively in the 1950s, as most likely did the generations before them. In the 1970s, bouldering was a big part of climbing for those concentrating on grit, as their routes were characteristically boulder problems high on the crag. The interesting thing from this distance is that the activists felt very little need to record their activities. It seems that if what would essentially be a boulder problem occurred on a crag, then it would be recorded. Activity on boulders was seen as just a bit of fun.

Allen and Bancroft were active on the bouldering front. Others – Mark Stokes, Nicky Stokes, Gabe Regan, Al Rouse – were very devoted boulderers, and all blessed with copious talent. In the 1970s these climbers scoured the Burbage Valley, the Millstone area, Secret Garden, Owler Tor, and without a shadow of a doubt, climbed many of what later became classics. The fact that their names never occur in first ascent lists is merely a reflection of their attitudes. Later, these early pioneers were joined by more who shared their attitude – Martin Veale, Allen Williams, Johnny Dawes, Greg Griffiths, Jerry Moffatt – and the exploration continued, records

only being kept by word of mouth. This has left the situation that these days, no-one can ever record a first ascent without some old timer rubbing their chin and scratching their head, then to declare that they probably did that in '78. This is no bad situation, and the lack of 'laying claim' as was the attitude of many generations of boulderers, perhaps suits the activity more. These days, the attitude of naming, grading and laying claim is set in stone, records are kept and all is known (an attitude, admittedly, perpetuated in this book). Things have not necessarily moved on, and perhaps a better outlook is to accept that almost everything was done a long long time ago.

In the last decade, bouldering has become big news, with almost as many people walking around the crags with pads as with ropes. Jason Myers was responsible for bringing bouldering more to the mainstream with his ascent of Brad Pit on Stanage in 1995, the first boulder problem to achieve celebrity status. In the years that followed, problems in the V9/10 and above range started to become more common, notably by Myers himself (Blind Fig, Submergence, Westworld), Jerry Moffatt (Zorev, Intense, Blazing 48s), John Welford (No Class, Blind Drunk, Darkstar, Famous Grouse, The Rib), Zaff Ali (Western Eyes, Zaff's Problem, Dick Williams), and others including Nik Jennings, Ben Moon and Ian Fitzpatrick.

So there you have it. Currently, in 2005, it's almost fair to say that the crags in this book are climbed out. Only a small handful of unclimbed lines remain, and arguably these are of much lesser stature than those that are already done. Most things have been repeated, and any new routes seem to be desperate voyages into pointless gaps that have been climbed many years ago. But this will only bother a very small minority bent on discovery. For the rest, what remains is one of the richest climbing histories in the world. These small crags have, since the initial delvings of JWP and the Kyndwr Club a hundred years ago, through all the successive stages of development, brought out the best from the climbers. These efforts are here for all to see, and by climbing their routes, you are almost brought back to their times. Sticky boots and camming devices can never change that. So, go forth, climb and experience the climbs. They are among the finest in the world.

The Routes

"There are, it is true, no laurels to be won on the edges and monoliths of Peakland, and there is little scope for sensational exploits or hairbreath escapes; the man who tumbles off one of these big boulders may hurt himself, but he will not have the gratification of falling through a hundred feet of breathtaking scenery."

EA Baker, 1903

The **Burbage Valley**

1

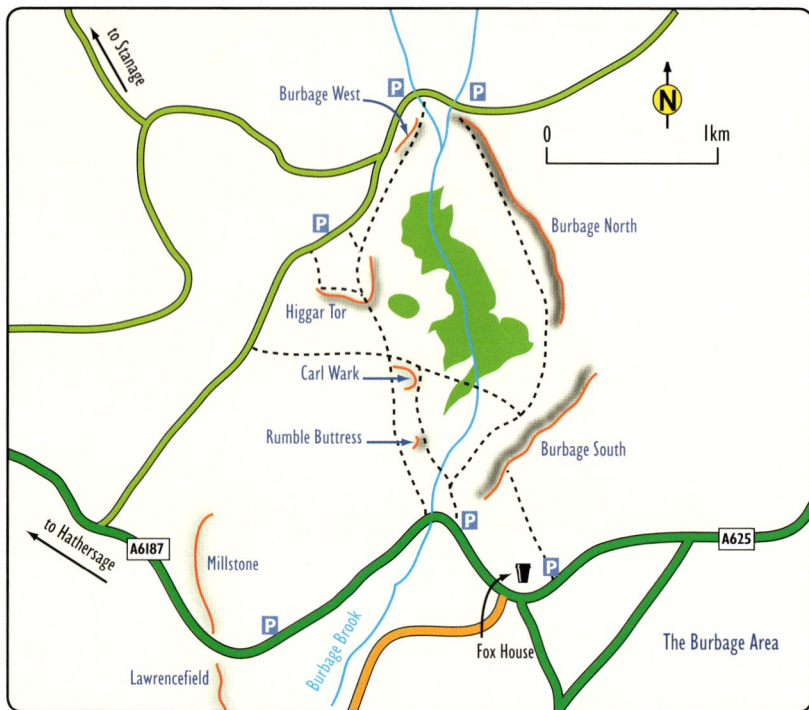

Burbage North

OS Ref. SK 263829 to SK 269820 | altitude 420m

by David Musgrove

One of the closest edges to Sheffield, Burbage North fills a wonderful niche in the Peak gritstone collection of crags. It is less imposing and impressive than the other major crags hereabouts, but on closer acquaintance it is a wonderland of small buttresses crammed full of high-quality routes, micro-routes and boulder problems. The crag is perhaps best loved as a soloing venue and many of its lines exist in the grey area between highball problems and short routes. These micro-routes can be enjoyed either as bold solos, as well-padded

and spotted boulder problems, or with a rope and runners. There are also a number of bigger buttresses with some proper gritstone classics. For quality crack climbs in the VD to E1 range, head for Ash Tree Wall, Sentinel, Hollyash Wall and Long Tall Sally areas. There is also a collection of hard routes that tend to be highly technical. Neither boldness nor burliness is sufficient here, though both may help.

The Climbing

Top class, with a great supply of very accessible and friendly routes. The rock is consistently brilliant, rough grit, and the moves are always interesting

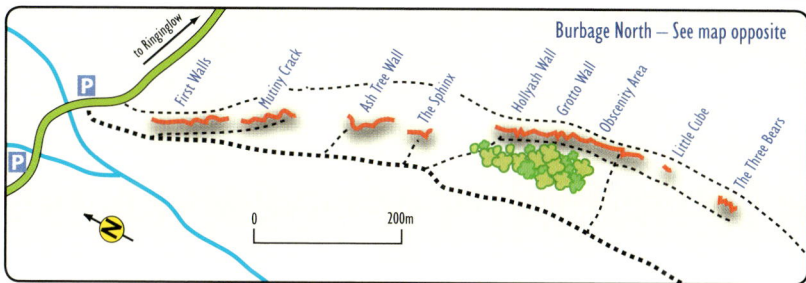

Burbage North — See map opposite

0   200m

with very little of the 'break-to-break' climbing that typifies less interesting crags. **Routes:** Almost 230 routes of every grade and style. **Bouldering:** Superb, with 90 problems of all difficulties ranging from tiny sit starts to full-bore heart-in-mouth highballs.

Conditions and Aspect

Burbage North is quite spread out and while some buttresses can be sociable, the smaller buttresses, particularly at the right-hand end, can be very quiet, allowing you to get to grips with the crag's secrets undisturbed. The rock is extremely clean, quick-drying and is climbable year round. Although the

Dave Norton on All Quiet on the Eastern Front, V3 (page 8). Photo: John Coefield.

crag can be a bit midgy on summer evenings, the fact that it catches any wind hurtling up or down the valley, will help to keep most of these evil creatures at bay. The crag faces southwest and receives the sun from lunchtime onwards providing some welcome warmth when other crags are cold.

Parking and Approach

Park at the Burbage Bridge car park and approach. Times range between a quarter of a second to a quarter of an hour. **By Bus:** Three services call at the Fox House (see Burbage South). From there, it is a 25 minute walk up the valley. In summer, and on bank holidays, the 257 service runs from Sheffield via Hunters Bar to Burbage North bridge.

First Walls

Could these be the most climbed-on pieces of rock in the world? The walls are popular as a soloing warm-up, though if you're not feeling so bold, most of them have perfect gear. There are many variations between the named routes so just go wherever your fancy and fingers take you. The obvious lines all get whole numbers whilst eliminates in between have to make do with decimals.

The first problem encountered lies 10m to the left of the first wall. ● **North Roof,** V3 (6a), finger-traverses the lip of the low roof to finish up the arête.

❶ Route I HS 4b ★   1934-51

6m The photogenic arête is a beautiful start to this crag, and a pointer to the technical nature of the routes. ● On the left side-wall of the buttress, **RT Wall** is a good little undercutting problem starting at some obvious carved initials, V2 (5c).

2 Route 1.5 VS 5b   traditional
6m The wall to the right.

3 Route 2 HVD 4a ★   pre-1934
6m The lovely wall passing a triangular pod.

4 Route 2.5 VS 5a   traditional
6m The wall between the cracks.

5 Route 3 VD ★   pre-1934
6m A little ripper up the obvious line finishing up the chunky zigzag crack.

The Skinpickers

We may ask what the purpose
Of the like of ticks and midges is.
We'll never know.

But one thing's for sure – the purpose
Of climbers is to shed
Skin for the Skinpickers.

A Burbage day leaves a feast
Of scrubbed-off fingerprints and patches

Of pimple elbow-hide. They come,
The Skinpickers, when we're all gone:

Very slowly scurry;

Turn over stones, scrabble around, sift
Brown bits of bracken frond and sand, glean
Crags' entire surfaces

For the frail coverings of human beings.

Mark Goodwin

6 Route 3.5 E1 6a   traditional
6m Contrived, but with a stretching move high up. ●**Route 4**, VS 5a (traditional), is the wall just left of the right arête. The right arête can be climbed at 4a. ●The low-level traverse of this buttress is about V2 (6a).

7 Cranberry Crack HD ★   1951
6m The left-hand crack is a gentle introduction to wide crack technique and could lead on to the more difficult wide cracks on the crag. Go on, bag it.

8 The Chant VS 5a ★   1958-59
6m Climb the left-curving overlap to the top break, step right and climb to the top past a tricky but protectable move. ●A squeezed-in eliminate can be had up the wall just right at HVS 5c.

9 Twenty-Foot Crack S 4b ★★   pre-1934
6m Could a crack this high be more perfect? ●**The Twenty-Foot Traverse** from here to the right arête is about V3 (6a).

10 The Curse VS 5b ★   1977-78
6m The wall has a super boulder problem start. ●**Lost in France**, VS 5c (traditional), is the face 1m left of the right arête.

Triangle Buttress: This is not much of a triangle.

11 Little Plumb D   1957-65
5m The cracked groove on the left is a bit bland.

12 Baseless VD 4a ★   1957-65
7m The straight crack, starting in a widening, has a gutsy finish pulling between two jutting blocks. Be brave. ●**Base over Apex**, VS 4c (1991), is an eliminate up the wall to the left of the crack.

⑬ Triangle Buttress Arête VD 4a ★   1932
7m The blunt arête becomes decidedly more pleasant after the sloping horrors at the start.

⑭ Triangle Buttress Direct HS 5b ★   pre-1934
7m The even-blunter arête has a powerful start (avoidable just left at S 4a), but again becomes quite civilised above.

⑮ Triangle Crack VD 4a   pre-1934
8m The corner-crack is quite tough to start. ● The wall immediately to the right of the corner can be climbed direct to the top at E1 6a.

⑯ Leaning Wall Direct VS 5a ★   1957
8m Gain the wide crack at the top of the wall via some steely pulls. ● The original version gained the crack by traversing in from either side (S).

⑰ Little White Jug VS 5a ★★   1977
9m A smashing route that blasts straight up the ever steepening wall and finishes with a scuffling mantel over the vague nose.

⑱ Big Black 'Un HVS 5a ★   1965-78
9m Another arm-blaster up the steep wall with a similar grovelling finish.

⑲ Steptoe M   1957-1965
6m The blocky crack will exercise the legs.

● **Triangle Buttress Girdle,** S 4b (1934-51), is a high-level traverse of this area from left-to-right.

Monkey Wall: This is the undercut slab 30m further on, with some classic problems and a couple of fine easier journeys.

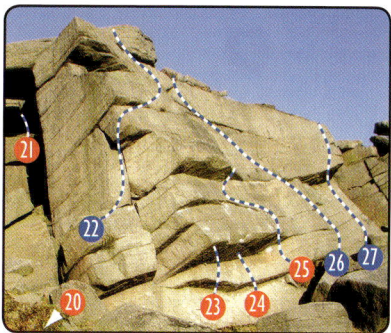

⑳ Definitive 5.12 V5 (6b)
For those who love a fight. Just down and left of this buttress is a triangular cave; jam and undercut out from the back of this. ● A left-hand exit can be had at V7 (6b).

㉑ Cinzano Roof V7 (6b)
Start on the ledge below the jammed boulder. From a flake in the roof, yard backwards over the bulge.

㉒ Monkey Corner VD ★   pre-1934
8m From the undercut groove in the left arête, swing right at a jug to climb the upper slab. Continuing up the arête direct is 5c. ● **Monkey Crack** in the sidewall on the left can be jammed at V1 (5c).

㉓ Banana Arête V2 (5c)
The bulging arête. ● **Banana Reverse**, V6 (6b), starts on the jug at the top of the arête, drops down and does Banana Finger Direct, then reverses the traverse of the original.

㉔ Banana Finger Direct V4 (6b)
Gain the end of the traverse from the sidepull. Impossible for some, 5a for others. Which one are you? ● Two problems of similar difficulty cross the roof 1m and 2m right using a flake and slopers.

㉕ Banana Finger V3 (6a)
A Burbage gem. Move up to gain the thin break. Fidget leftwards along the chalked crease until the crux move up can be made.

㉖ Monkey Wall M   1951-57
7m An unprotected right-to-left romp up ledges.

㉗ Monk On E1 5b   1982
7m A bold little problem. Climb the overhung arête on its left-hand side. Much easier on the right.

Overhang Buttress: Another fine buttress just right.

㉘ Ad Infinitum S 4a ★   1934-1951
14m An obvious left-to-right girdle above the roof gives some great exposure.

㉙ Little Brown Thug V5 (6b)
A super-reachy problem over the roof.

㉚ Wednesday Climb HVS 5b ★   1960-65
8m The big, baggy, undercut crack with a very steep start. Long trousers and determination may provide the key. Absolutely superb.

㉛ Life in a Radioactive Dustbin V5 (E3 6b)
Brilliant! Take the overhang at its apex, get both hands on the lip, control the swing and haul up; finish easily. ● From the lip, traversing right is fairly pointless; **Heather (Sea Monsters)**, E4 6b, (1993).

㉜ The Disposable Bubble E4 6a   1984
8m Cross the roof using a small slot underneath for protection. Pulling round is one thing – establishing yourself higher on the slab is another. A soft touch at the grade, although the moves feel pretty dicey.

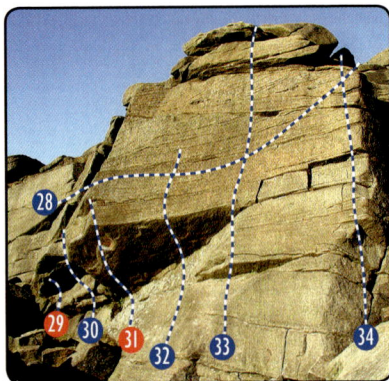

㉝ Overhang Buttress Direct S 4a ★   pre-1934
8m A fine route that climbs directly past a shiny start and the right-hand end of the long roof.

㉞ Overhang Buttress Arête M ★   1932
8m The right-hand arête of the buttress is a little delicate but quite lovely.

The next little buttress to the right has a number of attractive short lines: ● **Burgess Face**, HS 4c (pre-1934), is the face just left of the arête; ● **Burgess Buttress**, M (pre-1934), is the arête; ● **Burgess Street**, HD (1957-65), is the small corner 2m to the right.

Mutiny Crack Area

Fifty metres right is another area of perfect rock with a fine collection of routes of all grades and styles. The first climbs are on a flat-looking wall split by a wide crack. This buttress is yet another example of Burbage North at its best; quality micro-routes on perfect rock.

㉟ All Quiet on the Eastern Front V3 (E1 6a)
A sensational micro-route. A hard move might let you traverse rightwards past a pebble to gain the arête from which a joyful move leads to the top. ● **All Quiet Direct** is the obvious start with a couple of different means of success, both at around V7 (6c). A sit-start can also be done, adding a point.

㊱ The Busker VS 5a ★   1982
7m The bulging slab is mighty fine. ● Highball V1

hanging lip to finish with a rockover. Starting round on the right is much harder.

40 The Grogan HVS 5b ★ ★ 1964
8m A fierce little finger-ripper. Climb the slanting crack if you think you're hard enough.

41 The Groat E2 6b 1980-83
8m Good fun to climb, more fun to watch. A bizarre crux leaving the ledge gains an obvious crimp and allows the blunt arête just right to be climbed.

42 Wollock HVS 4c ★ 1964
8m Start as for The Groat, but saunter stylishly rightwards into the centre of the fine wall on good holds. ● The wall to the right goes direct at 5c.

43 Pulcherrime VS 4b ★ ★ 1951-56
8m The obvious crack is a wicked hand jammer.

44 Slanting Crack VD pre-1934
8m The well named crack is harder than it looks.

45 Small is Beautiful V6 (E2 6c)
Brilliant, but fierce. Start with your right hand on the sidepull in the break and climb the wall direct.

37 Bracken Crack S 1951-57
7m Found Cranberry Crack and Ash Tree Crack a breeze? Then try this offwidth for size. ● The left arête of the crack can just about be climbed independently at VS 4c.

38 Green Slab VS 4c ★ pre-1934
7m Another gem, steep and sweet.

Wallock Buttress: Across a broad gully is another series of steep walls.

39 Fallen Slab Lip V6 (6b)
Just left of The Grogan a boulder leans against the crag. Start sitting, left hand on the slab, right on the right arête. Move up, then swing right along the

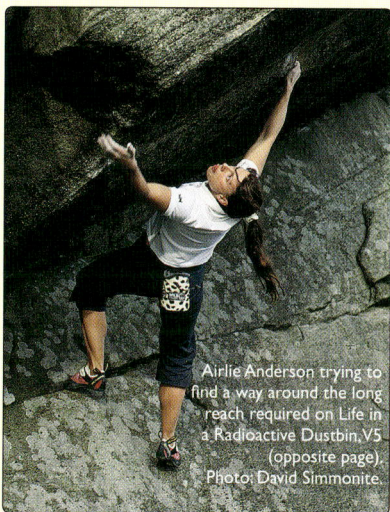

Airlie Anderson trying to find a way around the long reach required on Life in a Radioactive Dustbin, V5 (opposite page). Photo: David Simmonite.

"It is greatly to be recommended

to the girl novice, and to all novices, to practise 'bouldering' as much as possible, and for the girl, to select those boulder climbs where activity and balance are of greater value than muscular strength and arm-pulls. She will there, often be able to show a more experienced and much more powerful man, how a short piece of difficult rock can be climbed with ease and grace. Unless the climb is under ten feet in height, with a good turf landing, the rope should always be put on. Below that height no injury should occur to any young person who takes care to alight **a la chat**, on feet and hands at the same time."

Mrs. Harold Raeburn, 1920

46 Slanting Gully M   pre-1934
8m A climbing/caving biathlon. The gully tucked away at the back has a strange finish.

47 Chockstone Climb D   pre-1934
8m Another tortuous treat. Climb as far inside the dark chimney as you dare. How to tackle the chockstone? That's your decision.

Remergence Buttress: This buttress is excellent for bouldering with the two classic problems being the starting sequences of Remergence and Blind Date. There will be plenty of chalk around and in the winter, quite probably, a carpet of bouldering mats.

The next two routes step off a boulder onto the left wall of Remergence Buttress.

48 Stomach Traverse HVS 4c ★   1932
13m Gain the left arête from the gully then move up until beneath the roof. Hand-traverse the break rightwards to finish up Mutiny Crack.

49 Gymnipodes E4 6b ★   1988
13m Begin up The Hanging Rib boulder problem (see opposite) to gain easy ground. Continue up through overlaps to the top roof. Cross this leftwards to finish up the left arete.

50 Remergence E4 6b ★   1977
12m Climb the problem start and continue more easily to the top roof; haul over this (Friend 2) to finish.

51 Blind Date E5 6c ★   1984
12m A problem gains Tiptoe. Continue to the top roof at the same point as Remergence, but climb rightwards through the vague scoop to finish.

52 Mutiny Crack HS 4c ★ ★ ★   1934
12m An all-time favourite of which you will never tire. A steep start, which stops many, leads into a series of honest jams and big jugs. ●A poor 5a variation goes up left to reach a thin crack and short arête above. ●**Manatee Man**, E4 6b (1985), climbs through the roof to the right; artificial.

53 Meddle HVS 5a   1976
12m The right-hand side of the slabby rib (left of the short corner) is followed before moving right to climb with a touch of bravado through the weakness in the overhangs.

54 Detour S 4a ★   1957
12m A fine, varied lead. Go up the big corner to the capping roof then decide, wisely, to scuttle left, pulling round the arête until a step up can be made. ●The direct over the bottom roof is **Diversion**, HVS 5b (1964), finishing up a short crack.

"A **low class edge**; they lack style; they look as though the hens have been over them."

Patrick Monkhouse's opinion of Burbage Rocks in his book, On Foot in the Peak, 1932

Remergence Bouldering

A brilliant collection of hardcore problems, demanding strong fingers, good technique, and perfect friction.

1 **The Hanging Rib** V4 (6b)
Classic. From a crimp and sidepull under the roof, swing out to the hanging rib. Climb this, then lunge to the ledge off good crimps. ● The standing start is V2 (6a). ● **Zaff's Groove,** V7 (6c), is another fine eliminate, taking the undercut scoop between the rib and Remergence.

2 **The Slopers Eliminate** V6 (6b)
As for the last route, but instead of the crimps above the rib, gain the ledge off two poor slopers just left.

3 **Remergence** V4 (6b)
A testing old-school classic. From the sharp pocket, surmount the roof using a flake and pebbles.

4 **Blind Drunk** V11 (7a)
John Welford's mighty addition, forming a direct start to Remergence. Starting with the left hand on the good sloper and right hand in a small dish on the slab, rock up to the break.

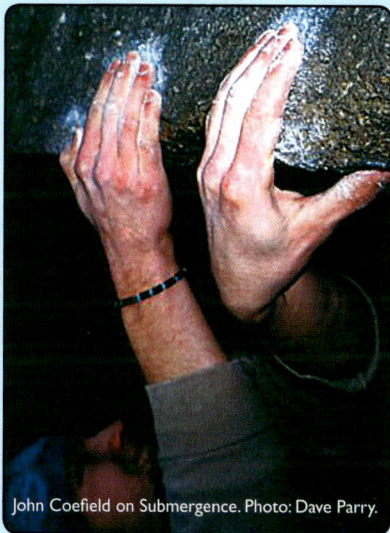

John Coefield on Submergence. Photo: Dave Parry.

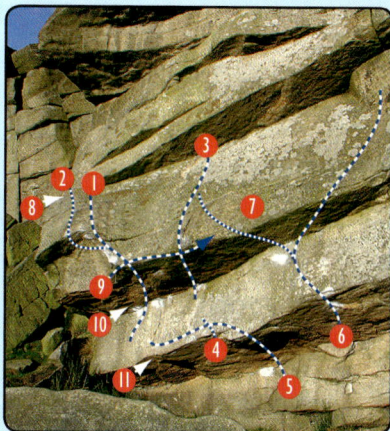

5 **Submergence** V10 (7a)
From the big jug under the roof, gain the lip. Swing left to match on a polished crimp and pull up to finish up The Hanging Rib. Tall people can miss out the final crux move at V9.

6 **Blind Date** V8 (6c)
A brutal, thrutchy and desperate thing of great historical value. From the holds at the lip, get the sloper and then the break. Squirm over the next roof and finish direct, or slink off right. Hard for the grade.

7 **Blind Fig** V9 (7a)
As for Blind Date to the sloper. Match this and swing left to join Remergence.

8 **Tiptoe** V0+ (HVS 5a)
Step on from the left and follow holds under the roof. At Mutiny Crack, either go up or down, or continue under the next roof to easy ground.

9 **Remergence Lip Traverse** V6 (6b)

10 **Break Traverse** V10 (6c)
Traverse the break under the second roof.

11 **Blind Ali** V10 (6c)
Traverse the lip from the polished crimp on the left using slopers and holds under the roof.

A normal day's bouldering? There's nothing normal
here. Adam Long captures the random goings on
during a typical Remergence bouldering session:
climbers, spotters, bystanders, demonstrators — and
somebody in the foreground doing something as yet
unidentified.

Twenty metres to the right is a short buttress with an attractive tree stump at the bottom.

55 Dead Tree Crack VS 4b ★   1957-65

7m   The wide crack provides a perfect layback, or terrifying offwidth experience.

56 Tree Stump Traverse V2 (6a)

Pumpy. ● The steep face above the traverse has so far stumped all attempts, and is a fine, fingery prospect.

57 Side Order Chaos VS 5b   1991

7m   The centre of the wall to the right is delicate and reachy above the break. The left edge of the wall is, ● **Side Face**, S 4a (pre-1951). ● **And Beaker**, HVS 5b (1993), is the right-hand side of the wall to a small groove.

The Little Slab: Immediately to the right is a small slab, which squeezes in four good, but worn, problems. Left-to-right these are: ● V0 (5b), ● V1 (5c), ● V2 (6a) and ● V4 (6b).

58 Solitude V5 (6b)

Thirty metres past The Little Slab is a little buttress. From the break in the cave, pull out left to a flake and rib. Go up this, then rock up and right to easier ground. ● A sort of direct is **Shazam**, V4 (6a), gaining the break from a jam below.

Ash Tree Wall Area

This area is home to a number of good quality clean buttresses. It is the obvious major section of crag to the right of the longest break in the edge. The first little buttress is up at the back near the left-hand side, above a small oak.

59 Oak Face HS 4b   1977

7m   Climb the crack above the small oak tree to a difficult and hairy finish over a bulging ramp. ● The wall to the left is **Sunlight Caller**, VS 5b (1985), ● and the scoop to the right is **Boggle Boothroyd**, a very reachy VS 4b (1985). 6a for the short.

60 The Last Great Problem HVS 5c   1992

7m   Climb the arête on its right side by weird moves.

61 Striker V10 (7a)

Ben Moon's hidden gem, dynamically undercutting up the desperate wall to the slot.

62 Beach Tea One HVS 6a ★ ★   1988

7m   A brilliant and gymnastic route up the distant breaks. From the arête, traverse left on the lowest slot. From the middle of the wall bounce up to perfect holds, and finish with a desperate mantel.

63 Ivy Tree HVS 5b ★   1977

7m   Climb the arête of the square buttress. The reachy start can be avoided by traversing in from the right (not so good) but there's no escaping the excellent crux move leaving the break. ● **Poison Ivy**, E1 6a (1994), finishes over the roof to the right.

64 All Stars' Goal E1 6a ★   1978

7m   Climb the bulging, left-hand side of the wall direct with some long moves on good holds. ● Highball V2. ● Just left, gain the **Pointy Nose Direct** at a committing V3 (6a).

65 Evening Wall E1 5b ★ ★   1964

7m   A fine but bold route. Start in the centre of the wall and climb up and right to the arête. The big breaks above are rounded and insecure. ● **Evening Wall Direct,** E2 6a ★, goes directly up the middle of the wall passing a two-finger pocket. Dangerous. ● A fine direct start, **Twilight,** E2 5c ★ (2000), starts on the right-hand side of the lower arête at a ledge and swings immediately round onto the front to continue up the arête to join Evening Wall.

66 Wall Chimney HVD ★   pre-1934

8m   Full-bore squeeze action up the narrow chimney. Finish inside or outside the capping chockstone. Desperate if you don't fit (and not many do!).

67 Happily Ever After E6 6c ★   1995
9m From the boulder, step on and climb directly up the hanging nose just right of the chimney. Pre-placed protection is used at this grade.

68 Nefertiti F6 6c ★ ★   1989
9m A fine line up the subtle scoop. Step off the boulder and gain the thin break. Move right and climb the scoop using thin breaks. Originally gained by a traverse in from the chimney and climbed with side-runners, it now makes a fine, scary, highball.

69 Wall Corner HVD 4a ★   pre-1934
9m A miniature mountain route up the small V-corner in the arête of the buttress.

Moving round to the front of the buttress the fine wall holds some great lower grade outings and a couple of thinner routes.

70 Ash Tree Variation HVS 5c ★   1965-78
12m Climb the centre of the wall right of the arête to the break then step right to finish up the delicate slab. ● A squeezed-in eliminate up the wall to the right is HVS 5b.

71 Ash Tree Wall S 4a ★ ★   1932
12m A great wandering route up the line of least resistance. Start up the slippery crack then traverse left to gain the prominent 'staircase' which leads to a ledge. Finish up the open groove.

72 Ash Tree Crack VD ★ ★   pre-1934
12m The major crack gives well-protected, physical climbing. Getting slightly harder due to the polish. Maybe even as good as Cranberry Crack. ● The face to the right can be squeezed in at 5b, **Bilberry Pie**.

73 Bilberry Crack VD ★   pre-1934
12m The second major crack is again well-protected and very classic. From the big ledge finish steeply, slightly to the left.

74 Bilberry Face S 4a   pre-1934
12m The narrow little face is delicate and bold.

● The twin cracks from a niche to the right are about VD. ● The slabby rib just right is **Learning the Ropes,** M. ● The steep rib right is **Rope Trick**, HS 4c, ● and the short wide crack is **Who Needs Ropes?** M. ● **Head-Banger,** S 4a, ascends the rib just right again to the capstone (all traditional). **Ash Tree Girdle,** S (pre 1934), is a scenic traverse of the walls.

The Leaning Block: This slopes in absolutely every direction and is home to some of the crag's hard power routes.

Left of the block, above the gully, is a short square arête hanging in space. The pockets in the arête look tempting, but they haven't yet been properly pulled on. It's highball, but surely someone is strong enough. ● Just left of the undercut arête is the short

The Troglodyte's Tour...

...being a whimsy of dark delvings and escapes from tight scrapes, the underground world of the Burbage Valley. Dare you enter...

by
Steve
'Offwidth'
Clarke

Starting at Higgar Tor, a crossroads in the rock is entered under Doddle to exit north through the back or, better still, west through a choice of holes in the roof (the middle being the easiest). The east branch opens to a canyon where Canyon Climb gives a variety of tight squeezes, starting at the merely improbable. Across the top to the east is a prominent Tor wounded by interlinked tunnels, the best being the top one gained from the middle. East across the top, a dirty hole in the ground leads down to the canyon of Giant Gaping Green Grotty Gash. Turn left at the exit and re-enter the crag under the big chockstone to an open chamber where tunnels and clefts abound: some are child's-play but true pilgrims will be sucked inexorably into the tight chimney gash on the left. Smaller distractions abound in the slots and boulders hereabouts but the journey to Carl Wark awaits. The verdant cleft of Lime Juice Chimney allows entry deep into the crag, whence a rock staircase at the back leads back out into daylight amongst startled tourists. Across to Burbage South, a pleasant diversion through Spyhole Crack leads on past minor fare to Ladder Gully. Here a staircase gains Connolly's Variation and an extensive system, with some frustratingly difficult variations, navigated through to an exit under Captain Sensible. Further on, almost at the end of the climbing and left of Prow Crack, is a small buttress with misaligned top blocks: at the top of the central side gully is a tight slot that demands some lateral thinking. To Burbage North now, where Grotto Slab is often climbed without thinking of its name, but behind is a caving through route: start on the right and shimmy left until it is possible to climb up through a hole and then exit upwards or left through another cleft. Ash Tree Wall is next and has the tempting inside route of Wall Chimney but the true journey is further inside taking a slowly rising line straight through the block. Numerous lesser squeezes and clefts are passed northwards but a fitting finale for the stricken is the exceedingly tight test threading the chockstone behind the top of Overhanging Buttress Arête.

John Dudley on the classic Ash Tree Wall, S 4a (previous page). Photo: David Simmonite.

rib of **Calvin Klimb**, E4 6b (1996). ●**A Phenomenological Problem**, HVS 5b (1977), climbs the short steep prow 10m up the gully.

75 Early Morning Performance HVS 5b   1978
9m   The green side wall of the leaning block gives nice reachy cranks. ●The left arête is **Late Night Antics**, HVS 5c (1990). ●The slanting crack to the right is **Leaning Block Crack**, VD (1934-51).

76 With a Little Help from my Friends
E1 5b   2000
14m   A bizarre but strangely enjoyable route that traverses the top break of the block from the short crack on the left all the way round to the arête on the far right. Watch out for rope-drag.

77 Navana E6 6b   1994
10m   A desperate move off the floor leads up for a couple of metres to a rightwards stretch to an obvious hold. A big reach via a slot gains the break. Finish direct to a scary mantel.

78 The Carved Block (Living in Oxford)
E7 7a ★★★   1989
10m   Hard, strenuous weirdness up the inhospitable blunt arête. Originally climbed on the left, it has lost pebbles and has since been climbed on the right side, with perhaps harder moves but a better landing. Some RPs can be placed in the low break.

79 Superstition E8 7a ★★★   1999
10m   Stunning! The hardest route on the crag so far and a fine line up visible, but tiny, holds. Gain the break from the left and then make very powerful moves to a high crux a good way above protection. Desperate, but surprisingly safe.

The blunt arête to the right has been top-roped (at about 7a), but is still awaiting a lead, and you can see the whole sequence from the boulder. It would knock Superstition into second place in the toughness stakes – oh the glory – just think about it.

80 Green Chimney VD ★   1934-51
10m   The cleft on the right-hand side of the block has a desperate start onto a chockstone. Well-protected and satisfying climbing above.

Sphinx Bouldering

This starts just 30m past Ash Tree Area on a jumble of blocks.

Jason's Roof Area

1 The Terrace V10 (6c)
The overhanging prow from a sit start.

2 Jason's Roof V9 (6c)
A long reach from the glued keel to the pinch. Height-dependent.

3 Jason's Stand-Up V6 (6b)

4 Right Arête V6 (6b)
Layback the right arête on its left. It can be started from the glued keel under the roof, making it a powerful V7 (6b).

5 End Face V5 (6b)
Pull straight over the square arête. V7 from the keel.

The Sphinx Area: This lies about 40m to the right.

6 Giza V8 (6c)
The wall above the start of The Sphinx gives a fingery highball.

7 The Sphinx V7 (E5 6c)
A superb, micro-route. Claw along the thin horizontal seam,

with the ground disappearing twice as fast as you are climbing, to finish up the arête.

8 Cleo's Edge V1 (5c)
The classic arête. Brilliant.

9 Cleo's Right Hand V1 (5b)

10 Roof Goofe V3 (6a)
A fun mantel over the lip in the gap behind The Sphinx. ●A similar problem just right is V4 (6b).

Safe Bet Area: This is just up behind The Sphinx

11 Jetty Aretty V2 (5c)

12 Jetty Buttress
HVD ★★   1934-51
Like a warm-up for High Neb Buttress, this is a little beauty up the front of the narrow tower with a tricky start.

13 Jetty Nose V3 (6a)

14 Pocket Passer V2 (6a)

15 Jetty Bulge V4 (6b)
A fairly desperate problem. ●The roof just right is V1 (5b).

16 Safe Bet V4 (E1 6b)
The arête, starting on its left side, is balancy, bold and beautiful.

17 Long Shot V4 (E2 6b)
The bulge immediately right of the arête is quite committing.

18 Bedrock V6 (6b)
Reachy moves past a small pocket in the break gain the top next to a tuft of grass.

19 Yabadabadoo V4 (HVS 6b)
The wall past the slot in the break. ●**Answer the Phone**, V1 (VS 5b), is the groove at the right-hand end of the wall.

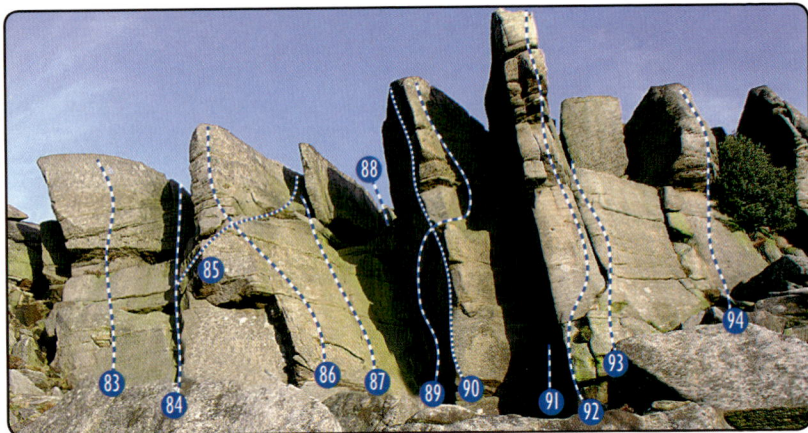

Roughly 15m right of Green Chimney is an area of blocky and slabby rocks. These can be, and have been, scrambled over at up to VS, but are very short. ●The ribbed bulge further right is a beautiful unclimbed feature, crossing the obvious roof.

The Sentinel Area

The fabulous Sentinel Area begins right from here. About 25m left of Gargoyle Buttress is a small but promising looking overhang, right of a narrow slanting chimney: ●**Chicken Broth**, HVD 4a (traditional), takes the chimney with tricky moves to get started and finished; ●**Sharks Fin Soup**, HVS 4c (1986), presumably takes the bold and reachy overhang direct on good but suspect holds.

Gargoyle Buttress: Right again is an isolated buttress with a square top, about 30m left of the main area.

81 The Gargoyle E2 5c   1985
8m   The left arête gives good climbing and the gear can be placed before leaving the ground. A squeezed-in eliminate ●**Daz Automatic**, E3 5c (1994), is directly up the face right of The Gargoyle.

82 Phillipa Buttress VS 4c   1934-51
8m   Gain and climb the fun offwidth.

Sentinel Main Area: The next routes are on the main area, 30m to the right.

83 Crystal Tips E3 6a   1989
8m   The wall right of the arête lacks an obvious line, but this problem tackles the centre of the wall from a crimp on the right; bold and high in the grade.

84 Stepped Crack M   1957-65
8m   The deep crack.

85 Black Slab Arête S 4a   1934-51
8m   From Stepped Crack, swing right with determination around the arête at the obvious line of holds to cross Black Slab and finish up an easy groove.

86 Black Slab VS 4b ★   1934-51
8m   A bold little number. Start up the slab (or traverse in from the right) and trend left over the overlap to finish up the arête. ●The direct start over the overlap is a reachy E1 5c.

87 Black Slab Variation D   1934-51
8m   Step up the fun (but reachy) slab on poor holds.

88 Green Corner VD   traditional

89 Now or Never E1 5b ★   1971
8m   An intimidating route. Start up the obvious flake in the black left-hand wall of the arête. A difficult move round the arête gains a ledge on the right-hand side. Place some gear and find out if you have the heart for the next awkward move up the arête.

Ella Russell enjoys the beautiful evening light on Wall Corner, HVD 4a (page 14), one of the many classic easier climbs to be found in the Ash Tree Wall area. Photo: David Simmonite.

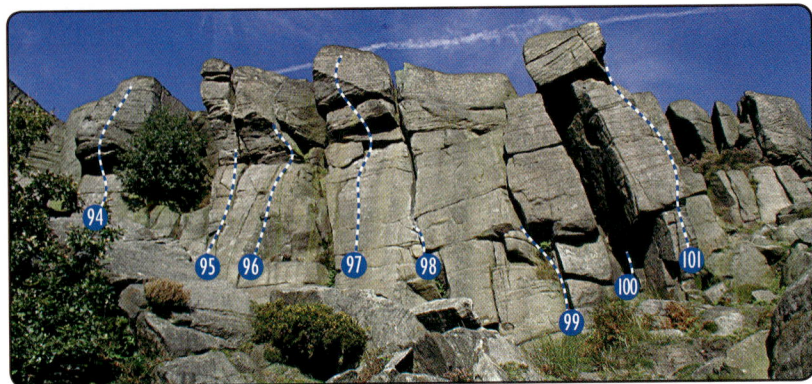

90 Kiss me my Darling E2 5c   2002
8m A direct route up the left-hand side of the arête. After a boulder problem start, continue up the left side of the arête to the top. ● **Too Good to be Forgotten**, E2 6a (1987), takes the same initial arête, but this time on its right.

91 Sentinel Chimney VD   1934-51
9m An unusual and protectable route which will severely test those climbing without proper thought or technique.

92 The Sentinel E2 5b ★★   1977
8m Taken direct, the biggest arête of this area is steep and very exposed. A super route although a little escapable in places and with just adequate gear. ● **Sentinel Indirect**, HVS 5b (1971), avoids the overhang by a traverse from Sentinel Crack.

93 Sentinel Crack VD   1934-51
8m The crack to the right of the big arête. ● A silly route, **Present Arms**, HS 4c (2002), climbs the slab to the right of the crack to the ledge and ascends the block at the back by embracing both arêtes with a final long reach.

94 High Flyer E3 5b ★   1978
8m The unprotected bulge right of Sentinel Crack is climbed trending diagonally leftwards. An easy E3 if nothing goes wrong.

95 The Grazer VS 4c ★   1957-65
8m An obvious jamming crack splits a bulge. With a big cam above your head you can afford to really 'give it some'.

96 Lie Back HS 4b ★   1957-65
8m A great little layback flake breaches the bulge just to the right of The Grazer. If only it was three times as long. ● **Think of England**, M (traditional), is the groove just right; a good, easy beginner's lead.

97 Ring my Bell E4 6b   1985
8m The left edge of the buttress. Inventive and very determined climbing might get you over the roof.

98 Ringo S 3c ★   1957-65
8m A pleasant and sustained climb. ● **Ring Piece**, HVS 6a (1991), is the wall to the right with side-runners; artificial.

99 Ring Climb HVD 4a ★   1934-51
7m Less sustained than Ringo, with a more distinct crux.

100 Ring Chimney M   1934-51
8m The wide cleft is not particularly exciting. The left arête of the chimney is a little artificial, but quite nice, and goes at about E1 5c.

101 Agnostic's Arête VS 5a ★   1977
8m The right-hand side of the blunt arête has some nice moves and is quite bold. It can also be started on the left-hand side with a move around right at 3m; finish direct. The wall right is ● **Pickpocket**, VS 5a (1978-83), ● and the cleft right again is D.

A Burbage Memory

We lived next door to this man called Les Gillott, and my dad asked him to take us out climbing, to burn off some excess energy, so he began taking me and Neil Stokes out. We'd just top rope stuff, Les would lead it, or if it was hard, we'd all top rope it.

The first thing you'd do were the little things around Burbage, but the big things to try to do were still the Brown and Whillans routes. You'd have a go at those, see how you'd get on, and after that it was the Peter Crew and Alpha Club routes. Les was good for that, he'd a real sense of history and of what had been done and what you should be trying, and as well as that, he knew all the things that Brown and Whillans had tried and not done. We'd just go through all those things.

I suppose at that time, if you'd done all the things that were supposed to be hard, and it would go from just being a bit of fun to thinking, 'right, I'm alright at this, let's see what else we can do', and we'd start looking round for new things to try. And I know this sounds funny, because so much has been done since, but finding new things wasn't all that obvious. I remember one of the first things we did was The Knack, and I suppose that got us started.

You'd nearly always abseil down something first, give it a brush and that. And at the time, ethics weren't all that strict. There wasn't all that much sense of trying to do something without looking at it. When you went down to clean it, you wouldn't top rope, but you'd always lock off your figure eight, and have a try at the moves. You know, nobody was bothered about that. Ethics have always changed. I think it's great the way things are now, that people try to do things well, but then, it was a different time, and things were different. Well, I mean, a lot of them used to chip back then, especially in the quarries. Not slagging, just saying that that's the sort of thing that went on. But for us, when you were trying a route, you'd try the moves, just to see if you could do it or if you were wasting your time. And of course the other thing was that

you didn't want someone else to get the route before you — you wanted to get it.

There were lots of people at it then, doing routes. Fawcett, Tom Proctor, Gabe Regan, Ed Drummond. And one of the first things we did was to start to eliminate aid points. We were all into outdoing the last generation, and aid points were like a red rag to a bull. So we'd do all that stuff at Millstone and Lawrencefield and that. And there was that big thing at the time of renaming things once you'd freed them.

Burbage was great, because, back then, you could get the bus to the Fox House for 2p — People's Republic of South Yorkshire and all that. I have a few favourites in the area. The Knock, of course. I can't remember if we top roped that first, but I don't think we did, because I remember jumping off it a lot. And West Side Story, that's tough, that one. It was maddening because the first time out, I nearly got it, but didn't think I should jump for the hold. I came down, and just thought, I'll get back up there and do it, but then I could never get back up. Another one I really like is Lost World over on Carl Wak, because, you see, that one has a crack to start. I've always liked that, because it gives it some direction, a bit of upwards. And runners. I've always liked runners, because it's your life, isn't it. And The Sphinx I like. Things like that, high stuff where you're not messing about with ropes, but you're still getting a cheap thrill. And of course, Silent Spring. I love that one, because it had the vision, to see that something went along there. You know, like what Johnny Dawes has. Like lots of people were really strong, but he had that special vision. I mean, Braille Trail, that's an amazing climb, and I never thought of it. And that's what Silent Spring had — a vision.

But yeah, we'd lots of days at Burbage then. Summer evenings. And as we'd climb, you could always see the last bus coming around Surprise Corner, and we always knew that if we packed up then, and legged it across the moors, we'd always just catch that bus back home.

John Allen

Hollyash Wall

This is perhaps the biggest buttress at Burbage North and is home to some great routes. It is easily identified by the large roof in the middle of the buttress with a big holly tree under its right-hand end.

102 **The Keffer** HVS 5a   1986
8m The blunt arête/rib on the left side wall of Hollyash Wall is delicate and poorly protected. ●The slab left is **With Juicy Bits**, HVS 5a (1990). Start up the stepped slab to gain the buttress proper and make tricky moves left of the blunt arête to gain a standing position in the break. Move left to nearly above the holly tree and climb up the pocketed slab. ●Now, ready with those blinkers? Try **Small Beer**, HS 4a (1992), up the narrow facet just right of The Keffer and a finish up the crack of Still Orange.

103 **Still Orange** S 4a   1956
10m A jolly route with an exciting finish. Climb the corner to the ledge before making an intimidating step right to finish up the vertical crack; well-protected. ●**Rise 'n Shine**, HVS 5a (1979), is a line up the centre of the wall just to the right.

104 **Green Crack** VD ★   1934-51
12m An excellent route, with good protection and sustained interest.

105 **Dover's Progress** HVS 5a   1932
12m A bold undertaking up the narrow wall. Side-runners are probably fair play.

106 **Hollyash Crack** VS 4b ★ ★   1932
12m A really interesting route up the wider crack. It can be thrutched, or climbed on the outside, using a variety of techniques. ●**En Passant**, E2 6a (1990), is the highly eliminate and rather bold line just to the right, avoiding holds in either of its neighbours.

107 **The Knight's Move** HVS 5a ★ ★ ★   1933
14m A classic route up the line of weakness at the left-hand end of the big roof. Use the big holes to gain the flake-line and continue straight up to its end at a bulge. Step left, up, and then right (the knight's move). Continue straight up to the top. A soft touch at the very bottom of the grade.

108 **Peter's Progress** VS 4c ★   1953
14m A fine, exposed route. Climb The Knight's Move until a long and airy traverse can be made on a break above the big roof. Finish up Great Crack.

109 **Arme Blanche** E5 6a ★   1980
14m This route goes straight through the big roof about 2m from its left-hand end. Either place a wire in The Knight's Move at the left end of the roof, or make do with a tiny cam at the back of the roof (or treat yourself to both). From the obvious undercut, reach round the lip to sloping holds before reaching (or slapping) for the big break. Mantel this and then go direct up the wall via pockets, some bomber cams and a thin section through a bulge.

110 **Great Crack** VS 5a ★   1932
14m From behind the giant holly, climb the corner

When John Allen returned to pioneering on grit,
a decade after the great 'Gritstone Rennaissance'
of the 1970s, he added some of the most technical
and visionary climbs of the day, many of which have
gone from obscurity to true classic status. Here, Ben
Bransby fights his way along the break on The Sphinx,
V7 (page 17). Photo: Adam Long.

to the roof. Hand-traverse out until a stiff pull gains the enjoyable upper crack.

⑪ King's Return E2 5b   1994

14m The slender pillar.

⑫ The Big Chimney HVD ★   pre-1934

12m Climb direct to the capping stone. Escape right, or be a tiger, and take it on the left at S 4a.

⑬ Windjammer E1 5b ★★   1980

12m Start at the cutaway and pull boldly out right to gain a stance and a break close to the right arête. Traverse carefully left along the break all the way to the left arête where a bomber cam is gratefully found. Make a lovely move up the arête before finishing easily. A really satisfying route.

⑭ The Rainmaker E1 5a ★   1977

12m Another airy route with fine moves. Start as for Windjammer, but move only slightly leftwards and boldly climb the centre of the face via a pocket.

Both of the previous two routes can be started more directly to the right of the cutaway at 5c. A direct start to the undercut left arête still awaits.

⑮ Big Chimney Arête HS 4b ★   1934-51

12m A fine exposed climb with good protection.
● The short wall above a ledge on the right can be climbed past slots at a beautifully dangerous V4 (6a).

The next route is on an isolated, narrow buttress 20m right of the last route.

⑯ Barry Manilow VS 4c   1985

7m An unusual, but good route, straight up the buttress. Picking through the nostrils is straightforward, but you wouldn't want to blow it higher up.

The Grotto Area

The edge breaks down into boulders and small outcrops over the next hundred metres. The routes here are short, often hidden by trees, and slightly obscure. However, in many ways, this is one of the best areas on the edge. There is a sense of isolation and privacy to be found here. The trees come right up to the base of routes making the setting unique for the crag. The routes are probably best enjoyed as part of a soloing circuit, although there are a lot of fine leads, especially in the lower grades. The first route is found 10m past Barry Manilow, set back slightly.

John Coefield on The Knight's Move, one of the biggest and best routes of its grade on the edge. It only just sneaks into the HVS bracket, and is a great route for the confident VS leader to have a go at (previous page). Photo: David Parry.

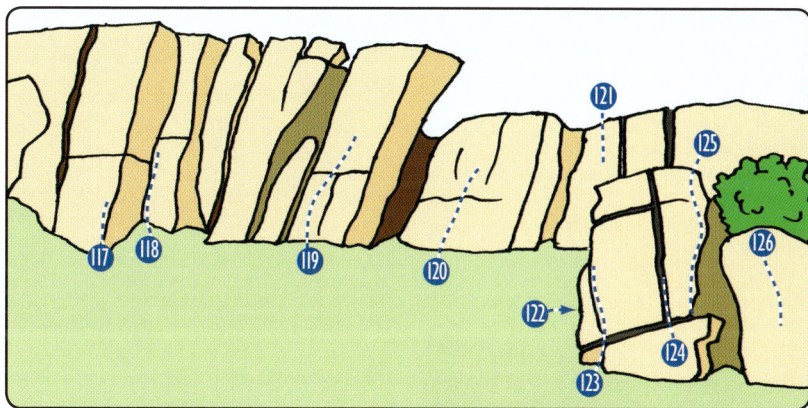

117 Survivor's Syndrome E3 5b   1984

7m The arête, climbed using neither the arête on the left nor the corner on the right, is serious but very artificial. ●The dirty cracks to the left are **Snowflakes** and **December Climb** (VD, 1957-65).

118 Twin Chimney's Layback HVD ★   1932

7m The obvious and attractive slabby corner-crack. Immediately right are two chimneys: ●**Left Twin Chimney**, D, and ●**Right Twin Chimney**, VD (both pre-1934).

119 The Happy Slapper VS 4c   1999

7m The wall is climbed via pockets and reaches.

120 Jimmy Riddle VS 4c   2000

7m Climb the centre of the pillar, starting at a short crack. A bold approach pays dividends.

121 Always Another One VS 5b   1992

7m On the short buttress right of Jimmy Riddle, follow a faint crack up the front. ●The arête on the triangular buttress just right is V1 (5b).

122 Bulletproof E1 6a   2000

8m The left sidewall of Split Slab Buttress. From two good pockets use a finger pocket to reach a flake out left. Mantel the flake to reach a break and the top.

123 Split Slab Crack S 4a   1957-65

8m Climb the leftward-leaning hand crack on the left edge of the buttress; finish direct.

124 Split Slab VD   pre-1934

8m The obvious wide crack is gained from the short green slab below.

125 Slide-Away E1 5a   1978

8m The unprotected blunt rib to the right of Split Slab has interesting moves but a nasty landing.

126 Grotto Slab M ★   1957-1965

8m An excellent route which takes the easy-angled slab direct to the holly. ●You might regret stepping airily across the chasm onto the hanging arête for the Severe extension finish (joining Submission).

127 Grotto Crack HS 4b   1957-65

8m This beast lies waiting for you in the grotto.

128 Submission VS 5a ★   1978
8m From the chimney, make a committing move left to the arête. Follow this, positive and straightforward, but still no place for the jitters.

129 Falstaff's Chimney VD ★   pre-1934
8m The clean chimney splits the tower to the right.

130 Falstaff's Innominate S 4a ★   pre-1934
8m The crack just right of the chimney has bomber jams and bomber gear.

Autumn magic. John Horscroft enjoys perfect gritstone conditions on Falstaff's Innominate, S 4a (this page).
Photo: Niall Grimes.

131 Falstaff's Crack M   pre-1934
8m The crack just right again.

132 Pale Face HVS 5a   2000
8m Climb the wall and cracked arête above, just to the right of the gully right of Falstaff's Crack.

Hidden Boulders: In the oak trees just below Pale Face are a few blocks of interest to the obscurist. The most obvious feature is the large, Sphinx-like block projecting toward the valley floor. ● **The Gibbet**, V2 (5c), is an exciting problem that lurches from a boulder to a jug on the point of the prow. A couple of hearty swings gains the top. ● **Iain's Prow**, V7 (6b), starts at the back of the roof and slaps along the double lip, to finish up The Gibbet. Below this is another large, squat boulder. ● **Mono Bulge** is a powerful V7 (6b) that grasps over the bulge on big holds. On the front of this boulder is a rippled face. The centre of this face would be a tough problem on snappy holds. ● Traversing the lip from right to left is **Ripple Riser**, V3 (6a).

Scarred Buttress: Above, and right of Pale face, is another pleasant buttress.

133 Bilberry Wall HD ★★   pre-1934
10m A brilliant climb. Gain and climb the short crack and then move left to climb the tower direct. A poor eliminate, ● **Bilberry Cake,** E1 5a, climbs the slab 2m left.

134 Bilberry Arête S 4a   1965-78
9m The right-hand arête of the buttress is bold.

135 **The Edging Machine** E1 5c 1978
6m The left arête of the buttress is problematic and reachy to start.

136 **Alpha Crack** HS 4b 1934-51
6m The left-hand crack has a tricky start.

137 **Omega Crack** VD 1934-51
6m The ill-defined groove line. Quite good.

138 **Scarred Buttress Climb** HD ★ 1934-51
6m A cracking little climb on perfect rock. Head direct for the obvious wide fissure.

Tharf Buttress: The next big buttress is home to a good concentration of easier climbs. None of them are mega, but a good time can be had trying to tick them all.

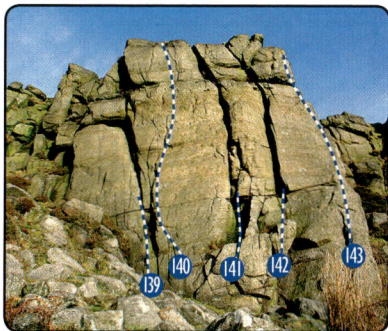

139 **First Crack** S 4b ★ 1957-65
9m The crack eases after a hard start.

140 **Tharf Cake** VS 5a ★ 1977
6m The slabby wall is thin and rather bold.

141 **Left Twin Crack** S pre-1934
9m A good climb with weird moves.

142 **Right Twin Crack** S pre-1934
9m Well-protected, technical climbing.

143 **Farcical Arête** HS 4a ★ 1957-65
9m Climb the unprotected right arête of the buttress with confidence.

Obscenity Area

The last major area of Burbage North is well worth the walk. Perfect rock and strong lines combine to give a great number of very high-quality routes, with a good variety of bold, technical and open climbs as well as some brilliant cracks.

144 **The Irrepressible Urge** E1 5b ★★ 1978
6m A little beauty up the middle of the wall, where precision and a cool head are mandatory. This is a taster of what micro-routes are all about.

145 **The Arctic Mammal** E3 6a ★★ 2001
6m The left-hand side of the right arête is pure grit magic, although the landing is poor. ● The original **Small Arctic Mammal**, E1 6a (1978-83), climbs the arête on the right, but is somewhat contrived.

Immediately to the right is a recess with a number of squashed-in little lines. They are: ● **Left Recess Crack**, HVD and ● **Right Recess Crack**, HS 4a (both 1957-65). ● The wall between has even been climbed at 5c; **Time for Bed Said Zebedee** (1999).

146 **Ace** VS 4b ★ 1965-1978
6m The prow. ● The fist crack and chimney to the right gives routes of VD and D. ● The sharp arête in back of the recess is V3 (6a), but keep your backside off the back wall.

> **"Ordinarily,**
> **a gritstone edge**
> is merely a chunk of glorified, petrified sandpaper. Of course, such material plays mischief with one's own skin and clothes, but, as compensation, there are few other kinds of rock you can hang on by your waistcoat and seat of your britches whilst you are feeling around for the next hand and foot-holds."
>
> Claude E Benson, 1906

The modern way. John Roberts headpointing
Three Blind Mice, E7 6c (overleaf), one of the
more popular E7s in the area.
Photo: Adam Long.

147 Thrall's Thrutch S   1957-65
6m The tight chimney is well-named.

148 Brook's Layback HS 4b ★★   1932
8m The corner-crack. You can layback if you wish but it does have perfect jams all the way. ● The arête to the right has been climbed at HVS 5a, but as escape is possible anywhere, it feels very eliminate.

149 Wobblestone Crack VD ★   pre-1934
8m A lovely route up the obvious crack in the front of the buttress, with a thought-provoking start.

150 Biscuits for Breakfast E4 6b   1993
8m The hanging slab, starting up the former route. Traverse right at the obvious pockets and mantel on two obvious pebbles. Finish up rounded breaks.

151 Red Shift E3 5c   1978
8m Traverse left out of Hollybush Gully and climb the top half of the left arête. It's a bit unsatisfying and really needs a lower start to the arête.

152 Hollybush Gully VD   pre-1934
8m Fun traditional climbing with steep, dirty and slippery moves up green holds.

153 The Screamer E1 5c   1978
8m The finger-crack in the right wall of the gully is unfortunately very escapable, which is a pity.

154 Gazebo Watusi E6 6b ★★   1993
10m From the large pocket on Obscenity (gear) move out left to the arête and make a hard move to gain a standing position on the sloping ledge. Gaining the top from there is a bit easier, but serious.

155 Obscenity VS 4c ★★★   1948
11m The fat crack. This is why climbing was such a laugh in the old days. Pull on your corduroys, grab some hexes and let rip.

156 Destructive Tendencies E7 7a   2004
11m An obvious problem that unfortunately requires a very strict approach. From Amazon Crack, step left and slap up the highly technical arête. Gear is placed at the base of the arête just above half-height at this grade.

157 Amazon Crack HS 4a ★★★   1932
11m The obvious crack. Perfect jamming and more sophisticated than its bully of a brother.

158 Don't Knock my Smock or I'll Clean your Clock E4 6a † ★   2002
11m The arête right of Amazon Crack is climbed on its right-hand side throughout, with bold moves up the upper arête. ● This supersedes **Artemis**, HVS 5a (1993), which escapes left at mid-height and finished up Amazon Crack.

(159) Amazon Gully M   1934-51

(160) Boney Moroney E1 5c ★   1969
10m The snaking crack and left arête of the narrow tower is quite awkward.

(161) Long Tall Sally E1 5b ★★★   1960-65
10m An elegant lady who is only interested in flawless technique and who has thrown off plenty of young (and old) hopefuls. The attractive groove yields to delicate footwork and a touch of blind faith. ●**Rockers,** E1 5c ★ (1985), is a variation, stepping left after the bulge to climb the arête.

(162) Three Blind Mice E7 6c ★★   1994
10m Beautiful, dangerous climbing up the commanding slab. Move left into a scoop from a large pocket. Crank directly up on vague pockets above (avoiding an easier, less committing alternative to the right) to a harrowing mantel onto the slab above; finish trending left. ●This supersedes **Short Fat Bastard**, E1 5b (1987), that foot-traversed the lip from Greeny Crack.

(163) Greeny Crack VS 4b ★   1934-51
10m An enjoyable old school romp up the corner crack. ●The arête to the right is poor and artificial, **Rhapsody in Green**, VS 5a (1978).

(164) Left Studio Climb VD   pre-1934
10m Follow a thin crack to a ledge. Climb the arête on the right (bold) and a crack above to finish. A good and varied challenge. ●**Right Studio Climb**, VD (pre-1934), is the inferior corner to the right. ●**The Artist**, VS 4c (1997), is the slab direct between the two studio climbs.

(165) Rose Flake VS 4b ★   1958
8m Good gear, burly jamming. Growl up the left of the two cracks on the left-hand side of the fin.

Velvet Cave

This cave lies about 40m below Nicotine Stain.

❶ Velvet Crab V7 (6c)
The left arête of the cave. The finish feels high and a bit gritty.

❷ Velvet Roof V2 (5c)
Quality thuggery.

❸ Right-Hand Roof V3 (5c)

❹ Zaff Skoczylas V9 (6c)
The low hanging rib, from a very low start. Starting slightly higher is easier (V8), although perhaps a bit more logical.

166 The Fin E1 5b ★★   1970/71
8m The ferocious hanging crack is superb. High gear can be placed before the crux but it will probably occupy the best handholds.

167 Ai No Corrida E5 6b ★   1984
8m A committing and testing route up the right side of the hanging arête, with a side-runner in the next route (or without at E6).

168 Right Fin HVS 5a ★   1957-65
8m Follow the attractive flake on the right wall. It's a bit of a soft touch, but only has one runner.

169 The Twenty Year Itch E4 6b   1993
8m The short wall just right above a poor landing via some small pockets. ●Highball V4.

170 The Enthusiast V3 (HVS 6a)
The left-hand edge of the wall is trickier than it looks. ●The blocky corner on the left is M.

171 Nicotine Stain V4 (E1 6b)
A brilliant extended boulder problem following the obvious seam. The hardest moves are low down, but it's solid 5c all the way to the break.

172 April Fool VD   1957-65
8m The crack. ●Laybacking the left arête is V0+ (5b). ●**Approach**, V2 (HVS 5c), has great thin moves up the narrow face to the right. No arêtes.

173 Spider Crack VS 5b ★   1957-65
6m The thin crack is more devious than it looks though you can, at least, protect this one.

174 The Be All HVD   traditional
7m The wide crack with the help of the thinner crack.

175 The End All HS 4a   traditional
7m The wide crack, taking care with a loose block. ●The technical wall to the left is **Pest Control**, V4 (6b).

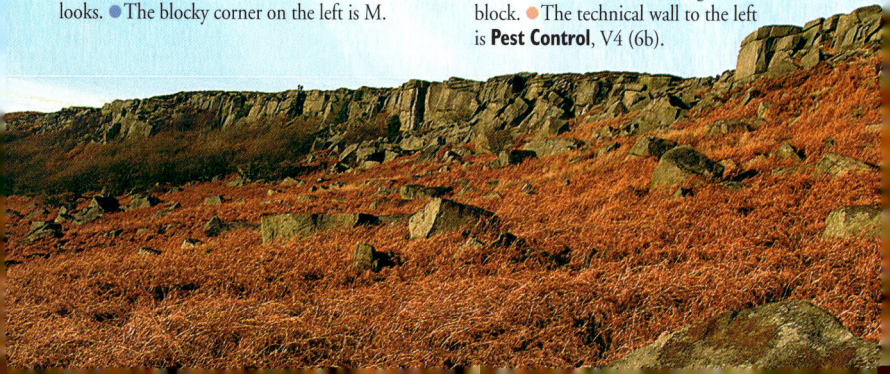

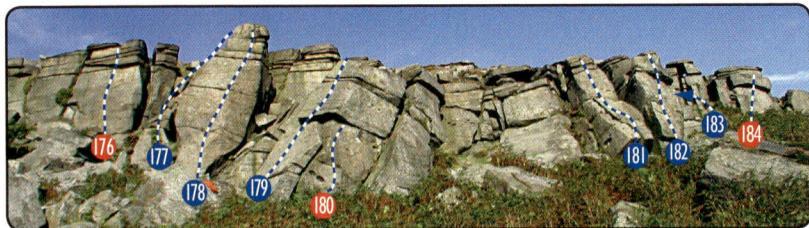

176 **Shelf Wall** V2 (5c)

177 **End Buttress** D   1957-65
8m   Climb the wide crack and then step confidently onto the slab on the left side.

178 **The Penultimate** E1 5b ★   1977
8m   A super technical route straight up the main face with a tricky start.

179 **End Slab** M ★   1957-65
8m   The slab with a wide break is easy but committing. A good introduction to friction climbing.

180 **Two Pocket Sitter** V3 (6a)

181 **Ender** D ★   1965-78
7m   The left-hand buttress is excellent, and another great route for beginners.

182 **Endste** D   1965-78
8m   The right-hand buttress has a balancey step right to a little flake and is quite bold.

183 **Almost the Last Word** HVS 5c   2004
8m   Around the corner from Endste is a blunt rib above a small roof. From the right, step left onto the obvious foothold before climbing the blunt rib.

184 **Capped Rib** V3 (6a)

The Little Cube: A fine square block 90m to the right .

1 **Little Cube Arête** V1 (5b)

2 **Once Upon a Time** V9 (6c)
A brilliant problem up the awesome smooth wall, very similar to Westworld at Burbage West.

3 **Beyond the End** V0 (5a)

The Three Bears: This is a little collection of blocks 50m right again, giving some easy problems.

4 **Daddy Wall** V0− (4c)

5 **Daddy Bear Arête** V0− (5a)

6 **Daddy Arête Right** V0+ (5b)
Too lumpy? ● The wall just right is V0− (4c).

7 **Mommy Wall** V1+ (5b)

8 **Mommy Bear Arête** V0+ (5b)

9 **Mommy Bear Right** V0 (5b)
Too soft? ● The wall right is V0− (4b).

10 **Baby Bear Wall** V0 (5a)

11 **Baby Bear Arête** V0− (4c)
Juuuuuusst right!

Burbage South

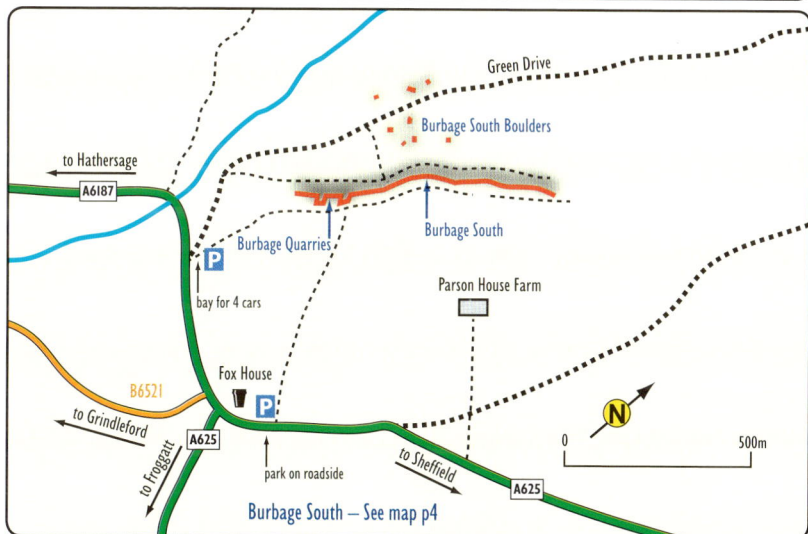

Green Drive

Burbage South Boulders

to Hathersage

A6187

Burbage Quarries

Burbage South

P

bay for 4 cars

Parson House Farm

B6521

Fox House

to Grindleford

A625

park on roadside

to Froggatt

to Sheffield

A625

N

0   500m

Burbage South — See map p4

by Niall Grimes

Burbage South could easily be overlooked among the great crags of the gritstone area. The edge, although long, seldom has great stature, and is often quite broken. It gets less sun than most, and often appears dark and dank. However, whilst it is perhaps not the greatest edge, it somehow manages to have a huge collection of many of the most beautiful and challenging routes on grit, as well as some of the best rock anywhere.

Tall, powerful challenges are to be found along the main central section, especially on The Tower and The Keep, giving phenomenal, exposed routes. Superb boulder problems are strewn the length of the crag, problems with great individual character. In-between lies one of the finest aspects of Burbage climbing, if not of grit itself – the micro-route. Endless short and ferociously technical challenges are to be unearthed everywhere, and – especially in these days of pads – these will give some of the most

memorable days out. The routes are pure gems, and even the most ardent Burbage fan will never run out of inspiration.

The Climbing

Routes: The edge has over 160 routes, ranging from Diff to E10, and a good spread of everything in-between. Every type of route is here: tall, forceful crack-lines, sizzling arêtes, thin slabs, technical wall-climbs and thrilling overhanging desperates. Routes also range from a few fun metres in length to ones giving a huge sense of exposure.

Bouldering: The gentle pasture of the Green Drive is a sort of mini-Fontainebleau, with lovely rounded blocks sitting casually in open surroundings. With its good landings and great number of problems, mainly in the easier levels, the Green Drive area is a lower-grade boulderer's paradise.

If more advanced boulderers find the Green Drive lacking in challenge, then this can easily be found on the edge itself. Along its entire length are many fine tough problems in little circuits or at the base of the routes. The far left-hand end is particularly good in this respect, where strong lines and some interesting landings combine to give some tough challenges.

Conditions and aspect

The crag faces mainly north-west and gets the sun from late afternoon. Despite its lack of sun, the rock is clean, and although some of the more recessed bays, especially the quarries, can become a little green, this presents surprisingly little problem. The far left end gets less light than the main edge, and some sections can be damp in winter. For all the above reasons, Burbage South makes a great escape from the summer heat. The crag is very sheltered, and even on wet days, some routes, particularly the harder ones, never seem to get wet.

Adam Coefield on Rascal Groove, V5 (this page)
Photo: John Coefield.

Parking and approach

Ample parking is available on the roadside above the Fox House. Cross a wall at a stile 150m above the Fox House, then strike straight across the moor to the top of the quarries, from where all parts of the crag can be approached in 10-15 minutes. There is also a small parking bay at the end of the Green Drive. **By Bus:** The First 272 bus runs hourly from Sheffield to Castleton, and stops at the Fox House. Also, the First 240 Sheffield to Bakewell and the TM Travel 65 Sheffield to Buxton, both call at the Fox House.

Burbage Earl

For many people, Burbage South stops at Roof Route. Adventurers will continue to Split Nose. Few ever go beyond. However, in these dark reaches, nicknamed Burbage Earl due to the resemblance to Earl Crag in Yorkshire, lie some of the best and hardest challenges on the edge. Little walls and arêtes spring up aplenty, and almost every inch of rock is climbable. It is very shady, making it a good place to escape summer heat, although some of the problems get dirty in winter.

The best feature hereabouts is The Little Rascal, the last steep, clean wall on the edge proper. The first problems lie to the left of this on an obvious capstone block, 50m away. ● **The Flat Cap**, V7 (6b), is on the north side. Starting from crimps, climb left and up. ● **The Whippet**, V5 (6b), is the line on the opposite side. ● Further right, 25m from the Rascal, is the short, but fun, **What a Way to Spend Easter,** V5 (6b), climbing a hemmed-in triangular slab.

1 The Little Rascal E4 6b ★   1986
8m Start up a small groove at the right-hand side of the buttress to gain the break. Traverse this left and make a hard stand-up to finish. ● **Rascal Groove,** V5 (6b), follows the bottom groove, then escapes right at the high ledge (or top out at E1). ● The sit start is a very fingery V10 (7a). ● The undercut arête 4m left is V1 (5c).

2 Flake 'n' Blob V0 (4c)
A brill highball. From the boulder, step onto the arête and gain the flake. Swing left, and top-out using a blob. Flake and blob! Geddit?

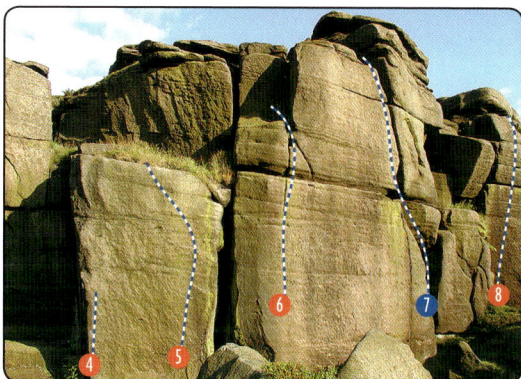

3 **The Housebrick** V2 (6a)
Just right, past a fine chimney (V0) is a short wall.
Climb this on fine crimps from a sit start.

4 **Standup Arête** V4 (6a)
The arête. ●The very bunched sit-start is **Fuji
Heavy Industries**, V7 (6c).

5 **Rail Thing** V2 (5c)
Dyno from the rail and mantel.

6 **Pocket Wall** V3 (6a)
Oddly, harder with the arête. ●V9 (6c) from a sitter.

7 **Pebble Crack** HVS 5a ★   1957-65
6m A good one for climbing archaeologists. The
hanging crack is gained with difficulty and followed
past a naughty foreign body.

8 **Flat Wall Dyno** V6 (6b)
To the right, climb the steep wall and bulging rib
above from the positive break. ●**Footy Rib** is the
slabby rib just right to the same finish, V2 (5c).

9 **Intense** VII (7a)
All-out frictionless desperation, started by jumping
for holds. A juicy Jerry gem. The all-too-obvious
start from the break is a well-tried project. ●**I'm
Tense**, V8 (6c), starts in the thin slot, then follows
the curving flake leftwards. ●**Basketball Bulge** to
the right is V3 (6a), gaining a jug by a jump.

*A few metres right is another small outcrop,
beginning with an arête on the left. This is:*

10 **Black Arête** V3 (6a)

To the right is a tall black block:

11 **Left Arête** V0 (5a)
The left arête of the black block.

12 **Snitch** V3 (6a)

13 **Prow Crack** S 4a   1957-65
6m A tough jamming sequence gains good holds
for the steep finish.

14 The Rib V8 (6c)
Welford's neo-classic, climbing the right side of the rib.

15 Fat Man's Misery HS 4b   1934-51
6m Indeed. ●Layback the right arête at V3 (6a).

16 Impossible Groove
The beautiful, unclimbed feature.

17 Desparête V8 (E4 6c)
Superb. Monkey up the tower to the break (crux).
Easier climbing and a sketchy top remain.

Ten metres right is a crack in a flat wall.

18 No Name Crack S 4a   1934-51
6m The wide crack. ●The crimpy wall to the right
is V1 (5c).

Ten metres right are more steep walls.

19 Clark's Route V1 (HVS 5b)
The sublime left arête of the face.

20 Sublime Indifference V2 (E2 6a)
Mantel the ramp and make a thin crank up the wall.
Superb.

21 Big Bad Wolf E5 6b ★   1982
8m Fairly mean. Climb the scooped, overhanging
wall, starting from the left. A hard move up from
the low break (almost 6c) gains the next break.
Finish much more easily, using the right arête.

22 Home Cooking V5 (E4 6b)
Slap up the narrow, overhanging tower, rocking
onto the slab at two-thirds height.

23 Eating Out V6 (6b)
Smear up the desperately technical slab on the right,
past a sharp tooth, avoiding the chock. ●**Chockstone Layback**, V0 (4b), is a terrific voyage around
the jammed chock just right. ●**Green S-Groove**,
immediately right, is V2 (6a).

*Ten metres below are some large boulders. The
next problems are on the downhill-facing face.*

24 Left Edge V3 (6a)
From a sit-start in the centre of the face, swing left
and layback the left edge on the right. ●The
dangerous slab on the left is V1 (5b).

25 Triangle Wall V5 (6b)
Climb the valley-facing face on sidepulls and rip-
ples. Fairly desperate. The sit-start is the same grade.
●Laybacking the right edge, on the left, is V4 (6b).

Back on the edge is:

26 Sweet Arête V3 (6a)
Start on the right. Climb up and left to the arête and
the top. ●The fissure just right is a VD chimney
problem or a filthy S 4b offwidth if you must.

27 The Wrestle V4 (6b)
A tasteless scrape up the front of the narrow
buttress. ●**Little Pig**, to the right, is V0 (4c).

28 The Alliance V6 (E4 6b)
A brilliant problem, monkeying up the two distant
arêtes. A committing grasp for a pocket leads to a
careful top-out. Spotter recommended. ●A problem exists on the underside of the boulder in front
of this problem, starting on the right, V4 (6b).

29 Friar's Wall V0− (4c)
A lovely wall on cushy holds.

30 Dominican V0− (4b)
The friendly jam crack.

31 Guppy Left V1 (5c)
Climb the left side of the long slabby arête.

32 Guppy Arête V2 (5c)
A great problem which guppies up the right side of the slabby arête. ●**Guppy Sitdown** is a quality V6 (6b) starting down right.

Five metres right is a buttress with a wide crack.

33 Renobulous Bongetl E5 6a   1982
8m   Climb the unprotected right arête of the buttress starting on the left and finishing with a long reach above a bad landing. Not for the faint-hearted. ●**Short Crack**, VD 4a (1965-78), is the crack to the left.

34 Breathless HVS 5b   1965-77
6m   Start on a boulder beneath the left-hand arête of the next buttress and follow the side wall just left of the arête to a reachy finish. ●**Breathless Start** climbs the lower arête from the ground, V2 (6a).

35 Lens Crack S 4a   1957-65
6m   Climb the left-hand crack, or the similar right-hand branch. ●**Lens Arête** just below is V2 (5c).

36 Wagger's Wiggle D   1952
6m   A crack in the buttress 30m right. ●The roof and steep wall immediately right is **Flip, Flop, Fly**, VS 5a (2004).

The Left End

A little further on, the edge proper begins in good style, giving a number of classy micro-routes on perfect rock.

37 Split Nose VS 5a ★   1957-65
6m   The hanging crack near the arête succumbs to a satisfying and gymnastic sequence. The same crack on the other side of the nose is 4c.

38 The Gnat E1 5c ★   1966-69/72
6m   A micro-delight up the pesky crack.

39 Midge E2 6a ★★   1972
6m   A cracking exercise up the fierce little slotted groove just right. ●**Kleg**, HVS 5b (1972), is the wall just right, traversing right at the break.

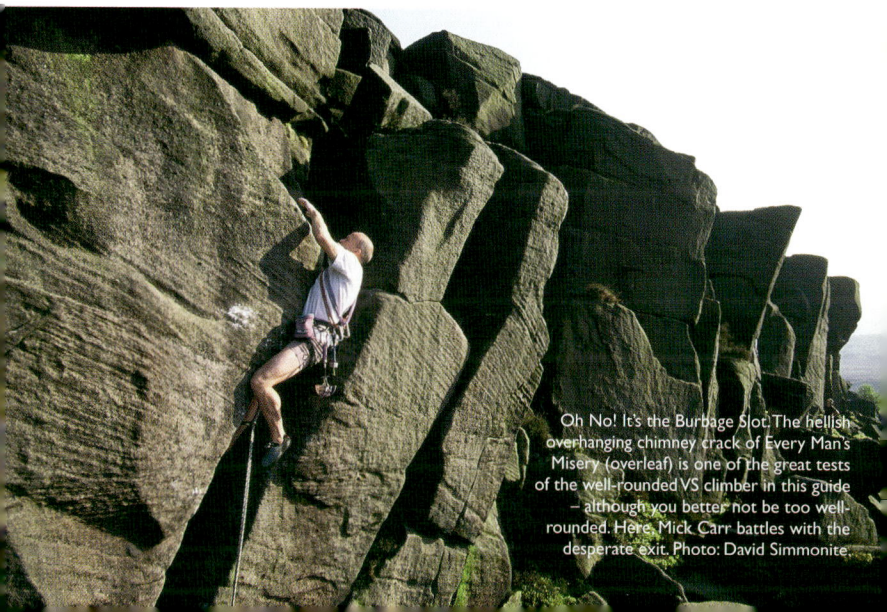

Oh No! It's the Burbage Slot. The hellish overhanging chimney crack of Every Man's Misery (overleaf) is one of the great tests of the well-rounded VS climber in this guide – although you better not be too well-rounded. Here, Mick Carr battles with the desperate exit. Photo: David Simmonite.

The **Advanced Beginner**

Having made your first moves on rock, learned how to place protection, manage ropes and generally move safely on rock, where do you go then? Well, here are some recommendations for advanced beginners, moving into the Severe and Hard Severe grades, routes that will test the skills already learned, but moves them into more pushy situations, although still, hopefully, in safety. Again, a basic rack of nuts, slings and extenders should be enough, although you may wish to add a few camming devices.

Burbage North, again, has a fine array of possibilities; try Route 2 and 3 and Twenty Foot Crack which, although only VD, are steep enough to make them pressing leads; also Wall Corner and other routes in the Ash Tree area, and Lie Back and other routes in the lofty Sentinel area. Nearby, at **Burbage South**, although there is not much in the lower grades, try The Staircase and Drainpipe Crack which are a couple of stern, muscular offerings. **Millstone** is a much less suitable crag for the beginner, being steeper, and less solid. However, Great Slab, Eartha and Hell's Bells are stiff Hard Severes for the competent. **Rivelin Edge** has a few steep cracks to test new skills, with Left and Right Holly Pillar Cracks, the forceful Root Route, as well as some pleasant smearing on Birch Buttress. On **Dovestones Tor**, Dovestones Edge, Slocum and Gargoyle Traverse are longer experiences, or try the shorter offerings around Groovy Moves. **Wharncliffe** has a great range of easier routes to try. Beta Crack, Puttrell's Progress, Tower Face and Hell Gate Crack are all great routes full of character, with positive moves on steep terrain. Finally, **Lawrencefield** has a small number of good, easier routes, which, while the climbing may not be desperate, takes it into slightly steeper and more hostile territorty, and demand a few extra skills: Pulpit Groove, Lawrencefield Ordinary and Snail Crack are the obvious ones to go at here, and try Three Tree Climb if you feel that there's a tiger in your tank.

40 **Every Man's Misery** VS 5a ★★ 1957-65
6m The Burbage Slot! Steep moves gain the wide crack-line. An awesome sequence of constricted squirming, which could easily last for hours, leads slowly to the top. A climb that could easily undress you.

41 **Triglyph** VS 5a ★ 1964
6m Another brute. Steep pulling on big features leads to a hellish yank into a niche.

42 **The Notorious BLG** E7 6c ★ 2003
6m From the ledge, step left to below the centre of the scoop, and make a delicate step onto the sloping footledge From there, move up and double-dyno for the top. Possibly 7a.

Eight metres right is a tall flat wall with a dirtier wall to its left. ● **Abu Simbel**, M (1964), is the twin cracks left of the dirty wall. ● The centre of the dirty wall is **Heidi Boo**, E2 5c (1995). ● The crack just right is **This Life**, VD (2000).

43 **Bobby Dazzler** E4 6a 1995
8m A direct line up the tall wall just right. ● The left-trending ledge is **The Connection,** VD (1965-78).

44 **The Thistle Funnel** S 1964
8m Climb a widening crack right of the last route to a ledge, then the wall right of the arête.

45 **Simba's Pride** E8 6b ★ 2005
8m An utterly bold route taking the fine left arête of the leaning tower direct, with the final moves forming the crux. ● This replaces the earlier attempt

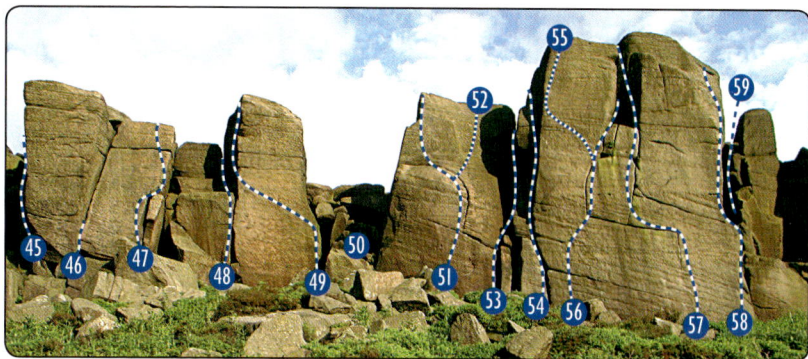

to climb this tower, **Stampede**, E8 6c (1995), which climbed the lower section of the arête, then moved left to gain and finish up the thin crack in the left wall. ● Those without a death wish may prefer the more sedate line up the unusual flake to the left; **Chimney Route**, HVD (1965-78).

46 **Roof Route** VS 4c ★ ★   1934
8m Shimmy up the fine wide crack in the angle, wearing the stoutest trousers you can lay your hands on. Sustained. ● **Daz Ultra**, E4 6a (traditional), is the desperately artificial slab on the right. Probably best enjoyed with logical side-runners at E2.

47 **Gable Route** HVS 4c ★ ★   1977
8m A real gem of a route which climbs the right arête of the slab via a wide crack and a horizontal break, using a variety of techniques.

48 **The Gutter** HVS 5a   1977
8m Climb a short crack to a ledge and continue up the corner.

49 **Press On** E2 6a   1987
9m Hand-traverse the ramp to gain the ledge. Climb the wall just left of the arête above.

The Tower

The next 50m of crag is Burbage South at its best, where the rock reaches its greatest height, and the routes, as well as being the best on the edge, have ranked among the greatest challenges of their generation. Several of the climbs would have earned

the title of 'the hardest route on grit' for their time. The first of these fine buttresses is known as The Tower, and the first route is on the slab round left from the front face.

50 **Mad Llehctim** E3 6b   1984
6m A fine, but dangerous, bit of bouldering up the steep slab left of the arête. ● V5 if well-padded.

51 **Charlie's Crack** HVS 5b ★   1961
10m The very attractive sickle-shaped crack is gained steeply and followed with great joy to a slabby finish up the arête. ● The arête on the left is **Lethargic Arête**, S (1951), a pleasant problem at the grade.

52 **Life Assurance** E6 6b ★   1986
10m From the flake on Charlie's, pad nervously up the steep slab on smears and poor pockets. Bold, but potentially survivable, and only E5 once you've done it.

53 **Tower Climb** HS 4b   1934
12m Gain the deep chimney by the leftmost crack and finish up a flake on the right wall.

54 **Tower Crack** HVS 5a ★   1957
12m The steep thick crack leads to a small ledge. Finish with a thrilling layback.

55 **Balance It Is** E7 6c ★ ★ ★   1995
12m This is one of the safer routes of its grade on grit, although it is utterly desperate. You can't have it all your own way. Begin by following Boggart Left-Hand as far as good protection just below the niche.

Mick Carr lost amid the marvellous architecture of the far end of Burbage South on Gable Route, HVS 4c (previous page). Photo: David Simmonite.

Skedaddle left, and layback powerfully up the right side of the arête.

56 Boggart Left-Hand E3 6a ★   1976
12m Gain the hanging crack by a worrying crank. For once, height is an advantage!

57 The Boggart E2 6b ★★   1960-65/75
12m Technically testing. A worn and frustratingly desperate crack leads up to a horizontal break. From here, traverse left to a better crack that leads to the well-positioned niche at the top of The Tower.

58 Equilibrium E10 7a ★★★   2000
12m The living end. The arête features powerful bouldering combined with an unjustifiable level of danger to produce a lead of gargantuan proportions. Begin by climbing the short lower arête to the ledge. (● This is **Yoghurt**, E3 6b (1980-83), which escapes left – a far more sensible option.) From there, gear can be placed out left. This is sound, and will just about protect the crux. Suitably psyched, launch up the arête via an unforgiving series of powerful snatches. Fun.

59 Tower Chimney M   1934-51
12m Start this old sandbag if you can: a real damp day challenge!

The Keep

The next prominent buttress is The Keep, a fine tall piece of rock, and a powerful twin to The Tower.

60 The Braille Trail E7 6c ★★★   1984
10m One of Johnny Dawes's first big grit routes, an audacious journey on nothing smears across a 'blank' slab with the bare minimum of protection. Begin on a ledge halfway up the gully. Smear desperately across the hanging slab on nothing toe-scrapes to a harrowing rest on the arête. A further hard move leads to the bottomless crack, and an overwhelming sense of relief. The route is protected by poor hand-placed pegs in slots and a six-inch nail.

● The ultra-keen will approach the last route directly up the right-hand side of the lower arête, **Blinded by Science**, E4 6a (1979), until a hand-traverse left leads to the stance. This line appears

'Keen Youth' James Pearson makes the third ascent of Bentley's mighty Equilibrium, E10 7a (this page). Photo: David Simmonite.

similar to **Child's Play**, E7 6c †(1995), claimed as a direct start to Parthian Shot. ●The short layback flake round left is **Byne's Flake**, VD.

61 Parthian Shot E9 6c ★ ★ ★   1989

15m Far and away the hardest grit route of its day, this mighty route bludgeons its way up the horrendously overhanging prow left of Brooks' Crack. The climbing is of the highest standard, being F8a+ even to top rope – and the protection is far from bombproof, consisting of a nest of runners placed behind a hollow flake at half-height. Although this flake has sustained several massive falls, it still comes with a health warning. Begin up Brooks' Crack, then, at 6m, finger-traverse left. An all-out dyno gains the aforementioned flake. With protection placed, press on towards the crux moves below the final slab. A harrowing rock-over onto this brings the final easier moves. One of the best routes anywhere. Ever!

62 Brooks' Crack HVS 5a ★ ★ ★   1934

14m A phenomenal route for the 1930s – the Parthian Shot of its day. Climb the left-hand crack directly to the top. The route is strenuous and sustained for its entire length, and only the most determined of leaders will sit successfully on the summit of the buttress.

63 Combined Heroes E2 5c   1983

14m A somewhat disappointing route following the arête, parallel cracks and a short fissure.

64 Byne's Crack VS 4b ★ ★ ★   1934

14m The right-hand crack is steep, strenuous and intimidating, although with its good protection, it is easy to enjoy the fantastic jamming and positions that it offers. ●A variation, **Easy Traverse**, HVS 5b (1969), goes right under the 'boulder' at half-height. ●A real beast, **The Kursk**, V5 (5b), starts at the back of the cave at the foot of the crack, and jams outwards. Rounding the bulge is hideous.

65 The Searing E3 6b ★   1987

8m Lovely inventive climbing, almost a highball. Gain the second break (gear). Crux moves to get stood in this gain better holds in the short twisting crack and a quick finish.

66 The Knock E4 5c ★ ★ ★   1975

9m This top-notch frightener up the blunt arête is John Allen's most elegant addition to the crag. Sloping shelves lead to some reachy crimping before a good hold is reached below the break. Although generally soloed, it is possible to place small, but hopeful, protection here, before making a precarious

stand-up that gains the top. Possibly E5 for the little people. ●**Ron Ring Home**, E5 6c (1986), is a left-hand variation on the lower section.

67 Keep Crack VS 5a ★   1960-65

11m   The stout crack in the corner right of The Keep is fairly tough. Once on the ledge, follow the thin crack in the groove above. ●**Keep Rib**, just right of the lower crack, gives a juggy V0+ (5a) problem.

The next routes climb the 'boulder' from the ledge.

68 Who's There? Titan's Grandma E3 6b   1982

6m   The bulge and slab in the middle. ●**WOW!**, E4 6b (1998), is the left arête on the right.

69 Fallen Block Sloper V8 (6c)

Starting from the lowest point of the block, traverse up and right until a hard snatch leads to the top.

Nosferatu Area

Just after The Keep is a broad gully offering an easy descent route. Beyond that the crag diminishes in height, but offers an uninterrupted stream of great, short routes on good rock. On the dark wall on the right of the gully is:

70 Captain Sensible E1 5b ★   1977

8m   The vague flake line on the right is satisfying, although bold for the grade. ●The grubby slab to the left is, **Bath House Pink**, E4 6c (1987).

71 Slow Ledge VS 5a   1965-78

11m   Follow the fine bouldery wall to a bold mantel onto the sloping ledge. Finish to the left.

72 Magog HVS 5b   1951

9m   Bridge desperately up the left corner of the angular cave to a tricky leftward exit. ●**Gog,** HS 4c (1951), climbs the constricted right-hand corner.

73 Gog Arête V0 (5a)

74 Ladder Rib V3 (6a)

A classic problem up the right side of the slabby arête. ●Climbed on its left it is V0 (5a).

75 Ladder Gully M   1934-51

8m   The gully has a tricky low move. ●**Connolly's Variation,** D (1934-51), takes the through route half-way up on the left and finishes up the slab in the canyon behind: esoterica personified.

76 Recurring Nightmare E4 6a ★   1982

8m   Absorbing climbing, technical and somewhat bold, up the ever steepening rib.

77 Macleod's Crack VD   1934-51

78 Crikey E5 6a ★   2001

8m   Monkey up the twin arêtes of the overhanging bookend until a committing slap gains the obvious hole. Swing left from here. ●The top was first gained from Dowel Crack; **Fade Away**, E1 6a (1982).

79 Dowel Crack VS 4c ★ ★   1964
8m A fine wrestle up the steep enclosed crack. Good hand jams lead pumpily to a wider crux. ● The little crack to the right starting off a pedestal is **The Iron Hand**, S. ● The two cracks 5m right are **Pollux**, HS 4b, and ● **Castor**, VS 4b (all 1957-65).

80 Movie Star E1 5b ★   1978
8m A good climb on the right of the clean face. Boulder up to a good jug on the arête, then stand on this. Follow the face just left of the arête with a bold grope to finish.

81 Surprise S 4b   1957-65
6m The left corner of the box-shaped recess on the right. ● The right corner is **Pythagoras**, HS (1957-65). ● The wall between the corners is **Shooting Star**, HVS 5b (1978). ● **Pie and Chips**, E1 6a (1987), finds its way up the wall to the right.

Boulders Under Sorb

1 Rock Bottom V4 (6b)
Hang the lip and rock onto the slab.

2 Definitive 5.11
From miles inside the mountain, tunnel out towards the light.

3 The Grazer V6 (6b)
An almighty stretch, rocking left onto the slab.

4 Sitting Duck V4 (6a)
Classy. Start sitting, in the cave under The Grazer. Reach up for the hold on The Grazer, then swing right to a jug and up the arête.

Mark Elliott in the atmospheric morning light during an ascent of Nosferatu E6 6b (opposite page), Burbage South's classic frightener.
Photo: David Simmonite.

●The long snake of rock running up from a large boulder on the right is **The Big Dipper**, S (1957-65).

82 **Sorb** E2 5c ★★ 1976
9m The left edge of the buttress is quite technical, and is much less willing to take protection than it would appear.

83 **Nosferatu** E6 6b ★★★ 1980
11m Sublimely bold climbing up the elegant rib. From the boulder jumble, snatch and crimp manically upwards to the salvation of a horizontal break and protection. Finish directly, or up the right arête. At the bottom of the grade.

84 **Reginald** VS 4b ★ 1951
9m A pleasant voyage into the depths. Steep, but good holds lead to a narrowing which is passed on the right.

85 **Bad Attitude** V5 (6b)
Climb the flake to the ledge with some steely pulls.

86 **The Attitude Inspector** V6 (6b)
A brilliant dynamic problem taking the sharp arête.

87 **Nathaniel** HVS 5b ★ 1951
9m The wide crack is fantastic – a proper battle that is at least 3 technical grades harder than the previous problem.

88 **The Knack** E1 5c ★ 1971
8m A great little micro-route which gains the shallow hanging groove from below and left. The crux is getting established in the crack, although this still feels steep and pressing. There may be some growth in the crack but this presents little problem.

89 **Nick Knack Paddywack** E2 6b ★★ 1982
8m A Burbage beauty, oft-ignored. A fierce flake, nearly a 6c move, gains the break (●V6). Swing left and climb the beautiful wall on flatties (5b). ●The direct finish to the flake is unclimbed, while a direct start is **Old Macdonald**, 6b (1982).

90 **Less Bent** S 1965-78
6m Follow the mellow arête and at the break, move a bit left to finish (or go direct at VS).

91 **No Zag** HVS 5b ★ 1957-65
8m Climb the right-curving flake to the break. Climbing wall bunnies will quiver here, while the well-rounded will make a couple of brisk jams up the short fist crack. ●**Zig-Zag**, HS 4c (1957-65), begins as for No Zag and finishes as for Less Bent.

92 **Unfinished Symphony** HVS 5b ★ 1974
8m Lots of fun can be had tackling the short hanging offwidth crack round to the right. Well-protected, and some day you'll be glad you learned how to climb a wide crack.

93 The Staircase HS 4b ★   1934-51

9m The impending wall left of the arête is climbed using a series of bold features. ● **Ribbed Corner**, M (1951), is the corner to the left.

94 Confidence of Youth E3 6a   2000

9m The square-cut arête on its right. The wall to the right may or may not be impossible.

95 The Drainpipe HS 4b ★★   1957-65

9m Beautifully simple. Climb the clean crack in the major corner. ● The wall to the right is **Booby Prize,** E3 6b (1982).

96 Parson's Crack S 4b   1957-65

9m Gain the pulpit from the slanting crack below and left.

97 Electrical Storm V7 (6c)

Climb the burly flake from a sitdown start.

98 Walker's Pulpit S 4a   1934-51

9m Follow the left-rising ramp, eventually getting stood on a large detached flake (The Pulpit). From here, avoid the fact that you are actually on top of the crag, and make a further mantelshelf onto a block to finish.

Oak Grove Boulders

In the hundred metres between Walker's Pulpit and a small grove of oak trees near Pebble Mill is a fine bouldering area. See topo opposite.

Pebble Mill Area

This is a short section of natural edge, giving a series of fine towers, and packing quality into every single change of angle. The rock is generally quite steep and the routes here have frequently been among the hardest of their day, and are a great testimony to the abilities of Whillans, Allen, Fawcett and Moffatt.

99 Little Limmock V3 (6a)

100 Broddle's Baby V6 (6b)

The right arête is incredibly uncooperative.

101 Broddle VS 4c   1964

6m The left arête, with a tough beginning and rounded top.

102 Limmock HVS 5b ★   1964

8m Start at the attractive flake, and, using this and a long reach, gain the break. Finish in an upwards direction.

103 Lino HVS 5c   1964

8m Climb the right arête to the break then the wall above.

104 The Birth of Liquid Desires HVS 5a   1977

6m Climb the technical and oft-green wall left of Wazzock on a series of disappointing holds. Variations are possible, but unnecessary.

105 Wazzock HS 4b ★   1964

9m The tall crack yields to some fine deep green jamming.

106 Playing Dangerous E7 7a   1996

11m A dangerous eliminate up the left side of the wall which, at this grade, presumably avoids the arête. Climb the desperate slab to the break and poor gear. Hard climbing on small pebbles remains.

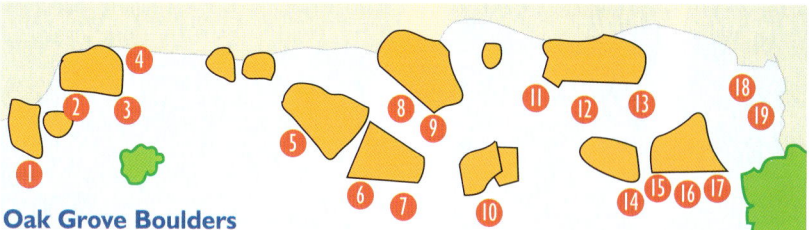

Oak Grove Boulders

This is a fine concentration of some of the best bouldering on the edge, stretching between the twisted grove of stunted oak trees beyond Pebble Mill, and the Drainpipe Area of the main edge, on the left.

1 Scratcher Sitdown V4 (6b)
From a sitting start on round jugs, gain and slap up the left edge of the fine slab.

2 Little Artless V7 (6b)
A desperate, but quick, slap from small crimps to the top.

3 Birch Tree Arête V4 (6a)
A peach, taking the tall arête.

4 Right Wall V0+ (5b)

5 Big Block Wall V4 (6a)
A sketchy bid for the summit.

6 Jason's Mantel V7 (6b)
Absolute hell!

7 Your Basic Mantel V6 (6b)

8 Curving Crimps V3 (6a)
From a sitter, crimp up and left to top-out.

9 Oak Tree Arête V3 (6a)
Another cracker. Start low and slap up the arête to a tasty top-out.

10 Block Layback V0 (4c)

11 7 Ball V5 (6b)
An exhausting wrestle up the square rib. Start low on crimps right of the cutaway, lean left, and slap up the rib.

12 Middle Wall V0 (5a)

13 Corner Pocket V4 (6b)
The right arête. ● The low start is V5 (6b).

14 Gentle Rib V0 (4c)
The arête. A sit start is V1 (5b). ● A good eliminate, **The Reach**, starts on the round orange hold and reaches right to the flake: V5 (6b). No arête at this grade.

15 Matterhorn Left VI (5b)
A great fingertip mantel near the left side of the slab.

16 Central Groove Thing V2 (5c)
Another mantel gains the shallow groove.

17 Right Matterhorn V0− (4b)

18 Green Arête V0 (5a)
A squalid arête in the trees.

19 Dark Hole Crack V3 (5c)
Another one of those roof crack battles that we have all grown to love.

108 **Pepper Mill** V5 (6b)
The superb arête on its right, as far as the thin break.

109 **Pebble Mill Traverse** V7 (6c)
A classic test of grit technique, crossing the open scoop in either direction. For the ●**Pepper Linkup**, follow the traverse leftwards, to join and finish up Pepper Mill, V9. ●**We Ain't Gonna Pay No Toll**, V4 (6b), climbs the right side of the wall and finger-traverses left to the arête. Jump off carefully, or join and continue up Pebble Mill at E5.

110 **Midget Tart** E5 6b   1987
5m From the boulder shoulder to the right of Pebble Mill, step off and climb the hanging arête above a cataclysmic chasm.

111 **Dork Child** E1 5c   1976
8m Down and about 9m right is a long slabby arête. Climb this to a ledge, then the reachy green wall above. Finish just left of the arête. ●**Goblin**, D (1957-65), is the crack system to the left.

112 **The Disappearing Bust of Voltaire** VS 5a   1977
6m The short stout crack facing Above and Beyond... is a good warm up. ●The horrible corner to the right is S.

107 **Pebble Mill** E5 6b ★ ★ ★   1976
11m A Burbage classic, a great test of technique and nerves, based upon the central arête of the buttress. Layback the lower arête on its slabby left side, until a swing right on a good hold allows a standing position to be reached. From here, tinkle up the wall above in a position of heightened anxiety.

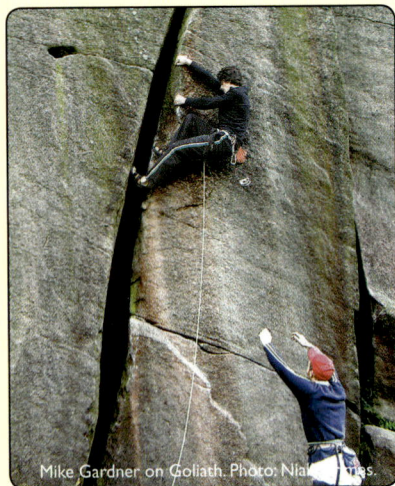

Mike Gardner on Goliath. Photo: Niall [...]es.

"Walking along Burbage Edge —

a trivial but pretty outcrop near Sheffield — Don came to a wide, and at first sight innocuous-looking, 25 foot crack, and speculated on whether it had been done. He thought to try it, arrived at the chockstone, called down to Doug [Verity] and said, 'It's a bit thrutchy, this — chuck us a sling.' He spent a fair time threading it with difficulty round the chock-stone, then huffed and puffed his way to the top. And didn't think much of it, didn't bother to give a name to what he'd done."

Jim Perrin, **The Villain**

"Head and shoulders above the rest." Neil Mawson soloing Pebble Mill, E5 6b (opposite page), on a perfect Burbage evening. Photo: Pete O'Donovan.

"I think in this day and age, everything's so safe, that you just need to escape from it every now and again, and gritstone gives you that. You can just get out there, have yourself a moment of madness, and then you can just come back afterwards to reality again."

John Dunne, **Hard Grit**

113 Above and Beyond the Kinaesthetic Barrier
E4 6b ★★★   1976

6m Although in some ways a boulder problem the height and difficulty mean that the E4 is well-earned. Gain the left arête of the buttress (possible small cam) from a hole on the left wall or the slab below, then follow the arête direct via a beautiful and committing sequence. ● Highball V6.

114 Samson HXS 7b ★★   1997

10m The lonely pockets on the wall left of Goliath are gained from that route (large cam), and passed leftwards by what is probably the hardest move on the edge. Finish up right of the arête.

115 Goliath E5 6a ★★★   1958

8m This brutal and uncompromising line is the perfect metaphor for its first ascensionist, Don Whillans. As such, you'd better be ready for a scrap! Climb the offwidth, starting with difficulty and getting worse near the top. By this point, even fist jams will be welcome. Those in possession of very large cams, two pairs of trousers, a leather jacket and fists the size of Higgar Tor will lose an E point.

116 David HVS 4c ★★   1950-57

8m The major dog-legged gash, while apparently of the most terrifying dimensions, yields to a posi-

tive, airy and satisfying layback. ● **Goliath Traverse** starts below David and traverses into Goliath, V4 (6a), whilst the arête above is a desperate project.

117 Sling Shot HVS 5b   1984

15m Follow the ramp into the corner of David. Climb this, then follow a break left into Goliath.

118 Messiah E7 6c ★★★   1984

8m A mighty challenge up the immaculate right arête of the buttress. Beautifully sculpted and over-hanging all the way, it calls for first bold, then brutally powerful (getting on for V9), climbing to reach the top. Small cam and nuts in the thin break (hard to place).

119 Messiah Traverse V6 (6b)

Traverse the steep wall rightwards to a flake.

120 Rollerwall V9 (E4 7a)

The desperate slab will appeal to fans of fingernail crimping, with thin moves leading to an exciting lunge for the ledge. Easier for reach monsters.

121 Saul VS 5b ★   1964

9m A satisfying solo, with a tough low crux, following the fingertip crack. At the ledge, move left and finish direct.

Burbage Quarries

Burbage Quarries swap the friendly technicality of the edge for strong foreboding battles. Their smooth, vertical and overhanging walls call for a determined approach, and amid some scruffy routes are some peerless tests of fitness and nerve. They can be quite dank in some of the more tucked-away nooks, although some walls get lots of sun. Consequently, the routes tend to be either very clean, or very dirty.

Northern Quarry

This is the larger quarry, with a good, steep and clean south-facing wall, containing many fine routes. The other two walls are less attractive. The first climb, **Deception**, HVS 5c (1976), a cracked corner, is 9m left of the quarry entrance.

1 **The Great Flake Route** D   1934-51
23m A fine ramble. Ascend the chimney and go across the ledge to a blocky belay (a direct start is possible to here). Climb the blocky corner above.

2 **Zorev** V9 (7a)
The quarried rib is a fine line, needing much tenacity and some care with the landing. ● A sit start is V10.

3 **Chinese Whispers** E3 6a ★   1998
8m From the ledge, gain and climb the flake to finish left over the roof. ● An earlier route, **Hidden in the Midden**, E2 5c (1980), continues traversing left along the break, finishing diagonally.

4 **Zeus** E2 5b ★ ★ ★   1969
11m A relentless battle from the word go. The superb crack-line will pump E2 climbers into the middle of next week, but at least it's well-protected, if you have the strength to hang on.

5 **Fagus Sylvatica** E8 7a ★ ★   2002
11m Don't expect any favours on this baby! The sharp arête slopes in more dimensions than physicists have ever dreamed of. With gear in the very low slot, power up the arête with great determination, skill, power, technique, and all those other things that you have not got.

6 **Hades** HVS 5b ★   1960-65
11m The corner-crack gives a tight, technical and slippery struggle. ● **It's Just Not Fair**, E5 6b (1997), is a reachy eliminate up the slab to the right.

7 **Fox House Flake** VS 4b ★ ★   1934
14m A very fine climb. Follow the fine friendly fissure and finish up the corner.

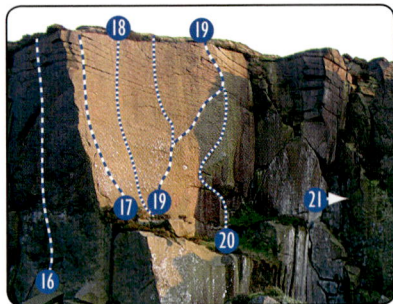

8 Fox House Fake HVS 5a   1999
12m A counter-diagonal to the flake with a steep finish up the wall. ●Finishing further left, near Hades, is **Disbeliever**, HVS 5a (1982).

9 The Cock VS 4c   1960-65
11m The steep blocky corner and crack.

10 Perched Block Route HVS 4c   1934-51
11m The corner and arête on the right.

11 Violence V7 (6c)
On the block below Hades, climb the angular, south-facing arête from a sitter.

12 Stockbroker on the Woodpile E5 6b   1987
10m Near the left side of the dark wall is a thin crack with pegs in. Climb the crack, and move right from the top peg, then back left on undercuts to finish.

13 French Kiss E8 6b ★   2003
10m The line just right has tough moves on small edges, and is protected by an old peg and a skyhook.

●The hellish loose chimney in the corner is **Odin's Piles**, HVS 4c (1980-83).

14 Shadows on the Wall E7 6b ★   2005
10m Just right of the chimney of Odin's Piles is a tall, dark arête, with a blank, shield-like flake. Climb the arête, bold and slappy, and with a runner placed, from the ledge, in the crack on the left.

●Ten metres right, taking very dubious rock, is **Curving Chimney**, VD (1934-51).Next to this is a thin crack curving rightwards up a pillar. This is:

15 Coldest Crack E2 5c ★   1976
14m Climb the thin crack with tough final moves. When clean, a very good route. ● The vertical scoop leading to the finish of this route is **Bashed Crab meets Dr Barnard**, E4 6a (1982), a serious test of dirty bridging. ●Laybacking the right arête of this on its right is **Little Monkey Hands**, E5 6a (2000).

To the right is a chimney (● **Sand Chimney**, VD, 1957-65). The walls leading right from here are now

Dave Parry on Milwheel Wall, E1 5b (opposite page). Photo: John Coefield.

mainly overgrown. ●Under the dirt are **Static Irritation**, E3 6a (2000), a thin crack just right of the corner, ●**Valk Corner**, S (1951), a groove in the arête, and ●**Nice and Tasty**, HVS 5b (1984), the wall left of the next chimney (●**Corner Chimney**), E (1957-65).●**Longest Day**, HVS 5a (1984) is the wall to the right. ●**Shale**, D (1957-65), is the crack to the right. ●**Prince Tarquin**, E2 5b (1978), is a flake and wall. ●Further right **Connoisseur's Crack**, HVS 5b (1976), is the thin crack. ●**Broken Wall**, VD (1957-65), is a dirty ramp, grass ledge and filthy crack. ●**Twin Cracks**, VS 4c (1957-65) gives good climbing above the ramp. ●**Broken Crack**, S (1934-51), is the double cracks near the front of the quarry. The last clean wall has a cleaner route:

⑯ Flaked Out E4 5c   1980

llm   The steep wall is not very well-protected. Climb a thin crack to the break. Move up and get established on a hollow flake with difficulty, then finish straight up.

Millwheel Slab: The next routes start on the grassy ledge and climb the clean slab above. This ledge is gained via the left arête, 5b, or by manteling off the millstone, 4b. The routes generally have a bold feel, but the horizontal breaks will all take tiny protection. ●**Middle-Aged Mutant Ninja Birtles**, E3 6a (1991), girdles the slab from right to left.

⑰ Dunkley's Eliminate VS 4c ★★   1957-65

9m   Great exposed climbing on positive holds. From the grass ledge, trend left to the arête, and follow it to the summit.

⑱ Pretzel Logic E3 6a ★   1979

9m   A very thin slab climb following the green streak with crux moves to gain the horizontal breaks.

⑲ Millwheel Wall E1 5b ★★★   1958

l0m   A superb route for confident E1 leaders, demanding steady footwork and trust in small protection. Starting at the centre of the clean slab, trend right to a steep juggier finish. ●**Cartwheel Wall,** E2 5c (1985), climbs directly up the slab from the start of the traverse, but is much less satisfying.

⑳ Hell For Leather E4 6b ★   1984

9m   A thrilling micro-gem. On the right of the

wall, boulder up to get stood on the clean ledge. One hard move up the ramp (amazingly, the greenness presents little problem) leads to much better holds. Continue direct to the top.

The broken and overgrown rock to the right has all been climbed and claimed from VD to HVS, and will give adventurous fans of grassy mantelshelves no end of pleasure. Most notable among these routes are: ●**Cardinal's Backbone**, HVS 5a (1973-79), is the crack to the ledge, then go right to Giant's Staircase, and follow this until a ramp leads out left to a scoop. ●**Scoop Crack**, VS 4b (1951), the lower corner crack to a ledge, then another corner giving access to a scoop on the right leading to the top; ●**Giant's Staircase**, VD (1934-51), a left-running ramp, into a right-angled corner, leading to a ledge on the right and an easy finish; ●**Spyhole Crack**, VD (1957-65), climbs a gully to the ledge, then up the overhanging wall on big holds. The gully gives an awkward descent. The tower to the right gives:

㉑ Burssola HVS 5b ★   1975

7m   The sweet little crack up the left-facing wall of the projecting buttress, just past the gully.

●The rib right of Bursola on its left side is **R9,** HVS 5b (1982). The juggy V0 (5a) wall immediately right of the corner is a gem as is the S 4b offwidth just right again. Right of this is a flattish wall with a curving overlap. Left of this wall, 6m left of the arête is:

㉒ Rabbit Claw V2 (6a)

Just right, step off a narrow ledge and balance boldly up left to the heathery scoop.

㉓ Sidepull Arch V2 (6a)

Classic. Climb through the arch from two poor sidepulls.

㉔ Hamburger Roof V4 (6a)

To the right, climb over the desperate low roof .

㉕ The Celtic Cross V3 (6a)

A beautiful problem up the natural arête 10m right.

㉖ Little Gem V8 (6c)

The steep wall just to the right on small flakes. The first holds are gained by a jump, or static (harder).

An unknown Australian latches the sloping jug at the top of Offspring, E5 6b (overleaf). Photo: Ian Parnell (who also owns the toe protruding into the edge of the picture!).

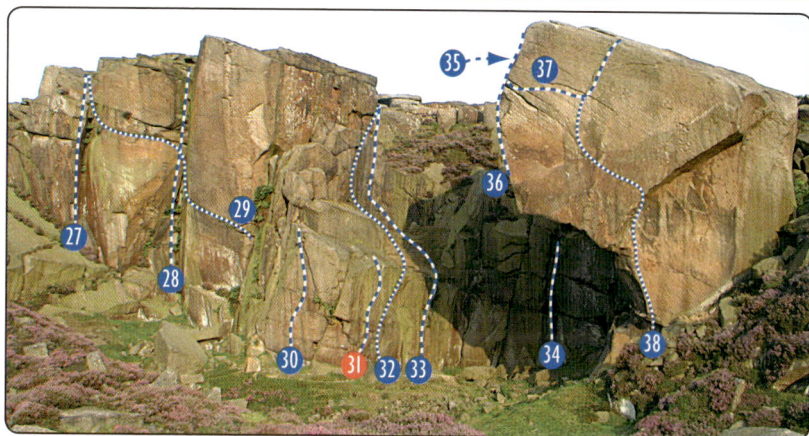

Southern Quarry

The smaller of the two quarries is dominated by the hulking projection of The Cioch, the huge perched block that casts its shadow across the steep inner walls. Several steep towers run up and left from the bay.

27 **The Verdict** E3 6a   1972

11m A desperate scuffle up the acute V-groove. ●**G.B.H.**, E4 6a (1981), is another fierce sequence up the painfully thin crack on the left wall.

28 **The Old Bailey** HVS 5b   1950-57

14m The obvious corner crack. A well-established project, **Wizzard Ridge,** gains the arête from two thirds of the way up, then somehow climbs to the top. Not very pretty, but if ever led, it will surely represent the technical boundaries on grit routes.

29 **The Simpering Savage** E5 6b ★   1981

18m A fairly mean bit of sideways shuffling, fingery and powerful. Mash your poor fingers into the all too obvious break, and sprint leftwards (crux), around the arête and into the corner. At a higher level, traverse the next wall leftwards to finish up a crack. Tiny cams protect.

●The broken crack to the right is **Bracken Crack**, (HS 4b, 1957-65), while the shattered crack to the right again is **Shattered Crack** (VD, 1934-51).
●The arête above the start of Simpering Savage, the right arête of the big tower, gives **No Flowers**, E5 6b (c.2000). This climbs the arête on its right to a peg below a sloping finish.

30 **Poisoned Dwarf** HVS 5c ★   1965-78

8m A cracking little problem up the clean cracked wall. ●Highball V1.

31 **Trellis** V6 (6c)

A fine highball up the overhanging wall, to a dynamic finish.

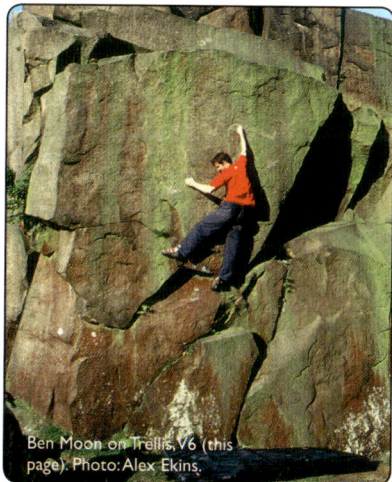

Ben Moon on Trellis, V6 (this page). Photo: Alex Ekins.

32 The Ramp HVS 5a   1964
15m Climb a slanting crack to the terrace (crux), then continue up the peapod crack above.

33 Gardener's Wall HVS 5b   1964
14m Climb a slanting crack to the right to the terrace, and possible belay. Continue up the thin corner crack above (crux). ● The corner-crack to the right is **Creaking Flakes**, VS 4c (1964). ● The crack 3m right again is **Noble Rot**, E2 5c (1972).

34 The Dover and Ellis Chimney E1 5b ★   1932
16m An historic route, of great difficulty for its time, that climbs the wide, leaning cleft just left of the gully. Climb a shallow right-facing corner to a ledge, then follow the curving crack and chimney out right with plenty of difficulty. The blunt arête to the right has been brushed and awaits a talented climber with nothing much to do.

The Cioch: This is the huge hanging, undercut block that looms over the right side of the quarry.

The next route girdles the mighty hanging slab on the right side of the quarry. Start from the top and drop down to a belay ledge on the left of the face. A hanging rope is useful for the belay. A first pitch climbed the thin and exposed diagonal crack on the sidewall with some significant trouble. Unfortunately this is very green, and is often avoided.

35 Silent Spring
E4 5c ★★★   1975
16m An exposed and highly adventurous traverse of The Cioch's Dark Half. From the belay ledge, make an exposed traverse right to a haunted block in the middle of the face, and a reverse mantelshelf. Finger-traverse right to the arête with better protection, and finish up this in a great position. Old bolts offer dubious protection on this pitch. ● **Grooveamarionation**, E4 6b (1988), ascends through this pitch, passing old bolts from a hanging stance.

36 Masters of the Universe E7 6c ★★   1988
12m The arête of The Cioch. Abseil to a foothold just above the lip and just left of the arête, and having clipped some old bolts (backed up by the abseil rope), climb the arête.

37 Offspring E5 6b ★★★   1985
11m A brilliant bouldery route in a position of barely justifiable exposure although, ironically, probably the safest route on grit. Abseil to a hanging stance on the arête, by deep cracks. Make a brutal traverse rightwards to a deep slot and cams. From here, give it all you've got, blasting up the slim groove. If combined with Silent Spring, this gives one of the best outings in the valley.

38 Captain Invincible E8 6c ★★★   1991
15m A gritstone E8 for sport climbers, but only ver bold sport climbers. The awesome front face has F8b climbing as well as some spicy cranking above dubious pegs. Start at the very bottom of the face, and climb to two poor pegs at the base of the groove. Pass these, and pull out left past two good pegs onto the face. Climb a series of thin cracks, past another peg and small wires, heading towards the relatively easy finish of Offspring, and glory.

The groove itself has been top-roped at 7a, but it is hard to imagine a more terrifying proposition than soloing it. The thin flakeline 3m right of the arête, leading to a ledge is an unclimbed problem. A final project is the blunt arête and small groove at the top of the block.

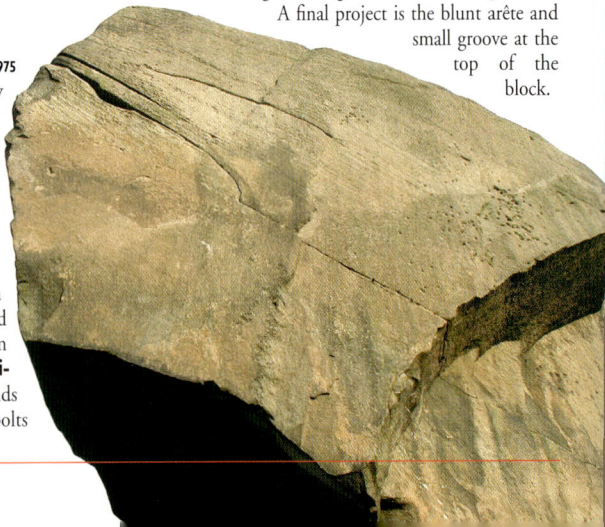

Burbage South Boulders

The boulders on either side of the Green Drive hold one of the most popular circuits in the Peak. Plentiful problems, perfect landings, easy access and quick drying, as well as being on proper 'boulders' give this area its special nature. It is especially good for boulderers operating at lower-levels, although many nasties lie in the area too.

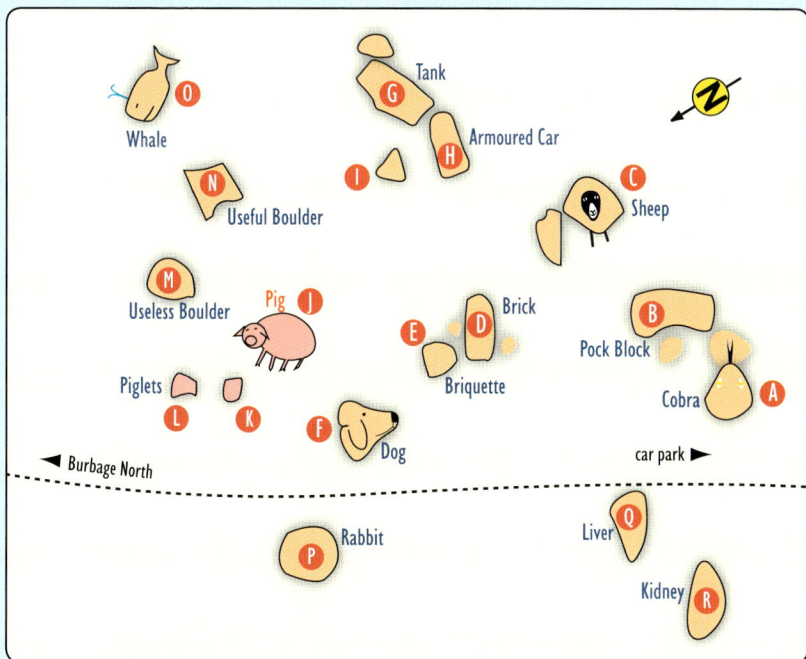

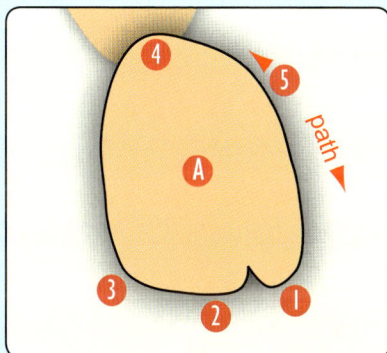

A – The Cobra

1. **Cheesy Nose** V0– (4b)

2. **Left of Crack** V0– (4c)

3. **Undercut Rib** V1 (5a)

4. **Cobra Mantel** V2 (5c)
With guaranteed leg-rash. Mmmmm!

5. **Cobra Traverse** V2 (5c)
Starting on slopes on the left, slap right, under the hood, to an easy finish.

Burbage South Boulders

B – Pock Block

6 Wall Past Slot V0 (5a)
A sweet move past the helpful chip.

7 Scratch Scoop V7 (6c)
Claw your way up the open scoop on invisible jugs.

8 Pock Man VI (5b)
A nervy little tickler. Step onto the very worn foothold and make a series of insecure steps up the steepening slab.

9 Pick V0– (4c)
Delightful. Step off the boulder and scoop up the blunt rib.

10 Pock V2 (6a)
A testy classic. Climb the wall on bullet holes.

11 Puck V3 (6b)
The high-step arête.

C – The Sheep

12 Talk to me Martin V9 (7a)
A nasty power move from tiny edges.

13 Sickle Crack V6 (6b)
From the crack, slap left to the arête and power upwards. The sit-start is V7 (6b).

14 The Sheep V5 (6b)
Getting established in the upper crack is a lot harder than it looks. A wolf, despite appearances.

15 The Shearing VI (5b)
Swing along the rising arête.

D – The Brick

16 Blunt Arête V0 (5a)
The left arête of the short back wall.

17 Pocket Wall VI (5b)
The centre of the narrow back wall.

18 Short Arête V0– (4c)

19 Reachy Wall VI (5b)

20 Little Air V2 (5c)
From the boulder opposite, leap across to latch edges, and top out.

21 Vague Rib V2 (5c)

22 Wall Past Pocket VI (5b)

23 Brick Wall V0 (5a)

24 Brick Arête VI (5b)

25 **Squeezy Wall** V0+ (5a)

26 **Slot Arête Left** V2 (6a)
Starting low in the slot is V4 (6a).

27 **Slot Arête Right** V3 (6a)

28 **Crash 'n' Gurn** V6 (6b)
From a sit start right of the slot, dyno into the puddle.

E – The Briquette

29 **Slabby Rib** V0– (4b)

30 **The Windmill** V2½ (6a)
Ascend the slab without the aid of hands or knees.

31 **Gentle Slab** V0– (4c)

32 **Huggy** V1 (5b)
Hug up the bulge from a sit start.

F – The Dog

33 **Rising Traverse** V4 (6a)
Slap along the rounded rising lip.

34 **The Gritstone Campus** V3 (6b)
Your basic move off the long pocket.

35 **Pockets and Edges** V7 (6c)
From a sitter, slap up rounded holds to the top. A harder variant goes left around the nose to finish above the deep pocket.

36 **Doggy Bulge** V0 (4c)

37 **Dog's Arse Left** V1 (5b)
On the right of the wide crack. ●A sit start, lay-backing the crack to here, is V6 (6b)

38 **Dog's Arse Right** V1 (5b)
A similar sit-start is V7 (6b).

39 **Doggy Style** V4 (6a)
Traverse along the lip then up the sloping arête.

G – The Tank

40 **Chieftain** V1 (5c)
The rib and flake.

41 **Catch 'n' Match** V1 (5c)

42 **Wall Past Flake** V1 (5b)

43 **Arête Sitter** V2 (5c)

44 **Big Flake Sitter** V1 (5c)

45 **Tiger** V4 (6b)
Snatch the top from blind pinches.

46 **Sitdown Arête** V2 (5c)

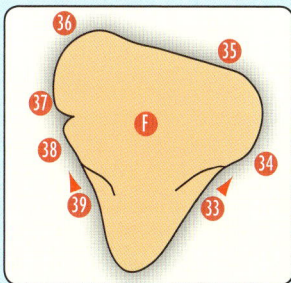

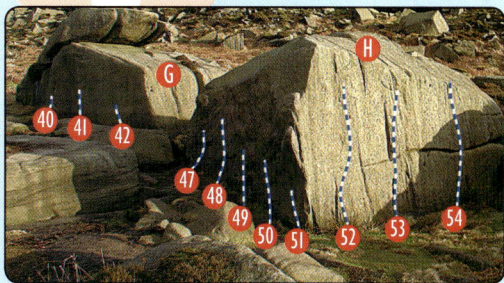

Burbage South Boulders

H – The Armoured Car

47 **Jigsaw Puzzle** V0 (5a)

48 **Mantel Past Slot** VI (5c)

49 **Sloping Mantel** V3 (6a)

50 **Sidepull Wall** V2 (5c)

51 **Big Flakes** V0– (4b)

52 **Armoured Cartwheel** V4 (6a)

53 **Blind Crack** V2 (5c)

54 **Rock and Mantel** V3 (6a)

I – The Little Point

55 **Arête on Left** V0– (4b)

56 **Arête on Right** V4 (6a)

J – The Pig

57 **The Basin** VI (5b)

58 **The Trough** V0 (5a)

59 **Bacon Foot** V3 (6a)
The bulge right of the crack.

60 **Little Pig** V9 (6c)
From a sitter, climb the bulge on poor slots.

61 **Ice Cream Cone** VI (5c)
Go up from a pointy pocket.

K – This Little Piglet

62 **Caley Slab** V4 (6b)
The arête on its left on smeary pebbles.

63 **Piglet Arête** V2 (6a)

64 **Fingerdish Mantel** V2 (6a)

L – That Little Piglet

65 **Arête on Left** V3 (6a)

66 **Arête on Right** V0 (4b)

67 **The Careful Trotter** V0+ (5b)
A lovely little pad up the scoopy slab.

68 **Oink Arête** VI (5b)
A quick move up the arête using a flake.

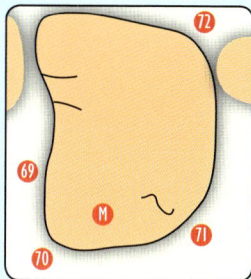

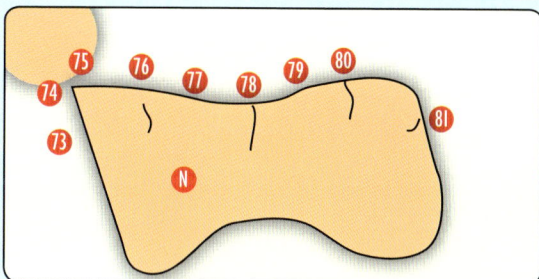

M – The Useless Boulder

69 **Pebble Wall** V1 (5c)

70 **Sloping Nose** V4 (6a)

71 **Grapple with Flake** V2 (6a)

72 **Arête** V4 (6b)
Slap up the nose from the low break.

N – The Useful Boulder

73 **It Hurts** V4 (6b)
Tricky wall climbing just right of the arête.

74 **Useful Arête** V1 (5b)

75 **Careful Arête** V3 (6a)

76 **Open Flakeline** V2 (6a)

77 **Scoop Eliminate** V3 (6a)
Tricky smearing with no cracks.

78 **Easy Flake** V0– (4a)

79 **Flakeless** V1 (5c)

80 **Peasy Flake** V0– (3c)

81 **Left Flake** V1 (5b)
Climb the flake and arete. ● A sit-start is V3 (6b).

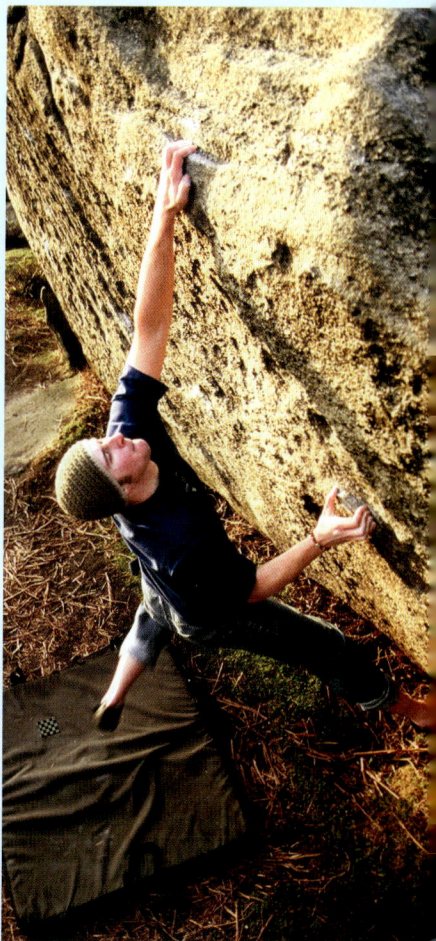

Right: Adam Coefield on Tiger, V4 (previous page),
one of the classic problems on the Burbage South
Boulders. Photo: John Coefield.

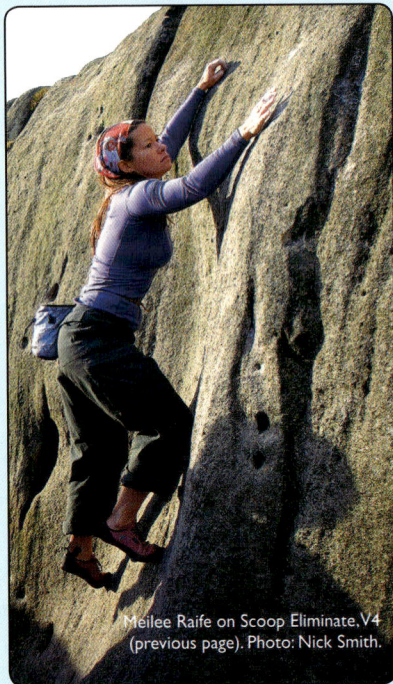

Meilee Raife on Scoop Eliminate. V4 (previous page). Photo: Nick Smith.

O – The Whale

82 **Whale Rib** VI (5b)

83 **Centre Whale** V0+ (5b)

84 **Right Whale** V0− (4c)

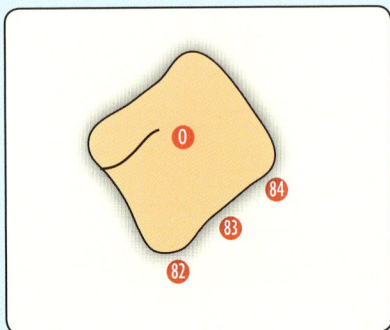

P – The Rabbit

85 **Reachy Arête** VI (5c)

86 **Top of Ramp** VI (5b)

95 Over the Top VI (5b)

96 Bald Top V0+ (5b)

97 Flake and Scoop V0− (4c)

R – The Kidney

87 **Deep Pocket** V2 (6a)
Lurch for the deep pocket and top out. Tricky.

88 **The Rabbit's Nose** V4 (6b)
Squirm over the bulge.

89 **Rabbit Wall** V2 (5c)

90 **Bunny Wall** VI (5c)

Q – The Liver

98 **Mantel the Bulge** VI (5c)

99 **Kidney Wall** VI (5c)

100 **Slot Entry** V2 (6a)

101 **4c Wall** V0− (4c)

102 **Kidney Traverse** V3 (6a)
The traverse, from left to right, is tenuous. Finish on the far right.

At the outbreak of the Second World War

many soldiers were billeted to the Burbage Valley. As part of their training, these soldiers engaged in target practice on the boulders (perhaps they reminded them of German soldiers), resulting in the many pock-marks which are now so crucial to many of the problems in the area.

91 **Green Scoop Mantel** V3 (6a)
Very hard till you find the knack.

92 **Left of Nose** V2 (5c)

93 **Nose Mantel** V2 (6a)
Another belly-scraper.

94 **Scoop Mantel** V2 (5c)

Carl Wark

OS Ref. SK 261808 to SK 258814   altitude 380m

by Stephen Coughlan

The next climbs all lie on the opposite side of the valley from Burbage South, around Carl Wark. The first area sits a few hundred metres south of the main area of Carl Wark.

Rumble Buttress

(SK 261808) A little matchbox of fine grit sits patiently a small way up the valley on the left. Best approached from the car park at the south end of the Green Drive.

① Guplets on Toast V4 (E3 6b)
Climb the right edge of the buttress, just left of the arête, to a rounded, easier, top.

② Guplets Sit Start V9 (6c)
From under the roof, follow the green streak past rounded crimps and poor pocks.

③ Slanting Crack VS 4c   1977
6m The crack – the one that slants, you know.

④ Darkstar V10 (6c)
A highball problem taking the shot-marked wall. The best climbing is up to the rounded break; topping out from here blurs the boundary between route and problem and it's worth cleaning the top holds on abseil before you start.

⑤ Rumble Groove VS 4b   1977
6m The overhanging crack/groove-style feature.

Carl Wark

(SK258814) Carl Wark is the flat-topped summit and ancient hillfort lying midway between Higgar Tor and the Toad's Mouth Bridge on the A625. It doesn't attract the number of climbers that the other crags in the Burbage Valley do. Despite this, there are some worthwhile routes here, and the crag offers solitude for the climber wishing to get away from it all. In fact, for the low grade leader a good day can be had.

The Climbing: The crag has 31 routes, mostly in the lower grades, although there are a handful of E3s and a great E6. There are a small number of boulder problems. **Conditions and Aspect:** Rocks on the eastern, valley side are very clean, and get morning sun. The Tower area faces north, and gets a modicum of late evening sun in the summer. Its aspect and lack of traffic does mean that some of the routes have a tendency to hold a covering of lichen. **Parking and Approach:** Either park as for Burbage South and follow the Green Drive, veering left on the fork, or approach from Higgar Tor. Both about 15 minutes.

Lookout Area

The first rocks are on the east of the escarpment.

① Lookout Ledge HD   1957-78

② Sensory Overload E1 5c   1991
6m The arête on the right, finishing with a slap.

③ Boulder Crack HD   1934-51
9m The recessed crack leads to a direct finish..

④ Ingle Nook HD   1957-65
9m The blocked chimney and wider crack above.

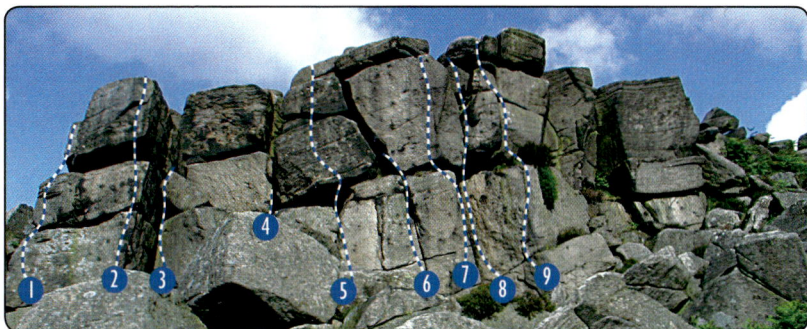

⑤ Lump Wall VD   1957-65
9m   The short crack and wall on the right.

⑥ Leaning Crack S 4b   1934-51
9m   The narrow crack and wider continuation.

⑦ Boy Wonder E3 6a   1997
9m   The arête. The lower part of the arête is a fine V1 (5c) problem in its own right.

⑧ Corner and Crack HS 4b   1957-65

⑨ Broken Buttress HVD   1934-51
9m   From the arête, move left to the short crack.

To the right are a number of problems identifiable by their names; ●**Broken Buttress Crack**, HS 4b, ●**Broken Buttress Corner**, VD, ●**Broken Buttress Chimney**, D, and ●**Broken Buttress Arête**, S 4a (all traditional).

The next recorded routes are 30 metres to the right on a slab.

⑩ Carl's Buttress S 4b ★   1934-51
6m   The right-hand side of the slab is climbed via a difficult initial mantelshelf, a break and a finishing slab. ●**Carl's Buttress Left-Hand**, HS 4c, is the left side of the slab. ●The right-hand side-wall is **Carl's Right Wall**, HVD 4a. (both traditional).

Twenty metres right is a small buttress: ●**The Corner** on the left is S, ●**The Arête** in-between HVD 4a, and ●**The Gloomy Corner** is VD (all traditional).

Legend has it

that the flat-topped escarpment of 'Ceorls Weorc' (Carl Wark) was once an Iron Age fort. After this, the Romans used it for its easily defended nature. It is this fortification that gave the valley its name. The word "Burh" in ancient English meant fortified, and "Bece" meant stream valley. Burbage, therefore, literally means "fortification by a stream valley."

Tower Wall Area

The next routes are 90m further to the right across the broken slope, facing Higgar Tor and provide the best routes at the crag. However, they can often be lichenous due to their situation and lack of traffic. At the left-hand end of this area is an obvious big fluted capstone block at the top of a jumble of rocks. The first routes start on the edge beneath this.

11 Layback Crack VD   1934-51
7m The corner below the fluted capstone with a choice of finishes.

"Rock climbing first began

at Burbage during a "Moorland Exploratory Walk" by members of the Kyndwr Club at the beginning of the present century. The club party, under the leadership of EA Baker (the head librarian of the Midland Institute in Derby) visited Carl Wark and Higgar Tor, scrambling upon the rocks which buttress these flat topped hills, and, crossing the moorland to the southwest, discovered the "Mother Cap" block and ascended this. Baker published several accounts of this expedition in such newspapers as the Manchester Guardian and the Nottingham Guardian. He never gave details of specific climbs but he mentioned Higgar Tor as a climbing ground in the current edition of Baddeley's "Peak District" guide."

Sheffield-Froggatt Guide, 1965

12 2b or not 2b HVS 5a   1983
7m Traverse the break leftwards until almost at the arête. Pull up to finish up a scoop.

13 Chockstone Crack S 4b   1957-65
8m The crack. ● The crack just right is D to the same finish. ● A route has been claimed to the right: **Chocks Away**, HVS 5a (1987).

David Parry on J-Warkin, V6 (opposite). Photo: Parry Collection.

14 **Carlos Warkos** VI (HVS 5b)

15 **Art of Silence** E3 6a   1982
6m Climb the blunt rib. The crux is the leftward reach at the top; don't fall off!

16 **Orange Juice Wall** VS 4b   1964
12m Climb the crack to an uncomfortable mantelshelf and finish up the short chimney. Unfortunately dirty, or it would warrant a star.

17 **Six Pack** E3 6a   1985
12m Follow the right-hand branch from Orange Juice Wall and climb the steep headwall using a small flake and an outrageous reach, originally via a pebble, which has since disappeared. This way is now possibly 6b. However, it can be done by a sneaky step left at the top of the crack and up via a pocket at a tough 6a. The rib/arête to the right is unclimbed.

18 **Lime Juice Chimney** VD ★   1900-20
11m Classic fare, the first route recorded at Burbage, passing the chockstone either on the inside or the outside. The chimney can also be 'climbed' by caving along the bottom and scaling the very back.

19 **Green Flag** V7 (6c)
Using a good hold in the vague break and two obvious sidepulls, somehow stand up to gain undercuts and reach the top.

20 **Tower Wall** HVS 5b ★   1965-78
10m A thin crack leads to a hand-traverse leftwards along a break at 4m. Make a trying move up to finish in the groove left of the arête.

21 **Lost World** E6 6c ★★   1985
10m An obscure classic. Tough, but very do-able. Climb Tower Wall and continue directly up the perplexing wall above. Good protection can be arranged in the horizontal break.

22 **Tower Crack** S 4a ★   1934-51
8m The crack system. ●A good VS finish moves left along the upper break to the short wide crack.

23 **Last Crack** HVD   1965-78
8m The last of the cracks.

"JW Puttrell also visited

the Tor, recorded nothing, but crossing to Carl Wark, he found the Lime Juice Chimney, and ascended this. What is surprising is that no-one seems to have noticed the much greater possibilities of the crags on the eastern side of the valley; not even Puttrell who was notorious as an explorer of "out of the way" places."
Dave Gregory, 1965 guide

A few metres right of Last Crack is a sharp arête. ●On its right-hand side from sitting is V1 (5b) using edges on the wall. ●The wall to the right is V0+ (5b), again from a sit start.

Roughly 30m right of Lost World is a short block with a rib/arête curving up the left side:

24 **J-Warkin** V5 (6b)
Start sitting from the low break and climb the rib using a couple of face holds on the right. ●The original standing start is V3 to V5 depending on how high you begin. ●Right is another short rib above a hole, V0 (5a). The short slabby wall over to the right of J-Warkin provides more problems in the V0 to V1 range.

Fifty metres right, close to the main path to Higgar Tor, is another set of short walls and boulder problems of lesser interest.

No route sums up the dominance of Joe Brown and Don Whillans as they redefined what could or could not be done on rock in the 1950s as The Rasp. This was climbing on terrain that was steeper and more hostile than anything that had gone before, and remains, today, as one of grit's finest E2s (page 73). Lucinda Hughes climbing. Photo: David Simmonite.

Higgar Tor

OS Ref. SK 255820

altitude 430m

by David Law and Simon Jacques

Higgar Tor is a fantastic crag giving a great supply of powerful routes, all full of character, across a good range of grades and length, as well as lots of great bouldering. Its centrepiece is the massive, dominating hulk known as The Leaning Block, one of the most famous buttresses in the Peak, with its fine front wall being one of the steepest faces on grit. This block is a very prominent feature and can be instantly recognised from most of the roads to the east around the Fox House pub area, and its prominence may be what got 'Hu gaer Tor' (The Hill of God) its name.

The Climbing

The crag has a well-deserved reputation for butch, fierce offerings and some of the best climbs around. The Leaning Block itself is quite awesome, over-hanging steadily by some 4m in its 12m height. Standing underneath the block it is quite easy to be deceived into thinking that the climbs are just off-vertical; it isn't until the block is viewed from the side that the true angle can be seen. **Routes:** Superb, with about 60 routes,

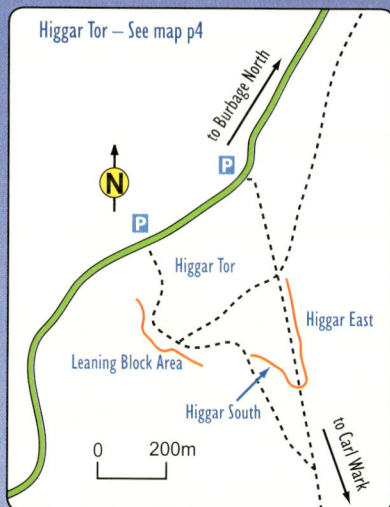

Higgar Tor — See map p4

mainly from VS to E6, and almost all well worth doing. **Bouldering:** While there is little on the main area, the southern, and especially the eastern reaches of the crag have a lot to offer. Higgar East has a large number of high-quality, and sometimes just plain high, easier problems, as well as a good handful of quality desperates. Over 70 problems, from V0 to V9.

Conditions and Aspect

Higgar Tor is situated in a prominent position on the watershed of the Burbage and Hope Valleys facing southwest and overlooking Hathersage. This exposed position provides little protection against the wind and rain, but ensures that the crag dries quickly after poor weather. The crag is climbable year-round, given friendly weather. Higgar East is notoriously sheltered from the prevailing west wind. This makes it a perfect option on blustery days, although it does mean that it retains dampness. The main crag gets lots of sun, and Higgar East gets it in the morning.

Parking and Approach

Park in the large bays by the side of the road. For the main area, ignore the obvious stile and walk down the road for 100m to another stile, climb over this and take the steady path trending around the hill: 5 minutes. For Higgar East, follow the large path by the parking bay: 2 minutes.

First Buttress

The first problems are found on the small north-east-facing buttress 20m north across the top and left of Hathersage Climb. It is characterised by an overhanging nose on the left.

● The wall left of the nose is V0− (4c); ● **Blizzard Nose**, V3 (6a), is the nose reached from the right; ● **Cheese Block Pinch**, V2 (6a), climbs the bulges just right using a triangular hold; ● **Wall Games**, V0 (4c), passes the short crack just right from a sitting start; ● **Flakes** is right again from the same start, V0+ (5b); ● right again, starting from a tiny right-facing corner climb the wall; V0 (4c). ● The wall right again from a crack is V0 (4b).

Hathersage Climb Buttress

Forty five metres left of The Leaning Block is a small buttress with an undercut left arête.

1 Small Beginnings S 4b   1999
4m   The diminuitive sidewall.

2 Hathersage Climb VS 4c ★   1957-65
6m   A short and powerful climb on some bold features. A good bite-sized chunk of Higgar Tor.

> ## "This Hill - the 'Hill of God'
> — is a little north of Carl's Wark. There are some small rocks here which give amusing scrambling, and one vicious crack near the huge Leaning Block, which may repay some attention."
> 1951 Sheffield Area Guidebook

3 All of a Quiver HVS 5a ★   2004
6m   A worthwhile eliminate with a hellish top-out.

4 Tossing a Wobbler VS 4c ★   1982
6m   A short route which packs it in, with steep yarding on positive holds.

Main Area Left

The main area of Higgar, dominated by the hulking Leaning Block, begins just right. Luckily, as a warm up, the first area is a little shorter and more friendly. The rock is perfect, although as everything slopes in every direction, the routes tend to be 3 grades harder than they look.

5 The Warding VD   1957-65
6m   The crack on the left side of the face, starting from a block. S 4b without using the block at the start.

6 Aceldama E4 6a   1980
8m   Two metres right, climb the steep fingery wall first direct, then slightly left, to a small flake and a hideously difficult crux finish. The only real gear is in the break below half-height. A serious route that feels high in the grade.

7 The Mighty Atom E2 5c ★   1975
8m   A good route with a distant exit. Starting at parallel cracks, climb direct to good cams and a broken flake. An exciting, difficult finish follows.

8 Brillo E1 5c   1987
8m   A deceptively difficult route starting on the left arête of the cave and taking the thin cracks above. ● The flake just left is a fingery V3 (6a).

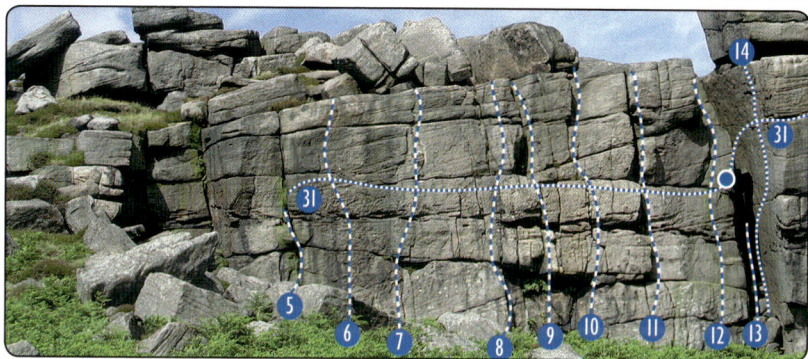

9 The Riffler HVS 5a ★   1957-65

8m From the centre of the small cave climb the overhang direct, finishing up a small corner. Strenuous and well-protected, but low in the grade – which makes a change here.

10 The Cotter HVS 5a   1957-65

8m Climb the wall just right of the cave to a break and huge jugs, then make a difficult move to the next break. Finish up the crack above, with a tricky top move.

11 The Rat's Tail VS 4c ★   1957-65

8m Steady, well-protected climbing leads to a testing hand jamming crack and the top.

12 The Reamer VS 4c ★   1964

8m The arête and wall on the left of the gully lead, via a curving crack and a delightful move, to a large ledge and the top. It gets better as height is gained, with a few reachy moves.

13 Leaning Block Gully VD   1957-65

9m Ascend the gully on its left side, exit outside the first chockstone and finish up the flake on the left wall. ● The gully proper can be used as a route up or down at M.

The Leaning Block

The overhanging wall to the right is what Higgar Tor is famous for. All the routes on the front face are thuggy, strenuous and demanding, requiring a great deal of stamina from any aspirant ascensionist.

There is nowhere to hang around or make mistakes. Protection is generally good and the routes get the 'E' for effort.

14 The Sander E4 6b   1976

12m Takes the steep left wall of the Leaning Block. Start by bridging up the gully and get established on the left side of the arête at an awkward break. Climb direct up the wall on the left of the arête via rugosities and a break to a large ledge.

15 Block and Tackle E6 6c ★★   1994

12m A brutal but safe route, tackling the front arête of the block. Start as for The Sander, then swing round to the front face from a good jug. Move up to good gear and then tackle the hard central section to reach the upper break. A difficult finish up the top part of the arête leads to a large ledge on the next route. The direct start is unclimbed.

16 Surform HVS 5b ★★   1958

15m A superb climb spoilt only slightly by the ledge at two-thirds height. Climb the prominent flake until it is possible to move left into a shallow recess. Leave this by climbing a short corner and continue diagonally leftwards up sloping ledges.

17 Bastard Cut/Prince's Dustbin
E4 6b ★   1991/1988

12m This combination makes a wild direct route up the cliff. Swing left from Surform to follow the shallow groove on small fingery flakes to rejoin Surform. Follow this, then make wild moves onto the arête of the massive hanging block, and fight up this. Hard.

A fierce test of jamming for the VS leader. The
File, VS 4c, (overleaf).
Photo: David Simmonite.

18 The Rasp E2 5b ★ ★ ★ 1956

14m A Brown and Whillans masterpiece, simply one of the best routes on gritstone. Start as for Surform, then move right and head up the line of flakes to a cave in the corner below the roof for a well-earned rest. Traverse right with difficulty (don't blow it now) to finish. Strenuous from the word go.

19 Arnold Schwarzenegger Stole My Body
E4 6b ★ 1988

15m Great name and very apt. Where The Rasp leaves Surform, go straight up past a large green jug, then climb a green slab and short corner finishing with a horrible mantel just left of The Rasp's cave (as for Flute of Hope).

20 The Rasp Direct E4 6a ★ ★ 1975

12m An even harder version of The Rasp! After a difficult start at thin cracks, climb straight up to join The Rasp at its crux, and continue to the cave. Climb directly over the roof above to yet another scary nose-grinding mantelshelf.

21 Flute of Hope E4 6a ★ ★ ★ 1971/77

20m A fine expedition taking a rising traverse of the Leaning Block with sneak previews of other hard routes (if you are not too pumped to look). Climb the short corner and thin crack. The impending flake above leads to the next break. Traverse left with difficulty to gain and follow The Rasp to the cave. Exit left and finish with great determination as for Arnold Schwarzenegger... Phew!

22 Bat Out of Hell E5 6a ★ ★ ★ 1979

12m An excellent, well-protected route up the front of the face that sees its fair share of air time. Follow Flute of Hope to the top of the flake. Hard moves up the wall above (possible 6b for shorties) gain the next break. Launch off slightly rightwards, somewhat pumped, ending as for The Rasp.

23 Linkline E6 6c ★ ★ ★ 1993

12m An outstanding climb, the equal of anything on the Tor. Start as for Bat... then traverse right to gain a prominent rugosity and stand on this to reach the next break. Continue direct (crux – totally desperate), and straight up to the niche above as for Bat Out of Hell. ●This supersedes **Pulsar**, E5 6c (1980), which gained the crux section from right of the right arête.

24 Pulsar Direct E6 6b ★ ★   1990s/1998

11m A quality route that takes the right arête of the block. Reasonable moves up the right side of the arête lead to good cams in the mid-height break. Swing left and climb the left side of the arête to the next break, and on to the top.

25 Leaning Block Traverse V9 (6c)

A desperate, powerful and very pumpy traverse across the base of the wall. Fairly rainproof.

26 The File VS 4c ★ ★ ★   1956

10m One of the classic cracks of the Peak – probably the best of its type on grit, and one that sees its fair share of failures. Just right of the arête is a fine continuous crack; jam this with determination and you will be at the top before you know it.

27 The Raven HVS 5a   1980

10m The arête, gained from the right via a break. A direct start would be rather more difficult.

28 Paddock HVD ★   1964

7m A thoroughly pleasant route climbing a series of cracks on the face just right of The Raven.

29 Greymalkin S 4a ★   1964

7m Climb the cracks right again, finishing over the obvious bulge.

30 Hecate HVD   1964

7m Climb a tricky shallow corner left of a large slabby boulder to gain a ledge and finish on the right.

The back of the Leaning Block can be climbed anywhere at around VD left of the obvious way up/ down (which is D).

31 Rock Around the Block
E4 5a, 6b, 5c, 4c ★ ★   1982-83

A girdle traverse of the Leaning Block, which would give some great views, if you're not too pumped to enjoy them.

1.10m Start on the block below The Warding. Step right passing The Mighty Atom and climb thin cracks. Continue to belay on the arête.

2.10m Move up and 'fall' across the gully to the prominent break. Traverse on good holds to the arête and move across the Leaning Block to gain the shallow recess of Surform.

3.10m Move right along the break on improving holds to the arête and belay around the corner before The File.

4.7m Follow the excellent break and dismount at the back of the block.

Right of the gully is a small quarried bay.

32 Wotan's Crack S 4a   1957-65

5m Follow the short, thin, doglegged crack at the back of the bay. The blocky corner on the left is D.

Right-Hand Area

The first buttress right of the bay contains:

33 Chance Encounter VS 5a   1982

7m Start 2m right of the left arête, use flat holds to reach a diagonal crack, climb this, to gain a ledge and climb the blocky arête above.

34 Rough Justice E4 6c ★   1995

7m A deceptive problem. Start just left of a boulder and climb the short technical wall just right.

35 Sickle Overhang VS 4c   1957-65

6m Climb a small wall and the overhang just left of the green corner direct.

36 Jupiter's Arête VS 4c   1957-65

6m The arête is climbed via a ledge on the left. ●This can also be gained from the left, **Jupiter's Slab**, E1 6a (1990).

37 Jupiter's Crack S 4b   1957-65
6m The crack widens awkwardly at the top.

To the right a is low cracked wall leading to a de-tached arête with an overhanging capstone. The wall provides five short routes: ● The pillar and left arête of the first crack is taken by **Easy Peasy**, E1 6a (1999), ● the crack itself is a **Doddle**, HVD (1978-83). ● The pillar between this and the next crack is the reachy eliminate **Lemon Squeezy**, HVS 5b (1999) and no arêtes are allowed at this grade. ● **Walkover**, S 4a (1978-83), is the central crack, finished on its right and ● **Piece of Cake**, HVD (1956-65), is the right crack.

Running through the crag at this point is a chimney/tunnel at the start of Doddle which forms an underground cross-roads with an east to west tunnel. Both north and west exits are interesting, the latter is at about the halfway point.

38 Achilles's Heel E2 5c   1960-65
12m Climb the centre of the face via flutings, up to the roof (harder than it looks with uninspiring pro-tection), to the break. Suitably protected, traverse rightwards round the face under the roof to finish easily via a ledge. Alternatively try the excellent strenuous direct finish; ● **Laze** E2 5c ★ (1975).

39 Spirito di Onki E3 6a   2004
12m Take a line up the centre of the wall right of the arête and finish direct over the roof.

40 Daley Bulletin HVS 5b   1997
7m To the right, climb the shallow grooved arête before moving left at the top to pull over the bulge Quite sustained and no gear until the ledges.

41 Canyon Climb HVD   1957-65
6m To the right of the 'canyon', climb the chimney burrowing inwards and upwards to finish through the hole created by the trapped boulder. Can be taken on the outside of the capstone for those who don't fit.

42 Zeus' Crack S 4a   1957-65

43 Root Decay E4 6b   1988
9m Climb the wall right of Zeus' Crack, with a very hard starting move above a hard landing to reach a good break. Move right to finish with difficulty.

44 Stretcher Case E2 5c ★   1979
9m From left of a hollybush, climb an awkward vague rib and break on the right with a stretch to rounded holds. Continue more easily to the top.

45 Splint HVS 5a ★   1979
8m The arête has some nice moves with a crux at just below mid-height.

46 Loki's Way S 4a ★   1964
7m Follow the delightful crack just right of the arête, moving round the arête to finish on the front face.

47 Fricka's Crack VS 4c ★   1964
6m An excellent little route following the fine finger crack to the top. ● The face to the right is **Nal's Face**, VS 4c (1999). Pleasant.

48 Jade Tiger HVS 5c   1984
The sharp arête on its left side. Sketchy landing. ● The crack on its right is **Freya's Climb**, VD (1964). ● The wall and the crack to the right have been climbed at around VD.

Higgar Tor South

This continuation of the Tor is a small collection of blocks and slabs, which are home to some pleasant boulder problems. To reach them from the Tor, continue across the top until you reach a curious stack of large rounded boulders. Drop down here for the bouldering. The problems face south and southeast, and get morning sun. They are clean, but not well-travelled.

49 The Harvester V4 (6b)
Start sitting with hands on the detached block and crank out the crack to an apocalyptic top-out. ● The top-out itself is **Pippin**, HVS 5b (1990).

50 Dyno V6 (6b)

51 Combine Harvester V5 (6b)
Traverse the low break to finish up The Harvester.

52 Harvester Dyno V4 (6b)

53 Arête on Left VI (5c)
Starting on the same holds as Harvester Dyno, roll up the arête. ● The arête on its right is V0+ (5a). ● The groove just right is the same grade.

54 Upper Traverse V4 (6b)

Just beyond the stacked boulders, and at a lower level, is a tall wall facing Burbage.

55 Your Round E1 5b ★   2003
6m Start at the right hand of two cracks and climb up and right with some exploratory long reaches between rounded holds. Small gear useful.

56 My Round E1 5a ★   2003
6m The rightmost crack leads to rounded holds above a poor landing. Move left to finish (or escape right at HVS).

Just below is a small slab. ● **Snow Blow**, V0 (4c), trends to the left-hand arête of the slab using the flake, and ● **Snow Bong**, V0 (5a), is direct up the middle. The right arête and pocketed sidewall are both V0 (4c). Twenty metres beyond this is a large

Adam Long on the sketchy Huge Slab. VI (opposite page). Photo: Long collection.

triangular slab. ● Between the wall and the slab is a jutting nose. Climb this nose direct, using a ripple on the right side, V3 (6a). ● The wall left and right of the nose can be climbed at V0 (5a). ● The jutting blocky prow immediately right again is V3 (6a). Ten metres right is a huge slab containing:

57 **The Huge Slab** VI (VS 5b)
The centre of the slab is a nervy voyage for boulderers. Using either arête is slightly easier.

● The small slab to the right is V0 (4c). ● Laybacking the right arête on the right is V1 (5b). ● On the centre of the block right again, jug and crease is V1 (5a). Behind these short walls is a small overhang. ● **The Prow**, V3 (6a), gains the top of the obvious prow and somehow mantels over the top of it. Entertaining! ● Ten metres further is End Slab, a small, but fine, slab resting against the end of the rocks. It can be climbed anywhere at V0 (5a).

Higgar Tor East

This is a fairly extensive collection of buttresses and boulders, which are home to some good tough problems, highball bouldering and micro-routes. Almost all the climbs here have been given bouldering grades. This reflects the way that people generally approach the climbs, and not the effect of a fall. In other words, don't go hurling yourself off anything that's too high. Facing east, the edge only gets the sun in the morning and can be slow to dry, but it is often a good shelter from the westerly wind blowing across the top of the Tor. It is generally quiet and unspoilt.

The Pillars Area: The first problems are found on the left end of the crag. Many of the problems are extremely high, and are more like solos.

1 **Seventy Degrees** V6 (6b)
The sharp arête at a higher level, from the break.

2 **Fingery Green Wall** V4 (6b)

3 **Bum Start Crack** VI (5b)

4 **Cherry's Crack** V0− (S 4a)

5 **Jason's Rib** VI (HVS 5b)

6 **Giant Gaping Green Grotty Gash** V0− (D)

7 **The Tower of Power** VI (HVS 5b)

8 **Golden Shower** V0− (VD 4a)

9 **Bigger Higgar** V0 (VS 5a)

10 **The Trunk** VI (HVS 5c)
The excellent arête gets high after a tricky, scary start.

11 **The Layback Crack** V0+ (VS 5a)

12 **The Corner Crack** V0 (VS 5a)

13 **Precarious Rib** VI (HS 4c)

14 **The Grassy Mantel** V0− (4b)

15 **Wide Crack** V0− (HVD 4a)

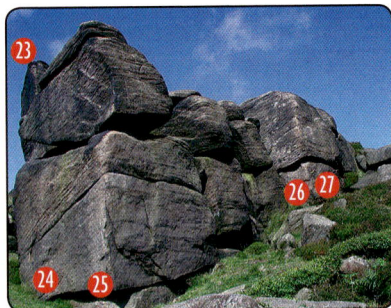

Black Choir Area

16 **Small Blunt Rib** V0+ (5a)

17 **Cracked Rib** V0 (5a)

18 **Open Thrutch** V0– (S 4a)

19 **Black Choir** E5 6b ★ 1997
6m The wide, bald rib is a much more significant proposition than its neighbours.

20 **Wide Crack** V0– (4b)

21 **Green Groove** V0– (4b)
Does what it says on the tin!

22 **Front Rib** V2 (5c)

23 **Sketchy Pillar** V3 (6a)

24 **Ledge Wall** V0+ (5b)
A harder start can be had off the crimpy rail.

25 **Tall Arête** VI (5b)
From small holds, climb the shapely arête on its right. ● V2 if climbed on the left.

26 **Scratchy Bun Left** V5 (6b)
The little arête is not very co-operative.

27 **Scratchy Bun Right** V2 (6a)
The left arête on its front side.

28 **Right Rib** V0 (5a)

29 **Sharp Arête** VI (5a)
The tall arête is a good little solo. The tall cracks in the wall just left are V0+ (5a).

30 **Toppled Block Arête** VI (5a)
Gets a bit high. ● The crack on its right is V0 (4c).

Triple Cracks Area

31 **Triple Cracks Arête** V3 (6a)
The large arête from a sitting start. ● From standing it's a good V0+ (5a). Either way it gets a bit high.

32 **Rounded Wall** V4 (6a)
From a sitting start on the low sidepull flake, climb the leaning wall, without using the right arête.

33 **Triple Cracks** V0 (5a)
Climb any combination of the three cracks.

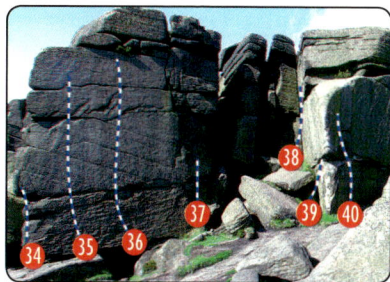

Flying Arête Area

34 **Left Arête** V0 (5a)

35 **Harry's Hole** V5 (E2 6b)
A charming, highly dynamic route, which covers the steep wall left of Krush Regime.

36 **Krush Regime** V6 (E3 6b)
The centre of the wall is blind and technical. Start low from the dirty hole if you must.

37 **Right Arête** V0+ (HVS 5b)

38 **Stretching Wall** V3 (6a)

39 **Flying Arête Left** V4 (6b)
The classic arête climbed on its easier side.

40 **The Flying Arête** V7 (6b)
The superb and highly frustrating arête, climbed on its right. It makes great demands on your dynamism and stickiness, as well as your ability to handle defeat. ● The wall to its right is V1 (5b).

The square buttress to the right has two very odd problems. ●**Winnie**, V2 (6a), starts sitting on the left and goes leftwards. ●**Pooh**, V8 (6c), starts sitting on the front. From crimps in the break, dyno for the top using neither arête! Dark.

41 **Sick** V3 (6a)
Gain the large ledge and mantel or dyno for the top. ●**Hemline**, V6 (6b), is a powerful low start. From jams at the back of the roof, climb out using pockets to the sloper on the lip (as for Shit). Traverse left to finish up Sick. Ledges on the left are out.

42 **Piss** V8 (6c)
An all-sloping horror-show. Pull over the bulge by lurching between the most perfect slopers. Anyone who uses heels on the ledge on Sick will spend a night in the box – and that ain't nice.

Jon Partridge on Piss, V7 (this page).
Photo: Alex Messenger.

43 Shit V9 (6c)

An awesome problem, the name referring to your language not the quality of the climbing! From jams in the back of the cave, use poor holds to somehow gain and finish up Piss.

44 Jump to Slopers V3 (6a)

45 The Low Prow V3 (6a)

The very low prow 8m right is climbed from under-cuts at the back.

Left: Oh come on, you're just not trying! Martin Dodds on Sick, V3 (previous page). Photo: Nick Smith.

Burbage West & Bridge Area

OS Ref. SK 261830   altitude 400m

by Percy Bishton

This is one of the best concentrations of high-quality boulder problems in the Peak, especially in the higher grades. Indeed, with so many desperate routes in such a small area, it could even be likened to Raven Tor, were it not for the fact that Raven Tor is a loose, polished, sweaty, grimy disgusting hell-hole, and Burbage West is rather pleasant.

The Climbing: Brilliant bouldering, with over 50 problems. Some are quite high and exciting, and were originally given route grades, but should generally be fine with a pad. The problems specialise in super-technical walls on pebbles and slopers, although there are some bulging testpieces. **Conditions and Aspect:** The problems on Burbage West face east, getting morning sun, and are generally very sheltered from the wind. Some drainage can come from the path above, although West Side Story can sometimes be the only dry grit in the Peak. The Bridge Area faces south-west and gets sun from mid-morning. Both give year round climbing. **Parking and Approach:** See map on page 4. Park in Birmingham and walk (2 days). Alternatively, park in the large car park at Burbage Bridge, directly above the bouldering, and walk in (1 minute). For bus travellers, see Burbage North.

Burbage West

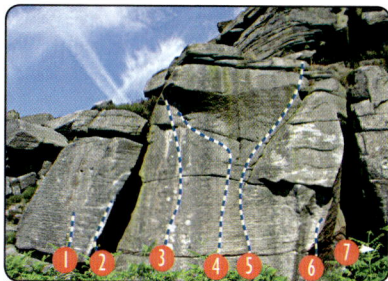

Famous Grouse Area: The leftmost area.

① Chipless V4 (6a)
Climb the arête on its left-hand side without the chips. If you use the chipped holds claim a V2 (5c).

② Breakfast V5 (6b)
The sharp, overhanging arête is climbed on its right-hand side from sitting. Can feel utterly desperate until you find the sequence.

③ Spartacus V9 (7a)
Harder than Kirk Douglas. Use the edges to get the distant hold in the small groove. Frustrating.

④ Brian V7 (6c)
Get the same hold using the disappointing ledge.

⑤ West End Girls V1 (E1 5c)
The central groove feels quite high.

⑥ The Famous Grouse V8 (7a)
The bulging arête. A good knack for slopers and incredibly flexible legs seem to be essential requirements for this one. A grim sit start is V9.

⑦ Square Arête V1 (5c)
The short arête just right.

Big Useless Boulder: Down the hillside from this area is a large squat lump of grit. This block is not as great as first appearances might suggest, but it does have one worthwhile problem ● **Big Useless Boulder Arête**, V0 (5a), as well as a few traverses.

Little Nose Area: This is a small low block that looks like the one in the picture.

⑧ Vague Nose V4 (6a)
Tricky. ● The wall left again gives some pleasant climbing, V0− (4b).

⑨ True Git V8 (6c)
Looks like it should be easy, but how wrong can you be? From the break, gain the big slopey layaway under the roof via two small edges. From there, either lay one on for the top, or using the footwork of a Frenchman, style your way to the summit.

West Side Area

⑩ Bullethole Wall V5 (6b)
Dyno up the sidewall.

⑪ The Arête of Cold Gloom V2 (E1 6a)
A bold classic, climbing the arête on its left.

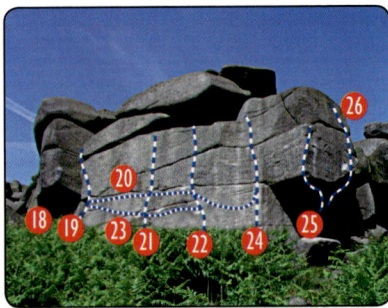

12 Crow Man Meets the Psychotic Pheasant
V2 (E1 6a)
The hearty arête on its right. ● **El Regallo del Mocho** is the slab just to the right of this, V6 (6b).

13 Crow Man Groove V0− (4b)
Easy enough, but balance and a cool head are useful at the top. ● The green wall to the right is V0 (5a).

14 West Traverse V5 (6b)
Traverse right from the arête to finish up Rumblefish.

15 West Side Story V9 (E4 7a)
A brilliant problem that has dozens of methods for success, but literally hundreds of different ways to fall off. Start on the well-chalked undercuts and style your way up the rib to gain the break. Although many people stop here, for the full tick you should push on to the top.

16 Ron Side Force-It V7 (6c)
A desperate eliminate which climbs the wall right of the rib, using it for the left hand, until a gaston move gains the slot.

17 Rumblefish V0+ (HVS 5b)
Climb the arête on its left. Often backed-off.

18 Western Eyes V10 (7a)
Start under the roof. Gain the twin arêtes and slap to victory like the proverbial monkey up a stick. The climbing eases a little once the break is reached; finish direct. Spotters essential.

19 Left Arête V1 (5b)

20 The Middle Traverse V4 (6a)
Traverse the middle break from the left arête to finish up Go West.

21 The Descent Route V0− (4c)

22 Easy Breaks V2 (6a)
Start sitting and use slopers to gain and climb the easy breaks. V0 from a stand-up.

23 The Low Traverse V7 (6c)
Traverse the low scalloped break leftwards to reach easier climbing to the top; harder for the tall.

24 Go West V3 (6a)
Frustrating until you find the knack.

25 The Nostril V7 (6b)
Using the undercut on The Nose, gain an undercut nostril-like hole, and climb the arête.

26 The Nose V6 (6b)
A local classic. From under the roof, undercut out to the slopey boss using cunning and sneaky footwork. The rib above is easier, although committing.

Westworld Area

27 Blazing 48s VII (7a)
A true Moffatt nasty – very crimpy and getting harder as the holds wear away.

28 Westworld VII (7a)
Jason Myers's desperate dyno, although it can also be done static. Very hard on the skin and very frustrating.

29 **Not Westworld** V4 (6a)
Undercut the wall just left of the arête to the unhelpful break. Can be double-dynoed.

30 **West Arête** V3 (6a)
Classic. Quite slopey and technical.

31 **West Arête Right** V4 (6a)

32 **Ledgy Wall** V0 (5a)

The next problems are on an easy angled slab situated just below this buttress. ● **Chipped Slab**, V0 (5a) wanders up the biggest part of the slab using everything. ● Alternatively climb it without the chipped holds at V1 (5b). ● Climbing the right-hand side of the slab to a crack is V0− (4c).

Burbage Bridge Area

The next buttress is found by following the path over the stream. The rocks are just below the path.

33 **Blocky Rib** V2 (5c)
A hard first move leads to easier climbing and a slopey grovel; V5 (6b) from sitting.

34 **Rocket Man** V8 (6c)
'*The fastest move on grit!*' The side-wall has a very strange dyno from the low break to the top of the block. Contorted and possibly harder for the tall.

35 **Mermaid** V6 (6b)
Climb the face from sitting following two vague cracks.

36 **Twin Cracks Arête** V6 (6b)
Climb the arête on the steeper left side from sitting. The big holds around the arête are off limits at this grade.

37 **Slabby Arête** V0− (4c)

Wobble Block Area

38 Bridge Wall V0+ (5b)

The steep sidewall of the buttress.

39 Bridge Arête V2 (5c)

Climbed from a sitting start with hands just left of the arête.

40 Little Roof V3 (6a)

Climb the face right of the arête from a sitting start.
● V3 (5c) if you use the arête.

41 Short Arête V0+ (5a)

Climb the arête on its right side; ● V4 from sitting.
● Traversing the break is V1 (5b),

42 Wobble Block V4 (6a)

A lovely problem that demands a bit of respect. Climb straight through both roofs, using a collection of slopey things and the wobbly block (don't worry, nobody has managed to pull it off – yet). ● Come in from the right at V2 (5c).

43 Beached Whale Crack V0+ (5b)

44 Sitdown Arête V0+ (5b)

Burbage Valley First Ascents

pre-1900   Ernest A Baker and his companions in the Kyndwr Club scrambled over Carl Wark, Higgar Tor and Mother Cap.

1900-20   **Lime Juice Chimney** James W Puttrell *Unbelievably the Burbage Edges were woefully ignored until:*

1932   **The Dover and Ellis Chimney, Hollyash Crack, Dover's Progress, Great Crack** Harry Dover, Gilbert Ellis *One of the best teams operating on gritstone around this time, the 'Chimney' is still rated Extreme today.*

1932   **Brooks' Layback** Rupert Brooks, Eric Byne, Jack Macleod **Amazon Crack** Jack Macleod, Rupert Brooks, Eric Byne **Stomach Traverse, Triangle Buttress Arête, Overhanging Buttress Arête, Ash Tree Wall, Twin Chimneys Layback** Eric Byne, Rupert Brooks, Jack Macleod

1933   **The Knight's Move** Gilbert Ellis, Harry Dover

pre-1934   In 1933 members of the Sheffield Climbing Club produced many new routes and published a guidebook to Burbage Valley in the 1934 Mountaineering Journal. Routes whose first ascent details are unknown include: **Route 2, Route 3, Twenty-Foot Crack, Triangle Buttress Direct, Triangle Crack, Leaning Wall, Monkey Corner, Overhanging Buttress Direct, Burgess Buttress, Burgess Face, Green Slab, Slanting Crack, Slanting Gully, Chockstone Climb, Wall Chimney, Wall Corner, Ash Tree Crack, Bilberry Crack, Bilberry Face, The Big Chimney, Left Twin Chimney, Right Twin Chimney, Split Slab, Falstaff's Chimney, Falstaff's Innominate, Falstaff's Crack, Bilberry Wall, Left Twin Crack, Right Twin Crack, Wobblestone Crack, Holly Bush Gully, Left Studio Climb, Right Studio Climb**

1934   **Brooks' Crack** Rupert Brooks **Byne's Crack** Eric Byne **Tower Climb** Byron Connelly, Bert Smith

1934   **Mutiny Crack** Eric Byrom, Douglas Milner **Roof Route** Jack Macleod

1934   **Fox House Flake (née Creeping Crack)** Frank Burgess, George Walker *At this time Frank Burgess climbed many of the routes on Carl Wark. After 1934 access again became a problem as the game keeping of the moors was stepped up.*

1948 July   **Obscenity** G (Nip) Craven, Rowland Pitts

1948   Publication of the 1951 Sheffield Area guidebook. Other routes whose first ascent details are unknown include: **Route I, Triangle Buttress Girdle, Ad Infinitum, Side Face, Ash Tree Girdle, Leaning Block Crack, Green Chimney, Jetty Buttress, Phillippa Buttress, Black Slab Arête, Black Slab, Black Slab Variations, Sentinel Chimney, Sentinel Crack, Ring Climb (née Ring Wall), Ring Chimney, Green Crack, The Big Chimney Arête, Alpha Crack (née Alfa Crack), Omega Crack, Scarred Buttress Climb, Amazon Gully, Greeny Crack, Quarry Gully, The Shattered Cracks,**

Giant's Staircase, Broken Crack, Curving Chimney, Perched Block Route (née Perch Block Chimney), The Great Flake Route, Walker's Pulpit, The Staircase, Macleod's Crack, Ladder Gully, Connolly's Variation, Tower Chimney, No Name Crack, Fat Man's Misery, Boulder Crack, Leaning Crack, Broken Buttress, Carl's Buttress, Layback Crack, Tower Crack

1951   Lethargic Arête, Gog, Magog, Valhalla, Ribbed Corner, Valk Corner, Isolated Buttress, Scoop Crack Joe Brown, Merrick (Slim) Sorrell *Valhalla was the most significant climb of this group, taking a large corner at the back of the Northern Quarry. However, showing no respect to the Master, it wasted no time in falling down.*

1951 May   Cranberry Crack Albert Shutt.

1951 Sept   Reginald, Nathaniel J R (Nat) Allen, Nip Underwood

1952 Nov 8   Wagger's Wiggle C W Ashbury, Eric Byne

1953 Aug 21   Peter's Progress Peter Biven.

1956 Nov   The File Don Whillans, Joe Brown, Nat Allen

1956 Nov   The Rasp (1pt) Joe Brown, Don Whillans. *This route by Brown represented a level of difficulty that had previously never been achieved. It was one of the hardest routes on gritstone at the time. Both Brown and Whillans were trying the route together and either of them might have been successful. In the event Brown succeeded first; though he did use a resting sling. The first free ascent is not known.*

1956 Autumn   Still Orange Dave Gregory, Ron Townsend.

1951-56   Pulcherrime Dave Gregory, Barry Fairest and others *Climbed whilst truanting from King Edward's School. Pulcherrime is a poor translation of 'fairest'. Gregory recalls that it was Fairest who had first go, but it was the team that gave the route its name.*

1957   Publication of the 1957 Further Developments including **David, The Old Bailey, Monkey Wall, Bracken Crack** – first ascent details unknown

1957 Mar   Tower Crack (née Night Climbers' Crack) Geoff Sutton, Tony Moulam

1957   Detour, Leaning Wall Direct Ron Townsend, M Padley

1958   Surform Joe Brown Rose Flake Sheffield University Mountaineering Club party

1958   Millwheel Wall Len Millsom (solo) *An impressive lead for its day, especially as it was led in big bendy boots.*

1958   Goliath Don Whillans *At the time of its first ascent, it was almost certainly the hardest route in the country, although it was almost certainly climbed with protection from inserted chockstones. A characteristic Whillans affair!*

1958-59   The Chant Alan Clarke

1961   Charlie's Crack Charlie Curtis

1964 Summer Wollock, Evening Wall, Lino, Limmock, Broddle, Wazzock, Orange Juice Wall, Dowel Crack,

Triglyph, The Thistle Funnel, Abu Simbel Dave Gregory, Andrew Brodie, George Kitchin *Limmock was named as the assembled party thought that you would have to be supple to do it. To quote a phrase of Kitchin's father.... 'He were that limmock, he could fit in a roll of lino.' Dowel Crack was so called because a section of thick wooden rod was wedged in it.* The Grogan Gerry Rogan *Dave Gregory and Andrew Brodie were failing in their efforts when Rogan came along after work. He climbed the route in his work boots and a tattered, mortar-stained Burberry.* Loki's Way, Fricka's Crack, Freya's Climb, Paddock, Greymalkin, Hecate Dave Gregory, George Kitchin (various leads) The Reamer, Diversion, Saul, Creaking Flakes, Gardener's Wall, The Ramp Dave Gregory, Andrew Brodie *All climbed during guidebook work... and Gregory is still involved forty years on! A enormous appetite for one of the most thankless jobs in climbing.*

1960-65   Wednesday Climb Pat Fearnehough Long Tall Sally Alan Clarke *FFA after an ascent by Jack Street using pegs.* Hades, The Cock, Achilles' Heel Gerry Rogan Keep Crack, The Boggart (2pts) Alan Clarke *Clarke used a shoulder and a nut for aid to force the first ascent of the latter. FFA 1975.*

1957-1965   Publication of the 1965 Sheffield Froggatt Area guidebook. Other routes whose first ascent details are unknown include: **Little Plumb, Baseless, Steptoe, Burgess St., Dead Tree Crack, Stepped Crack, Ringo, Snow Flakes, December Climb, Split Slab Crack, Grotto Slab, Grotto Crack, First Crack, Farcical Arête, Left Recess Crack, Right Recess Crack, Right Fin, April Fool, Spider Crack, End Buttress, End Slab, Bracken Crack, Spyhole Crack, Dunkleys Eliminate, Twin Cracks, Broken Wall, Shale, Corner Chimney, Sand Chimney, Goblin, Parsons Crack, The Drainpipe, No Zag, Zig-Zag, The Big Dipper, Pythagorus, Surprise, Castor, Pollux, Vulcan, The Iron Hand, Rombald's Staircase, Every Man's Misery, Split Nose, Lens Crack, Chockstone Layback, Prow Crack, Pebble Crack, Lookout Ledge, Ingle Nook, Lump Wall, Corner and Crack, Chockstone Crack, Hathersage Climb, The Warding, The Riffler, The Cotter, The Rat's Tail, Leaning Block Gully, Wotan's Crack, Sickle Overhang, Jupiter's Crack, Piece of Cake, Canyon Climb, Zeus's Crack**

1957-65   The Grazer, Lie Back, Doddle Dave Gregory Thrall's Thrutch Pat Fearnehough

1966-1969   The Gnat (some aid) Alan Clarke. FFA Neil Stokes, 1972.

1969   Skive (A1) S Chadwick, B Briggs *One of the bolted routes on the Cioch.* Boney Moroney, Zeus Jack Street *The latter route was reputedly called Tramlines by Street. Originally there was a peg runner. Later that year it was claimed as Zeus by Tom Proctor and that name stuck.*

1969   The Fin (some aid) Tony Barley *FFA Neil Stokes, John Allen, 1971*

1971 July 4 **Flute of Hope** (2pts) Ed Drummond, Hamish Green-Armytage *Typically, Ward-Drummond was eager to try the hardest problems around and with it, he brought his controversial style to the Peak District. Alas he used two aid slings to force the route. FFA Ron Fawcett, Geoff Birtles, 1977.*

1971 **Now or Never, The Knack, Sentinel Indirect** John Allen, Neil Stokes

1972 **Noble Rot, The Verdict** Ken Jones **Kleg, Midge** John Allen, Neil Stokes **Tiptoe** Chris Craggs

1974 **Unfinished Symphony** John Allen, Steve Bancroft

1975 Summer **The Mighty Atom, Silent Spring** Steve Bancroft, John Allen *On the first ascent of Silent Spring, no bolts were clipped, only 'natural' gear was used.* **The Rasp Direct** Steve Bancroft, John Allen **Burssola, Laze, The Boggart, The Knock** John Allen (solo)

1976 April **Sorb** Dennis Carr, Al Parker, D Sinclair *Now changed due to a rockfall, although the original grade still stands.* **Deception, Coldest Crack** Mick Fowler, John Stevenson **The Sander** Jerry Peel

1976 **Above and Beyond the Kinaesthetic Barrier, Pebble Mill** John Allen (solo) **Connoisseur's Crack** (née Sniper) Nicky Stokes, John Allen **Dork Child** John Allen, Nicky Stokes **Meddle** Dennis Carr, Jon de Montjoye **Boggart Left-Hand** Steve Bancroft, Chris Addy

1965-77 **Breathless** Details unknown

1977 Jan 12 **Little White Jug** Andy Hall, Keith Sharples

1977 June 7 **The Rainmaker** Keith Sharples, Liz Blakemore

1977 July 2 **Remergence** Steve Bancroft, Neil Stokes *Named in deference to Neil's Nth comeback*

1977 Aug 4 **Captain Sensible** Steve Webster

1977 Oct **The Gutter** Dave Gregory, Mark Vallance **Gable Route** Mark Vallance, Clive Jones, Dave Gregory Dave Gregory, Dominic Lee, Jeremy Lee **Rumble Groove** Dominic Lee, Dave Gregory, Jeremy Lee

1977 Autumn **Tharf Cake** John Parkin, Dave Gregory **Slanting Crack, Ivy Tree, Oak Face** Dave Gregory, Andrew Brodie **The Disappearing Bust of Voltaire, A Phenomenological Problem, Agnostics Arête, The Birth of Liquid Desires** Clive Jones (solo) **The Sentinel** Dennis Carr, Ted Rogers, Tony Cowcill **The Penultimate** Keith Sharples (solo)

1978 Oct 11 **High Flyer, Slide-Away, Submission** Gary Gibson

1978 **The Irrepressible Urge, Early Morning Performance, All-Stars Goal, Red Shift, Furiously Sleepin', The Screamer, Rhapsody in Green, The Edging Machine, Shooting Star, Movie Star, Approach, Prince Tarquin** Colin Banton **Ender, Endste** Dave Gregory

1965-78 **Poisoned Dwarf** Alan 'Richard' McHardy, Terry King

1977-78 **The Curse** Details unknown

1978 Publication of the Froggatt Area guidebook. Routes whose first ascent details are unknown include: **Ash Tree Variations, Bilberry Arête, Ace, Less Bent, Slow Ledge, Chimney Route, The Connection, Short Crack, Slantside, Clark's Route, Tower Wall, Last Crack, Big Black 'Un.**

1979 April **Bat out of Hell** Paul Bolger

1979 Aug 11 **Pretzel Logic** Dave Jones, John Codling

1979 **Rise 'n' Shine** Phil Baker, Nick Fenwick **Stretcher Case** Chris Craggs, Colin Binks **Splint** Colin Binks, Chris Craggs **Blinded by Science** Chris Gore

1973-1979 **Cardinal's Backbone** John Allen, Mark Stokes

1980 July 4 **Nosferatu** Andy Barker, Pete Lowe *Barker led the route on sight after Lowe backed off. Originally a large block leant against the crag allowing Barker to place a runner in a pocket up and left, making this a significantly safer proposition. The fall of the block, which has also affected Sorb, effectively made this route a solo. A frequently-on-sighted route at the grade.*

1980 Sept 12 **Arme Blanche, Windjammer** Gary Gibson

1980 Sept 22 **Pulsar** Jonny Woodward

1980 Oct **The Raven** Gary Gibson, Dave Tempest, Richard Kerr **Aceldama** Gary Gibson (solo)

1980 **Hidden in the Midden** Paul Mitchell, Dave Greenald **Flaked Out** Paul Mitchell, Ian Jones, Jon Kirk

1981 May **The Simpering Savage** Paul Mitchell, Andy Barker.

1981 Aug 14 **G.B.H.** Andy Barker, Paul Mitchell

1982 Jan **The Busker, Monk On** Steve Bancroft *Steve often had a monk on.* **Art of Silence** Steve Bancroft, John Allen

1982 Mar **Fade Away** Paul Mitchell

1982 April **Knick Knack Paddywack** Andy Barker, Paul Mitchell **Old MacDonald** Andy Barker (solo)

1982 May **Bashed Crab meets Dr Barnard** Paul Mitchell **Tossing a Wobbler** Jim Rubery, Dave Gregory **Chance Encounter** Dave Gregory, Jim Rubery **Disbeliever** John Arran, Andrew Osborne

1982 Aug **Big Bad Wolf, Who's There? Titan's Grandma** Paul Mitchell **Renobulous Bongetl, Recurring Nightmare, Booby Prize** Andy Barker *On the first attempt of Renobulous Bongetl, Barker was pulled over the top clinging to Martin Veale's arm.*

1982 Nov 7 **R9** Dennis Kerr (on sight solo)

1978-83 **Small Arctic Mammal** Mark Millar (solo)

1980-83 **Odin's Piles** Paul Mitchell *Mitchell re-ascended the gap where Brown's Valhalla once stood.* **Yoghurt** Daniel Lee **Groat** Al Rouse, Paul Haszko **Lost in France** Steve Bancroft

1982-83 **Rock Around The Block** Chris Craggs, Colin Binks *Done with a rest point but later freed by Craggs*

1983 Publication of the 1983 Stanage Millstone guidebook. Other routes whose first ascent details are unknown include: **Pickpocket, Doddle, Walkover.**

1983 Mar 9 **Combined Heroes** Paul Evans, Doug Kerr, Jon Handley

1983   **2b or not 2b** Nick White

1984 April 21 **Survivor's Syndrome** Richard Davies (solo)

1984 Easter **Nice and Tasty** Paul Pepperday, Chris Hayles **Longest Day** Chris Hale, Paul Pepperday

1984 Aug 26 **Jade Tiger** Richard Davies (solo)

1984   **Mad Llehctim** Paul Mitchell **Sling Shot** Chris Craggs, Colin Binks

1984 Oct 13 **Blind Date** Al Rouse

1984 Oct **Hell for Leather** John Allen (solo) **Ai No Corrida** John Allen, Mark Stokes

1984   **Messiah** Jerry Moffatt *Jerry knew Johnny Dawes had tried it, but summer temperatures meant that conditions weren't favourable. Jerry had also inspected it and, although he felt that the top would go, he thought the bottom looked like it might be a project. One day, as a storm was brewing, it was very windy and the temperature was just right. 'It took about two hours to find someone to go out and give me a belay. Anyway I soloed up to put the gear in, then lowered off, rested five minutes and then did the route first try, much to my surprise.' Climbed ground up by Ben Bransby, Neil Gresham, Pete Robins, Ivan Tresch and Tobias Wolf, and perhaps more.*

1984   **The Braille Trail, The Disposable Bubble** Johnny Dawes *The Braille Trail was one of Johnny Dawes's first major new routes on a rock that he was to make his own. Originally claimed at E5 6c, it subsequently lost 'lost pebbles'. This, according to Dawes, was a single, brittle pebble on the arête, used for the last moves. However, he thought that its brittle nature, although it made the move easier, probably meant that the route was E8.*

1985 April 24 Offspring Johnny Dawes (unsconded).

1985 June 12 Sunlight Caller, Boggle Boothroyd M J Bridges

1985 June 15 Lost World John Allen, Steve Bancroft

1985 Sept 19 Ring my Bell John Allen, Steve Bancroft **The Gargoyle** Steve Bancroft, John Allen

1985   **Pest Control** Greg Griffith **Rockers** Al Rouse, Steve Sustad **Manatee Man** Paul Pritchard **Cartwheel Wall** D Wilson **Guplets on Toast** Jonathan Wyatt (solo) **Six Pack** Steve Bancroft, John Allen **Barry Manilow** Steve Bancroft (solo)

1986 May 16 Life Assurance John Dunne, Dean Eastham. *Often on-sighted.*

1986 Aug 5 **The Little Rascal** Johnny Dawes (solo)

1986   **The Keffer** Kevin Thaw, Neil Beverly

1986   **Ron. Ring Home!** Ron Fawcett (solo)

1987 June 23 Too Good to be Forgotten Keith Sharples (solo) **Pie and Chips** John Allen **Press On** John Allen, Dave Fearnley

1987 July **Bath-House Pink, Midget Tart** John Allen

1987   **Brillo** Chris Craggs, Dave Spencer **Chocks Away** Malc Baxter (solo) **Short Fat Bastard** Malc Taylor, Terry Godum **The Searing** Pete Oxley **Stockbroker in the Woodpile** Paul Mitchell, Paul Evans **Pippin** Malc Baxter

1988 April 7 **Masters of the Universe** Andy Pollitt *Second ascent by visiting German Tobias Wolf in 2004, with two falls. Wolf was one of many talented, strong and ultra-keen foreign visitors who started visiting the grit around this time, and, like many others, wasted no time in cranking through the upper reaches of gritstone desperates, with a few spills along the way. On Parthian Shot, he took 14 huge falls onto runners behind the poor flake, runners that a Brit had to place for him, as Tobias had never learned how. After many successes, including End of the Affair, he finally came a cropper on Ray's Roof when his gear pulled out and he broke a wrist.*

1988 June **Grooveamarionation** Stuart Mackay **Prince's Dustbin** John Allen, Martin Veale

1988 Oct **Arnold Schwarzenegger...** Nigel Prestidge, Mike Lea **Root Decay** Mike Lea, Nigel Prestidge.

1989 April 18 The Carved Block (Living in Oxford) Johnny Dawes (solo) *Dawes, returning to his native gritstone, records a route of uncompromising seriousness. Named by the previous Volume Compiler who had tried repeatedly to contact Dawes during the preparation of the guidebook. Dawes since offered the name The Carved Block. First repeat by Mike Lea in 2000, doing the lower arête on its right, after crucial pebbles had disappeared from the original, left-hand side of the lower arête.*

1989 Aug 22 Crystal Tips Chris Horsfall

1989 Sept 19 Parthian Shot John Dunne *Made famous in the television programme, 'Stone Monkey', as Dawes top-roped the climb, taking a near-ground fall, and declaring himself years away from the lead. The route was then climbed by John Dunne, a claim that sparked much controversy among the Sheffield mafia, who doubted his ascent. This was dismissed as bitterness by Dunne, who by his own reckoning, was so fit from his Yorkshire sport climbing, that the route was not so hard for him. Personalities clashed and arguments raged, much to the amusement of the majority. The second ascent, by Seb Grieve in 1998, became even more famous, as it was the subject of the film Hard Grit. In the film, Grieve takes 5 falls onto (pre-placed) marginal gear in the flake before success. Repeated, placing gear on lead, by Neil Bentley and Nic Sellars.*

1989   **Nefertiti** John Allen *Climbed with side-runners. Soloed ground-up with a more direct start, by Dave Musgrove in 2003. A direct start has also been claimed as On a Wing and Prayer, E5 6c by Darren Thomas, 1994 'A technical direct start to Nefertiti. Start just right of the centre groove and climb upwards on various smooth breaks. The same side runners as Nefertiti are used.'*

1990 Apr 25 Jupiter Slab Malc Baxter

1990   **En Passant** Al Evans

1990 Summer Late Night Antics, With Juicy Bits David Simmonite

1991 Jan 13 Sensory Overload Stephen Robinson.

1991 May 12 Middle-Aged Mutant Ninja Birtles Steve Bancroft, Dave Nicol, John Cullen

1991 May **Captain Invincible** Sean Myles *With only one*

known repeat, by Robin Barker c.1997.

1991   **Bastard Cut**   Martin Veale, Chris Craggs   **Ring Piece, Base over Apex**   Jim Rubery

1991 July 7   **Side Order Chaos**   David Simmonite (solo)

1992 Jan 12   **The Last Great Problem**   Alex Thackway, David Simmonite

1992   **Small Beer**   Dave Gregory (solo)   **Always Another One**   Dave Gregory, Dave Farrant

1993   **Linkline**   Neil Foster

1993   **And Beaker**   Iain Farrar   **Gazebo Watusi, Heather (Sea Monsters)**   Jonny Needham   *A similar line to Gazebo Watusi was climbed on sight by Darren Thomas (9/10/94) and called Sweet Sixteen E5 6b. The description; 'Climb the face left of Obscenity direct all the way. Use a low side-runner in Obscenity, otherwise the grade is E6. It starts on a thin break then launches upwards on holds, rockovers and egyptians into the top groove.'*

1993 July   **Biscuits for Breakfast**   Mo Overfield, Chicken Chev, Dodgy Rogers   **The Twenty Year Itch**   Andy Barker   *Climbed with a runner in Right Fin.*

1993 Aug   **Artemis**   Bruce Goodwin, Nigel Bishop

1994   **Poison Ivy, Navana, Daz Automatic**   Darren Thomas   *Daz Automatic was often climbed traditionally as a variation on the corner. Navana was done with an indirect start and a pre-placed runner at 3m. The direct start was added later by Thomas. At this point some mention should be made of Darren Thomas. Often a climber will operate outside the established 'scene', and when they go on to add very hard new routes, questions are often asked. However, the series editor has frequently been frustrated in his attempts to even locate the whereabouts of many of his climbs. Others took areas of rock that would barely justify the word 'climbing'. Where identified, grades have veered wildly from that claimed. The editor would like to point out, however, that none of this is intended to cast doubt on his ascents. Darren, who was very young at the time, was definitely talented, and Johnny Dawes reported him 'burning Ben and Jerry's asses at the Foundry'. All effort has been made to gave Darren the credit he most likely deserves, and apologies for any ascents missed out.*

1994   **King's Return**   Bill Birch, Roger Birch

1994 Sep 3   **Three Blind Mice**   Dave Pegg   *Pegg was one of a new breed of super-fit limestone-trained climbers who turned his attention to some of grit's last great problems. Second ascent by Zaff Ali soon after. Flashed by James Ibbotson in 2004.*

1994 June   **Block and Tackle**   Neil Foster, Howard Lancashire

1995   **Child's Play, Heidi Boo, Bobby Dazzler**   Darren Thomas   *Child's Play claimed as a direct start to Parthian Shot, joining it at the flake, soloed on sight, at E7 6c. It is not certain what happened when he reached Parthian Shot.*

1995   **Rough Justice**   Simon Jones

1995 Apr 8   **Stampede**   Simon Jones

1995 Apr 13   **Balance it Is**   Neil Foster, Keith Sharples   *A fine line. Climbed, ground-up, with one fall by James Ibbotson c.2002, and flashed on sight by Richard Simpson.*

1995   **Happily Ever After**   Ritchie Patterson   *Preplaced protection, including a hand-placed peg, in the break.*

1996 April 3   **Playing Dangerous, Calvin Klimb**   Darren Thomas   *Playing Dangerous had been climbed many times in the 1970s as a variation on Pebble Mill. At the time it had some pebbles.*

1997 Mar 31   **Daley Bulletin**   David Simmonite, John Daley

1997 Sept 20   **It's Just Not Fair**   Matt Heason

1997   **Boy Wonder**   Andy Healy, B J Couch   **Black Choir**   Joe Brown (the younger)   **The Artist**   John Judson

1997   **Samson**   Jerry Moffatt   *Unrepeated*

1998   **Chinese Whispers**   Paul Mitchell, Paul Evans

1998 Nov 25   **WOW!**   Johnny Dawes, Andy Peat   *'Both hard moves are sustained'.*

1999   **Superstition**   Miles Gibson   *The hardest route on Burbage North fell as Gibson applied his plentiful bouldering skills to some of the last great problems on grit. Unrepeated.*

1999   **The Happy Slapper**   Chris Moor (solo)   **Small Beginnings**   David Simmonite   **Fox House Fake**   Leon Zablocki, Cathy Meads

1999 Aug 26   **Time for Bed Said Zebedee**   Michael Vincent

1990s   **Pulsar Direct**   Ben Moon   *Moon climbed a more direct version of Woodward's Pulsar staying on the left side of the arête above the mid-height break. Percy Bishton climbed the arête in 1998, staying all the way on the right, naming his effort Rowley Birkin QC.*

2000 Feb 24   **Equilibrium**   Neil Bentley   *The first E10 on grit, and the subject of an obsession for Bentley. Previously climbed by Ben Moon as a top-rope problem, at F8b+. Second ascent by Neil Gresham in 2003. Third ascent by 'Keen Youth' James Pearson in Mar 2005.*

2000 June 11   **Confidence of Youth**   John Jeed

2000   **Twilight**   David Simmonite (solo)   **Bulletproof**   Rob Harper   **With a Little Help from my Friends**   David Simmonite, Dave Viggers   **This Life**   Graham Hoey

2000 May 26   **Little Monkey Hands**   Nik Jennings

2000 Aug 22   **Static Irritation**   Nik Jennings

2000 Sept   **Jimmy Riddle**   Doug Kerr   **Pale Face**   Simon Lockwood, Peter Goult

c.2000   **No Flowers**   Paul Mitchell

2001 July 16   **Head-Banger, Rope Trick, Flaked Out, Learning the Ropes, Who Needs Ropes?**   Steve Clark   *These had almost certainly been climbed before.*

2001 Oct   **Crikey**   Niall Grimes   **The Arctic Mammal**   Dave Musgrove

2002 May 31   **Don't Knock my Smock or I'll Clean your**

Clock Ben Jones (solo)

2002 Feb 15 **Fagus Sylvatica** Miles Gibson *Yet another powerful and dangerous addition from one of the area's strongest climbers. Gibson, a tree surgeon, called the route after the beech tree. Unrepeated.*

2002 **Present Arms** Mark Stephen Davies **Kiss me my Darling** David Musgrove

2003 Oct 12 **French Kiss** Simon Moore

2003 **My Round, Your Round** Steve Clark, Lynn Robinson.

2003 **The Notorious BLG** Pete Hurley *This could well be the same line as Freak Power by Darren Thomas, 1995, at E5 6b, and soloed on sight! See note on Poison Ivy, 1994.*

2004 Jan 18 **Destructive Tendencies** James Pearson *Named, tongue in cheek, by the editor after criticism of James on a climbing website chat room after breaking a pebble on Smoked Salmon.*

2004 **Almost the Last Word** Tom O'Rourke **Spirito di Onki** James Pearson **All of a Quiver** David Simmonite (solo)

2005 Mar **Simba's Pride** Toby Benham

2005 Oct **Shadows on the Wall** Ally Smith

Boulder First Ascents

All Quiet on the Eastern Front Ed Ward-Drummond, 1960s
The Alliance Pete Oxley, 1987
Answer the Phone Graham Hoey, 1985
The Arête of Cold Gloom Gary Gibson , 1979
The Attitude Inspector Mark Wilford, Derek Bolger, 1979 *Later claimed by Martin Veale, whose name now stands. Veale continued up the buttress between the cracks.*
Blind Ali Zaff Ali
Blind Date Al Rouse Oct 1984 *Soon after the first ascent, the boulder which just allowed a desperate 'splits bridge to begin the route' strangely migrated towards the crag making the start easier. This boulder has now gone altogether, thereby making the start appallingly difficult.*
Banana Finger Ed Ward-Drummond, June 1971
Bedrock Stephen Li
Blind Drunk John Welford
Blind Fig Jason Myers
Blizzard Nose Duncan Eagles, 2004
Breakfast Martin Veale, 1980s *Originally named Boulderado, although now known as Breakfast.*
Cinzano Roof Andy Harris, Richard Heap
Crow Man Meets the Psychotic Pheasant Mark Stokes, 1979
Desparête Johnny Dawes, 1996
Dominican Dominic Lee, 1977
El Regallo del Mocho Ben Bransby, 2004
The Enthusiast Nick Hallam, 1978-87
The Famous Grouse John Welford
The Flying Arête, Flying Arête Left (Higgar East) Paul

Mitchell, Andy Barker
Friar's Wall Dominic Lee, 1977
Fuji Heavy Industries John Welford
Green Flag Richie Patterson
Giza Ian Fitzpatrick
Guplets Sit-Start John Welford
Gymnipodies John Allen, 1988
Home Cooking Johnny Dawes, 1984
Intense Jerry Moffatt
Jason's Roof Jason Myers
J-Warkin John Coefield, 2003 *Sit start by Dave Parry*
Krush Regime Greg Griffith, 1985
Life in a Radioactive Dustbin Paul Mitchell, 1984 *It took Mitchell three moves, including swinging 'one arm to get both hands on a hold on the lip'. Bob Berzins could reach it from the ground, but was too gripped to do the next move.*
Little Pig Domonic Lee, 1977
Nicotine Stain Al Rouse, 1983
Rascal Groove Sit Start Neil Travers
The Rib John Welford
Rocket Man Rob Smith
Rollerwall Ron Fawcett, 1987 *Previously chipped in the early seventies and subsequently cemented in by Andy Barker.*
Ron's Traverse Ron Fawcett
Rumblefish Mark Stokes, 1979
Safe Bet John Allen, 1985
Shazaam James Hogg
Small is Beautiful John Allen, 1985
Snow Blow, Snow Bong Duncan Eagles, 2004
Solitude Dave Parry
The Sphinx John Allen, 1985
Spartacus John Welford
Striker Ben Moon, 1990s *This is probably the same as Demeter More Direct, climbed at E3 6c in 1995 by Darren Thomas. It is not known which was done first.*
Sublime Indifference John Allen, 1984
Submergence Jason Myers
The Terrace Paul 'Huffy' Houghoughi
Trellis Ben Moon, 1990s *This may correspond to the Darren Thomas route Razzle Dazzle, which also claimed to be the wall left of the Ramp, at E5 6b. However, in Thomas' description, RPs protected the route, which throws some confusion on the subject.*
True Git John Welford
Velvet Crab John Welford
West Side Story John Allen, 1985
What a Way to Spend Easter John Welford
Yabadabadoo Graham Hoey, 1985
Zaff's Groove Zaff Ali
Zaff Skoczylas 'Polish' David Skoczylas/Zaff Ali

Dave Heselden on Edge Lane, E5 5c (page 109). Photo: Pete O'Donovan.

The **Millstone** Area

2

'This is the first Gritstone guide to a piton climbing ground. It thus marks a new stage in Peakland climbing. Previously artificial aids have been frowned upon when used on the older traditional Gritstone Edges, but Millstone has no tradition, its magnificent walls are not for the free climbing purist.'

Eric Byne, luckily getting it quite wrong, Further Developments in the Peak District, 1957

Millstone Edge

OS Ref. SK 248801 to SK 248807	altitude 340m

by Niall Grimes

Millstone Edge, with its endless towering angularity, is rightfully one of the most popular crags in the Peak.

The Climbing

Routes: Brilliant, with over 200 climbs. Millstone routes feel tall and exposed for their grades. The rock is usually almost vertical, and sometimes overhanging, and its smooth walls are split by numerous natural finger, hand and fist cracks. As well as this are the characteristic pegged-out cracks which give thrilling, positive finger-lock climbing. The other characteristic features of Millstone are the right-angled corners and arêtes that zigzag along the entire length of the crag, giving either strenuous bridging routes or perfect, bold arêtes. Slab climbers will

have slim pickings. The climbing tends to be more positive than on more weathered gritstone crags, a fact that makes the crag popular for visiting climbers unused to the more normal roundness of natural grit. Also, the positive crack-lines tend to be easy to protect, something else that obviously appeals to gritstone visitors. **Bouldering:** Not masses, although there are a few of the Peak's classic testpieces here.

Conditions and Aspect

Millstone sits proudly on the hill overlooking Hathersage. It faces west, and the majority of its walls get lots of sun from the early afternoon. These faces are clean and sound and dry quickly. However, due to the zigzag nature, many walls face north and get little sun, providing welcome shade in the heat (especially around North Bay), although they stay quite green in winter.

The crag

is climbable all year round, although on cold grey days, it can feel a bit bleak. On wet days, the Keyhole Cave area stays remarkably dry. It is a beautiful place to spend a summer evening.

Parking and Approach

Park in the large pay & display car park above the crag on the A623. Take one of the paths across the moor to the crag. The areas are reached in 10 minutes. An alternative approach, especially if visiting the north end, is to park in limited parking on the road that leads down from Higgar Tor. Follow a scenic path through the birch trees to the crag.

Public transport: The First 272 bus from Sheffield to Castleton stops by the pay & display car park. For train travellers, take the Sheffield to Manchester train, alight in Hathersage, and walk up the hill in the direction of Sheffield to the crag in 25 minutes.

Access

Voluntary restrictions to access are agreed annually if ravens or peregrines nest here. Please look out for signs during the nesting season. Any restrictions are regularly reviewed and lifted once the birds have fledged, at which time the signs will be removed.

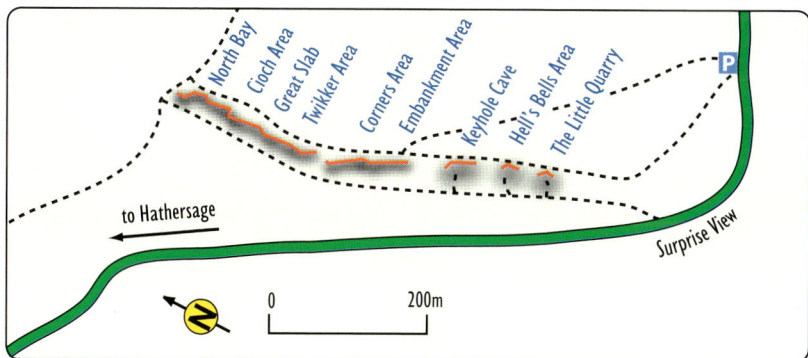

North Bay Area

This area represents the northernmost extremity of the crag. Its tall towering walls are steep, and a good number of high-quality lines force their way here. The routes have a big feel about them, and will seem challenging for their grade. The area gets less sun than other areas, with the Brimstone wall only receiving sun late in summer evenings. This makes it cold in winter, but a good option for a warm summer. **Descent:** A path comes down under the Brimstone wall, or between North Bay and the Cioch areas.

1 Brindle VS 4c   1957-65
8m The wide crack is best appreciated from the ground.

2 Scrimsel VS 4c   1957-65
12m Climb this baby, which will push the major muscle groups to the limit, until a constriction

again allows good jams. Finish on more conventional holds.

3 Brimstone E1 5b ★★   1957-65/73
13m An absolute corker up the fine overhanging crack-line, which will have you as pumped as you're ever likely to get on an E1.

4 Satan's Slit E1 5b   1964
13m The wide kinky crack has an especially pressing move low down. ● Leaving no hold unheld, **Anything is Possible in Cartoons**, E4 6b (1988), traverses right from the kink on Satan's Slit, past a peg, crux, then into and up Gates of Mordor.

5 Gates of Mordor E3 5c ★★   1969
15m A genuine thunderpump. Climb the groove to its end at half-height. Above this, attack the very steep thin hand crack, where you will most likely be glad of the perfect protection.

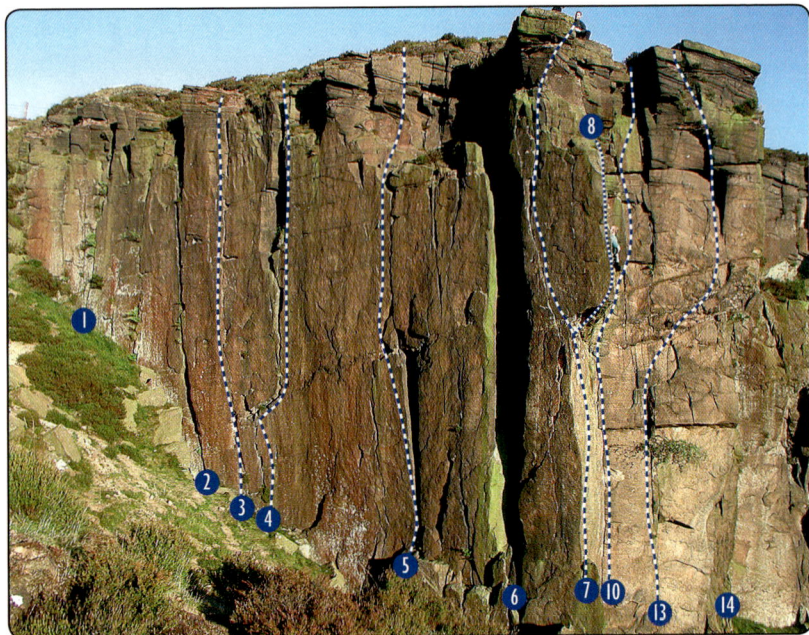

6 Hacklespur HVS 5b   1957-65
15m The wide chimney/groove. ● **Pin Prick**, E2 5c
(1957-65), is a poor route up the crack system to the
left.

7 Cauldron Crack E3 5c ★   1957-65/76
15m Good chunky climbing. The right side of the
arête is followed, hollow but mellow, to a jug
beneath the overhang. Swing left to gain and follow
the nut-friendly crack to the top.

8 Freight Train E4 6a ★   1988
15m Very Gogarth. From the overhang on
Cauldron Crack, lurch right past an 'iffy' peg (good
wires to the left), to gain the overly-exposed arête.
Claw round right to gain a good peg, and a sense of
relief. Easier above.

9 Estremo HVS 5a ★★   1957-65
16m An obvious wide fissure snakes up the left wall
of the corner. Climb this with all hands on deck as
far as a niche. From here climb the quick corner
above in a position of refreshing exposure.

10 Gimbals HVS 5a ★   1957-65/76
18m Ascend the technical crack in the corner as far
as a niche. Step right and tackle the bulging wall
aiming for the skylight.

11 London Pride E5 6b, 5c ★★   1957-65/76
An adventurous journey, with a fairly out-there feel.
1. 15m Climb the peg-scarred crack until a traverse is
made under the roof to the arête. Belay there on
old bolts and other protection. (A hanging rope may
also provide some comfort.)
2. 10m Traverse steeply right for 4m on biggish holds
to a crack. Pull up into this, cross the overhang and
finish easily.

12 Which way up Mr. Rothko E5 6b ★   1988
16m Tough climbing with adequate protection.
From the belay of London Pride, pull up and left
into a shallow hanging groove. This is climbed
desperately, past 3 peg runners.

13 Mother's Pride E6 6b ★★★   2001
24m A superb hybrid route doing the first pitch of

London Pride then Which Way Up…, giving a long and sustained pitch with reasonable protection.

14 Perplexity E6 6b ★★★   1957-65/84
24m A superb climb, taking a stately line up the domineering arête. Boulder up the arête to the first bulge, and a nut. Crux moves up and left lead to improving holds immediately over the second bulge and so to the overhang. Good protection can be had there from old bolts, nuts and cams. Climb the groove and wall above.

15 Plexity HVS 5a ★★★   1957
22m A big route for the HVS leader, with thrilling, tough and exposed climbing all the way. Climb the steep crack up the centre of the wall as far as a recess. From here, an unhelpfully sized crack is gained by stepping right then back left above the overhang, and followed rapidly to the top of the mountain. The excursion can be avoided by gaining the finishing crack directly above the niche at a stiff 5b.

16 Remembrance Day VS 4b ★   1959-61
20m Jam joyously up the wide crack in the main corner of the bay, passing a ledge.

17 Day Dream VS 4c ★   1957-65
20m A technically interesting route based on the clean arête just right of Rememberance Day. Climb this with good protection to a grass ledge. Follow a shallow corner to the summit.

18 Rainy Day VS 4b   1957-65
20m The corner-crack to the left of the dark recess has not one, but two grass mantelshelves.

19 Southern Comfort E3 5c ★   1957-65/76
22m Very Cumbrian. From the right end of the ledge, take a direct line up the dark groove above; good steep moves. Beware loose rock near the top.
● A right-trending hand-traverse from the ledge has been climbed, **Owzaboutthatthen**, E4 6b (1988), following a line of pockets into Saville Street.

⓴ Commix E2 5c ★★   1957-65/76

20m Very fine and well-protected climbing with a trying crux. From 3m up Southern Comfort, move right to a crack. Follow this steeply until a mantelshelf-type manoeuvre leads to better holds then a ledge and an easier, though hollow, finish. Much better than it looks.

㉑ Toploader E7 6c ★★   2001

28m Top-notch cranking up the smooth wall. Climb the thin peg-scarred crack. Carry on past several pegs up and slightly right to a semi-rest and a junction with Saville Street. Move back left from here and climb past bolts to the top. ● This supersedes the route **Scumline**, E5 6b ★ (1969/84), which, after the start, trended left to the previous climb.

㉒ Bohemian Grove VII (7a)

Slippery wall climbing just right of, and avoiding, the arête.

㉓ Drifter E7 6c ★★   2000

9m Hard climbing above dubious gear, packing a fair punch for its short length. The grooved arête is followed with difficulty to sandy pockets and protection. Continue up the left side of the arête to a hideously sloping finish.

㉔ Saville Street E3 6a ★★   1957-65/75

28m A tough Millstone classic with continually forceful climbing and adequate protection centred on the thin crack. A short awkward crack gains a ledge. From here, follow the fine crack to the overhang. A very determined attitude is now needed to gain a standing position on the ledge above and an easier finish. Hard for E3, and 6a.

㉕ Soho Sally E1 5b ★   1975

28m Climb a flake crack to a grassy ledge. Make a committing series of moves left and up into a very shallow groove and a runner. More trying moves lead left to the airy arête, and so to easier ground. Protection for the groove is not fantastic, and the prudent leader will carry RPs.

Several lines have been claimed on the broken rock to the right(**Chaos** and **Derision**, 1957-65 and **Spider Crack** and **The Web**, 1951-57), although Mother Nature is making a much stronger claim. R.I.P.

Little Lower Wall: The next routes lie on the series of low walls running left from the level below Plexity. At the far left of these is a flat wall. Round left from here, facing Stanage, is a flat slab whose left arête is currently the last great problem on the edge. Get to it. ● Going back to the last flat wall, the short left arête is VS 5a, ● and the twin cracks just right are VS 5b. Another 20m right is a taller flat wall;

㉖ Salinela Sunset E4 6a   1987

10m A bold solo up the clean left arête of the wall. ● The wall just right is climbed by **Fat and Jealous**, E5 6c † (1989), although the peg used on the first ascent is now missing.

The shorter walls to the right and left give some scrambling.

The Cioch Area

This is one of the more friendly areas of the crag, named after the prominent cracked 'spike' in the middle of the wall. It is very open, and less steep then you tend to get elsewhere at Millstone. Some of the rock on the unpopular routes is a bit delicate, although the better routes are all well-travelled. **Descent:** A path skirts this section on its left.

'As far as is known,

the first climber to practice his art on this impressive and commanding escarpment was the late George Bower during the early 1920s. He confessed to ascending an odd route at the Surprise end of the edge, and then after inspecting the tremendous blank walls that reared above him, "raised his hat and retreated to Stanage in good order".'

Eric Byne,
1965 Sheffield-Froggatt Guide

Mike Lea making the first ascent of his dark neo-classic, Toploader, E7 6c (opposite page), one of the safer routes of this grade on grit. Photo: David Simmonite.

The rock to the left is somewhat overgrown, and contained ● **Slack Alice**, E1 5c (1982), the thin crack through a bulge and ● **Bamboozle**, VS 4c (1957-65), taking the groove and overhang then moving diagonally right to a rib, and to the right. ● **Dolorous Gard**, E2 5b (1982), is the undercut arête on its left. ● **Fluted Corner**, HS 4b (1957-65), is the grassy corner.

27 February Fox E2 5b ★   traditional
12m Make a series of long reaches up flat holds 2m left of the arête. Highly enjoyable.

28 March Hare E3 5c ★★   1957-65/75
14m The left arête of the flat wall; the climbing is far from easy, with the crux at half-height.

29 April Arête HVS 4c ★   1957-65
16m A Master's Edge for the enthusiast. From the ledge, climb the main arête. A fine sense of exposure is felt, especially during the crux mantelshelf. The crack to the right is VS. ● The old aided start up the flake below has been freed at a dirty 6b (1970s).

30 Dextrous Hare E3 5c ★★   1957-65/76
16m A fine route which climbs the sneaky little pegged wall left of Dexterity. It is not uncommon for one's heart to murmur on the moves left to the hanging corner. RPs useful.

31 Dexterity E1 5b ★★   1957
20m The splitter crack will test leaders' biceps to the limit. Superb, straight-in jamming leads exhaustingly to a slap-in-the-face crux at the top. Those of lesser moral fibre have been known to scurry out left below this, but you wouldn't do that, would you?

32 Cioch Corner S   1956
22m Climb the corner left of the Cioch to the ledge, then climb any of the easier finishes to the top.

33 Mayday HVS 5a ★   1957-65
22m A technical exercise up the arête of the Cioch. Not a brilliant line, but fine moves nonetheless.

34 Supra Direct HVS 5b ★   1957-65/75
20m Climb the peg-scarred crack on the front of

'Here the **piton** and **etrier**
can be used without shame; no raised
eyebrows or supercilious glances will be cast
at the ringing sound of hammer on peg, for
here, on these great smooth exposed walls,
no one could sense a defilement which could
be felt on such natural edges as Stanage and
Gardoms.'

Peter Biven, **Further Developments
in the Peak District**, 1957

the Cioch, with a couple of thin pulls, as far as the ledge. Finish more easily above.

35 The Hacker VS 4c ★ 1983
20m Follow the little pegged crack just right of Supra Direct as it curves right to a ledge. Move up a corner and then follow the steep, cracked arête as much on its right-hand side as your mood allows.

36 Close Shave HVD 4a ★ 1956
30m A good route following the sweeping groove formed at the right side of the Cioch. From the ledge, finish up the back corner.

37 Boomerang S 1957-65
24m The easiest route up the steep wall is unfortunately loose and dirty. It climbs leftwards until half-height, then slightly rightwards to a ledge. Traverse right and finish up the corner. ● Alternatively, for **Cioch Diagonal**, HVD (1956), continue left to the big ledge then climb the wall left of the corner.

38 Brumal VS 4c 1956-65
22m Climb the steep crack above the rightwards slanting section of Boomerang.

39 Eskimo Blue Day VS 4c 1971
17m One of the best mixed routes on Millstone, featuring superb dirty crack climbing in its first half and peerless turf action on its second. Climb the corner direct. ● **Strait Jacket**, E5 6b † (1989), climbs the steep slab just left to a nut placement. From this, move left and finish direct. ● **Corner-stone Climb**, HS 4a (1971), is the crack right of

Eskimo Blue Day. ● **Shamrot**, S (1957-65), is the dirty crack just right again.

40 Only Just E1 5a ★ 1959
15m Gain the ledge and climb the clean groove to the left of the wall. The climbing is easy, but protection limited. (Side-runners sometimes used in Eartha.)

41 Eartha HS 4b ★★ 1957
16m Fine climbing up the attractive flake system in the centre of the slab. It is gained by climbing delicately up near the left side of the lower wall. Among the best HSs on the edge.

● **Slime Crime**, E4 6a (1983), is the slippy slab on the right of the upper crack. ● **Bowling Green**, VD (1959), is a wide, shallow groove right again.

42 F. A. T. D. HS 4a ★ 1969
13m A good, bold route taking the main arête .

Round to the right is a crumbling wall, with a corner 10m right of the arête.

43 Dune Flake VS 4a 1957-65
12m Left of the corner, layback the dramatic ear of rock. Care needed near the top. ● The dangerously loose crack to the right is **Dune Crack**, VS 4a (1957-65). ● The thin crack system 2m left is **Sudden Impact**, E1 5b (1984). (And there's a clue in the name.) ● **Flakey Pastry** and ● **Rough Puff** (1957-65), both cover the unattractive ground to the left, at HS.

44 The Pittsburgh Enigma E4 5c — 1985

15m A good line based on the arête, though the rock is a little brittle. Climb to a peg, then gain a second one on the left, and finish direct.

To the right is a forked crack with a projecting block at 12m.

45 Wuthering Crack HVS 5a — 1957-65

18m Delve into the obvious wide crack on the left, and muscle up to a steepening. Jam up the left side of the projecting block, beefy, to a respite on the ledge. Finish more easily.

46 Evening Premiere VS 4c ★ — 1976

19m Good steep crack climbing. Climb the thin crack on steep jams and finger locks. After getting stood on the horizontal breaks, avoid the loose finish up the blocky crack by heading for the final crack on the last climb. Another direct finish has been claimed as **Evening Premier Direct Finish**, E1 5b (2002), climbing directly up the wall above the initial crack. ● The corner to the right is **Creaking Corner**, HS 4b, ● and right again is **Crumbling Corner**, HS 4a (both 1957-65).

The Great Slab

This is the big sheet of quarried grit, containing the only real slab climbs at Millstone. Fans of rockovers will enjoy routes of all grades from HS to E6. Some of the climbs are virtually solos, and many climbers have taken the slide down the entire height of the slab. In this event, you may wish to have a fire-extinguisher handy, as the friction generated could easily send your feet up in flames. The rock above and around the slab is of a more suspect nature, and requires some care. **Descent:** Take the path left of the Cioch area.

47 Svelt HVS 5a ★ — 1962

20m The smooth corner has a couple of slippery bulges. From the top of the slab trend left and up a steep juggy corner. The original line took the open corner to the right, but this is usually dirty.

● **Crumbling Cracks**, HS (1957-65), is the shallow groove left of the last route. ● A girdle, **Gibbering Heap of Puss**, E3 5c (1984), follows Svelte to the roof, then traverses right past the large hold on The Snivelling Shit to finish across Sex Dwarves and down Cake Walk.

48 **The Psycho Path** E6 6b ★   2000

10m Non-existent and widely spaced holds lead up the flawless slab, to a high crux. Unprotected. ● This route bears strong resemblance to **Velvet**, which climbed the slab 2m right of Svelt, but escaped into the corner at a lower level, at E2 5c (1984). E2 leaders would do well to note this small but significant difference.

49 **The Snivelling Shit** E5 6a ★ ★   1977

10m This unique test of nerve and footwork climbs the bald slab on the smallest of holds, aiming for a deep slot and an easier finish. Strangely classic.

50 **Greasy Chips** VS 4b ★   traditional

10m An alternative start to the next route can be made up a line of chips. Unprotected. ● The slab to the left is **Election Special**, E4 6b (1987), using side-runners.

51 **The Great Slab** HS 4b ★ ★   1952/57

28m A good big route, with an adventurous feel. Climb the thin left-trending crack with slippery difficulty to the top of the slab. From here, climb straight up via a wide crack and a careful top-out, as the rock is a little hollow at the top.

52 **Sex Dwarves** E3 6b   1982

10m Painfully thin climbing up the slab on razor blades and polished smears leads to the break. Escape here. ● A thinner line just left is **Dino**, E4 6b (1984). If you liked Sex Dwarves, you'll love this. Begin as for that route but move left to climb a line parallel with Great Slab.

53 **Lorica** VS 4c ★   1957-65

20m Climb a crack to the top of the slab. Above and left is a right-curving flake. Follow this, then the hand crack above. ● An alternative, **Cake Walk**, HS (1957-65), continues left to the top of Great Slab.

54 **Bun Run** HVS 5a   1969

20m Follow Lorica to the top of the slab. Gain a hanging corner to the right and follow this steeply to a final wide crack.

55 **Windrête** E2 5b ★ ★   1969

14m The left arête of this wall, climbed face on, is a pretty full-on affair. Some gear can be had at a

Andi Turner on Great West Road, E2 5b, 5b (page 109). Photo: David Simmonite.

third height, and while this will cover the crux, it still feels a long and lonely way to the top. On a more positive note, it is neither strenuous nor pumpy, which allows you plenty of time to worry about each move. A very fine climb.

Twikker Area

In the next couple of bays, the cliff steepens up again, and gives lots of good, forceful climbs. The rock is not always perfect, but the quality of the lines easily makes up for this. **Descent:** Scramble down between Billingsgate and The Corners Area.

56 Breeze Mugger E5 6b   1990
15m Boulder up to a deep slot and good wire. Above, bold fingery climbing leads upwards before easier moves lead left to a finish up Windrête.

57 Meeze Brugger E5 6b ★   1984
15m Crimpy fear up the steep crispy wall. Pass a break, then boulder up to an isolated jug, and worrying wire. More trying moves gain easy, but loose ground.

58 Eros HVS 5a ★ ★   1957-69
15m Pummel up the rough and ramshackle flake in the centre of the wall with great joy and care. Fine chunky climbing in a great position.

59 Frank Sinatra Bows Out E5 6b   1987
15m Tough, worrying wall climbing. Climb the wall to a massive peg and cam. Hard climbing above this leads to a scrabbly ledge where you can either traverse off or continue up the slightly loose wall above. ● To the right, **Acheron**, VS 4c (1963), is the main corner. ● **Mean to Me**, HVS 5b (1980), takes the shallow groove and the left side of the arête.

60 Lyon's Corner House HVS 5a ★ ★ ★   1956/57-65
30m A fantastic rock climb based on the fine arête. Gain the cave, then continue up the corner to the roof, where a swing left leads to a ledge (as for Erb). From here, trend up and left to gain and follow the arête in a superb position. ● A superb direct start is possible up the lower arête at HVS 5a. This is more independent then the original, but care must be taken with a loose flake.

61 Erb E2 5c ★★
1957-65/75

28m Another good route, serving up a delightful smorgasbord of strenuous thuggery and delicate technicality, sometimes both on the same plate. From the floor of the cave, climb the left-hand corner and exit onto a stance on the left. From here, a line leads up and right to a hungry gash in the lip of the roof. Beef through this to a rest, then still surprisingly difficult going to the top.

62 Twikker E3 5c ★★★
1956/75

28m This awesomely steep route gives one of the best E3 challenges on the edge. It takes the big roof crack, both exhausting and exciting, and then continues to a niche below an overlap. A disappointingly difficult manoeuvre over this on pin scars leads more easily to the top. A large bird often builds a large nest in the cave on this climb. This can be unsightly, but, amazingly, doesn't really get in the way. Two starts have been climbed up the lower flake (5c) and wall (6b).

63 Lubric HVS 5b
1957-65

30m From the recess, climb the major, stepped right-hand corner.

64 Pinstone Street E2 5c ★
1956/69-78

28m Climb a peg-scarred corner then the overhang, to a ledge. Follow the easier crack system all the way to the top.

65 Diamond Groove HVS 5a
1957-65

30m Open moves lead up into the groove, whence a struggle leads one onto another ledge. Finish up the easier cracked wall above. The ramshackle wall to the right contains three poor efforts. ● **Shady Wall**, VS 4c (1957-65), climbs to a grassy ledge, continues past a niche then follows a groove on the left. ● Going right and climbing the cracked tower is **Helliconia Spring**, HVS 5a (1983). ● The gash to the right is **Black Crack**, S (1963).

66 Flapjack VS 4b ★
1956

24m Climb the stepped feature, until a mantelshelf gains the ledge. From here, a series of bold stretches leads up the shallowest of grooves as far as another ledge, whereupon a quick move leads to the top. ● The left edge of the slab above the ledge is **Optimus**, E1 5a (1978), a fine, bold climb that unfortunately is often green. ● **Neatfeat**, VS 5b (1977), is a fine little problem taking the lower arête on its right.

EEK! Mad Tobias Wolf on an on-sight solo of Millstone's brilliant Knightsbridge, E2 5c (page 110). Photo: Alex Messenger.

67 **S.S.S.** VS 4b   1957-65
18m The stepped corner has good bridging moves.

68 **Winter's Grip** E6 6b ★   1983
17m Fine, scary climbing up the arête. A couple of hopeful blade pegs can be hand-placed *en route*.

69 **Keelhaul** VS 4c   1957-65
15m Gain the flake from below and climb it. Finish on the right, as the direct is a little loose. ● **Crusty Corner**, S (1957-65), is the crack in the corner to the right. Unfortunately the crust has gone stale.

70 **Quiddity** HVS 5a ★   1957-65
16m The steep rib right of the corner is a good technical challenge with just about adequate protection. ● The groove on the right leading to this route is **Findus**, HVS 5b (1983).

71 **Billingsgate** E1 5b ★ ★   1951-57/69
18m The big open groove has solid rock and gives highly absorbing technical climbing. It can be adequately protected by small wires. ● A poor eliminate, **Sea Creature**, E4 6a (1984), climbed the thin crack to the right then moved left into the corner.

72 **Piledriver** E3 5c †   1976
16m The big arête, climbed on its right, has been damaged by rockfall, and has probably not been ascended since. It has reputedly been climbed on its left at 6b/c. The unstable rock to its right has been climbed on, named and graded, but these passages can hardly be seen as routes. (● The loose chimney of **Mopsy**, ungradeable (1957-65), bounds this section on its right.)

The Corners Area

Classic Millstone terrain now, with a long stretch of flawless corners and arêtes. The rock quality here is generally perfect, and some of the finest challenges in the Peak, from VS to E7, lie within the next hundred metres. The routes are steep and often very bold, and follow the most brutal of lines. **Descent:** A path comes down the spur left of Stone Dri.

The routes begin with a square-cut bay on the left, characterised by a deep crack in its right corner. The next climb follows the left corner of the bay.

73 **Stone Dri** E2 6a ★   1976/78
15m The tight left-hand corner has most of its difficulties packed into a short section passing some satisfactory nuts above the ledge. ● The shot-holes and flake to the left is **Nib-Nob**, HVS 5b (1982).

74 **Crew Cut** HVS 4c ★ ★   1963
20m The salivating fissure. Medieval thrutching, or bold laybacking, leads past a chockstone to a lifesaver ledge. With loins suitably girded, attack the upper crack, passing another chockstone *en route*. The whole voyage feels particularly brave without the aid of an oversized cam or two. From the ledge, escape left, or, better, do one of the following:

Below: Just in case you thought it wasn't dangerous enough already – try doing it in a Whillans harness and smoking a fag! Loz Francome on Green Death, E5 6b (page 109). Photo: Brian Cropper.

The Corners – A History

The 1965 *Sheffield-Froggatt* guidebook makes a quick mention of what has now become the Corners Area: "The blank walls to the left of Knightsbridge have seen borings and bolting – a practice many ardent fans of artificial climbing decry when no line exists up the crag" – evidence that, at the time, the thought of free climbing these corners and arêtes was beyond imagination.

This soon changed. In 1969, when Tom Proctor, partnered by Keith Myhill, forced the stunning Green Death up the blank central corner, to give a route very much at the cutting edge for its time. On the first ascent, Proctor, one of the most powerful climbers of the era, nicknamed The Hydraulic Man, placed a peg. This came out with a gentle nudge, and for a second ascent, which was televised and rocketed The Hydraulic Man to instant fame, he drilled out a hole and cemented in a good peg. A despicable act and one for which many later climbers have been grateful for. Procter returned once again to make the first winter ascent in heavily iced conditions. Myhill, also returned some time later "on a glorious shimmering summer's day" for a lead, although, as he had spent an enjoyable morning in the boozer, unfortunately fell off from below the peg resulting in three months in traction.

Proctor, with Geoff Birtles, next turned his attention to the sharp arête to the left of the corner, and top roped this with intentions on a solo. Before he could, however, and in one of the most impressive climbing achievements of the decade, Alan 'Richard' McHardy, steamed in and made an on sight ascent of the climb. Steve Bancroft, one of a group of seconds on the climb, recalls it as "definitely the boldest ascent I have ever seen, by a long way. On the crux [final] moves, McHardy was only hanging on by his knees and his entire body was going into convulsions." McHardy had placed a peg in the half-height shot hole, but this offered very much 'token' protection. The problem of protection was later overcome by one notable local climber. After a claim of an early repeat, a photograph emerged showing the hero on lead, with an abseil rope hanging down with a series of loops in it, into which the leader had clipped his rope. Now why didn't McHardy think of that?

Next up were Proctor and Birtles again, who had their eyes set on the upper arête on the right of the bay. For some reason, this was gained when Birtles led Green Death to the peg, then pendulumed from there to gain the upper, easy section of the sharp arête on the right. This led to the ledge, where Proctor took over to produce Great Arête, a climb so frightening that the Hydraulic Man "put his hard hat on for the first time in years". 'Nuff said!

This left the square-cut arête beneath Great Arête, and this began to see action in the competitive era of the early 1980s. At this time, Jerry Moffatt, the new pretender, was battling it out with the established hero, Ron Fawcett, for dominance on British Rock. As one of the finest unclimbed lines around, the Millstone Arête was an obvious target for the two climbers. Moffatt, after much effort, finally succeeded in top roping the line without tension. Having spent some time previously in the US along with top American climber, John Bachar, Moffatt had adopted Bachar's philosophy that if you top roped a climb, to go back and lead it was unfair, the only decent thing being to solo it. A combination of this risky philosophy and Jerry's belief that he was the only person capable of climbing the line, left an open goal.

Ron Fawcett had spent the autumn of 1983 nursing a broken wrist, and later in the year, recovery left him keener than ever. Sensing his years at the top were nearing an end, he wanted to make a mark. "It was something I was desperate to do. I had looked at it before Jerry, but [the challenge] spurred me on.' Fawcett abseiled the line and practised the moves and, on December 29th, when any sensible person was in front of the telly burping up turkey sandwiches, led the route. After his successful top roping of the route, Moffatt had publicly declared that 'only a true Master could solo this route on sight'. Fawcett had no choice over a route nam – Master's Edge was born.

Since that date, Master's Edge has become the consummate hard route on grit, with all the grandeur, history, difficulty and boldness that such a title demands. Repeats only followed from the most talented of climbers such as Mark Leach and Shaun Hutson, who climbed the route after abseil inspection. Martin Atkinson climbed the route ground-up and gives a graphic account of long falls from below the protection, and thundering into the hard ground below, eased only by a layer of Karrimat. The late great Wolfgang Gullich broke his back falling off the climb and more than one person have broken their ankles. In the Hard Grit revolution of the early '90s, extensive top rope practice and bouldering mats threw the route open to the masses. Others then made better style ascents, until finally, in 2004, the talented young Liam Halsey finally closed the book on the climb by doing the long awaited on sight flash.

Nic Sellers climbing Master's Edge on sight, managing it with only one fall. A fine effort, lad. Photo: Adam Long.

A choice of worthwhile second pitches for Crew Cut is available from the birch ledge. ● **Yourolympus**, HVS 4c (1969), starts near the left arête, climbs a heathery crack rightwards to a slopey shelf in the middle of the wall, then traverses the shelf left to the arête, to finish boldly up this. ● **Myolympus**, HVS 5a (1969), starts just left of the corner (Xanadu), and boulders up to a left trending flake-line. Trend left to meet Yourolympus and continue up the thin crack directly above with some difficulty.

75 **Under Doctor's Orders** E2 5c ★ 1951-57/87
20m Good climbing, bold and forceful. The arête and crack right of Crew Cut are followed past a peg to slopey shelves and a rest. Climb the thin crack above until it is possible to swing out right onto a ledge. Mantleshelf to glory.

76 **Jealous Pensioner** E4 5c ★ 1978
20m Ascend the centre of the shot-peppered wall as far as a narrow ledge. From a standing position on this, climb the upper wall using a blank flake to the next ledge (hard for shorties). Protection can be had at foot level, but the move is still a heart-stopper.

77 **Xanadu** E4 6a ★★ 1969/74
35m Technical wizardry up the overly-blank corner at the back of the bay. Gruesome bridging off the ledge leads to a little shelf. Further desperation lands one on a good ledge. The corner above can be followed as a second pitch at HVS, with a possible finish along the wide break near the top.

78 **The Trumpton Anarchist** E6 6b ★ 1988
12m Great moves up the lonely wall above Xanadu. From the ledge, move right, clip some pegs, then sequence out the right-trending feature, passing possible small cam placements *en route* to the ledge on Great West Road.

79 **Adios Amigo** E5 6b ★★ 1985
15m Unique cranking up the big flat wall. From the ledge at the bottom of the Xanadu corner, a lengthy lean or a gymnastic jump rightwards gains shot-holes in the middle of the wall. *'Ascend these then crank like a disease to a nothing finger edge from which a bucket can be reached.'*

80 **Great West Road** E2 5b, 5b ★★★ 1956/69/75
Two contrasting pitches, one strenuous and well-protected, the other bold and delicate, combine to produce a route every bit as classic as its exalted neighbours. Both pitches would probably merit E2 by themselves, the second being very high in that grade.
1. 19m The clean peg-scarred groove is followed, with a strenuous layback leading to a perfect belay ledge. An easier alternative skirts the layback to the left.
2. 19m The arête above is followed past an old bolt (gulp) to a ledge (possible cam in a pocket round to the left) and a bit of a heart-stopping finish.

81 **Edge Lane** E5 5c ★★★ 1974
18m You can boulder about on this one for years, but some day you're going to leave the ground knowing the only way is up. Then God help you. The square-cut arête bounding the left side of Green Death is followed, calmly if possible, to a crux at the top. Nowhere is the climbing more than 5b/c and the crux is only the crux because it is at the top.

82 **Green Death** E5 6b ★★★ 1969
18m The all-too-well-named corner provides a stern test of technique and commitment, and as such, is avoided by most. The 6b bit comes right off the deck, although a running jump would also be a fair way of accessing good flat holds a few feet up. From here, a series of surprisingly good holds soon gets one into danger. A bulge in the corner marks the 5c crux, after which positive holds allow a peg to be clipped on the right wall. Above this, while the climbing is still technical, life seems somehow sweeter...

● The shallow scoop just left of the corner has been claimed as **Stranger Breaks Right**, E6 6b (1994). Follow the line of scooped overlaps, trying very hard to avoid the easy corner. Where it becomes difficult, join Green Death. A ruthless rejection of any ideals of line and quality.

83 **Green Death Superdirect** V8 (7a)
The classic bridging testpiece up the blank corner. ●**The Left-Hand Start**, V3 (6a), traverses in from the start of Edge Lane. ●**The Green Death Start**, V4 (6b), climbs tiny edges between the corner and the arête (the normal stsrt to the route).

84 **Master's Edge** E7 6b ★★★ 1983
18m Fawcett's masterpiece. The stunning square-cut arête gives one of the finest hard challenges in the Peak, with sustained difficult climbing and painfully limited protection combining to produce an unforgettable lead. Increasingly difficult moves lead up to shot holes at half-height (protection) from where more increasingly difficult moves lead to a heart-stopping lunge for a flat jug at the top. A fast belayer may be needed to protect this section. Incidentally, the arête has been top roped on its left-hand side – *one handed* – by... guess who?

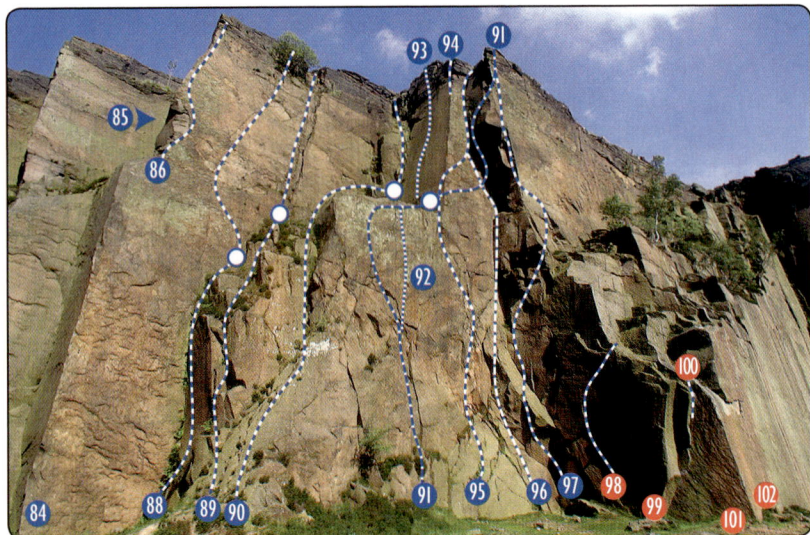

The previous routes can be escaped from via the dirty corner at the back of the ledge at V Diff. But if you're still in the mood...

85 **The Bad and the Beautiful** E7 6b ★ ★ ★ 1987
15m '*You can fall, but you'd better not bounce!*' One of the best hard routes on grit, despite its shy setting. The blind flake on the wall left of Great Arête is climbed with increasing difficulty until a desperate and irreversible move leads to a ledge and an easier finish. Utterly committing.

86 **Great Arête** E5 5c ★ ★ ★ 1974
16m If you still have anything left after the lower routes, then a superb second pitch follows the hulking continuation of the Master's Edge arête. From the ledge follow the sharp arête, mainly on its right side, to an easing at half-height. The climbing is fairly steady, and while not quite the chop-route that the grade would suggest, it is unlikely that the leader's personality would ever be the same again in the event of a fall.

87 **Stranger in Paradise** E5 6a † 1994
16m An ability to avoid holds and protection may be needed for this narrow voyage up the wall between Knightsbridge and Great Arête. Start for

Knightsbridge and climb the wall passing a sloping ledge. A pathetic excuse for a climb.

88 **Knightsbridge** E2 5b, 5c ★ ★ ★ 1951-57/73
35m An absolutely fabulous climb, which is, somehow, both sustained and cruxy – work that one out! Climb the lower corner (often overgrown), or

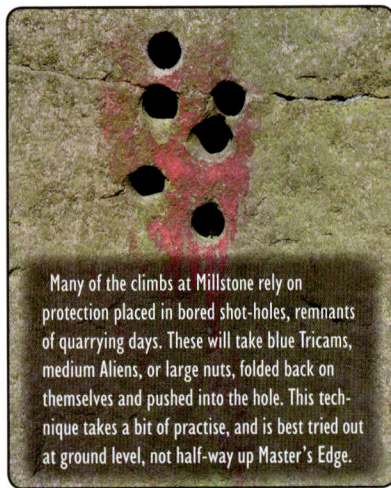

Many of the climbs at Millstone rely on protection placed in bored shot-holes, remnants of quarrying days. These will take blue Tricams, medium Aliens, or large nuts, folded back on themselves and pushed into the hole. This technique takes a bit of practise, and is best tried out at ground level, not half-way up Master's Edge.

scramble up The Scoop. Climb the thin pegged-out crack above via interesting moves on perfect rock, to an easing just short of the top. Good protection can be earned in the form of many small wires.

89 Scoop Crack VS 4b ★   1957-65
32m Climb a shallow corner in the arête then the crack above the ledge.

90 The Scoop D   1951-57
35m Disjointed climbing with some good positions up the slab, ledges and corner with a bold finish.

91 Detour E2 5c ★   1975
40m A phenomenally indirect line, but one that finds some good climbing along the way. Climb slabby rock and a thin crack above to the ledge and possible belay. From here, move into, and follow, Great North Road until established over the little overhang; a straddle right gains good finishing holds on the arête.

92 The Hunter House Road Toad E5 6b ★ 1985
15m This takes the significantly thinner crack right of Detour. The two *in-situ* pegs are old, but good, and can be backed up by small wires.

93 Clock People E6 6c ★   1984
15m The miniscule slotted crack on the flat wall left of Watling Street. A desperate start leads to a good hand-jam slot. Continue up the absorbing line on spaced and positive holds. Well-protected by a mountain of micro wires.

94 Watling Street E2 5b ★★   1957-65
15m The square-cut arête is an overlooked gem, with balancey moves on good holds. Marred by its proximity to the corner in its upper reaches, although some will be glad of the protection this offers.

95 By-Pass HVS 5a ★   1963
40m Climb the wide crack, past a salvo of loose blocks to a big ledge. From the ledge traverse right to the corner and continue up this.

96 Great North Road HVS 5a ★★★   1956/57
35m This, the Cenotaph Corner of grit, climbs the fantastic stepped corner. Everything that HVS should be, and then some.

97 Quality Street E5 6b, 6a ★   1983
30m Climb onto the smooth ramp with difficulty. Climb it then move directly up to the ledge. Belay. Climb the arête above to reach a small groove. Go up this then move left at the lip of the capping roof to finish direct.

98 Deaf Dog VI (HVS 5b)
The big flake.

99 Master Chef V8 (6c)
The superb hanging arête. A sit-start is V9. ● **Hic Up Pick Up** is an eccentric problem on the sloper just right of Master Chef. Hang footless from the woeful sloper and say 'Hic Up Pick Up'. Far out.

100 Technical Baiter VI (HVS 5b)
The big fun flake, used as a descent by boulderers.

Loz Hudson on Technical Master, V4 (overleaf), one of the Peak's most celebrated boulder problems. Photo: David Simmonite.

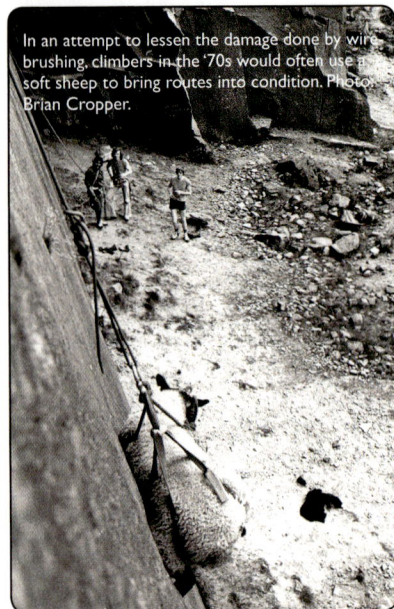

In an attempt to lessen the damage done by wire brushing, climbers in the '70s would often use a soft sheep to bring routes into condition. Photo: Brian Cropper.

101 **Technical Master Left-Hand** V5 (6b)
Latback the arête with the help of the crack.

102 **Technical Master** V4 (6b)
A flawless test of technique following the angular arête on its right. Has been climbed one-handed, and in Reeboks (see the *Stone Monkey* video).

Embankment Wall Area

The quality continues in this area, starting with a sheer, cracked slab, well-dotted with peg cracks. This was named after its resemblance to the Thames Embankment in London. Some individual pitches exist on the upper wall, as well as some second pitches to those on the lower wall. However, you may well prefer to pick 'n' mix your first and second pitches, as there is no particular logic to the original pairings.

103 **Embankment Route 1** E2 4c, 5c ★   1957-65/75
27m Follow the short crack to a horizontal flake, then swing awkwardly right and up past a helpful iron bar (VS in its own right). Belay. On the upper wall follow the tricky peg crack (the E2 bit).

104 **Blind Bat** E4 5c ★★   1965-72/76
20m A protected crux is followed by tense wall climbing. Begin by placing a side-runner a few metres up the second pitch of Embankment Route 1. (Oi, Not that far!) Go back down and climb the wall direct to the peg. Pass this with a hard move. From flat holds, continue reverently to the top.

105 **10,000 Maniacs/Elm Street** E8 6c ★   1994
10m Horrifically thin, steep slab climbing up the blankness between the cracks with the barest minimum of holds, and much less protection.

106 **Who Wants the World?** E5 6a   1981
10m Climb the steep wall. The initial moves are hard, reachy and poorly protected, which is a shame, as the open climbing above is very enjoyable.

107 **Embankment Route 2** VS 4c, 4b ★★   1957-65
25m Twin cracks, big brother and little brother, lead to the belay ledge. Using little brother alone is **The Compromise**, E1 5b (traditional). On the upper wall, climb the right-facing corner.

108 **Scritto's Republic** E7 6c ★★   1951-78/82
15m Hard, thin and technical. The seam was never pegged hard enough to become an Embankment Route; instead it is a searing test of technique and finger strength. Climb the seam on shallow pocks. The crux is in the first half, and tiny gear can protect the still difficult upper section.

109 **Embankment Route 3** E1 5b, 5b ★★   1957-65/70/75
25m The perfect peg crack leads past two pitons to the terrace, belay. Straightforward Millstone quality, making up for the sore feet. The second pitch takes a short steep crack just left of a shallow right-facing corner of Embankment 2.

110 **Time for Tea** E3 5c ★★   1974
20m Further right is one of the wall's few natural cracklines, which the quarrymen forgot to complete. So, climb the crack, and with good gear at its apex, move confidently left to a ledge in the middle of the wall. From here, balancey, open climbing on flat holds leads up and left to the summit. Short people would prefer to upgrade this one, but tough. ● **Time for Tea Original** attained Embankment Route 4 from the top of the crack, E1 5b ★★ (1974).

Phil Robins high on Embankment Route 4, E1 5b (overleaf), possibly the most varied and interesting of the Embankment routes. Photo: Pete O'Donovan.

Paul Mealor and Nening Dennis on Great Portland Street, HVS 5b (overleaf), one of Millstone's many outstanding routes at this grade. With the desperate mantelshelf below, the leader is now tackling the more technical and delicate upper corner. Photo: Pete O'Donovan.

111 **Tea for Two** E4 6a ★ ★ 1982
20m Emotionally, much like doing a double tour of duty in Vietnam. From the terminus of the crack on Time for Tea, career directly upwards via thin moves to the top. A route to clear the cobwebs. Superb.

112 **Embankment Route 4** E1 5b ★ ★ ★ 1951-57/75
22m As good an example of peg-pocketeering as gritstone has to offer. Climb the tall crack, straight-forward at first, then with a frisky scuffle near the base of the vague groove. This leads less strenuously to a final crack and then the top.

113 **Whitehall** HVS 5a ★ ★ 1951-57/69
25m The major corner at the back of the bay is climbed direct, providing a fine test of laybacking technique.

114 **Lotto** E1 5c ★ 1957-65/75
25m Varied climbing in an exposed position. Ascend a faint groove which curves up, past a thin section, to the arête. Swing right to follow Covent Garden.

At the roof, go back left along the wide break and beef the overhang at a slotted crack. A better, harder and more independent variation, ● **Lotto Direct**, E3 5c ★ ★ (traditional), avoids Covent Garden by laybacking the arête on the left until stood on a little ledge. From here, finger-traverse a flake leftward to the middle of the black wall, whence a committing move up gains the original finishing crack. The climbing is lonely but positive.

115 **Little Lotto Arête** V2 (5c)

116 **Seventies Style Wall** V4 (6a)
A technical exercise up the quarried crimps.

117 **Covent Garden** VS 4b, 4b ★ ★ 1956
25m A scrappy first pitch is more than made up for by the delightfully exposed second pitch. Climb easy ledges and a pedestal to a big ledge. An alternative follows the arête just to the left. Belay. Cross a narrow terrace to the left arête. Balance up this with glee to a slightly hollow finish.

Millstone > Embankment Wall Area

● The walls have been girdled from Covent Garden to Badly Bred; **London Marathon**, E5 6c, 6b, (1988). Totally desperate.

⑪⑧ Scruples E5 6b † _1987_
22m Climb Bond Street until established in the first sentry box. Move left to climb a bulge and slab. A crucial peg runner used on the first ascent is missing.

⑪⑨ Bond Street HVS 5a ★ ★ ★ _1951-57_
22m Cancel your trip to Yosemite; this Millstone classic has it all on your doorstep. The perfectly-formed hand-jamming crack is simply superb, marred only by not being ten times longer. Scramble off the finishing ledge or do the lovely second pitch of Covent Garden.

⑫⓪ Monopoly E7 6b ★ _1983/84_
2lm A very bold line following the shallow features up the wall. A skyhook may offer some protection, but the chances are that if you fall off, you won't be passing 'Go' anymore.

⑫① Great Portland Street HVS 5b ★ ★ ★ _1951-57/63_
20m Yawn! Not another brilliant HVS? This one ascends the fine groove to the left of White Wall. This delicate bridging is unfortunately guarded by a desperate mantelshelf manoeuvre, a bit like getting out of an overhanging swimming pool, and harder than anything on Regent Street.

● **The Impetus for Stranger Faeces**, E5 5c (1994), climbs the perched arête to the right, although unfortunately it is mostly within easy reach of the corner.

⑫② White Wall E5 6b ★ ★ _1969/76_
22m A worthy sister route to London Wall takes the pegged crack in the smooth face left of The Mall. While not quite as fine, being less sustained, it still has great climbing and impressive situations. Climb steadily up kinked cracks until a desperate move gains a standing position below the overlap. From here, thrilling cranking over the small roof leads to a piton and less difficult climbing to finish.

⑫③ The Mall VS 4c ★ ★ ★ _1951-57/57_
22m Heave-ho your way up the big chunky corner. This contains a lot of climbing, all of it enjoyable, although it can be sandy in the post-monsoon.

⑫④ London Wall E5 6a ★ ★ ★ _1956/75_
22m The London Wall of the Peak! This classic product of the '70s free climbing revolution is also one of the best lines on grit. Finger lock your way up the searing pocket-studded seam with never-ending difficulty. One of the greatest trophies on gritstone.

⑫⑤ Urban Sprawl E6 6b _1997_
22m Relatively safe climbing at the grade, although very physical. Having clipped the pegs on London Wall, crank rightwards and upwards to reach the easy groove leading to Badly Bred.

⑫⑥ Badly Bred E1 5c _1977_
24m From the chimney, step left and climb to a large ledge. From here, climb the tricky right arête with some trepidation.

⑫⑦ Lambeth Chimney HS 4b ★ _1951-57_
22m Follow the broken chimney, then the easy arête above, until an exacting straddle to the left gains a smart little groove leading to the top.

The Keyhole Cave Area

This is one of the great venues in the Peak, with a great collection of searing, vertical crack-lines to suit all levels. The routes are long, pumpy and unforgettable. The wall gets lots of sun and dries extremely quickly if it ever does get wet. It is worth being careful on the tops of the routes as the soil is loose. This is an important note for belayers. The first section of wall, on the left, is not quite as fine as the main area, but is worthwhile all the same. **Descent:** Scramble down the corner in the far right-hand corner of the bay.

Crusty Wall: The first routes are on the crusty wall just right of Lambeth Chimney.

⑫⑧ Old Kent Road D _1951-57_
25m More of a risky ramble than a rock climb. At the left end of the wall, move up to a good ledge. Follow this rightwards to a flake chimney and up, taking as many stances along the way as you wish.

⑫⑨ Alopecia HVS 5a _1957-65_
18m A thin crack a few metres right of a large flake, leads to a non-finish. ● **Brittle Road to Freedom**, E1 5b (1976), is the random wall just right, putting

The Man. Johnny Dawes surveying his kingdom from London Wall, E5 6a (opposite page), one of the mighty desperates from the generation before his. Photo: Adam Long.

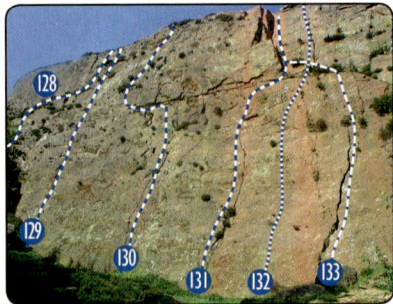

yourself in as much or as little danger as your mood demands.

130 **Petticoat Lane** HVS 4b ★   1956
25m A route requiring a steady leader, given its spaced gear and sometimes hollow rock. For the same reasons it is also a rewarding lead. Climb a thin crack to a break at a steepening. Traverse 4m left and climb the wall to a ledge. A long rightward diagonal leads, with some anxiety, to the plateau.

131 **Bow Street** HVS 5b   1956/67
20m Climb a crack below the corner to a little roof then escape right. Continuing direct is more like a nasty E4.

132 **Metal Rash** E1 5b   1978
25m Climb the wall and vague crack to the ledge. Finish up the thin crack directly above.

"I'd be careful
on that slope above the Keyhole Cave. I remember once I led Coventry Street and got to the top of the crag. I was going up the slope to the belay, when I stood on a big flake, and suddenly it started sliding back down toward the edge, with me on it. I was sort of surfing backwards towards the edge, and all I could think was that I only had one RP in that top wall, miles down. I must have slid down about eight feet, and then it just came to a stop, and I was able to just stand off. But I would be careful up there."

Tony Ryan

133 **Brixton Road** VD ★   1951-57
20m Climb the ledged crack to a cracked ledge. Move left and climb the shallow corner., taking care with some loose scree near the top. ● **Ekel**, S (1957-65), is the horrible corner to the right.

134 **Skywalk** VS 4b ★   1957-65
25m A drastically exposed voyage for the grade (although with easy climbing) that will have you sleeping with the light on for weeks. Gain the highest ledge on the arête (go up Brixton Road and turn right), take a deep breath, and traverse right along the face on positive holds to finish up Oxford Street.

135 **The Economist** E6 6b ★   2004
20m An alternative start to the next climb takes the curving flake which trends right to meet Adam Smith's... at the peg. Bold, powerful climbing.

136 **Adam Smith's Invisible Hand**
    E6 6b ★ ★ ★   1984
20m At last! Sport climbing without the safety. The arête is climbed, desperately, past three pieces of industrial archaeology. By the top one, swing left (crux) around the arête, and climb the wall on better holds to a peg. Slightly easier climbing leads to much easier climbing.

137 **The Rack** E5 6a ★   1957-65/82
13m Crimps and cranks its way up the steep wall left of Oxford Street. Follow holds slightly right, (possible gear in Oxford Street). Work back up and left, heading eventually to a peg, and then sanctuary in the cave. Bold, but at least it's positive. Has been done without gear in Oxford Street at a very mild E6.

The next routes climb to the cave via friendly crack-lines and then reach the top of the wall by more challenging means. Many climbers tend to lower off from an in-situ spike in the sandy cave. This will obviously change the grade and most definitely lessen the experience. Note: This spike is an unknown entity; use it at your own discretion.

138 **Oxford Street** E3 5a, 6b ★   1956/69
22m A lovely HVS crack followed by a classic roof struggle. Superb, steep hand-jamming leads to the sandy cave. Beef over the roof crack to the right then

mince up the easy wall above. The difficult section is phenomenally well-protected. ● **Littleheath Road**, E3 5c (1976), is the bombed out crack through the roof to the left. Stay away!

139 The Keyhole Traverse up to V8 (6c)
Don your best lycra, biggest chalk bag and stiffest Firés for this sterling test of good old fashioned crimping. Starting from Oxford Street, crimp your way sharply rightwards as far as you can, picking up V grades with every crack that you pass.

140 Piccadilly Circus E2 5a, 5c ★   1957-65/76
25m Two contrasting pitches combine to yield the easiest way up the wall. Climb the delightful natural finger crack to a landing in the sandy cave (● a great HVS 5a by itself). Belay. From here, beetle leftwards to a thin crack which leads to a ledge. Exciting while it lasts. Finish up Skywalk.

141 Coventry Street E5 6b ★ ★ ★   1956/76
22m Now, let's see if you can climb finger-cracks! After an encouraging start, poor fingertip jams and

critically unhelpful footholds lead to a desperate lunge for the ledge. Here, having clipped various artefacts, including one of the Peak District's few Bong runners, muscle over the roof crack with determination, and wobble directly to the top. Doing the bottom section alone and lowering off gets E4, but isn't *real* E4. (Oh yes it is!)

142 Jermyn Street E5 6a ★ ★   1956/75
25m A big adventurous route only marred by sandy sections and an indirect line. Climb the crack and groove into the cave. Move right and scuff your way up the right arête of the cave, placing a wire along the way. Hand-traverse the lip leftwards, (good Friend 1), and pull into a standing position on the more solid rock above the cave. From here migrate into the relative security of Coventry Street and finish. Better than anything on Gogarth.

● **The Direct Finish**, E5 6b † (1984), carries on up the headwall above the sandy arête to finish via twin thin cracks. Seldom repeated, and perhaps affected by the loss of holds and gear placements.

143 Regent Street E2 5c ★★★   1956/68
20m Quite simply one of the best Extremes in the Peak, with superb protection and sufficient rests making up for its uncompromising steepness; as such it probably holds the same position in Derbyshire as Left Wall holds in Wales, although the walk in is easier. Follow twin cracks past a cheeky move. More delicate climbing leads up and right to below the headwall crack. From here an onslaught of savage cranking on perfect finger locks leads to a gasping point below an easier finish. Unforgettable.

● **Transmetropolitan**, E3 5c (1988), is a traverse from Regent Street to the top of The Rack. ● **Keyhole Cops**, E2 5a, 5c (1973) traverses the wall, from Oriel to Skywalk, above the level of the two caves.

144 Regent Street Direct Start E3 5c ★   1975
20m The slender groove that runs directly to the upper crack provides a very worthwhile, and harder, start to the classic. Pressing moves over the initial bulge are followed by exciting, though protectable, moves up the groove. An illogical upper section took the ramp right of the top crack. ● A poor eliminate has also been climbed to the left of Regent Street. **Appletree Yard**, E4 6a (1988), uses side-runners.

145 Wall Street Crash E5 6b ★   1983
20m This climbs the blank wall on unique iron rugosities. Start up the thin crack. When this finishes, a desperate sequence of crimps will lead the technically adept to a break where the climb runs out of steam. Finish by the easiest line which will most likely be a pre-placed abseil rope. Originally protected by old bolts, which have now been re-placed by (fairly good) pegs.

146 Shaftesbury Avenue HVS 5a ★   1956/67
20m Bovine jams lead up the straight, wide crack to an overhang. Climb steeply over this. Enjoyable open climbing now leads to the summit.

147 The Whore HVS 5b ★   1975
20m Follow cracks to the little overhung corner. Overcome this strenuously, good solid 5b, then steep finger locking leads to an easier finish.

148 Gimcrack VS 4c ★★   1962
24m Romp delightfully up the jamming crack and

finish up the corner above. The slope above this is mildly biodegradable. Beware.

149 At-a-Cliff VS 4c   1977
25m The hand and finger crack leads to the niche in the overhang at half-height. Power through this to an easier finish. ● **Wings of Steel**, E3 5c † (1979), is a non-line just right.

150 Happy Wanderer VS 4c   1957-65
25m Climb the narrow crack with some difficulty to the left end of the cave. Traverse left and finish up Gimcrack, avoiding any sand skiing.

151 Oriel VS 5a ★   1957-65
15m The jamming crack has a stubborn section leading to the beach in the cave. Exit this right and climb pleasantly to the talus slope at the top. This slope is quite magnificent, and a good a place as any to practice one's step-cutting technique.

● The thin crack to the left, **Charing Cross Road**, HVS 5a (1956/67), gained the cave and then took any of the cracks above. ● The technical wall left again is **Wash and Brush Up**, E1 6b (1985). ● To the right, the poverty stricken corner-crack above the bottom of the descent is **Trio Crack**, S (1957-65). Earthy. Just right is the descent gully.

The next climb lies on the steep wall across the other side of the descent gully.

152 Pot Leg Wall V2 (HVS 5c)   1976
A very fierce move up the steep little wall on peg holes. Finish easily. Good prastise for Coventry Street.

Dave Viggers on Regent Street, E2 5c (opposite page), a line of uncompromising steepness, and one of the most thrilling tests of E2 in the Peak. Here, the climber has just done the fierce move to pass the projecting block, and is making his way towards the resting ledge. The climactic finger crack is all-too-obvious above. Photo: David Simmonite.

Mike Lee and Matt Rudkin making the steep moves onto the ledge on Chiming Cracks, HS 4b (this page), one of the small number of good easier routes to be found at Millstone. Photo: Nick Smith.

Hell's Bells Area

Some shorter, easier climbs are located in the next bay 30m to the right. The first routes are high on the left side, in the corner left of the narrow projecting buttress on the left.

153 **Bent Crack** HS 4b   1963
6m Quite sustained climbing up the widening crack left of the corner. ● The corner itself is **Piper's Crack**, VD (1957-65).

154 **Butter-ess** HVS 5b ★   1959
8m The crack system on the front of the projecting buttress. ● The corner to the right is **Crossways**, S 4a (1957-65), having traversed the ledge from Flank Crack. ● The corner, with a direct start and finish is **Key's Climb**, HVS 5a (1957-65). ● The two cracks above the traverse are **Straight Leg**, VS 4b (now overgrown), ● and **Flared Bottom**, HVS 5a (both 1977).

155 **Flank Crack** VD   1957-65
8m The short corner to the ledge. Walk off right or take the direct finish up the sandy wall at S.

156 **Chiming Cracks** HS 4b ★   1959-61
8m The steep cracks are short but pumpy.

157 **Hell's Bells** HS 4b ★ ★   1963
8m The best route hereabouts taking the tall

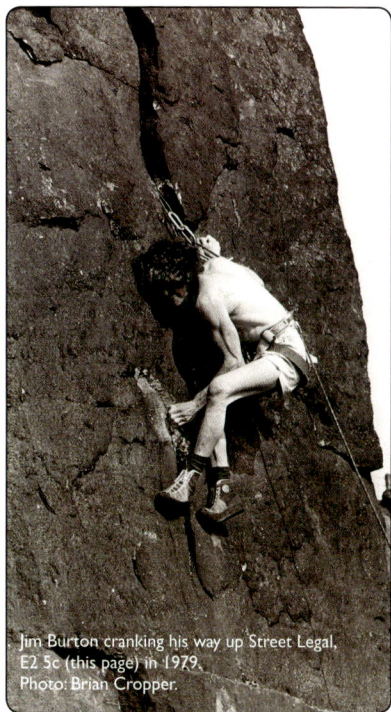

Jim Burton cranking his way up Street Legal,
E2 5c (this page) in 1979.
Photo: Brian Cropper.

162 Blood and Guts on Botty Street E5 6b   1987
8m Hard and unprotected slapping up the right arête of the buttress.

The broken rock to the right gives a convenient descent. The shallow bay to the left again has two poor routes taking the two corners, ● **Frond Crack**, VD, and ● **Crane Fly Climb**, S (both 1957-65), but hardly rank as routes in the modern idiom.

Wilfred's Wall: Another 10m right is another area of clean rock, with a smooth arching slab bounded on each side by deep cracks. ● The deep crack on the left of the slab is **Squeak**, VS 5b, (1959), which is especially good fun at the overhang. ● **Wilfred**, S (1957-65), avoids the crux by climbing the crack left of the overhang. ● **Annabella Superstella**, E2 6b (1986) is the thin slab just left of Wilfred. ● **Helping Hands**, E1 5b (1985), is the slab left of this, with slightly more holds, and a crux mantelshelf at two-thirds height. ● **Beneath the Pavement Lies the Beach**, E4 6a (1986), takes the centre of the smooth slab right of Wilfred. ● **Pip**, S (1959), is the crack right of the slab – a good honest thrutch.

The Little Quarry

The last climbs are to be found in the minor bay, about 70m from the road. It can be identified by a pointed boulder on a little hillock at the entrance. At the back left-hand side of the bay is some rock: ● **Fireworks**, V5 (6b), is a pointless and lethal problem up the slab above the big pointed boulder on the left; 5m right, climb the bulging crack and arête at V0 (5a); ● **Damage**, V4 (6a), is the arête above a careful landing; ● **Halloween**, V4 (6b), is the painfully thin face to the right; ● **Big Al**, V0 (5a), is the finger crack on the right. ● Facing these routes, on the opposite side of the quarry, is **Humpty Dumpty**, E1 5b (1995), taking the slab and crack left of the heathery corner-crack.

corner. Sustained and well-protected, it deserves to be somewhere else. ● The right arête of the short upper wall makes a good bold finish at HS 4b.

158 Juniper E1 5b   1978
8m The arête, with good balancey moves. Often climbed with side-runners at HVS.

159 Midrift VD   1957-65
7m A good beginner's route up the short corner. ● The chimney up the short wall above is D.

160 Giant's Steps D   1957-65
8m A gentle frolic up large features. ● The crack systems in the upper wall are VD, providing a good finish.

161 Street Legal E2 5c ★   1978
8m Climb the wall with stiff moves passing a hanging flake. Little protection until after the crux.

Lawrencefield

OS Ref. SK 250795 to SK 250800   altitude 300m

by Simon Jacques

Lawrencefield is an impressive old quarry lying just under Surprise Corner. It exists slightly in the shadow of Millstone, and although it lacks the grandeur of its greater neighbour, it has enough good points to make it a worthy destination. These include a friendly aspect, better easier climbs, the dark and mysterious pool, and a very sheltered and cosy setting.

The Climbing

The quarry has over 110 routes from VD to E6, although the majority are in the VS-E3 range. The routes tend to be fairly steep corners and cracks, with some fine examples of peg-pocket-pulling to rival anything on Millstone. There are also a few good slab climbs, especially on the unfortunately polished Gingerbread Slab. The climbs above the pool have a fine situation. However, some suspect rock exists and care is needed at the top of routes, especially in the Great Harry area. Often the only belays are the refurbished fence posts well back from the edge, or iron stakes above the routes round the pool.

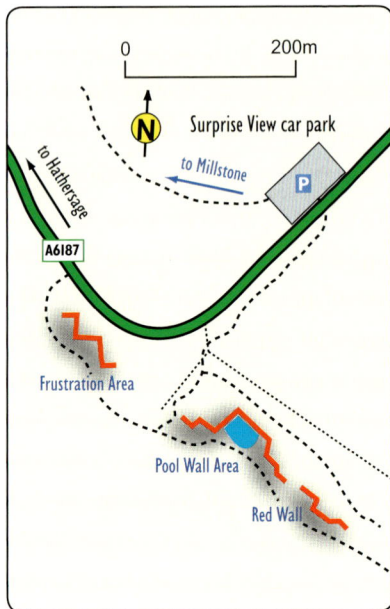

0   200m

Surprise View car park

to Hathersage
to Millstone
P
A6187

N

Frustration Area

Pool Wall Area

Red Wall

Conditions and Aspect

The crag is very sheltered and can be a sun trap during the winter, making it a great option on cold, windy days. However, in summer it can be like an oven, so choose days with some breeze. Unfortunately it can be slow to dry, and rain tends to bring sand down onto the cracks and ledges. Some parts of the crag are now returning to nature, and watch out for the giant wood ants, they are hungry blighters. The crag generally faces southwest, with the Great Harry area getting the sun from first thing and the rest coming in the sun later in the morning.

Parking and Approach

Park as for Millstone Edge. Cross the road and go over a stile to follow the quarry lip rightwards to an easy descent. For the first bays, stay on the road and go round the Surprise Corner and carefully climb over the stone wall opposite the Millstone Quarry

track, taking care not to lean on the buttress when doing so – the other side of it fell down in 1981! This path also contours round to the main quarry. **Approaches:** All about 5 minutes. **By Bus:** The 272 First stops right above the crag on the A625. **By train:** Alight at Grindleford Station and from the Station Café go left and over the rail bridge, Burbage Brook and then past Padley Mill before striking right up a dirt track and left at the old water station. The track then goes steeply uphill but keep right and you will soon hit the Delectable Area.

The Roadside Bays

The first climbs encountered are in the two millstone-littered bays leading straight off Surprise Corner, before the main crag. The first bay, below the road, houses a highly suspect left wall. The first route is on the wall 2m left of the corner.

1 Brain Attack HVS 5a   1980

11m Follow a tricky peg-scarred crack to a ledge. Finish up parallel cracks above a tree to loose rock and the top. ● The main dirty corner to the right is **Itslide**, VS 4b (1964), ● and the twin, grassy cracks just right are **Sunday**, HVS 5a (1965-78).

2 Surprise, Surprise VS 4b   (1957-65)

9m Ascend the groove 6m right of the corner passing a grassy ledge. ● The enjoyable flake right of the upper groove is **Friday**, VD (1957-65). ● **Shallow Chimney**, VD (1958) is the chimney on the right, and ● **Split Second Timing**, E1 5c (1981), is the technical wall to the right of shallow chimney.

The next routes are on the second, larger bay.

3 Spec Arête E2 6a   1957-65/76

9m Climb the imposing arête left of Frustration, using a sneaky side-runner in that route.

4 Frustration E1 5c ★   1958/76

9m We are in Millstone territory now for the peg-scarred crack up the overhanging tower. This has a difficult start, goes direct, and is a real energy sapper.

5 Straight Crack VD   1958

9m The broken cracks have some suspect rock.

6 The Big Red Jacket VS 4b   1986

9m The steep crack with a tiny pinnacle.

7 Rocking Groove HVS 5a   1958

11m Another well-named pitch.

8 Redbits E2 5c   1978

11m The hideously strenuous quarter moon crack in the centre of the steep wall is what we northerners call a 'reet bugger' of a climb.

9 Slippery Wall HVS 5b ★   1957-65

12m The wide crack in the upper wall can be gained from the left or right cracks, or direct at 5c. Fight the fissure to a hard, sandy exit.

10 Quantum Crack HVS 5b ★   1957-65

9m The thin, overhanging crack system. '*A strenuous finger exercise.*'

11 Vaseline HVD   1957-65

9m The corner is quite pleasant.

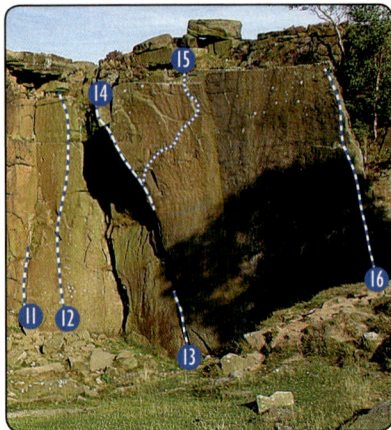

The Pool Area

About 100m right is the most extensive part of Lawrencefield with its infamous dark pool. Surrounding this is a steep cauldron of superb routes, most of which present tough, physical challenges for their respective grades. The easiest descents are either side of the quarry, most popular and gentle at the left.

Great Harry Area: This is the steep area of walls and corners on the left side of the pool. The first 2 climbs begin halfway up the steep slope to the left, from a large, square rock platform. Above this is a large, clean corner. Left of this is a smaller corner with a narrow slab to the left. This is taken by:

12 Positively 4th Street HVS 5b   1989
9m   Climb the wall direct via a series of ledges with a crux at two-thirds height involving a horizontal break. ●**Grass Groove**, D, is 4m right of the corner. ●**Seta**, HS 4c (1957-65), is a green route 1m right leading to a flaky corner.

13 Proud Crack VD   1957-65
11m   A Freudian and claustrophobic climb. Follow the wide crack to the ledge then move behind the mega flake to the right. Back to the womb.

14 On Deadly Ground E6 6b †   1995
12m   Climb the left arête of the flake, starting at the base of Proud Crack. Somehow tackle the leaning arête via presses and hooks with no protection to save you lest you fail.

15 Brain Cells in Collision E3 5c ★   1981-83
12m   From the grassy ledge, boldly break out right across the wall. Exposed, to say the least.

The large blank wall right is Lawrencefield's last challenge. Every move has been done by Johnny Dawes, who believes the route to be solid E11 when climbed in full. '*When that goes, things will really have moved on!*' Any takers?

16 Last Day of Freedom E4 6a   1991
10m   The serious, though escapable, right arête.

17 Gregory's Slab S 4a   1955
13m   A worthwhile easier climb. Climb the short corner-crack to a jutting flake. Use this to gain the ledge and an easier, broken finish.

18 Summer Climb HS 4b ★   1956
15m   A quality climb on clean rock with good protection. From the square platform, make a tricky move right into the large clean corner. Follow this with a thrilling layback until a perplexing move gains easier terrain.

19 Three Tree Climb HS 4b ★ ★   1952
21m   A fine climb with an exposed, exciting finale. Climb a problem crack to gain a series of grooves. Follow these, and, near the top, grope right to a crack round the arête. Layback this to the ledge and a finish off left. It is possible to continue up the groove, avoiding the step right, but this is not as good. ● A much better variation, **Branching Off**, HS 4c (traditional), steps right at a much lower level, to get a narrow ledge 3m below the short crack. Layback the arête to reach the crack, and jam this to the ledge. The HS man's Suspense.

20 Pulpit Groove VD ★ ★   1952
27m   '*A pleasant route, especially for an average party*'. A superb multi-pitch journey, with a refreshing sense of space. After a tricky start (variations possible), follow the leaning groove to a well-positioned pulpit stance. Good thread belay. Deep breath, and launch right across the void, then follow the leaning scoop to a large shelf and a rowan tree belay.

21 Great Peter E1 5b ★★   1956/76

18m A pumpy Lawrencefield classic, and a good introduction to the crag's harder finger-cracks. Attack the thin crack, minding out for the loose block, and crank towards the ledge. Go direct from the larch tree.

22 Great Harry VS 4c ★★★   1953/56

21m A stout line with brilliant, sustained climbing. The wide corner-crack is jammed and bridged to the pulpit. Continue to the large tree ledge with difficulty. Tackle the corner direct to a friable finish.

23 Too Good To Be True E4 5c   1978

21m Start in the centre of the wall right of Great Harry and climb direct on sloping flakes to the ledge on Scoop Connection. Finish up a shallow corner.

24 Scoop Connection
E3 5b ★   1965-78

22m About as worrying as walking gets. From the centre of the slab, climb diagonally up and right to ledges on the arête (as for Suspense). From here, step up, and left onto the sloping shelf. Continue philosophically across this – easy, but no place to sneeze – to finish up Pulpit Groove.

25 Suspense E2 5c ★★★   1956/75

21m A rousing local testpiece that will live long in the memory. Follow Scoop Connection to the arête. Move boldly round this onto the steep wall to positive holds (don't look down). From here, follow the pegged crack and finish past a (sometimes) *in situ* peg (other sufficient protection exists). The climbing wall rats will quiver on this one.

26 Brainstorm E4 5c ★   1981-83/89

21m Climb the right arête of the slabby wall on its left-hand side until the shelf is reached. Continue boldly up the upper arête (dubbed the **Brain Death Finish**).

27 Pool Wall
E5 6a ★★   1958/81-83

21m A fantastic wall climb, which starts at the low-water level (if the weather has been dry), giving great technical moves just about protected by wires and small cams. Climb up to a thin break, then move right (crux) then back left to finish up Suspense. This was Suspense Direct, the old aid route, with *'Poor Pitonage – and Wellington Boots if the water is high.'* - 1965.

The next climbs are reached by traversing behind the pool, from its right-hand side, across a ledge system known as the Great Shelf. This can be tricky when the water level is high. For the first 4 routes climb the short corner, VD, at the left-hand end of the Great Shelf. For Side Pocket and Cascara Crack, traverse left to a thread belay in the wide fissure of Cascara Crack, behind the large sycamore tree right of Pool Wall. Above are four leftward-facing corners, which get bigger as one goes from left to right.

28 Cascara Crack HS 4a   1953

18m Climb the strenuous chimney-crack behind the sycamore to a large ledge, then move right into the second corner to finish.

● The crack 1m left of the crack is **Side Pocket**, HVS 5a (1953), with an awkward mantelshelf to any of the finishes. ● **The Table Leg**, VS 4c (1990), takes the ledge at water level below, to the broken crack and the tree. Only for Topomaniacs or masochists who must swim or abseil into the start.

29 Mildly Laxative VS 4c   1990

9m The rusty crack right of the sycamore tree is followed by the third corner.

Thea Williams on the exposed upper face of Suspense, E2 5c (previous page). The protection here is just about good enough to allow the climber to enjoy the exposure of the perplexing crux sequence. Photo: Nick Smith.

30 **Austin's Variation** VS 4c ★   1956
9m The fourth corner, with the overhanging flake, gives an alternative finish to the previous two routes. Take a big cam along, it proves useful.

31 **Lawrencefield Ordinary** VD ★   1952
22m A scenic ramble. Ascend the short corner just right of Mildly Laxative to its large ledge at 10m. Move left across the rising steps and go up the first short corner above and finish as desired.

The Great Wall

The next routes are on the impressive main wall, and are gained via the ledge system.

32 **S.A.E.** HVS 5b   1956/64
21m From Lawrencefield Ordinary, climb the main corner, or stepped rocks on the right. ● For **Crystal Clear**, E1 5b (1979), follow S.A.E to a grassy ledge below its main corner ledge. Move right and climb the broken corner and crack above on bad rock.

The next routes belay on an iron stake near the fence, which also can be used on its thicker posts.

33 **High Plains' Drifter** E4 6a ★ ★   1977
21m Saddle up to start at the left-hand end of the large ledge then climb a groove to a sapling. Ascend the wall above, small wires, via a short ramp to an old peg. Move left then go up to the large ledge, crux. Drift off left to finish up the wall to the right of the flake. Fire up your cigar, pilgrim.

34 **Boulevard** E3 6a ★ ★   1956/75
18m From easy ledges, move right to attack the thin peg-scarred crack in the upper wall with conviction. Low in the grade and well-protected.

35 **Von Ryan's Express** E6 6b ★   1985
19m A serious route winding its way up the centre of the Great Wall. Start directly up the slab, to gain the break (side-runners possible). A hard move gains a small, lonely ledge in the centre of the face. More hard moves follow, passing a thin crack.

36 **Billy Whiz** E2 5c ★ ★ ★   1957-65/75
19m One of the Peak's best cracks, a ferociously pumpy route at the very top of its grade, taking the prominent slanting fissure. Follow the slabby groove to a break. Climb the curved flake above to reach

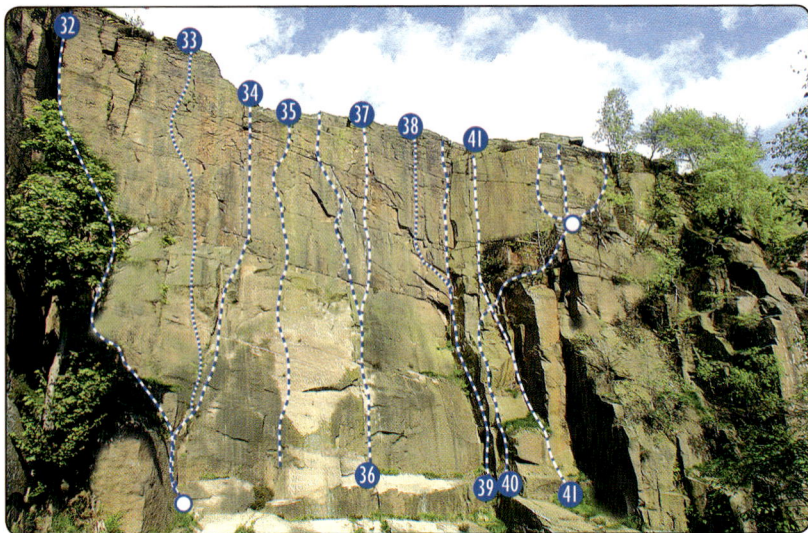

right to a pod and a well-chalked crack. Crank up this to its end, bang in a runner – anything from a medium sized hex to a small nut, then Whiz your way up the final holds to the top on rapidly tiring arms. Magnificent! ● **Silly Billy**, E4 6b (1996), takes the main route to the pod, then moves left to climb the obvious flake. Sometimes climbed by mistake whilst trying Billy Whiz.

37 High Street E4 6a ★★ 1956/75
20m More thrilling finger-jamming. Start as for Billy's slab to the break. Move right to a battered peg-scarred crack. After vicious first moves, crank your way to glory. ● **High Times**, E5 6a (1994), is a serious direct start up the slab, 2m right of the groove, to the break.

38 Holy Grail E4 5c 1977
22m A steep and pushy route, with just adaequate protection. From Excalibur, move left at the steepening to climb the steep wall direct, with crux moves passing the low roof. Small cams useful, as is a very high side-runner in Excalibur (at E3).

● **Heavy Plant Crossing**, E5 6b (1986), is a high level traverse of The Great Wall from Excalibur to High Plains' Drifter. Feet are in the thin horizontal break above the main break. ● A lower-level traverse, going right from 10m up the Ordinary along the slabby ledge system, is **Great Wall Traverse**, S (1953), which gains Excalibur to finish as for Jughandle.

39 Excalibur VS 4c ★★★ 1953
21m Rising up from the lake, the tough corner-crack at the right of the wall is reached by the grassy groove below it. Layback to the top in fine style in a superb position, with plenty of jugs and gear.

40 Jughandle HVD 1957
12m Climb up via giant steps on the right of the main corner, then traverse ledges rightwards to a

During the first ascent
of High Plains' Drifter, Jim Campbell accidentally dropped his second's, Robbi Mallinson, prized collection of new Moac nuts into the pool. Campbell decided that the water was too deep, and that they were lost, and led off to the pub. Not wanting to lose his precious nuts, Mallinson returned the next day with his girlfriend and a full frogman's outfit just to find that the water was ankle deep!

ledge (The Tumbril) and a choice of finishes: **Pimpernel**, S, is the left-hand crack; **Guillotine**, S, the centre of the wall; **Reprieve**, D, the slabby rocks at the right-hand side of the ledge (all 1951-57).

41 J.J.2 E1 5b   1976
21m   Start up the red groove to the right of Jughandle, then layback the thin crack 2m right of Excalibur.
● An alternative finish, **The Gordons, The Gordons**, E3 6a (1985), climbs the square arête on the right from the ledge, first on the right then on the left.

● The dirty grooves to the right are climbed by **Louisette**, S (1952), and **Guillotine Groove**, S (1952), but are now in a poor state.

Gingerbread Slab

The most popular piece of rock in the quarry (due in no small part to hordes of top-ropers), and every crease, crack and crimp has been climbed on. Only the most definite lines are recorded here, so please let us claim no more. From the top of the slab, scramble easily to the top of the crag using a chimney on the left.

42 Once Pegged Wall VS 5a ★   1955/57-65
9m   Not climbing hard enough for those tough peg cracks? Fear not, for here's one Don Morrison made for the mid-graders. Climb the scars direct to the ledge on the left. Gain this and move round the arête to the top. ● The direct finish is a tad harder at HVS 5b.

43 Morning Glory E2 5c   1983
9m   The parallel line of peg holds to the right gives tough, but good, cranking. Take care not to make recourse to holds on adjacent routes.

44 Limpopo Groove VS 4b ★ ★   1955
9m   Grapple with Gregory's 'Great, Grey, Green Greasy Groove', with thought and care at the top (the crux). Bomber protection but it can be a bit slippery.

45 Gingerbread VS 4c ★ ★   1952
9m   A lovely climb albeit demoted from HVS, but with wear and tear it will rise in the grade eventually. Climb the delicate left-hand arête of the slab arranging protection at half height. VS or HVS? You decide. Laybacking the arête on its left is 5b.

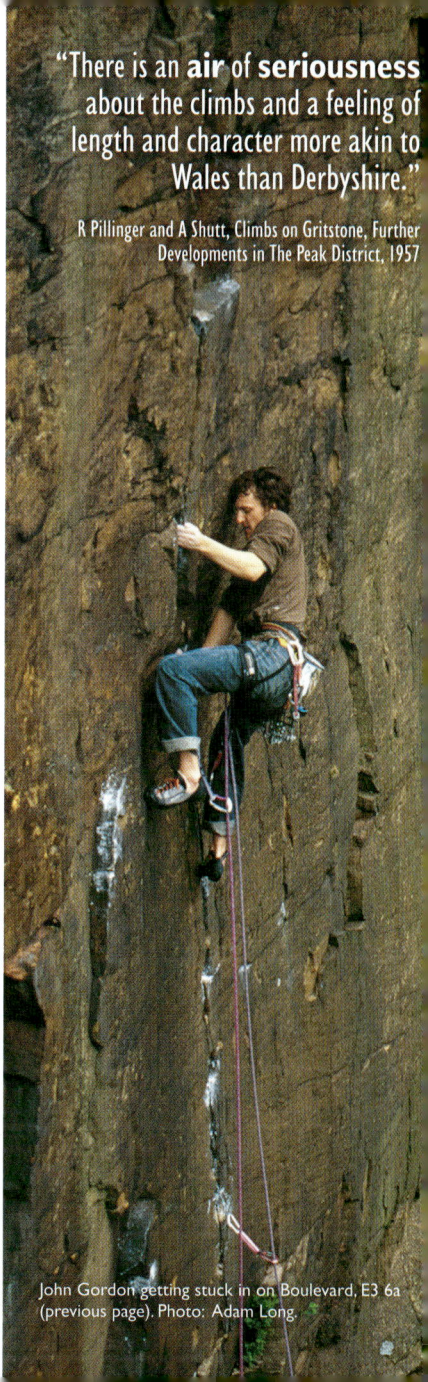

John Gordon getting stuck in on Boulevard, E3 6a (previous page). Photo: Adam Long.

John Cook storming the fearsome upper wall on Billy Whiz, E2 5c (page 129). Photo: Alex Messenger.

Every Man and His Dog, E1 5b (1983-91), has claimed the slab to the right. Let that be an end to it.

46 Meringue HVS 5a ★ 1953/55
9m   The thin crack has taken a bit of a battering and is a touch easier after the appearance of a positive hold. Tiny cams in the break will just protect the top moves. Still bloody awkward at the shiny start.

47 Éclair E1 5b 1957-65
10m   Unprotected climbing on smooth holds.

48 Vanilla Slice E1 5c 1965-78
10m   The slab just right again. Side-runners have been used in Snail Crack, but make it artificial and easier and wires can be arranged in the hairline crack to the left of this keeping more in line with the route. Another serious and slippery slab climb.

49 Snail Crack HVD ★ 1952
18m   The well-defined crack is climbed direct to the ledge. A good beginner's route.

50 Nailsbane VD 1952
20m   The leftward-slanting crack is followed to an awkward mantel. ● **Bole Hill**, VD (1989), takes the crack right of Nailsbane to a large hole. Gain a crack

on the left, finishing just left of the upper arête.

51 Tyron HVS 4c 1957-65
18m   Climb the cracked wall to an awkward move to the ledge. Move a little right into the groove and the upper curving crack to a ledge. From here, a worthwhile second pitch takes the bulging wall above. ● **Chilly Days And The Purple Acorns**, E1 5b (1996), takes Tyron's groove at half-height left-wards along the ramp to its end. Finish direct up the headwall with difficulty.

52 Nova HS 4b 1956
18m   Take the line of choice right of Tyron to twin cracks high in the wall, to an awkward move to a shelf, to gain the large ledge. For a VS 4b finish, climb the traditionally named Trio Wall behind.

● Back down to earth is a mucky corner, with a de-tached and dubious flake. **Flake Climb**, D (1951-57), climbs the flake. ● **Grooved Arête**, VS 4c (1957-65), does the dirty groove just right, ● with the short arête right being **Elytrocele**, highball V3 (6a) (1987). ● **The Ashes**, S (1955), starts 2m right and climbs parallel cracks to a ledge, ● while **Urn**, HVD (1965-78) is a red sandy crack 2m right. ● **Scotia**, VS 4b (1957-65), ascends the dusty,

Lawrencefield > Gingerbread Slab

The Peg-Pocketeer

The steep quarried walls of Millstone and Lawrencefield are home to a very particular style of climbing – peg-scar cranking. These are the holes eked out of hairline cracks by the aid climbers of the 1950s that these days are more welcoming to fingers and toes. The climbing on these routes tends to be pumpy and powerful due to a usual lack of footholds, and on steeper walls turns quite savage. However, there are few things more thrilling than scorching up an otherwise blank wall of grit, cranking out long reaches, fussing in good protection, with that ever-threatening pump approaching. Below is a series of tests of this style, to see of you are a peg-pocketeer.

Once Pegged Wall, VS – a fine introduction to the style. Finish up the arête or stay direct for a bit more practice; **Delectable Direct**, HVS – a steep excursion on the right-hand side of Lawrencefield; **The Supra Direct**, HVS – small holds but at a lesser angle make this a technical one; **Pot Leg Wall**, HVS – only a couple of moves, but as hard as anything on Coventry Street; **Embankment Route 3**, E1 – peg scars up a long smooth slab requiring a determined approach. A route with no hiding places; **Knightsbridge**, E2 – less travelled than the nearby Regent Street, and also a lot less straightforward, being a bit more technical and fingery; **Dextrous Hare**, E3 – short, and the technicalities are well felt; **Boulevard**, E3 – a journey onto Lawrencefield's fabulous Great Wall, with its savage crux then sustained, but easier peg work; **Coventry Street**, E4 – the first section of this fine classic sees many falls where the footholds run out and the pockets get tiny; **London Wall**, E5 – the all time classic test of peg cranking – overhanging, no footholds, long and desperate. You are truly a master.

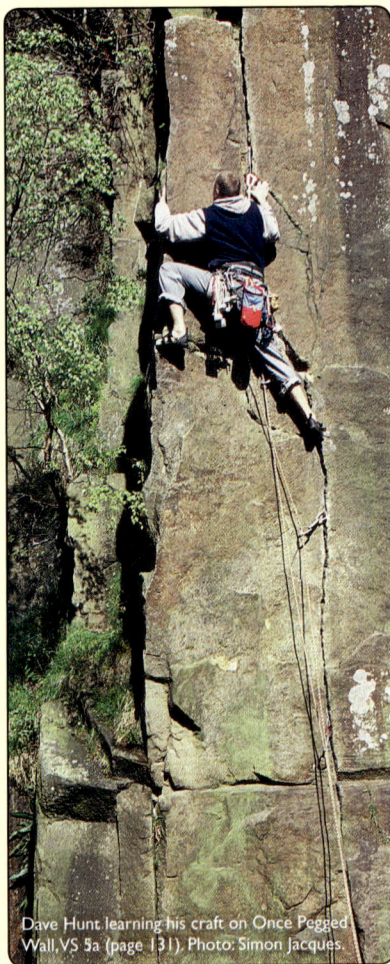
Dave Hunt learning his craft on Once Pegged Wall, VS 5a (page 131). Photo: Simon Jacques.

blocky red cracks just right to finish either up the cracks in the slab or the right-hand corner. ● The broken blocks and cracks to the right are **Fractus**, S (1957-65), ● while **Howarth's Wait**, S (1978), trends rightwards across broken rocks to a large corner containing a tree, climbing direct. All these climbs are overgrown and not worth the bother. A past rockfall has left the next section highly unstable, and led to a more recent huge rockfall a few years ago.

Stonemason's Buttress: Fifteen metres right, the ground is hollowed into a stone-filled depression, often with stagnant water. It has a large grassy ledge at half-height. Above the left-hand edge of this ledge is a shattered wall broken by vertical seams. ● **Tony's Chimney**, VD (1955), is the chimney below the left edge of the ledge. ● **Callus**, VS 4c (1978), is the arête just right. ● **Verve**, VS 4c (1964), is a corner-crack system just right ● **Stonemason's Climb**, HVS 5a

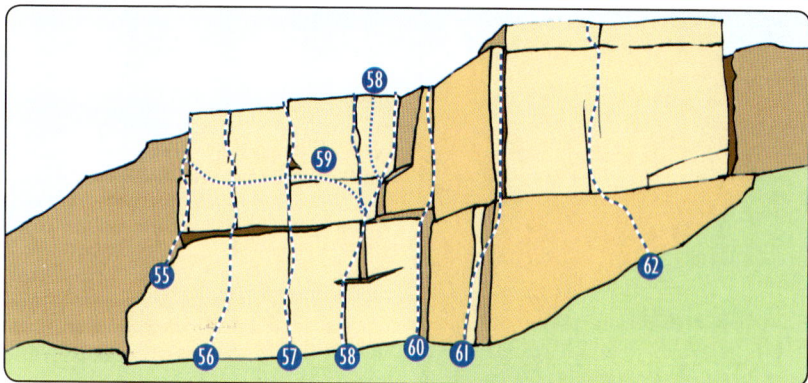

(1952), is the ledgy arête to a finishing corner on the right or the wall direct. ● **Going For The One**, E2 5b (1981-83), passes dirty ledges just right.

53 Blacksmith's Climb VS 4c   1956/57-65
21m   The steep corner is climbed direct past a tree to a second tree. Finish up the broken crack-line.

54 Tuesday's Child VS 4c   1964
21m   From a ledge slightly higher and to the right climb a crack to the first ledge then the arête above the third ledge. Exit up the crack in the arête left of a curved flake, or escape up the corner to the right.

● **Vector**, HS 4b (1955), is right and higher again: a prominent crack, reached via easy ledges. Follow it to the corner-crack or the curved flake just right.
● **Sinister Crack**, VS 4b (1964), climbs Vector for 6m, moves right then follows a crack to an oak.

Red Wall

Further right is a steep wall with a shallow sandy cave at half-height. ● **Moss Corner**, VD (1957-65), is the main corner to its left. ● **Finale**, VS 4c (1956), bisects this route by climbing the left end of the lower slab, and the steep crack left of the upper corner. ● The sorry crack between this and the upper corner is **Reckless**, HVS 5a (1991), which moves left to the arête near the top.

55 Rockhopper El 5c   1984
8m   Climb the arête from the ledge. Contrived.

56 Rattus Norvegicus E5 6b †   1981
15m   Climb the lower slab to the break. Climb the upper wall past two tricky sections.

57 Delectable Direct HVS 5b ★   1956/64
15m   Excellent, well-protected climbing that takes the peg-scarred crack to the 'Red Cave' and continues direct up the headwall, past a small sentry box.

58 Red Wall El 5b ★   1956
17m   Follow the groove and flakes rightward to the ledge in the corner and a choice of finishes: the main corner is 4b (making the route VS overall); the wall with its scary mantel 1m left of the corner, 5b, or the thin crack 1m left again, tough 5b.

59 Delectable Variation VS 4c ★★★   1957-65
22m   A wildly exposed outing. Follow Red Wall to its ledge, then traverse left, all the way across the wall, treating holds with care, and finish up the fine arête.

60 Cordite Crack HS 4b ★   1955
15m   From a corner 2m right, move up to the obvious steep corner-crack. Blast up this to the top.

The face right, Cordite Wall, has been used as a target for Dad's Army for their spigot-mortar during the war years. The last remnants of this mortar, a stain-less-steel mounting, is still in the undergrowth opposite the wall. It also makes an obvious project.

The next routes are all gained from the right along a huge sloping ledge below the wall.

61 Skyline E3 5b   1965-78/81

12m The well-positioned crack is a tad loose.

62 Block Wall E4 6b ★   1965-78/81

12m The best line on the wall gains the pegged-out crack on the upper wall. Finger-knackering cranking on peg holes leads to an easier finish.

● **Varlet,** VS 4c (1958), takes the dirty groove just right of a jutting flake leading to the grassy terrace. Have at ye quagmire of a crack to finish. ● **Knave**, HVS 5b (1983), charges in to the right of Varlet, climbing the right arête of a cutaway and the dirty slab to the terrace. Finish up the fourth crack on the wall. ● **Slab and Groove**, HVS 5b (1957-1965). Gain the small slab near the right-hand corner via a tricky mantel in the corner, moving into this at the top. From the terrace go right to take '*A very shallow corner sparsely furnished with holds*' – 1965. This was claimed in the last guide as Formic Escape. The crack left of the corner can also be climbed at this grade.

Two boulder problems exist here: ● **The Anthill Mantel**, V4 (6b), mantels the sloping shelf at its widest point, below the very smooth slab left of Slab and Groove's mantel, and ● **The Anthill Traverse**, V3 (6b), traverses the shelf left from the corner to finish up the arête on its front.

● **Lone Ridge**, S (1957-65) is the stepped ridge just right, while ● **Tricky Cracks**, S (1957-65) is the projecting buttress via two parallel cracks.

Little Upper Tier

Moving up and right there are a number of short buttresses providing some moderate bouldering in the trees above good landings. Scramble up the rocks immediately right of the last routes. A series of cracked walls, about 4m high, run along here.

At the left end of the tier is a large block with a sloping top and an undercut base, with several possibilities, including a traverse and mantels over the bulge. ● Round to the left of this is an amazing slab project, a flawless sheet of clean natural grit above a good landing. The holdless line just left of centre is fairly inspiring. Thirty metres right of the undercut block is a quality overhanging crack: ● **Finger Locking Good**, V3 (6a), and just to the right is the delightful ● **Erb Arête**, V2 (5c), from a sit start.

Back to the lower tier, the crag now deteriorates giving numerous problems and two further routes

on a dirt-speckled buttress 100m to the right. ● **Howard's Slab**, HVS 5a (1957-65), takes a scooped wall, while ● **Middle-Aged Spread**, E3 6a (1989), is a mantel and slab 3m left. ● For the completist, **Playtex**, VS girdles from Cordite Crack to Great Harry, although the middle bit has fallen down.

Bole Hill Quarry History

Lawrencefield is actually locally known as Bole Hill Quarry, which has been quarried for Millstones from as early as the thirteenth century (as their presence shows on the lower track right of the quarry). Later, the quarry was chosen to supply around 1.25 million tons of prime gritstone for the building of the dam walls for the 3 reservoirs in the Derwent Valley in the early 1900s.

The quarry face was 1,200 yards long and in 1905 some 439 men were employed there, operating cranes, three locomotives, the winding drum and almost 100 tipper wagons. Two men were killed whilst working in the quarry; one fell from a bench of rock and died from concussion, the other fatality occurred in an accident in a cutting when three loaded trucks broke loose and ran into an area where around 20 men were working. If you look hard enough you can find traces of the old

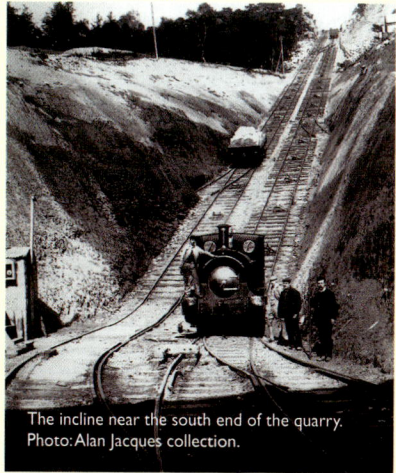

The incline near the south end of the quarry.
Photo: Alan Jacques collection.

industry towards the south of the quarry, with a large incline and remnants of the old winding house which controlled the rail wagons as they took stone from the plateau. Both the tremendous dam walls in the Derwent Valley and the fine wall and crack climbing at Lawrencefield stand firm as a testimony to the skill and hard work of the quarrymen of Bole Hill.

Alan Jacques

Quarry workings in the Delectable Area of Lawrencefield. Photo: Alan Jacques collection.

Crags Above Millstone

OS Ref. SK255804 to SK 251808   altitude 300m to 380m

The Secret Garden

By Niall Grimes

OS Ref. SK 255804   **altitude 300m**

A little nugget of bouldering gold, nestled like a paradise of slopers amid a sea of sheltering birch trees. If beefing over roofs on the most vertical of holds is your thing, then Secret Garden is for you, brother.

Conditions and aspect: Faces east and gets the morning sun. The crag is very sheltered, so is climbable year round but can remain damp after a bit of rain. Of late, the crag is showing signs of wear, both on the rock and the landings. Try to always use a mat, and avoid climbing on damp rock. **The climbing:** Brilliant for bouldering, with 35 problems from V0 to V10. Mainly steep bulges or roofs on slopers or pockets. Great landings. **Parking and approach:** From the Millstone car park, walk east (that's towards Parthian Shot, if you've forgotten your compass) along the road for about 200m until, about 80m past a big boulder on the left, a track crosses a stile and leads into the trees. This track is very near the end of the birch wood. Follow the track for 100m until the crag, resembling a huge chalked-up cow pat, can be seen on the left. Ten minutes walk. The 272 First runs along the road, giving easy access.

The Main Garden

The first rock met is a low double buttress.

1 First Bulge V1 (5b)

2 Sitdown Groove V1 (5c)

3 The Harder Side V6 (6b)
Start sitting with hand in a slot, and slap desperately up the left side of the bulging arête. A good problem.

4 The Easier Side V4 (6b)
From the same start, swing up and right to the tiny groove and climb the still-tricky wall above. ● V2 (6a) from standing.

5 Topless Crack V2 (6a)
The crack and stretchy wall above.

6 Chockstone Crack V1 (5b)

7 Up From Recess V3 (6a)
Start low and battle leftwards up sloping holds.

8 Beach Bum V5 (6b)
Start under the roof at a cramped pinch (or the lip for happy people), and burl to and up the vague arête.

9 Zaff's Problem V9 (6c)
From the back of the roof, gain the lip 1m right of the vague arête of Beach Bum. From here, gain the next slopers directly above and then get to work.

10 Pistol Pinch V7 (6b)
Cross the roof to gain the awkward vertical pinch/pocket. Using this, float effortlessly to the top.

11 Beach Ball V6 (6b)
Classic. Yard across the roof to jugs then lurch gaily up the bulging nose; or, just follow the chalk.

Right: 'Polish' David on Zaff's Problem.
Photo: Alex Ekins.

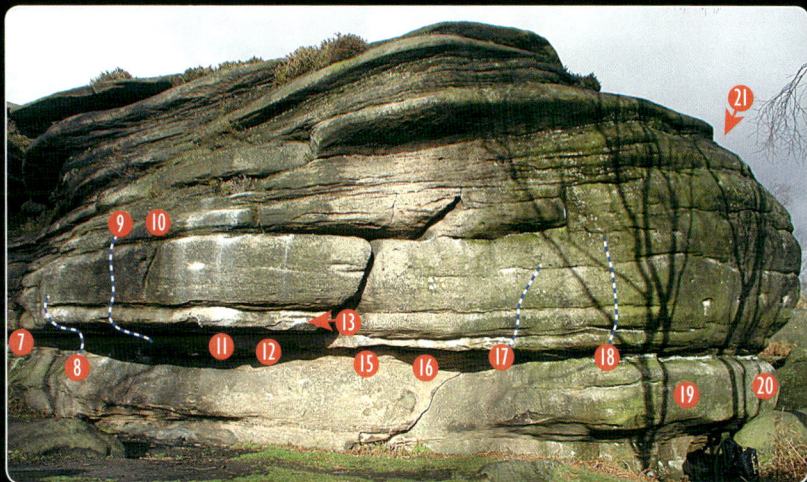

'Our Sheffield friends

are in the habit – from strictly scientific motives of course – of eliminating the most convenient holds from any given climb, much in the way a crafty examiner leaves out the handiest logarithms; and so they can set the newcomer some particularly severe exercises.'

Dr EA Baker on the delights of the eliminate boulder problem, 1903

12 **Not Zaff's** V2 (6a)

13 **Secret Garden Traverse** V4 (6b)
An absolute classic test of sloper technique and body tension; a fine shoe-shredder. From the crack, slap left along the lip to finish easily up the recess at the left. ● Alternately, finish up Beach Bum at V6.

14 **Zippatricks** V10 (6c)
A desperate and rarely repeated testpiece from the master of all things horizontal. Do the last problem footless – sheer delight for legless midgets, and torture for gangly beanpoles – to finish up Beach Bum.

⑮ Beach Crack V1 (5b)
Jam out from a sitter to finish up left.

⑯ The Runnel V5 (6b)
From jugs, move up past the shallow runnel to the flake. A sketchy top-out follows, or certain death.

⑰ Secret Uphill Gardener V7 (6b)
From the jug in the break, squirm up on slopers to the flake. Another hearty top-out follows.

⑱ Nige's Problem V9 (6c)
A bit of an unconfirmed entity. From a sitter, climb the desperate wall just left of the arête to gain the flake as before.

⑲ Left-Hand Man V9 (6c)
From a sitter, climb the wall and arête on its right on slopers and blind pockets. Variations possible.

⑳ Dick Williams V9 (6c)
This time, climb the right arête. ● A variation up the middle of the wall is possible at V10.

㉑ Buoux Style Pockets V0+ (5b)
To the right, climb the wall on sinker pockets.

The Pointy Hat: This is the triangular buttress just right. ● There is a V1 (5a) on the back, ● and the downhill bulging nose is V4 (6b).

The Flower Pot: This is the boulder found by walking directly away from the road from Buoux Style Pockets for 30m. The problems face Burbage.

㉒ Pulley Hulley V8 (6c)
In the centre of the boulder is a scoop. Climb the scoop, from a sit-start, and passing a pocket the size of a coin slot. ● The very bulging arête to the left is unclimbed.

㉓ Fireball V8 (6c)
The hanging arête just right of the scoop.

㉔ Walnut Whip V6 (6b)
The hanging arête to the right again.

The Window Box: This is just behind the left side of the main buttress.

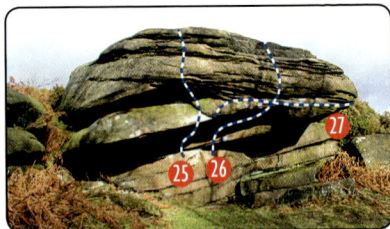

㉕ The Duck V4 (6a)
From jams at the back, cross the roof to quack quack pinches and slap to the top.

㉖ Right-Hand Duck V6 (6b)
From the jams, cross the roof rightwards passing a crack to crimps near the lip. A staunch top-out follows. ● A leftward finish is also possible.

㉗ Zaffatricks V8 (6b)
From The Duck, traverse slots and slopers below the lip, to finish round right.

'Bouldering is reputed
to be bad for the skin. Gloves should always be worn. These ought to be thin and easy, without being loose. The shins may be protected by puttees. Unless the knickers have double knees, it is well to tie on protectors, both for the sake of the knees and of the knickers. These can be made of a couple of large handkerchiefs or old scarves. With gloves, puttees and knee guards on, an hour's hard boulder practice should not result in the smallest damage to the tenderest skin. Bouldering is of great use in teaching what small holds can be employed with safety - at a pinch - on great climbs. It has also a wonderful effect on improving the balance, and in teaching the correct attitude to assume, and efforts to make, on various kinds of holds. On a single fifteen foot boulder one may find a series of climbs containing all the characteristic difficulties one will encounter in a whole day's climb on a great rock peak.'
Mrs. Harold Raeburn, **Mountaineering Art**, 1920

Mother Cap Quarry

by David Law

OS Ref. SK 251805   altitude 320m

This is a small quarry located just left of the path between the car park and Mother Cap. The routes are all approximately 6m in height. Landings are generally good and most lines are short solo climbs.

On the left side of the quarry is a square bay with a prominent arête on its right side. ● Two metres left of the arête is **Flat Cap**, E1 5c (1991), which initially takes a flake-like weakness up the steep wall. ● The arête taken on its left side is **Andy Cap**, E1 6a (1991). ● **Dog Brush**, HVS 5c (1991), climbs up the ramp on the right of the arête finishing left of the crack above. ● The crack itself is HVS 5a finishing left or VS 4c finishing right. ● The wall right again is **Night Cap**, E2 6a (1991), which starts near the end of the graffiti using two thin slots and moving left to a good hold and a decisive finish. ● The best and hardest route hereabouts is **Just Done It**, E5 6c (1993), which climbs the easy wall and obvious overhang to the right. A pocket under the roof leads to a desperate rock over and the top. ● Finally, **Live Mountain Rescue TV**, E5 6c (2001), climbs the groove in the boulder which caps the right wall of the quarry. Step off the quarry edge and move left into the groove. Scary.

The Boulder: Above the right side of the quarry is a boulder containing some problems. ● The bulging arête is V4 (6b). ● Climbing the bulging wall on the left on slopers is V4 (6a), ● while the slotted wall on the right is V5 (6b).

Mother Cap

by David Law

OS Ref. SK 252805   altitude 340m

Mother Cap is a small exposed square monolith on the moor at the back of Millstone Edge. It is composed of well-weathered natural gritstone. The sides are steep, rounded and slopey – there are no crimps here. Many of the climbs were originally claimed as routes, although all are best enjoyed by boulderers. An easy descent is possible off the short side.

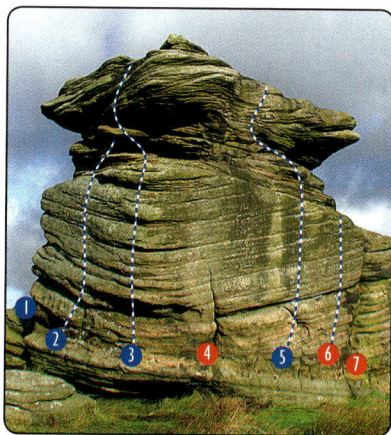

1 Blue Cap   HVS 5a   1991
6m   Climb the pleasant left arête on its right side to a sloping top out. ● Highball V0+.

2 Elf Cap   E2 6a   1991
6m   The big shelving face is scratchy and unprotected. ● Highball V2 to the ledge.

3 Oyster Cap   E2 5c   1991
6m   Very sloping holds lead, weirdly, to the shelf (● Highball V2). Swing left and boldly tackle the overhang on slopers.

4 David   V8 (6c)
From the short crack, climb the steep wall on very poor holds.

5 Conan The Librarian E3 6b ★★   1986
6m A technical testpiece of the highest quality. Climb the very fingery wall to the ledge. ● A great V4 to here. For the full route tick, continue up over the looming bulge above, an act guaranteed to raise an eyebrow from onlooking boulderers.

6 Thin Wall V3 (6a)
The wall left of the crack. No arête.

7 Milk Cap V0− (4a)
The crack.

8 Ink Cap V0− (4b)
The juggy arête is fun. ● **Baby's Traverse**, across the break rightwards from Ink Cap, is V0 (4b).

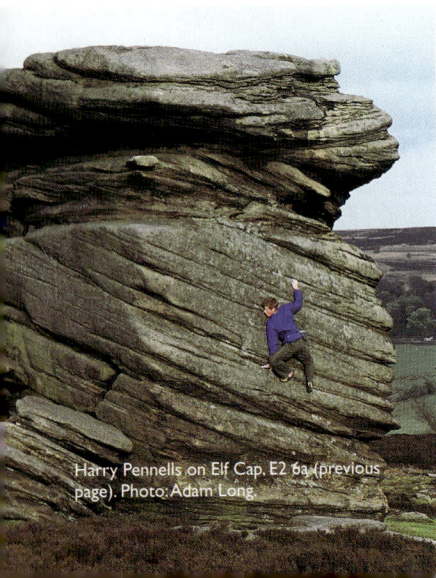

Harry Pennells on Elf Cap, E2 6a (previous page). Photo: Adam Long.

Mother's Pet Rock

This lies just below Mother Cap, on the opposite side of the path.

1 The Blue Whale V4 (6b)
Steep moves over the deeply uncooperative bulge lead to sloping, slapping joy on the hideous desert of woeful nothingness that constitutes the top.

2 Mother's Pet Project.

3 Mother's Pride V8 (6c)
Classic sloper mauling, bang up the middle to a tenuous top-out.

4 Pet Cemetery V7 (6c)
Less butch than Mother's Pride, but just as good. From the break, trend up and right on a sea of slopers.

5 Ahab V2 (6a)
Grasp up the short rib. ● Traverse in from the stsrt of Pet Cemetery at V4.

6 Moby V3 (6a)
Make an awkward mantel onto the right end of the shelf. ● Gained from the shelf under the roof is V6 (6b).

7 Proper Grit V5 (6b)
The wall just right of the shelf.

8 Pets Win Prizes V7 (6c)
The steep wall just right from a sitter. Cunning.

9 Pet Whale V4 (6a)
Traversing the shelf and breaks is a bit of a thrash.

'Fraid there ain't no jugs up there, brother! Modern day local bouldering guru, John Welford sticking hard to Mother's Pride. V8 (opposite page). Photo: David Simmonite.

Over Owler Tor

by David Law

OS Ref. SK 251808   **altitude 380**

A joyous little plug sitting cheekily on the moors above Millstone Edge, giving generous pocketfuls of problems and routes. It is best visited as part of the circuit above Millstone, or for an evening visit. It has a great supply of boulder problems, micro-routes and solos, as well as the fine arête of Aeroflot, the E2 merchant's End of the Affair, which looms threateningly on the approach from Millstone.

Conditions and Aspect: The tor sits in an exposed position, is windy and quick-drying. The rock is good quality, and seldom green. It faces northwest, and gets sun from late afternoon. **Routes:** A great place for a quick visit, with 17 good, short routes, mainly in the lower grades. **Bouldering:** A great little circuit, quiet and varied, with good landings, with 25 problems from V0 to V7. **Parking and Approach:** Park at the Millstone car park and follow the track past Mother Cap, or approach easily from the North Bay end of Millstone: 5-10 minutes. For public transport, see Millstone introduction.

Skydiver Buttress: This is a fine little outcrop just left of the main tower, with a flake in its centre.

1 Skydiver VS 5a ★   pre-1965
7m Fun, gymnastic climbing. Climb the prominent flake and make a mighty musclebound stretch to a wider crack, which still puts up a good fight, to a round top. ● The arête to the left is 5a.

2 Hang Glider HVS 5b   1999
7m Just right, the green overhanging offwidth crack is climbed with an awkward struggle to reach better holds and easier climbing. ● The crack right of the overhang is **F-Plan**, HS 4b (1960s).

3 Green Light Go E1 5b   1991
9m The overhang is climbed via a pocket on the right on good holds leading to a superb finishing jug.

A few metres right is a small wall split by a large cleft. ● The wall on the left yields two short routes. **Right Eye** (4c) starts from the boulder and **Left Eye** (4c) starts just left from the ground. ● The cleft itself is taken by **Breaststroke**, M (1991), which 'swims' up the cleft and exits at the back; climbing it on the outside is a little harder at VD. ● The pillar face on the right is **Frontcrawl** (5a), avoiding the block on the right.

Thirteen metres right is another small buttress with three routes:

4 Elephantitis E2 5c ★   1991
6m From a prominent, hole ascend the left rib to a rounded and scary finish. ● Struggling up to the right arête from the same start is HVS 5a, which finishes delicately on the right of the arête. ● The easy-angled face on the right is **Zorro**, D (1991).

The Ship: This is a large angular boulder just below the next climbs. The first problem is on the lower side of the boulder, facing away from the crag.

5 Sailing V4 (6a)
A good problem. Start sitting under the left arête of the long face, snatch the lip, and traverse right on slopers to rock up into the scoop using the sharp right arête. ● Doing the first move and mantelling the lip is V2 (6a), ● and a mantel just right is V2 (5c). ● The last move of the traverse in a quality V1 (5c).

6 Rod Stewart V1 (5c)
The sharp arête of the boulder facing Aeroflot, from a sit start.

The Main Area: After a broken section, the crag springs up again. On the left side of this is a short vertical wall above a shallow jumbled pit.

7 Owler Pit Project
The desperate-looking wall has holds, and will be mighty hard. ●Further left is a V0 (4c) mantel.

8 Really Exciting Flake V0 (4c)
A wild problem starting up and right on a boulder. Swing left onto a flake and exit up and left. ●**The Arête Direct** from the boulder is a good V0 (5a).

Further right is The Pinnacle with a deep chimney on its left, M. On the left is a straight deep crack capped by a large rock giving

9 Brass Monkeys VD   1987
6m   Exit left under the chockstone.

10 Three Men on a Rock HVS 5a ★   1987
9m   The enjoyable left side of the pinnacle is climbed via a short blind crack at the top. ●The narrow wall to the right is **Tuck and Roll**, E2 5c †
(1999), with runners in the next route.

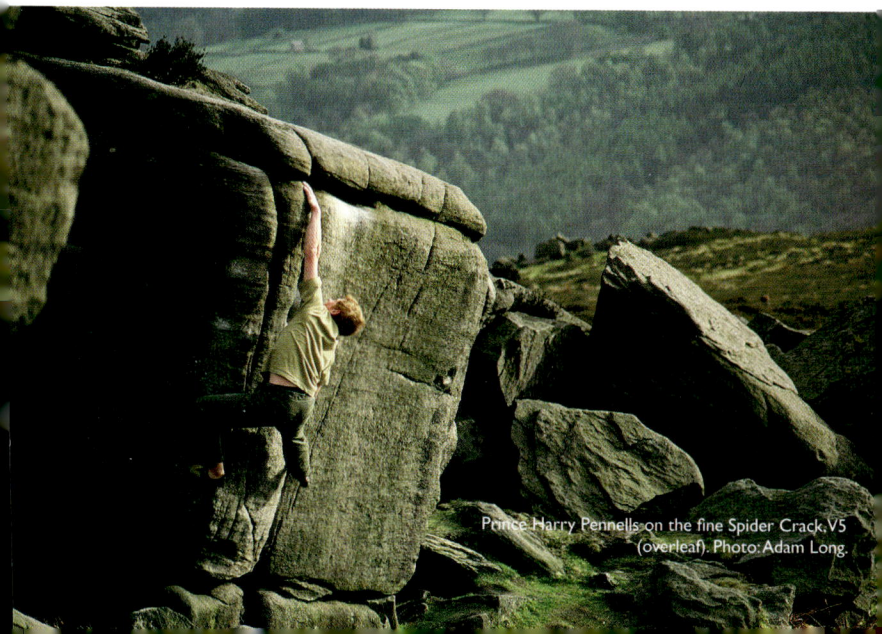

Prince Harry Pennells on the fine Spider Crack, V5 (overleaf). Photo: Adam Long.

11 **Aeroflot** E1 5b ★★   1991

9m The route of the crag, with good climbing and superb views, which takes the fine right arête on its left side. Climb to the break and make scary moves to the top via a pocket and flake. The flake will take small wires but these are difficult to place. A superb, obscure gem.

Around the side of the pinnacle on the right there is a pock-marked wall: ● the right arête is **Jet**, a scary V2 (5c), ● and around the back, taking the obvious crack, is **Propeller**, V0– (4b). ● **Merlin** is the arête and slot just right; V3 (6a).

Right-Hand Area: Ten metres right is a reasonably large buttress.

12 **Zeppelin** E2 5b   1999

10m A good but escapable climb. From a short crack, follow the pillar-like end wall on good pockets to a rounded finish. ● A problem, **George Smith E7**, V2 (6a), starts very low on a jug and climbs the bulging wide crack to the break.

13 **Balloon** HS 4a ★   1991

10m A good climb taking the arête and face. Start from the blocks leaning against the wall and climb up the reasonably-angled arête using pockets and a thin flake.

14 **Goodyear (Vienetta)** HS 4a   1987

10m Climb the wall via a large pocket at mid-height.

15 **Scrunchy Slopes** V4 (6b)

Climb the front face on poor holds.

16 **Lil' Arête** V0 (4c)

The left edge of the small flat wall.

17 **Wafery Flake** V3 (6a)

The fine technical wall, on small, thin flakes.

18 **Plop** HVS 5a   1960s

7m Climb the arête on generally good holds to an awkward move to gain the upper arête.

19 **Marshall, Morris and Faulkener (Plip)** VS 4c   1987

7m A rounded climb. Climb the centre of the wall just right of Plop past a large pocket and an awkward rockover finish. ● A traverse across the top of the wall has been climbed as **Pockets**, VS 5a (2004), going from right to left using the pockets to finish just left of the arête.

20 **Flake Arête** V0– (4b)

The short arête 4m right.

21 **Roof I** V4 (6b)

Awkwardly struggle out and over the roof using a flake.

Millstone Area First Ascents

Early 1920s At Millstone, George Bower did a few routes up now forgotten weaknesses. He then retreated to Stanage Edge.

Late 1920s Reg Damms, Jack Macleod and Eric Byne also visited Millstone, but again only left one un-recorded route before leaving.

1952 **Cornerstone Climb, Great Slab** (some aid, FFA 1957) Alan Maskery **Three Tree Climb, Nailsbane, Pulpit Groove, Guillotine Groove, Gingerbread, Lawrencefield Ordinary** Albert (Bert) Shutt, Reg Pillinger **Stonemason's Climb** Peter Rickus, Reg Pillinger

1953 Feb. **Cascara Crack, Great Wall Traverse** R A (Dick) Brown Cascara (Sagrada) is a natural laxative, like climbing grit really. **Great Harry** Harry Hartley, Reg Pillinger **Jughandle, Meringue** (1pt) Bert Shutt, Reg Pillinger, Tony Davies Meringue FFA 1955 by John Fearon.

1955 March **The Ashes** John Henry Fearon, Bert Shutt (AL) **Peg Wall** (A1, FFA 1957–65) Don Morrison, Al Hall, Pete Marks **Tony's Chimney** Tony Davies

1955 **Gregory's Slab** Wilfred (Wilf) White, Reg Pillinger, D Bradley *A large team from Sheffield and some lads from the Valkyrie were sheltering from the sun under the birches. Dave Gregory recalls that he kept protesting desultorily that someone ought to do some climbing. Eventually Wilf did and passed the name of his tormentor down to posterity attached to this route* **Limpopo Groove** Dave Gregory *Named before it was climbed, after Kipling's great grey, green, greasy river. After the ascent, Gregory attempted the arête right of Jughandle but fell to join a dead sheep in the pool. Poor chap. The sheep that is!* **Vector** Dave Gregory, Bert Shutt, Tom Collins

1955 Summer **Cordite Crack, Excalibur** Peter Biven, Trevor Peck *The name, Cordite Crack, comes from the machine gun or mortar scars on the wall to the right. The mortar/machine gun, used in practice by the military, was placed on the stainless steel mounting still visible among the trees.*

1956 Summer **High Street** (A1), **Boulevard** (A1), **Suspense** (A1 & VS), **Great Peter** (A1 & VS), **The Great North Road** Peter Biven, Trevor Peck FFAs 1975-76

1956 **Blacksmith's Climb** (2pts) Reg Pillinger, Bert Shutt, Alan Clarke **Nova, Red Wall** Don Morrison, John Fearon. S.A.E. (1pt) Don Morrison, Al Hall, Pete Marks **Finale** Don Morrison

1956 **Petticoat Lane, Lyons Corner House** (A3) George Leaver, Kit Twyford

1956 **The Great West Road** (A3), **Twikker** (A2 and VS), **Pinstone Street** (A2) Dave Johnson and Sheffield University Mountaineering Club party FFAs 1969-76

1956 **Flapjack** Jack Soper.

---

22 **Roof 2** VI (5c)

23 **Left Tower** V0 (5b)
The left edge of the tiny skyscraper.

24 **Fingersplitter** V0+ (5a)
The stunning central crack-line.

25 **Right Tower** V0 (5a)
The right edge. A tricky sit-start is possible, avoiding the crack.

26 **Friend Slot Wall** V0+ (5b)
The fine, steep wall left of the arête.

27 **Golden Arête** V4 (6b)
Climb the fine bulging arête with the aid of the thin crack. A powerful classic.

28 **Spider Crack** V5 (6b)
A desperate problem climbing the thin crack, avoiding the arête. ● Can be done from a sitter at V7 (6b).

29 **Jawbone** VI (5c)
Climb the overhanging arête from a sit-start on the big flake.

30 **The Eye Socket** V2 (5c)
From the same start as the last problem, swing right past the deep pocket.

1956   **Bow Street** (A2, FFA 1967)   Frank Fitzgerald

1956   **Close Shave, Cioch Corner, Cioch Diagonal**   Alan Clarke, Ben Wilson, Ted Howard

1956   **Shaftesbury Avenue**   (AI, FFA 1967), **Regent Street** (A2, FFA 1967), **Jermyn Street** (A2, FFA 1975), **Coventry Street** (A3, FFA 1976), **Oxford Street** (A3, FFA 1969), **Covent Garden, Charing Cross Road** (AI, FFA 1967), **London Wall** (A3, FFA 1975), **The Girdle Traverse** (Aid)   Peter Biven, Trevor Peck   *Obviously a frantic year with several teams working hard. In the event, Peter Biven and Trevor Peck established an effective technique and almost entirely dominated the development, especially so in the Keyhole Cave area. London Wall was climbed using especially thin pegs for the then hairline crack. The ascent took about four hours. The hardest climb on the crag ... a thrilling and spectacular route.*

1957   Publication of the *Further Developments In The Peak District – Climbs on Gritstone*. Other routes whose first ascent details are unknown include: **Austin's Variation, Variation I and 2, Flake Climb, Billingsgate** (AI & VS), **Hammersmith Road** (A2, wedges), **Knightsbridge** (AI wedges), **The Scoop**, **The Embankment** (AI, now called Embankment 4), **Whitehall** (AI), **Bond Street** (AI), **Great Portland Street** (A3), **The Mall** (A2), **Lambeth Chimney, The Old Kent Road, Brixton Road**.

1957   **Supra Direct** (AI, FFA 1975)   Parnassus Climbing Club

1957   **Great North Road** (FFA), **The Mall** (FFA), **Plexity**   Joe Brown, Joe (Morty) Smith

1957   **Dexterity**   Harold Drasdo

1957   **The Great Slab** (FFA), **Eartha**   AI Parker, Peter Bamfield

1958   **Shallow Chimney, Straight Crack**   Eric Byne, Jean Turner **Rocking Groove**   Fred Williams **Frustration** (AI, FFA 1976)   M A James **Suspense Direct** (AI)   Alan Clarke, Walt Hulka   Varlet   Don Morrison

1959   **Pip, Squeak, Bowling Green**   AI Parker, Peter Bamfield **Butter-ess**   AI Parker, Bob Brayshaw **Only Just**   Ernie Marshall, Wilfred (Wilf) White

1959-61   **Remembrance Day**   Ted Howard   **Chiming Cracks**   Alan Clarke

1962   **Gimcrack**   Barry (Baz) Ingle   **Instability**   John Loy **Gripe**   Harry Wood **Derision**   Clive Rowland **Svelte**   AI Parker, Martin Boysen (alternate leads)

1963   **Crew Cut, Bent Crack, Hell's Bells, Great Portland Street** (FFA), **Windrête**   Alan Clarke   *Windrête was only top-roped.*

1963   **Acheron, Black Crack**   Don Morrison   **By-Pass**   John Loy **Duo Crack**   Harry Wood

1964   **S.A.E** (FFA), **Delectable Direct**   Don Morrison, Les

Gillot, Alan Clarke

1964   **Playtex**   Don Morrison, Les Gillott   **Satan's Slit, Tuesday's Child, Itslide, Sinister Crack**   John Loy   **Verve**   Pete Crew, W Ward

1957-1965   **Frond Crack, Crane Fly Climb, Piper's Crack, Crossway, Trio Crack, Skywalk, Ekel, Lotto** (AI & HS, FFA 1975), **Scoop Crack, Rotten Row, Mopsy, Quiddity, Crusty Corner, Diamond Groove, Creaking Corner, Dune Crack, Dune Flake, Flaky Pastry, Shamrot, Boomerang, Rough Puff, Brumal, Fluted Corner, The Web, Commix** (A2 & VS, FFA 1976), **Day Dream, Brindle**   John Loy, solo, or with Alan Clarke, Don Morrison, Harry Woods or J Widdowson   **Blacksmith's Climb, Once-Pegged Wall** (FFA)   Anon   Howard's Slab   Ted Howard

1957-65   **Erb** (AI & VS, FFA 1975), **Keelhaul, Shady Wall, Lubric, Crumbling Cracks, WIfred, Wuthering Crack, May Day, April Arête, Rainy Day, Hacklespur** (aid, FFA John Loy, 1962), **Scrimsel**   Alan Clarke, with John Loy, Don Morrison or Harry Woods

1957-65   **Watling Street**   Len Millsom   **Humpty Dumpty, Spider Crack**   Don Morrison   **Happy Wanderer, Oriel**   John Brailsford   **Embankment Routes** (AI & VS, FFA 1975)   probably Biven and Peck   **Estremo, Bamboozle**   Ted Howard   **Chaos, Derision**   Clive Rowlands   **Saville Street** (A2, FFA 1975)   probably Reg Pillinger   **Lorica, Scoop Wall** (AI, FFA 1969)   John Conn   **The Rack** (Hard A2 & HS, FFA 1982)   Tanky Stokes   **Flapjack, S.S.S.**   Jack Soper   *S.S.S. is an irreverent geological term meaning shit and small stones.*

1965   The 1965 Sheffield Froggatt guidebook went to press with Millstone having reached so-called maturity. Many other climbers, including W Ward, K Rhodes, Ted Howard, Clive Rowland and Les Gillott, were also active during this period. Who did what is not clear but the guidebook also contained the following uncredited routes: Giant's Steps, Midrift, Flank Crack, Keys Climb, Cold Comfort, Alopecia, Rakes Progress (AI & VS), Eros (AI), Cake Walk, Sweater (AI), Gimbals (AI), Cauldron Crack (AI), Pin Prick (AI), Brimstone (AI), Friday, Slippery Wall, Quantum Crack, Vaseline, Grass Groove, Seta, Proud Crack, Suspense Variation (top-roped only; later recorded as Scoop Connection), Éclair, Tyron, Grooved Arête, Scotia, Fractus, Moss Corner, Skyline (AI), Lone Ridge, Tricky Cracks, Delectable Variation, Slab and Groove, Skydiver Numerous shorter and scrappier routes were also included and are not described in this edition.

1967 Apr I9   **In Memoriam** (Ipt)   Paul Grayson, Jack Firth. *A rurp and a drilled peg runner were used. Later claimed by Keith Myhill, Al Evans. Now the top pitch of Great West Road. FFA in 1975*

1967   **Charing Cross Road** FFA   Anon   **Shaftsbury Avenue** FFA   Jim Campbell   *Rumour has it that although many people thought that they had made the first ascent, no-*

one was willing to argue with 'Big Jim'. Bow Street FFA *Alan (Richard) McHardy*

1968 **Regent Street** (FFA) Terry King *A brilliant lead, ahead of its time.*

1969 Apr 17 **Xanadu** Keith Myhill, Al Evans (AL) *This original line started up Crew Cut, then traversed into the main corner along easy ledges. The direct start added in 1974.*

1969 Aug 24 **Gates of Mordor** (1pt, FFA 1969) Phil Burke **Bun Run** Al Evans, Nick Elliott

1969 **Oxford Street** (FFA) Phil Burke, John RQ Jeany **Great West Road** (FFA) Al Evans, Keith Myhill *Only the first pitch was climbed by following the left-hand variation. The direct finish was added later by Keith Myhill* **Eros** (FFA), **Myolympus** (1pt) Paul Grayson *Myolympus FFA 1969* **Myolympus** (FFA), **Pinstone Street** (1pt), **Scoop Wall** (1st pitch), **Windrête** (FFA) Al Evans, Z Dyslewicz *Pete Crew may have soloed Windrête at the same time.* **Devil's Delight** (Brimstone) (1pt) Keith Myhill, Nick Elliott FFA 1973 **Whitehall** (FFA) Keith Myhill, Al Evans (alternate leads) **Yourolympus** Dave Gregory, Andrew Brodie **Billingsgate** (FFA) Steve Chadwick **Gates of Mordor** (FFA) Hank Pasquill **F.A.T.D., White Wall** (AI) Anon FFA 1976 **Nostrils** (AI) R Buckley, Al Thewless *Climbed with pegs and 7 bolts! FFA of the first section in 1984 as Scumline, the rest in 2001 as Toploader.*

1969 **Green Death** Tom Proctor, Keith Myhill *A stunning new route up rock hitherto not thought to be suited to free-climbing. The start was originally made from a pile of stones.*

1960s **Skydiver, F-Plan, Plop** Malc Baxter *He may have climbed other lines hereabouts?*

1970 **Embankment Route 3** (FFA 2nd pitch) Ken Jones

1971 Mar 17 **Eskimo Blue Day** R Hayward, R Sedgewick

1965-1972 **Blind Bat** (A2, FFA 1976) Les Bonnington

1973 **Brimstone** 'Hot' Henry Barber FFA of Devil's Delight **Knightsbridge** (FFA) Tom Proctor, Geoff Birtles **Keyhole Cops** John Allen, Neil Stokes

1974 **Edge Lane** Alan (Richard) McHardy, Bill Birch, Neil Stokes, John Allen, Steve Bancroft

1974 **Xanadu** Hank Pasquill, P Penketh *The aforementioned direct start but really the meat of the route.* **Time for Tea Original** (FFA) Ken Wilkinson, R Thomas

1975 July 30 **London Wall** (FFA) John Allen, Steve Bancroft *A superb free route which resisted the pack until the eighties. Drummond, vying for the FFA, was stunned by Allen's ascent since his own fingers wouldn't fit into the crack! The great Pete Livesey had a similarly trying time on the route.*

1975 July **Great West Road** (FFA 2nd pitch) John Allen, Chris

Addy **Embankment Route 4** (FFA) Chris Addy, John Powell

1975 Aug 31 **Great Arête** Geoff Birtles, Tom Proctor (AL)

1975 Oct **The Whore** Jim Reading, Clive Jones, D Hyles **Detour** Jim Reading, Clive Jones

1975 Nov **Regent Street Variant** Jim Reading, Mark Stokes

1975 **Boulevard** (FFA) Ed Drummond, Jim Reading **High Street** (FFA) Jim Reading **Billy Whiz** (née Harlequin) Geoff Birtles, Ernie Marshall, Tom Proctor, Giles Barker

1975 **Erb, Lotto, Twikker, Jermyn Street** (all FFAs) Tom Proctor, Geoff Birtles *'Tom didn't have those side-runners in Regent Street when we did it, he just had the iron spike down in the cave!' Birtles, recalling the FFA of Jermyn Street, having seen a photo of Bancroft repeating it with side-runners. Bancroft later said 'Believe it or not I didn't see the spike.' Even the spike has gone now: removed by a falling climber!* **Soho Sally, Saville Street** (1pt) Geoff Birtles, Tom Proctor *Believing that the final aid point on the latter couldn't be eliminated, Birtles watched Proctor follow the pitch. 'The bastard freed it', was Birtles comment as Proctor climbed right past it. FFA 1975 by John Allen.*

1975 **Embankment Route 1** (FFA 2nd pitch) John Allen, Tom Proctor **Suspense** (FFA) John Allen, Nicky Stokes

1975 **Embankment Route 3** (FFA), **Time for Tea** Ed Drummond **March Hare** Gabe Regan

1975 **Supra Direct** (FFA 1st pitch) Pete Brayshaw, Pete (Pod) O'Donovan

1976 July 4 **Pot Leg Wall** Neil Stokes *Climbed by Stokes when his leg was in plaster!*

1976 July 27 **White Wall** (FFA) Steve Bancroft, Jim Reading. *Freed after an earlier ascent the same day by Jim Reading who had reduced the aid to one point, although he did not quite finish the route. Soloed by Tony Ryan in the 1980s.*

1976 Sept 3 **Piccadilly Circus** Steve Bancroft, Nicky Stokes, Chris Addy. FFA of the finishing crack of The Rack

1976 Oct/Nov **Littleheath Road, Piledriver, Cauldron Crack** (FFA), **Gimbals** (FFA), **Evening Premiere, London Pride, Blind Bat** (FFA) Mick Fowler, John Stevenson, along with Geraldine Abrey, Mick Morrison or H Crompton **Commix** (FFA), **Southern Comfort** (FFA) John Stevenson, Mick Fowler *A remarkable domination of new routes by Fowler et al. after they arrived in the Peak District from 'The Smoke'. Southern Comfort had its moment of glory when for some unknown reason it was the only route to be awarded the XS(+) grade in the 1978 guidebook.*

1976 **Coventry Street** (FFA) Steve Bancroft, John Allen (AL)

1976 **Spec Arête, Frustration, J.J.2** Nicky Stokes, John Allen, Steve Bancroft

1976 **Thorpe Street** Al Parker, Ted Rogers **Stone Dri** (1pt) John Regan, Paul Kirk, Iain Hibbert. FFA 1978 **Dextrous Hare** (FFA) Martin Taylor (roped-solo) *Done using a hanging rope with a strategically placed knot at half-height to protect his ascent. Since then, nut placements have appeared.* **The Rack** (2pts) Jim Reading *Both points used for resting only.* FFA 1982 **Great Peter** (FFA) Clive Jones, Jim Reading

1977 June 23 **Badly Bred** Steve Bancroft, Nicky Stokes

1977 **Flared Bottom** Al Parker, Graham Fyffe **High Plains' Drifter, Holy Grail** Jim Reading, Rob Mallinson

1977 **The Snivelling Shit** Jonathan Lagoe *The route was credited to Bob Millward and Tony Dillinger from an ascent in 1978, whose name has stuck. However, Lagoe's ascent pre-dated this. His name was Slideshow.*

1978 Publication of the Sheffield-Froggatt guidebook. Other routes whose first ascent details are unknown include: Straight Leg, Rake's Progress, All The King's Horses, At-a-cliff, Neatfeet, Pinstone Street, Pin Prick, Sunday, Surprise Surprise, Vanilla Slice, Urn, Block Wall (AI).

1978 Apr 15 **Redbits** Pete Blackburn, D Ferguson

1978 June 3 **Jealous Pensioner** Jim Burton, Paul Cropper, Chris Dent *Rumour has it that this route was stolen from Phil Burke and then named in his honour. On an early repeat attempt Quentin Fisher fell off the headwall soloing, but remarkably landed on the narrow ledge, thereby maintaining his reputation for leading a charmed life.*

1978 Oct **Brittle Road to Freedom** Gary Gibson, Derek Beetlestone, Mark (Ralph) Hewitt **Callus, Metal Rash** Gary Gibson (solo) **Street Legal** Paul Cropper, Nadim Siddiqui **Too Good to be True** Mark Walton, Phil Wilson, Paul Delaney

1978 **Juniper** Nick Halliday, Tony Sawbridge **Stone Dri** (FFA) Dave Humphries **Optimus** Gary Gibson, Mark (Ralph) Hewitt, et al **Howarth's Wait** Dave Gregory

1965-1978 **Scoop Connection** Keith Myhill

1979 Oct 29 **Wings of Steel** Paul Cropper, Brian Cropper

1980 **Mean to Me** Gary Gibson, Steve Keeling, Derek Beetlestone **Brain Attack** Martin Crook, Dave Farrant

1981 Aug 29 **Split Second Timing, Who Wants the World?** Gary Gibson, Martin Veale, Jon Walker

1981 Oct 31 **Rattus Norvegicus** Gary Gibson, Neil Harvey

1981 **Skyline** (FFA), **Block Wall** (FFA) Daniel Lee

1982 **Scritto's Republic** Ron Fawcett *FFA of the thin crack-line left of Embankment Route 3. Fawcett 'created' a technical masterpiece just as the 1983 guidebook went to press. The route was originally protected by two old bolts placed by Tom Proctor in shallow drilled-out holes. It went unrepeated for a while until, in 1984, the route recieved its 2nd, 3rd, 4th and 5th ascents in a single day from Chris Gore, Martin Atkinson, Andy Pollitt*

and Tony Ryan. *Not long after, the first bolt was broken off by an aid-climber, whilst the second was removed by Malcolm Taylor who then replaced the pair with a single bolt. This was subsequently removed by Andy Perkins. The route is now unprotectable until after the crux. The route was then soloed in the late 'eighties by Pete Cresswell after extensive top-roped practise. The landing was packed with ropes, duvet jackets, rucksacks and the rear seat of a car and its efficiency tested when he fell off from around the crux. It is still not known if the route has been climbed ground-up.*

1982 July 8 **Slack Alice, Nib Nob** Paul Mitchell *Nib-Nob was soloed, on-sight, barefoot.* **Dolorous Gard** Andy Barker (solo)

1982 **Tea for Two** Ian Riddington, Nigel Riddington **Sex Dwarfs** Mark Miller **The Rack** (FFA) Loz Francomb *The route has been done without side-runners, perhaps by Sean Myles?*

1983 May 12 **Helliconia Spring** Chris Jackson, Adey Hubbard

1983 Sept **Knave** Dave Gregory, Jim Rubery **Morning Glory** Dominic Stainforth

1983 Dec 6 **Findus** Al Rouse, Phil Burke

1983 Dec 7 **Winter's Grip** Neil Foster (solo) **Quality Street** Al Rouse, Phil Burke (AL)

1983 Dec 29 **The Master's Edge** Ron Fawcett *The ultimate: Ron was unseconded, unfettered and unequalled. Having spent the autumn nursing a broken hand, Fawcett came back with a vengeance. Ron later wrote that it was 'E6 or E7, hard 6b or even harder, I don't know what to grade it.' Ron reportedly practised some moves but did not top-rope the route in its entirety. The arête has been top roped on its left side, one handed, by Johnny Dawes.*

1983 **Monopoly** Johnny Dawes *Originally climbed by Dawes with side-runners, then during a subsequent ascent in 1984, Dawes returned and used a low peg runner for protection. This has since been removed. Climbed on-sight by Ben Heason in 1999.* **Wall Street Crash** Johnny Dawes, Nigel Slater *Pre-placed and pre-clipped wires on old bolt heads were used to protect the first ascent. The bolts were removed with very little mandate by Dave Thomas around 2002, and replaced by pegs.*

1983 **Slime Crime, Diamond Daze** Gary Gibson **The Hacker** Brian Mosley, Tony Eady

1981-83 **Pool Wall** (née Suspense Direct, FFA) Roger Greatrick, Al Carn **Brain Cells in Collision, Brainstorm** Paul Mitchell **Going for the One** Phil Barker, Adey Hubbard

1984 Jan **Clock People** Ron Fawcett **Velvet** Dominic Stainforth, Nigel Slater (AL)

1984 Feb 12   **Sudden Impact**   Nigel Slater, Alastair Ferguson

1984 Apr   **Meeze Brugger**   Ron Fawcett   **Dino**   Paul Pepperday

1984 July   **Gibbering Heap of Puss**   Johnny Dawes

1984   **Sea Creature**   Al Rouse, Andy Bailey   **Scumline** Paul Tattersall   **Rockhopper**   B Davidson, S Biskhill

1984   **Jermyn Street Direct Finish**   Ron Fawcett, Dominic Staniforth

1984   **Adam Smith's Invisible Hand**   Johnny Dawes *The route was named after a photograph Dawes had, on which shadows and a rock formation formed a large hand on the wall left of the arête. Adam Smith was an economic philosopher who proposed that economies were steered by the 'invisible hand' of what we would now call 'market forces', hence the present-day enthusiasm of right-wing politicians and economists for his work.*

1984   **Perplexity**   Johnny Dawes   *Free-climbs part of the old aid route, Sweater. Second ascent soon after by Shaun Hutson. Sadly the route was chipped in 1988, although this has not changed the grade much. Further ascents followed during the Foot & Mouth epidemic of 2001, including the first in its current state by Mike Lea and an on-sight by Ian Vickers, as a warm-up for his on-sight of Toploader straight after, a feat matched by Dave Musgrove.*

1985 May 7   **Wash and Brush Up**   Al Rouse

1985 Aug 28   **The Hunter House Road Toad**   Mark Pretty, Richie Brooks

1985   **The Pittsburgh Enigma**   Paul Mitchell   **Helping Hands**   John Feltrup, Jamie Harper   **Frigged Anonymously** Jamie Harper

1985   **Von Ryan's Express**   Tony Ryan, Mick Ryan   *Soloed on-sight by Kevin Thaw in the 1980s.*   **The Gordons, The Gordons**   Johnny Dawes, Paul Clark

1985   **Adios Amigo**   Mark Leach   *Leach recalls that having borrowed Fawcett's Amigo to attempt the second ascent of The Master's Edge, he climbed Adios Amigo instead: 'I only did this route because I was too gripped to do Master's that weekend.'*

1986 Sept 23   **Annabella Superstella, Beneath the Pavement Lies the Beach**   Mark Delafield, Ivor Delafield

1986   **Skyhigh, Heavy Plant Crossing**   Chris Plant, Mark Pretty   **Conan the Librarian**   Johnny Dawes (solo)

1986 Oct 26   **The Big Red Jacket**   Tim Rolfe, David Simmonite *The name comes from a later claim. Previously known as Last Wet Wednesday..*

1987 Apr 23   **Under Doctor's Orders**   Keith Sharples, Ian Riddington, Geoff Radcliffe, Graham Hoey, Martin Veale. *FFA of the initial section of Hammersmith Road*

1987 May 16   **Election Special**   Dominic Staniforth, Dave Tidman

1987 July   **Scruples**   Paul Evans, Neil Buttle   **Salinela Sunset** Simon Cundy

1987 Oct   **Three Men on a Rock**   David Simmonite, Tim Rolfe, Roy Bennett   **Brass Monkeys**   David Simmonite (solo)   **Goodyear**   Dave Simmonite   **Morris, Marshall and Faulkener**   Roy Bennett, Tim Rolfe, David Simmonite

1987   **The Bad and the Beautiful**   Mark Leach (solo)   *It is reported that on one of his attempts Leach retreated from a sky-hook, only for it to rip, depositing him on the ledge. Leach felt that he needed both a 'spotter and a photographer'. In the event Dale Goddard convinced Leach that even if he fell he would stay on the ledge, so Goddard photographed the ascent.*

1987   **Blood and Guts on Botty Street, Frank Sinatra Bows Out**   Allen Williams

1988 Spring   **Transmetropolitan**   Steve Bancroft, Sue Bird

1988 June   **The Trumpton Anarchist**   Paul Mitchell, Steve Wright

1988   **London Marathon**   Steve Bancroft, Harry Venables **Appletree Yard, Owzaboutthatthen, Freight Train**   Paul Mitchell

1988 Sept 10   **Anything is Possible in Cartoons**   Paul Mitchell

1988 Sept   **Which way up Mr Rothko?**   Paul Evans

1989 Apr 1   **Positively 4th Street**   David Simmonite, Tim Rolfe *Named later by Simon Jacques*

1989 May 18   **Strait Jacket**   Paul Reeve

1989 Sept 20   **Middle-Aged Spread**   Al Evans

1989   **Fat and Jealous**   Dave Pegg   **Brain Death**   Anon **Bole Hill**   Simon Jacques, Dan Jackson

1990 Apr   **Mildly Laxative, Side Pocket**   Dave Gregory, Alastair Ferguson   **Table Leg**   Dave Gregory, Bill Taylor

1990 July 8   **Breeze Mugger**   Paul Deardon

1990 Oct 14   **Dog Brush**   Malc Baxter (solo)

1991 July   **Night Cap, Flat Cap, Andy Capp**   Doug Kerr (solo)

1991 Aug   **Elf Cap, Milk Cap, Ink Cap**   Gavin Taylor, Malc Baxter   **Oyster Cap, Blue Cap**   Malc Baxter, Gavin Taylor   **Balloon**   Malc Baxter

1991 Oct 20   **Last Day of Freedom**   Bill Gregory

1991   **Reckless**   David Simmonite (solo)   **Green Light Go, Breaststroke, Zorro, Aeroflot, Vienetta, Elephantitis**   Jon Lawton, J Middlebrook

1992   **Top Banana, Mushroom Crumble**   Andy Crome

1993   **Just Done It**   Robin Barker

1994   **Stranger Breaks Right, Stranger in Paradise, The Impetus for Stranger Feaces**   John Marsden   *John Marsden descended upon Millstone and laid claim to some 15 new routes. Amazingly, the three listed above*

Helen Gibson on the crux of Bond Street, HVS 5a (page 116). Photo: Niall Grimes.

– *poor non-lines, squeezed in to the narrowest of gaps between good routes, and often within reaching distance of VS territory - are the pick of the bunch. While in many ways even these three are not worth recording, it was felt that some record of this man's activity should be included.*

1994   **Elm Street**   Adrian Berry   *The route was previously claimed as 10,000 Maniacs by Chris Parker in 1986. The claim, for some unknown reason, appears to have been dismissed, and Berry is widely acknowledged as the first ascensionist.*

1994 Aug   **High Times**   Percy Bishton

1995   **Humpty Dumpty, On Deadly Ground**   Darren Thomas

1996 Oct   **Silly Billy**   Malcolm Taylor, Alison Taylor   *Almost certainly climbed before in 1977 by Jim Reading and John Store*   **Chilly Days and The Purple Acorns**   Ian Loombe, Percy Bishton

1997   **Urban Sprawl**   Rich Heap, Paul Mitchell

1999   **Tuck and Roll, Hang Glider, Zeppelin, Goodyear**   David Law

2000   **Drifter**   Thomas de Gay

2000   **The Psycho Path**   Julian Lines   *Climbed on-sight by Adam Long in 2002. Attempted, on-sight, by James Pearson, who took the full skid from the crux.*

2001   **Top Loader, Mother's Pride**   Mike Lea   *Millstone was one of the first crags to be opened up after the Foot & Mouth epidemic of 2001. On-sight ascents soon followed from the super-fit, including Ian Vickers and Steve McClure.*

2001   **Live Mountain Rescue TV**   Dan Honneyman

1991-2002   **Who Wants to Be Lucky Pierre**   Iain Farrar

2002 July   **Evening Premier Direct Finish**   Nick Taylor, Alan Taylor

2004   **The Economist**   Tom Randall   **Pockets**   Steve Clark, Gordon Stainforth

Mother's Pride   John Welford
Master Chef   Johnny Dawes
Master Chef Sit Start   Mo Overfield
Nige's Problem   Nigel Prestige
Pet Cemetery, Pets Win Prizes, Proper Grit   Jon Fullwood
Pully Hulley   Tim Hulley
Technical Master   Keith Myhill, late 1960s
Walnut Whip   Tim Hulley
Zaff's Problem   Zaff Ali
Zaffatricks   Zaff Ali
Zippatricks   Mark Pretty

Boulder First Ascents

Bohemian Grove   Mo Overfield, 2003
David   Richie Patterson
Dick Williams   Zaff Ali
Elytrocele   Pete Oxley, 1987
Erb Arête & Lawrencefield Upper Tier Boulder Problems
Duncan Eagles, Justin Pettifar, Simon Jacques et al, 2003-05
Fireball   Mick Adams
Left-Hand Man   Ian Fitzpatrick
The Little Quarry Problems   Darren Thomas, 1995
Mother Cap Quarry Problems   Pat King

3 The **Rivelin Area**

"We have at last robbed ourselves of the great incentive at Rivelin: the Needle is no longer unconquerable, and we are the poorer for it."

RA Brown, 1950

Kim Leyland soloing the great historical classic on the Rivelin Needle, Spiral Route, VS 4c (page 181), the first free climb to get to the top of this great feature. Photo: John Coefield.

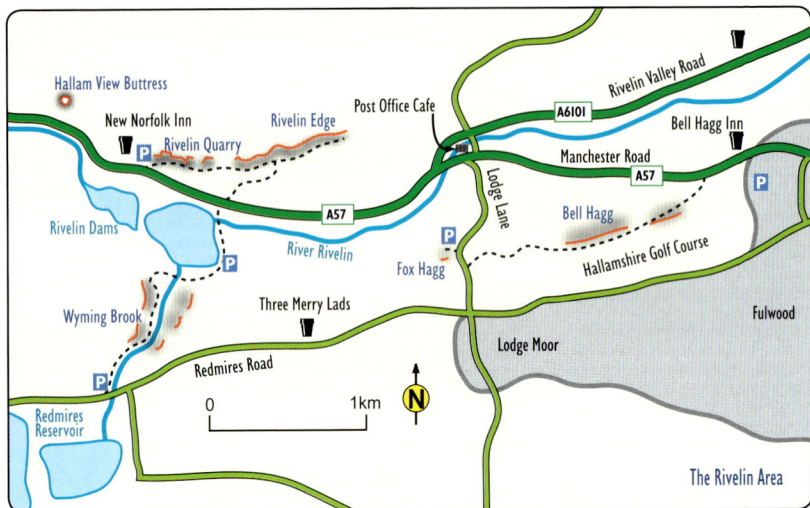

The Rivelin Area

Bell Hagg

OS Ref. SK 303861 to SK 288863   altitude 180m

by Mike Snell

A local crag for local people. Bell Hagg is a long, strung-out collection of short steep buttresses running along the crest of the ridge overlooking the A57. It is probably the closest rock to Sheffield, and it gives a number of fine gymnastic exercises that can be reached in only a few minutes from the city. As well as being a good venue for bus travellers, and even being a pleasant walk from the city limits, it also benefits from being climbable when other crags are dripping.

The Climbing

The Hagg has over 120 climbs ranging from boulder problems to short routes with a maximum height of 10m. Some can be led, but it is rare to see a rope here. It is best seen as a venue for bouldering and for short, technical solos. The climbing is quite friendly and there is a great range of easier problems, making it suitable for beginners.

Conditions and Aspect

The rock faces northwest on tree and scrub-covered slopes. Its low altitude means that it gets less bad weather than other crags and can be a good bet on bad days. However, it gets little sun and consequently some routes remain green and lichenous throughout the year. There are many, however, that are climbable in most conditions, although a soft brush may be a useful addition to one's pack. In general the rock is sound, although care is needed on some lines.

Parking and Approach

The crag is easily accessible by a variety of approaches. The three main ones are:

i) A public footpath crosses the Hallamshire Golf Course, from just west of the clubhouse (do not park in the golf club car park, unless you are a member). Follow the footpath with care to a walled path, which emerges at a stream at the eastern end of the crag. From there either scramble down to the Amen

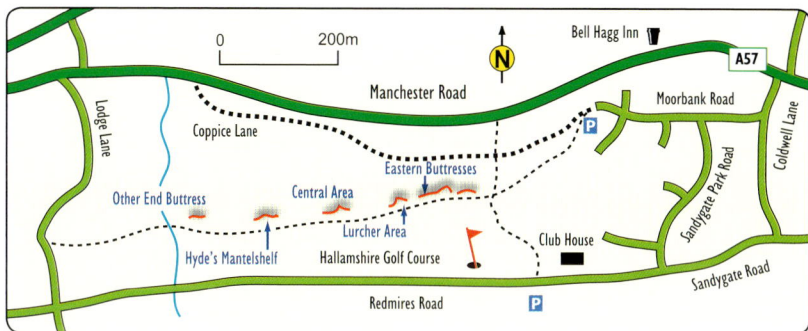

Corner buttress, or take the cliff top path for other areas: 5 minutes.

ii) Walk 100m down the A57 from the Bell Hagg Inn and take the bridlepath on the left. This leads uphill to a byway known as Coppice Lane. Either go right, to join a footpath up to the eastern end of the crag, or go left, to meet the next approach at its steps: 5 to 10 minutes.

iii) Coldwell Lane runs uphill from the A57 beyond Crosspool. Take the first right turn into Moorbank Road and follow it until it turns into a track (Coppice Lane). Parking is available there. Follow the track, bearing left at some steps and continue along the ridge until the golf club path is met at the Amen Corner area: 5 minutes.

By bus: Buses run from the City to Lodge Moor, via the Golf Club (bus number 51); to the Bell Hagg Inn on the A57 (bus number 51A); and to Coldwell Lane on the Sandygate Park Estate (bus number 51)

> **"Some apology might be needed**
> for a series of chapters on climbs that hardly ever exceed a hundred feet in height, were they not situated in some of the most attractive scenery in England, and at the gate of several big cities."
>
> EA Baker, Moors, Crags and Caves of the High Peak and the Neighbourhood

The Eastern Buttresses

A good concentration of small buttresses lies at the eastern end of the Hagg. The first routes are 15m to the left (east) of the stream on an obvious buttress. ● **Maju**, D, is the east face; ● **Mbili**, VD, climbs the front face, via the nose then finishes on the arête to the left (both pre-1953). The crack to the right is M.

End Buttress: Beyond the stream is the main edge. The first four routes are all situated on a small green buttress. ● **End Crack Arête**, VD, ● **End Crack**, VD, ● **Elbow Room**, VS 4c, the wall to its right (all pre-1953), and ● **Church Spire**, VS 5a (1957-63), the overhang and arête right again. Further right is ● **Church Tower**, M (pre-1953), which climbs the valley face of the squat tower.

Amen Corner Buttress: Broken rock leads to the first major area. This has an enormous well-polished flake at its base with overhangs above. Known to the mat brigade as Burglar Buttress, this popular bouldering venue often stays dry in the rain and has numerous low grade problems and eliminates.

① The Hand Traverse El 5a ★   1963

9m   Easy rocks on the left end of the buttress lead to a horizontal flake below the overhang. Swing boldly right for 4m then climb the groove above.

② Furherbuch VS 4c   1968

12m   An alternative to the previous route climbs the corner just left to a hand-traverse rightwards, a step round the rib above the overhang, to finish up a gangway.

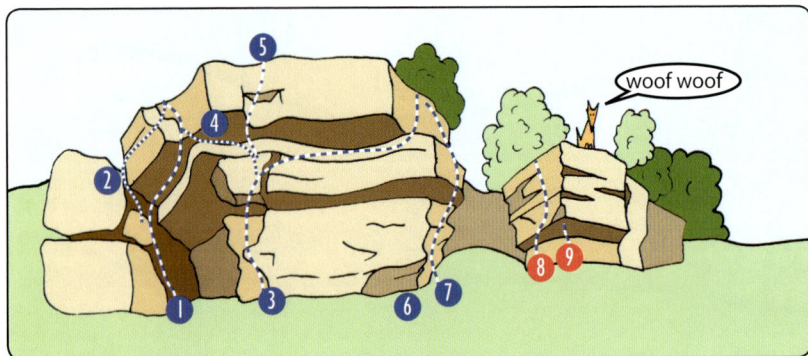

woof woof

3 Amen Corner VD   pre-1953
12m The left-hand end of the huge flake forms a crack. Ascend this to the roof, traverse right, and where the roof ends move awkwardly up to a large sloping ledge.

4 The Wigg E2 5c   1962
8m Climb the crack of Amen Corner then gain the end of the traverse on The Hand Traverse by a tricky move up and left; beware the suspect flake. Finish as for The Hand Traverse.

5 Burglar In My Bedroom E5 6b   1988
9m The roof above Amen Corner and right of The Wigg is desperate; move left then right above. Side-runners may help maintain composure.

6 Amen Corner Right S 4a ★   pre-1952
9m Start 6m right of Amen Corner below an overhang at 3m. Pull over this and continue direct to and through Amen Corner.

7 Men Only HS 4c   1964-76
7m A route to the right, which climbs the bulging wall to the large sloping ledge.

●Other quality problems and variations exist hereabouts including an excellent low-level traverse of the buttress at V4 (6a), ●and a head-height traverse at V1 (5b).

8 Len's Edges V3 (6a)
Crimp up left of the arête. The short crack to the left is **Jan**, VD (1968).

9 Len's Areet V1 (5c)
The arête direct. ●A low start is V4 ●and the wall 2m right is **Alleluia**, V0 (5a).

Twenty five metres rightwards is a slabby green wall with three cracks on its right-hand side.

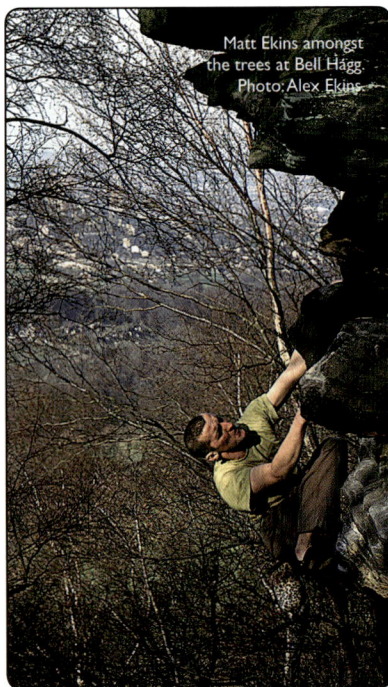

Matt Ekins amongst the trees at Bell Hagg. Photo: Alex Ekins.

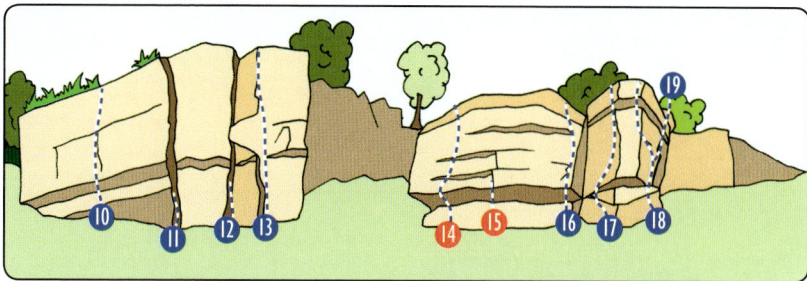

10 All Hallows HVS 5b ★   pre-1953
6m   Gain the mantelshelf ledge on the left side of the wall, using a small flake, and continue directly to the top. ● The wall just left is V2 (HVS 5c), and the bulge to the right is ●**Green Thinking**, E5 6b (1991).

11 Broomstick S 4a   pre-1953
8m   The left-hand crack.

12 Greymalkin S 4a   pre-1953
8m   The central crack.

13 Cauldron Crack S 4a   pre-1953
6m   The last crack. ● The flake just right is **Witch's Wall**, HS 4b (pre-1953). ● The arête to the right, climbed on its right, is **Bewitched**, E1 5b (2004).

Nunn's Eliminate Wall: This lies approximately 10m further right.

14 Monk's Bulge V1 (5b)
The roof left of the Eliminate.

15 Nunn's Eliminate V3 (6a)
A classic that is certainly harder than 6a if you can't do it. Two layaways in the centre of the wall lead strenuously over the roof.

● The wall just right of Nunn's is a worthwhile V4 (6b), which entails a long reach over the roof. ● Right again is another V1 (5c) problem that gains a spike above the roof to finish left. The next route is:

16 Griff's Variant VS 5a ★   1963
6m   The blunt arête right of Nunn's Eliminate is overcome by an obvious jug; finish direct.

17 Hangman's Arête VS 4b   1957-63
7m   Attain a standing position on the wedged block with style or, more usually, by other means. Finish up the arête. A direct start is 5b.

18 The Noose E2 6a   1980s
7m   The right-hand side of Hangman's Arête is gained by a thin finger-traverse from Phlegm.

19 Phlegm VS 5a   1962-63
6m   The impending sidewall direct. The holly-choked rock just right is **Holly Crack**, S (pre-1953).

● Ten metres right, **Birch Slab**, D (pre-1953), is the green slab to a birch tree. ● To the right is a wide crack; **Mantelshelf Slab**, D (pre-1953), is the slab 2m right. ● Three metres right, **Mantelpiece**, VS 4c (1963), starts on a jutting finger of rock and moves up and left over bulges using a good jug. ● Moving up and right from the finger, but staying left of the arête, is **Toytuss**, E1 5b (1963), ● while the arête itself is **Rodger's Arête**, VS 5a (1962-63). ● The scruffy corner right again is VD. ● Five metres further right are two slight routes; **Prow Arête**, VD (pre-1953), starts from a V-groove and continues up the corner above, ● and **Prow Wall**, VD (pre-1953), ascends the wall just right.

The Lurcher Area

The next routes are some 30m further on, beyond an obvious, easy descent.

20 Banner's Ridge E1 5b ★★   1957-63
9m   The prominent steep arête, started on the left, provides exhilarating climbing. ● The right-hand side of this is a fine highball V1 (5c).

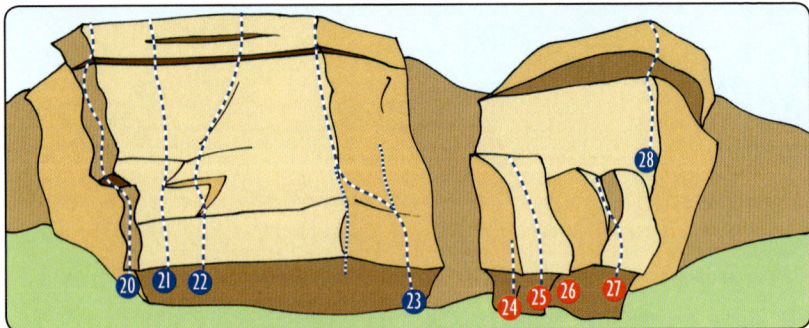

A number of traditional variants are possible around here: ●**Dim 'n Dismal**, VD (1991), grovels up the crack and ledges left of Banner's Ridge, ●while **Black Crack**, VS 5a (pre-1953), traverses into the upper part of Banner's Ridge from this. ●Finally **Steptoe**, S 4a (1957-63), takes a low traverse from Black Crack through Brown's Unmentionable.

㉑ The Brig E1 5c ★   1976
9m Start just right of the arête with sharp pulls and continue confidently above.

㉒ Brown's Unmentionable HVS 5a ★★ 1950s
9m Overcoming the severely undercut break is fun or frustrating. Mantel convincingly and float up the airy groove above. Another contender for the best route on the edge.

㉓ The Lurcher HS 4c ★   1953
8m Gain the undercut right arête of the buttress by a mantel further right and a traverse left to climb the arête. ●**Lurcher Direct Start** is a brilliant V5 (6b), and is becoming very worn. ●It is also possible to climb direct from the original start at 4c.

㉔ Lurcher's Nose V1 (5c)
The little arête. ●The sit start is V4 (6b).

㉕ Lurcher's Nose Front V2 (5c)

㉖ Nose Arête Right V2 (6a)

㉗ Sitdown Groove V4 (6b)
On the block just right, climb the angular groove from a sitter. ●Doing it without the arête is V5 (6b).

Behind these problems is a large scooped slab:

㉘ Scoop Arête VS 5a ★   pre-1953
9m The arête which forms the right edge of the scoop, leads to an overhanging finish, or a move right and up via a jammed block at HS 4b. ●**The Scoop**, VD (pre-1953), is the slab on the left.

Ash Tree Wall: The next wall is 10m further on and has a number of short worthwhile lines. ●On the polished wall on the left, the wall past the flake on the left is V0− (4c); ●the fingery wall in the middle is V0 (5a), ●and the small edges on the right are V0+ (5b). ●The dark wall past some cracks on the right contains **Black Flake**, V1 (5b) up the centre.

The Central Area

The rock gives way to vegetation for 100m, then reappears in the form of a poor buttress, characterised by a grassy bower on the left. ●**Haggled**, S 4b (1991), goes direct to the tree; ●**Flaky Wall**, VS 4b (pre-1953), is the wall to the right and ●**Green Wall**, VD (pre-1953), follows the verdure up the slabby right wall of the buttress.

The Barrel: Below the crag is a boulder sticking out of the hillside. ●**The Barrel Slap Problem**, V4 (6b), moves off a ledge, via an undercut, leading to the eponymous move from a layaway. ●The problem to the left is V2 (6a).

Inverted Arête Buttress: Another 10m on is a better buttress, with a deep dank chimney on the left. ●Just left of the chimney is **M and S**, S 4a (1990).

Leon Zablocki getting dynamic at the Hagg, on a direct start to Hangman's Arête, 5b (previous page).
Photo: Alex Ekins.

● The chimney is **Birch Tree Chimney**, VD (pre-1953), which is not compulsory, but probably is obligatory. ● **Marvin Haggler**, HVS 6a (1991), is the steep wall, wide break and capping overhang on the right. ● The fine arête to the right is **The Inverted Arête**, HVS 4c ★ (pre-1953), a bold line following the arête directly to the overhang, which provides the crux, taking care with the rock on the way. ● Right of the arête, **Green Gold**, HVS 4c (1964-76), is another bold, direct line, via the obvious hole, to a dirty finish. ● Right again at a flake right of the hole, **Rowan Wall**, VS 4a (pre-1953), climbs direct to the tree. ● In another 10m, a fang-like rock nose protrudes. This holds **Fang**, D (pre-1953), which starts below the nose and just right of a crack; climb direct. ● The wall 3m right is **Denture**, VD (1957-63).

Dave Parry on the reclusive Barrel Slab Problem, V4 (previous page). Photo: Parry collection.

Nameless Buttress: The next routes are some 15m further on. ● **No Name**, D (pre-1953), is the crack in the left edge of the buttress. ● **Nameless**, VD (pre-1953), is the corner and arête just right; loose holds. ● **No Words to Say**, HVS 5a (1990), mantels the bulge just right and continues up the wall. ● **The Innominate**, S (pre-1953), mantels the bulge right again to climb a groove.

Belle Buttress: The next routes, identified by the luminous green glow, are found 30m right. ● **The Belle,** D ★ (pre-1953), is the evergreen arête climbed on its left, providing a pleasant route. ● **The Flying Pig Variant**, HVS 5a (1964-76), is the arête from the right; green. ● **The Hagg**, HVS 4c (pre-1953), is an overgrown, damp and dirty swing over the overhang, right of the arête. Continue via the pocket. ● Four metres right of this is a verdant slab; **Dribble**, D (1957-63). Vegetation overwhelms any outcrops for the next 30m, but thankfully the rock that follows is of excellent quality.

Hyde's Buttress Area

The Hagg pulls itself together again for this little collection of buttresses, formed of three short, clean walls. Some can be led, but most are best enjoyed as highball problems.

㉙ Sputum Traverse V5 (6b)
Step off the ledge on the left and traverses the thin breaks with very little in the way of footholds.

㉚ Sputum V0 (5a)
The centre of the buttress from a hole. ● The steep wall immediately left of this is **Spunky**, V0+ (5b), and ● **Hole Wall**, V0− (4a), is the wall to the left of this again. ● **Spigolo**, V0− (4b) is the wall on the right, past Sputum.

㉛ Spasm VS 5a   1962-63
On the next buttress, climb the fine wall via the pocket at half height.

㉜ Spasm Right HVS 5b   traditional
The wall just right of the pocket. Further right, the slight arête is 4b. ● **Cave Wall**, D (pre-1953), is the green slab just right.

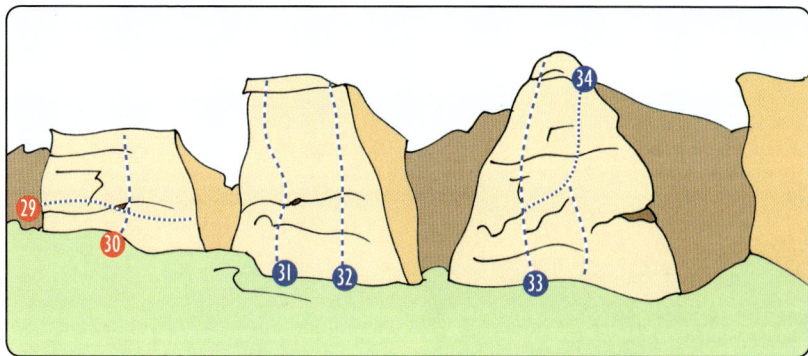

Next is an easy gully with a slabby right wall. The following routes are on the fine steep front face, immediately right.

33 Hyde's Mantelshelf HVS 5b ★★ pre-1953
8m Start in the middle of the wall and mantelshelf to reach a crack above and left. Finish up the crack and juggy breaks.

34 Leo HVS 5b ★★ 1957-63
8m Use Hyde's Mantelshelf to start: at 4m, traverse right on the horizontal break for 2m and climb the wall above. A direct start is available, at between 5b/6a, depending on one's height.

● **Gangway**, D (pre-1953), is 5m right below a projecting flake. Climb the bulge and finish on the edge of the flake. ● The bulge can be ascended further right, with a direct finish: **Byway**, S (1999). Open grassy slopes prevail for the next 70m, before the rock reappears as a low slabby outcrop, which provides various short problems at VD standard. Below and right of these, a detached block gives a worthwhile line:

35 Birch Buttress S 4a pre-1953
8m The front of the buttress.

36 Son of a Birch V3 (6a)
A good problem taking the right arête of this buttress from a low start at a flake.

The next routes are 10m further right, on a very green slab. ● **Philosopher's Slab**, VD (pre-1953),

climbs the left arête of the narrow slab, left of the main slab. ● **Alchemist's Slab**, VD (pre-1953), is right of the groove, which separates the main slab from Philosopher's Slab; finish at a birch. ● **Alkali**, VS 4b (1964-76), is 2m right. ● **Varappe**, HS 4b (1968), climbs slightly right of the centre of Alchemist's Slab, via the shallow scoop to the right.

The Other End Buttress

The final buttress of note, lies 10m right and is split by a wide crack. Although the problems are somewhat stunted, the landing makes them a serious proposition but mats and careful spotting should help.

37 The Lost Arête V2 (HVS 5c)
Classy. The blunt left-hand rib provides a fine thin problem. ● The slab on the left, gained from the rib, is a delicate V1 (5c); **Hanging at the Hagg**.

38 Savage Dog V4 (E2 6a)
The wall just right of The Lost Arête, has few, if any, real holds. ● The dirty rib just right is **Muzzled**, HVS 5b (1999), ● while the crack is **The Goblin**, S 4a (pre-1953).

39 Master's Revenge V4 (E2 6a)
The right arête of The Goblin, is climbed on its right side. It is also possible, to climb up the wall, from the obvious large hold, at the same grade.

40 The Missing Rib V1 (HVS 5b)
A fine problem up the right arête of the buttress. ● **Finale**, S 4a (1985), is the wall to the right.

Fox Hagg

(SK 293868) This is a solitary buttress, which is a continuation of the Bell Hagg escarpment. It provides good sport for an hour's bouldering for those who may have visited Bell Hagg and are hungry for more.

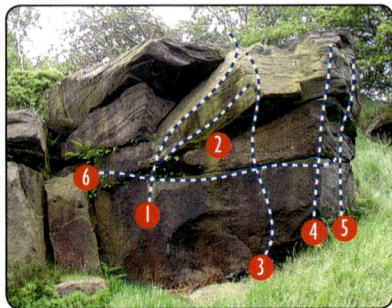

To approach the buttress, either walk along from the end of Bell Hagg, or follow the A57 road until just before the junction with the A6101 Rivelin Valley Road and follow Lodge Lane uphill to a car park on the right. Continue up the road for 50m until a path breaks off right, which gains the path along the top of the edge. The block is just after a house. Access details are unknown but a low profile won't hurt.

1 Slanting Groove V0 (5a)

2 Twentieth Century Fox V4 (6a)
From the bottom of the groove, move out right along a small break to finish up Thought Fox.

3 Thought Fox V4 (6b)
From a sit start, climb the bulges above direct.

4 Foxy V1 (5b)
From a sit start, climb the bulges above direct.

5 Foxy Loxley V1 (5b)
From a sit start using the pocket, climb the sidewall.

6 Life Gets Easier V5 (6b)
Traverse the lower break from left to right to finish up Foxy Loxley.

Boozer's Buttress

OS Ref. SK 291878   **altitude 220m**

This buttress, originally known as The Old Man's Head, is situated prominently above the Rivelin Hotel on the A6101 out of Sheffield. It might be best approached across the rough land to the right of the Inn and associated houses. The owners and their attitude to the use of the rocks are not known, but there have been access difficulties in the past as the crag lies at the foot of the gardens of nearby houses, which is unfortunate due to its closeness to the pub. Due to the access problems the grades have not been re-checked and the crag is included only for completeness. This script has been reproduced from previous guidebooks. The climbs were all first ascended in the 1950s.

Starting in the bay just left of the main buttress the climbs are; ● **Pint O' Mild**, VD, a steep crack to the hollies. ● **Brown's Brew**, HS, the wide central crack and right again ●**Muses**, HS, right up the prominent shelves to join the arête. The next two routes are the longest here; ●**Apollo**, HS, takes the thin crack in the undercut front face, moving left to the arête. ●**Bacchus,** HS, is 1m right climbing a bulge and flakes. ●The corner-crack is **Pink Gin**, S, whilst ●**Angostura**, HS, goes over the undercut base of the buttress to join an easier crack. ● Finally **Odin**, S, climbs the short crack 6m right.

To the right a quarried wall extends for some 100m. Routes have been climbed here in the past, but are friable and overgrown. Further right, below the minor road, lies **Rivelin Glen Quarry (OS Ref. SK 307898)**. Access is forbidden as it is used as a store by a stone firm.

Rivelin Edge

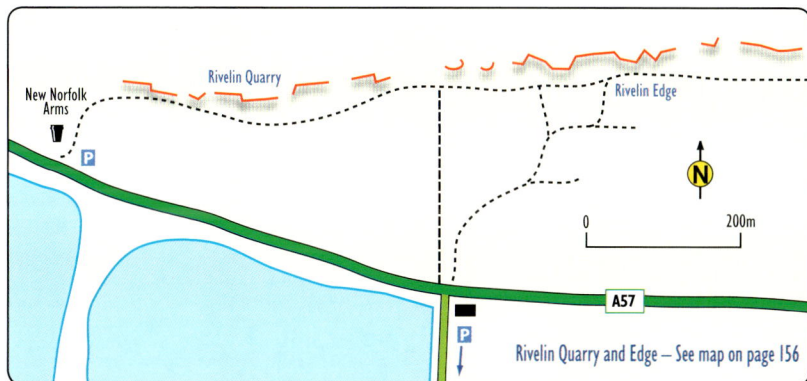

by David Simmonite and Percy Bishton

Rivelin Edge is one of the finest crags in the whole Sheffield area. Despite its modest stature – few routes reach 10m, and it is not very long – it manages nevertheless to cram in a great amount of quality into very little space. The rock is peerless, being rough, fine-grained and extremely sound, and the routes are bursting with character, giving continually interesting moves on generally very strong lines. As if that wasn't enough, the crag lies in a beautiful wooded setting of birch and oak that gives its many individual buttresses a fine sense of seclusion. All in all a gem of a crag, and there can be few happier experiences in the Peak than being sat on top of the Needle at the end of a summer day.

The Climbing

Really good climbing, tending towards the steep and the technical, mainly on cracks and positive edges. **Routes:** With 180 routes from beginners' bumbles to hard man horrors, the edge has everything. Cracks, walls, arêtes and corners are the thing, with a small number of slab climbs. One aspect of Rivelin climbing, especially noteworthy in its harder climbs, is the presence of protection. A good proportion of Rivelin's harder climbs can be enjoyed in relative safety. **Bouldering:** Although there are only about

20 problems, in true Rivelin style, these are almost all interesting high-quality challenges. Few are regular boulder problems, most tending to be highballs, or micro-routes high above good landings.

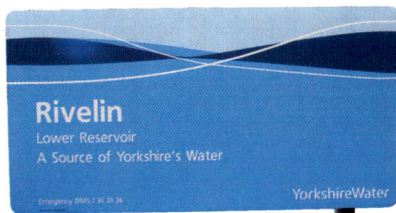

Conditions and Aspect

This is a very clean edge, with only a few routes suffering from vegetation, often in the form of an unwanted tree or gorse bush. It has an idyllic setting with woodland beneath and overlooking the dam below, although these also provide a good breeding ground for the dreaded midge. It is extremely sheltered, making it an excellent cold weather venue. It isn't unheard of to climb in T-shirts when the Peak is gripped by inclement weather. The sun comes onto the main edge in the late morning, and lingers for most of the day. Great in winter. **Note:** Most of the descents here can be tricky and the nervous might want to check them out in advance.

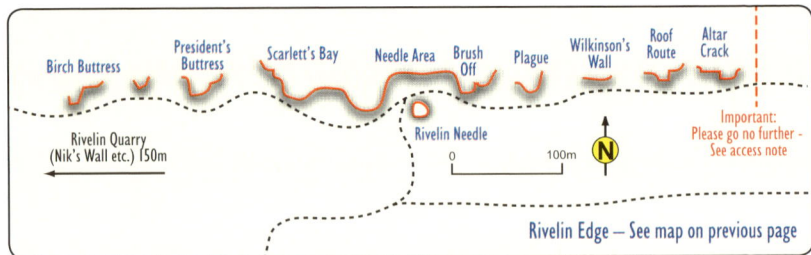

Birch Buttress | President's Buttress | Scarlett's Bay | Needle Area | Brush Off | Plague | Wilkinson's Wall | Roof Route | Altar Crack

Rivelin Quarry (Nik's Wall etc.) 150m

Rivelin Needle

0   100m   N

Important: Please go no further - See access note

Rivelin Edge — See map on previous page

Parking and Approach

Park in the large car park across the dam. Return to the A57 and cross the wall and follow the footpath uphill, then right, across a small stream, to a fork by a post with a yellow arrow. Go left and wind through the trees to the Rivelin Needle. Note: it is very important not to wander off the path through the woods (see access note). **Approach:** Up to 15 minutes. **By bus:** The Mainline 54 stops at the New Norfolk Arms pub.

Access

The felling of trees by unknown individuals in 2004 almost caused climbing at Rivelin to be banned. Negotiations saved this situation. However, access is now very sensitive as the owner is now very concerned about further damage and erosion to this special woodland area as it is a nature reserve.

After a meeting with BMC Access reps, it has been agreed that:

- **informal access** to the crag for small parties can be maintained (NO groups).
- The BMC&**ACT** (the Access and Conservation Trust) will meet the cost of making good the damage done to trees. Limited clearance of additional trees, with the exception of oaks, has also been agreed.
- **access to the crag** is via the footpath that starts opposite the dam road and emerges left of the pinnacle. Do not wander through the woodlands below the crag.
- **the footpath will be sympathetically developed** to preserve surrounding woodlands and ensure that it is easily visible.
- **climbers/boulderers must avoid** the edge right of the Altar Crack area and respect its integrity as a nature reserve. Failure to do so will jeopardise all access to the rest of the crag.

Left-Hand Rocks

The left-hand end of Rivelin contains many fine gems, both for boulderers and routers. The rock is every bit as good as that in the main areas, the climbs are in a lovely leafy setting, and there is a pleasant feeling of solitude to be had. Approach along the diminishing paths along from the Needle area.

Boulderers may wish to note that the fine collection of problems at the end of Rivelin Quarry lie only 150m further across the hillside.

Birch Buttress: The first buttress has a fine collection of easier climbs.

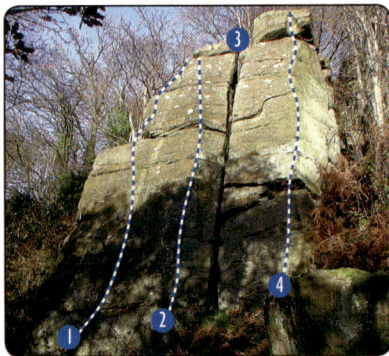

1 Birch Buttress S 4a ★   1935-51
7m Pleasant smearing up the centre of the slab leads to a ledge. Finish up the arête above. ●**Birch Bark**, VS 5a (1970s), is the slight arête to the left. ●**Birch Side**, VS 5a (2004), climbs the left arête of Birch Buttress on its left side, until established on the second mantelshelf ledge.

2 **Don't Birch the Doc** HVS 4c   1994
8m   A eliminate, with some good moves. Climb a slight rib to a break then finish up the wall above.

3 **Birch Crack** HD ★   1935-51
8m   The central crack will take you back in time.

4 **Birch** HVS 5a ★   1964
7m   The arête is a good route with the only protection in the slot at half-height. The crux is reaching a wide break below the final runnel. ● An eliminate, **Silver and White,** HVS 5a (1994), has been climbed between Birch Crack and Birch (side-runners), ● while **Birch Branch,** E1 5b (1997), moves right from the gear slot onto the sidewall and climbs this.

Five metres up and right is a small buttress.

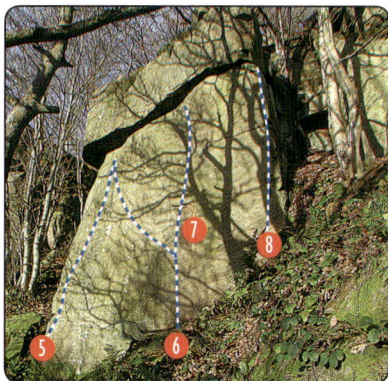

5 **Cool Rib** V3 (6a)
The rib on the left of the wall is harder than it looks.

6 **Cool Running** V3 (6b)
Step up to an undercut and balance out left to the top of Cool Rib. Good technical stuff.

7 **Faze Action** V7 (E2 6c)
A classy test of finger strength. From the undercut of Cool Running make a technical sequence direct up the rib, via some stiff pulls on a pebble and a crease, to gain a break. Top-out optional.

8 **Hot Dog** V0+ (5b)
The arête on the left. ● V0− (4c) on its right side.

The Bivouac Cave: Thirty metres right is a steep quarried block containing two significant problems.

9 **Purple Haze** V7 (6b)
Traverse the lip from the left to finish up just left of the right arête.

10 **Master Kush** V10 (7a)
A modern desperate up the right arête from the block at the back. A massive wing span is crucial.

"One day in 1928

a group of three equipped with a clothes line toiled up to Rivelin Edge. The three knew nothing of rope technique, and the rope was for moral support only. After doing a number of the easier lines in more or less the orthodox manner, the leader was attracted to a fifty-foot chimney that had every appearance of being unclimbed. He attempted this on a rope held above by one of his companions. Halfway up the cliff face he found himself confronted by a screaming apparition with saucer eyes and a wide-open beak. It was a young owl, still in the downy stage, and it screamed with the full power if its voice, either from terror or defiance. The climber was so frightened that he instinctively drew back. The next moment he found himself swinging in mid-air on the clothes line which stretched until it was as thin as twine. Luckily it held, despite an ominous twang, and regaining his holds, he finished the climb. This was Harry Scarlett's introduction to climbing."

High Peak, by Eric Byne

Rivelin Edge

Boulderers! KNOW YOUR HOLDS!

All these are holds on named problems in this guide. Know them? Answers on page 322.

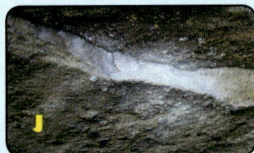

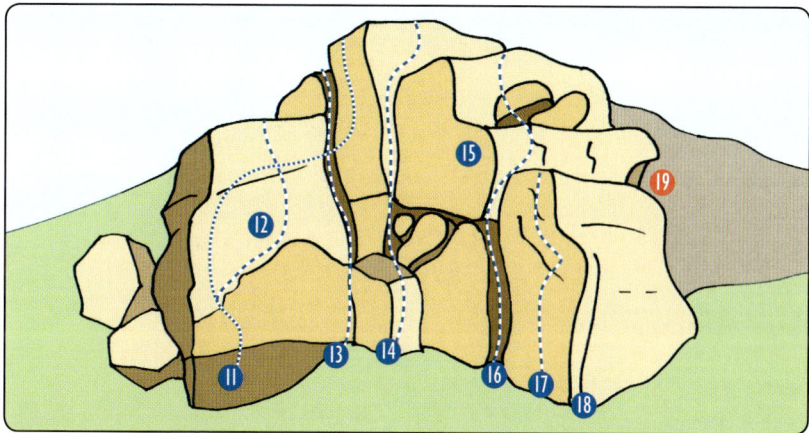

President's Buttress

Thirty metres further right is a larger buttress bounded on its left by an undercut slab. It has a good concentration of routes at many grades.

11 Red's Slab Variations VS 4c ★★ 1952

11m A good series of alternatives on an older route makes for a varied and exposed climb. Mantel the bottom of the ramp, then make bold moves up to the ledge. Foot-traverse the break to the corner and climb the tower directly above to a grasping exit. The original route followed the arête all the way (HS 4b).

12 We're Only Here for the Smear E4 5c ★ 1984

9m A bold, unprotected route. Make a tenuous foot-traverse directly above the vertical wall, to the centre of the slab and make lurching smears for the salvation of the break. Finish direct.

13 White House Crack S ★ 1935-51

7m The slabby corner crack is harder than it looks. A good challenge, and a fine piece of exercise for long-trousered beginners.

14 The President's Crack VS 4b ★ 1935-51

8m A strenuous offering, up the crack on the right of the corner, which expands towards the top. Move up the crack and once it begins to widen, continue with the aid of the left wall.

15 Milena E6 6b ★ 1999

8m The hanging arête above Senator's Gully is climbed 'by way of pebble-pulling, smearing and slapping to a horrible mantelshelf to top out'. Lovely!

16 Senator's Gully S 4b 1935-51

8m The wide crack and tricky flake above.

17 Money for Old Rope E3 6b 1999

7m Boulder up to a slopey break and place gear in a flared slot to the right. Pull into a left-trending seam and launch for the obvious ramp to finish.

18 Ray Crack VS 5a ★ 1956

10m The shallow crack leads stiffly to a platform. Finish up Senator's Gully. ● The dirty wall to the right is **Parallel Universe**, E3 6b (1984), ● and the short dirty rib to the right is **Ukase**, HS 4b (1961-63).

19 Friday Club V6 (6b)

On the right of the ledge is a small cutaway roof. Start under the roof at a sharp flake. Using a pocket, reach the arête and slap up this to the top.

Thirty metres further right is a buttress now well-hidden by a holly tree which contains two routes: ●**Beginner's Buttress,** S (1952), begins at the lowest point right of the tree and goes up to a small crux roof and ●**Beginner's Route,** D (1952), takes the same start to the roof but avoids this by going right for 3m before moving up. Now overgrown.

Scarlett's Bay

This is the buttress 30m right of President's Buttress, giving great, tall routes on the finest Rivelin Grit. Testpieces of all grades abound, and you will have to work for them. The first routes are up and left. ●The much lamented **Jade**, HVS 5b (1976), used to climb an oak tree and the wall above via a pocket and the arête. Unfortunately, the tree was felled and all that remains is a stump.

20 **The Caress of the Blubbery Hand** E2 6a 1987
6m Begin up the right-hand side of the arête to a ledge/break and either attack it on its left-hand side to a sloping finish (E3 5c), or on its right-hand side (E2 6a), depending on whether you feel bold or technical.

21 **Vice Like Grip** HVS 5b 1999
5m A piece of class up the sharp right arête. ●V1

22 **Twister** VS 4c 1961-63
6m Start below a crack starting halfway up the wall (belay advised for second). Mantelshelf a flat hold to reach the crack and follow it steeply.

23 **Seville Flake** HVS 5a ★ 1956
7m A good route up the snaking flake to the right. Gain the flake from the jug on Twister, then climb the flake past a slot and finish to the right. ●Gaining the flake direct is a tough 5b - **The Barber** (1999).

24 **Ausfahrt** E2 5b ★ ★ 1991
11m Exposed and unlikely. From the ledge on the left, (consider a nut in the roof crack to the right) swing right and mantelshelf onto the small ledge. Step left and follow the exposed rib, which eases with height. The main challenge of the unprotected, narrow face to the left remains unclimbed.

25 **Exit** E3 5c ★ ★ 1983
11m A great route, with exposed moves on good rock. From the niche, mantel over the bulge with some gusto, and continue directly, in a lonely position, up the line of the crack (small wires/RPs protect).

26 **Jaded** E4 6b ★ 1986
11m Climb the short wall to the break. A thin pull on slopers (somewhat scrunchy) allows the centre of the upper wall to be gained and followed, past a nut slot to the top.

A rare delight for the lover of fearsome wriggles. The dark delights of Kremlin Krack, HVS 5a (page 174). Mick Carr climbing. Photo: David Simmonite.

The Highballs List

Surely the best thing about Grit – highball problems, micro-routes – all the buzz, all the height, over in a heartbeat. If you are new to the highball game, here is a list, roughly arranged in grades, to get you going. All the problems in this list are either slightly high boulder problems, very high boulder problems, or routes where a bouldering mat is your best hope – and a couple that might just need one quick runner. Don't take it that if a problem occurs on this list that it is therefore okay to fall off the top – far from it. These problems require all the control needed in doing any route. The only guarantees are the fun that you will have. So go on, careful boulderers, enjoy yourselves.

VS and under

Route I, V0–
Cherry's Crack, V0–
Golden Shower, V0–
Flake 'n' Blob, V0
Precarious Rib, VI
Shelf Wall, V0–

About HVS

Wednesday Climb, VI
Ash Tree Variation, VI
Early Morning
  Performance, VI
Yabadabadoo, V4
High Flyer, V2
The Enthusiast, V3
Clark's Route, VI
Poisoned Dwarf, VI
Carlos Warkos, VI
Jason's Rib, VI
The Tower of Power, VI
The Trunk, VI
Rumblefish, V0+
Deaf Dog, VI
Technical Baiter, VI
Hyde's Mantelshelf, V0
Leo, V0
The Lost Arête, V2
The Missing Rib, VI
Cool Rib, V3
Vice Like Grip, HVS
Wobbly Wall, VI
Steph, VI

About E1

All Quiet on the
  Eastern Front, V3
All Stars' Goal, V2
Safe Bet, V4
The Irrepressible
  Urge, VI
Nicotine Stain, V4
Rascal Groove, V5
The Gnat, V3
Captain Sensible, VI
Crow Man Meets the
  Psychotic Pheas-
  ant, V2
Technical Master
  Left-Hand, V5
Technical Master, V4
Cool Running, V3
Trivial Pursuits I, V3
Trivial Pursuits 2, V2
Fluff 'n' Stuff, V3
Altered, V3
The Business Boy, V4
Master Blaster, V2

About E2

Small is Beautiful, V6
Evening Wall Direct, V2
Twilight, V2
Sublime
  Indifference, V2
Midge, V4
Nick Knack
  Paddywack, V6

Pepper Mill, V5
Harry's Hole, V5
February Fox, V2
Savage Dog, V4
Long Shot, V4
Faze Action, V7
Acid Reign, V5
Where Bulldykes
  Daren't, V4
Chimp 'A' , V7
Chicken Head, V2
Something Silly, V5

About E3

Life in a Radioactive
  Dustbin, V5
The Arctic
  Mammal, V3
Mad Llehctim, V5
The Searing, V6
Pretzel Logic, V3
Trellis, V6
Guplets on Toast, V4
Krush Regime, V6
March Hare, V2
David, V8
Conan The
  Librarian, V4
Down to Earth, V3
Trango 2, V2

About E4

Giza, V8
The Twenty Year

Itch, V4
Desparête, V7
Home Cooking, V5
The Alliance, V6
Recurring
  Nightmare, V2
Above and Beyond
  the Kinaesthetic
  Barrier, V6
Rollerwall, V9
Hell For Leather, V5
West Side Story, V9
Salinela Sunset, V2
I'm Back, V2
Takes the Biscuit, V5
Europe After Rain, V5
Sex Drive, V5

About E5

The Sphinx, V7
Black Choir, V5
Blood and Guts on
  Botty Street, V3

About E6

Nefertiti, V8
Darkstar, VIO
Western Eyes, VIO
Sick Arête, V7

Kim Leyland practising his art on Shelf Wall, VS 4c, or highball V0– (page 182) depending whether you're climbing above a mat and spotters, or if you fancy leading with a rope and taking a belay in those nice bushes overhead. Photo: John Coefield.

27 **Der Kommissar** E4 6a ★ 1983

11m A long-ignored pitch, straightened out, but still the most logical line of the wall. Climb Kremlin Krack then swing left to gain the flake. Go up this then swing left to join Jaded.

28 **Moontan** V7 (6c)

Boulder up the wall on tiny edges to the spiky flake.

29 **Kremlin Krack** HVS 5a ★★ 1952-56

11m Brill! One of those routes that a climbing wall can't prepare you for. Ascend the steep crack by strenuous jamming and laybacking and even the occasional hidden hold. Large gear is useful.

30 **Scarlett's Chimney** HS 4b ★ 1928-30

10m Very much a traditional offering (i.e. awkward but in a fun kind of way) from one of the crag's first explorers. Enter the widening chimney with some difficulty and not without a battle and some cursing.

31 **Left Under** HVS 5a 1970s

11m Good. The small groove beneath Left Edge leads awkwardly to a standing position below the flake of Left Edge. Layback up to join that route.

32 **Left Edge** HVS 4c ★ 1961-63

11m A good route climbing the left arête of the slab.

● At half-height it is possible to teeter straight up the slab without using the arête, **Better Late Than Never?** E1 5a (1982), which is a bit bold, but with genteel moves.

33 **Rivelin Slab** M 1935-51

10m A wandering line up the broken slab on good holds to the right and is often used as a descent for those able. Can be dirty.

34 **Angle Rib** HVS 5a 1976-82

7m Climb a crack left to a large ledge. Step right and back left to ascend the exposed right-hand side of the undercut rib. A good grade harder if climbed more direct through the bulge.

35 **Angle Crack** D 1935-51

7m The corner crack has a good finish.

36 **Solitaire** VD 1961-63

7m Ascend the crack in the wall just right.

37 **Isolation** S 1935-51

7m The wide fissure is demanding.

38 **Rodney's Dilemma** S 4a ★★ 1961-63

7m The arête is an exposed gem with joyous holds and just enough protection.

Neil Strawbridge sampling the delicate delights of Rodney's Dilemma, S (this page), giving fine open climbing with a great bold feel. Photo: Nick Smith.

Dave Nodder soloing among the birch trees on the bold and slabby Left Edge, HVS 4c (opposite page).
Photo: David Simmonite.

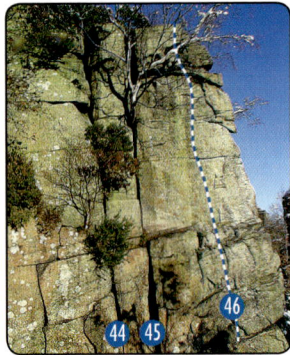

39 **End of the Road** E1 5c   1992
7m   Climb the centre of the lower wall to the break. Utilising the arête above, attain a standing position in the break and good holds to finish. Good stuff.

40 **Clinker** E5 6c ★   1998
7m   A technical number up the blank-looking scoop that the previous route avoids. Attain the small ledge of Temple Crack and climb the blunt rib above to a break. Make a weird move on a poor pebble in the middle of the scoop to rock over to the blunt right arête and progress to the top. Very reachy.

41 **Temple Crack** VD   1935-51
7m   The slanting crack to a juggy exit.

42 **Crafty Cockney** E2 5c ★   1984
7m   Climb the scoop to a thin break. Step right and reach up to small crimps. A stiff pull brings positive holds then, all too quickly, the top.

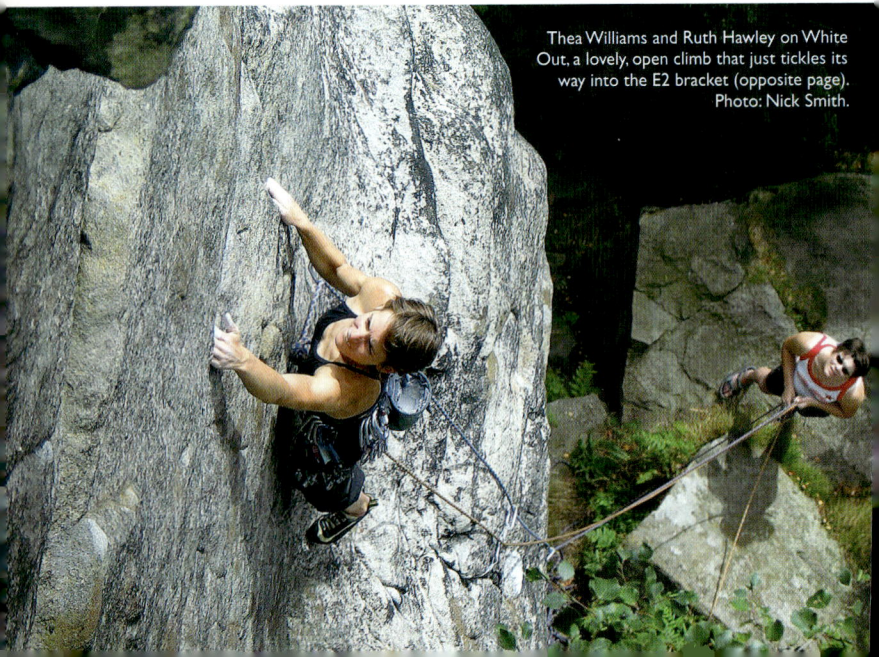

Thea Williams and Ruth Hawley on White Out, a lovely, open climb that just tickles its way into the E2 bracket (opposite page).
Photo: Nick Smith.

43 Pious Flake S 4b   1961-63

7m A good route up the thin corner crack on the right. A hard but well-protected move gains the ledge below the tree and an easy finish up the blocky cleft. ●The flake on the right to the same finish is **Tree Crack**, D (1935-51). ●The overgrown wall just right held **Long Hot Winter**, E1 6b (1984).

44 Ulex S   1933

45 Gardener's Pleasure S   1935-51

10m Climb the lower wall past a hollow flake. The wide crack above is the crux and is HS without large protection. Above the tree, the squeeze chimney may cause leaders to regret taking too large a rack.

46 White Out E2 5c ★★   1983

12m Justly popular and generally well-protected climbing up the steep wall 2m left of the arête of Blizzard Ridge. Move carefully up to a horizontal break at half-height. Stretch past this and keep left of the arête to finish. Low in the grade for the tall. ●An eliminate up the wall just left of White Out is **Interminable Drizzle**, E3 6c (1987).

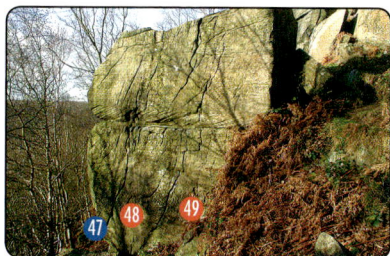

Below and left of White Out is a large block.

47 Trivial E3 6a   1998

7m The left arête is climbed on its left-hand side. Lack of protection and a grave-like hole filled with boulders directly underneath make the consequences of a miscalculation anything but trivial.

48 Trivial Pursuits 1 V3 (E1 6b)

The leftwards-trending crack is stiff but good fun.

49 Trivial Pursuits 2 V2 (E1 6a)

The right-hand crack via increasingly difficult moves.

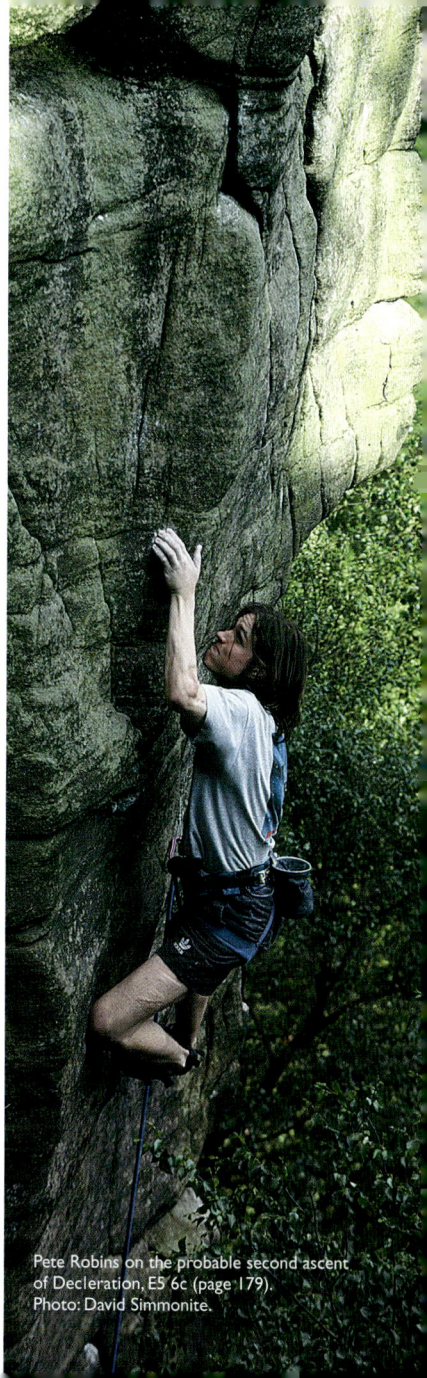

Pete Robins on the probable second ascent of Decleration, E5 6c (page 179).
Photo: David Simmonite.

The Needle Area

There now starts the longest concentration of quality climbs on Rivelin, the justifiably popular area around the famous Needle. The climbs are all clean, good and quick-drying.

50 **Blizzard Ridge** HVS 5a ★ ★ ★   1958

14m The prominent arête provides a climb of outstanding quality and is a much sought after tick. However, it isn't overly endowed with protection and requires a steady approach. The arête is gained from the right (or more direct at 5b). Follow the arête airily on its left-hand side to welcome protection below a small nose. Move right around this and climb straight up to the top. ●A boulder problem, **Bleausard Ridge** V4 (6a), climbs the short arête at the very toe of the buttress.

51 **The Tempest** E4 6a ★   1983

12m Bold climbing crammed in between easier routes – technically low in the grade. Arrange various pieces of marginal protection behind the flake (a hand-placed blade-peg can be 'dropped' in behind this, but how solid is the flake?) and continue up the centre of the slab.

52 **Jonathan's Chimney** HS 4b ★   1928-30

11m One of the first routes to be climbed at Rivelin, the fine corner crack has a hard start around the undercut near its base.

53 **Jonad Rib** VS 4c   1955

10m Climb directly up the dividing rib with somewhat spaced protection to a very reachy top.

54 **David's Chimney** VD ★   1928-30

9m More traditional fare from Harry Scarlett. The wide crack with a tricky move over a chockstone.

55 **Mad as Cows** E1 5c   1990

9m The rib and face are climbed on blind flakes and breaks.

56 **Layback Crack** VD   1933

7m Climb the glossy left-hand crack, step left and finish up its wide continuation. ●Continuing direct is **Corner Crack**, HS (1951).

57 **Twin Hole** VS 5a   1976-82

From the ledge, lean out to gain two good pockets, and make an energetic lunge for the ledge – (●V1). Finish up the crack. Or don't.

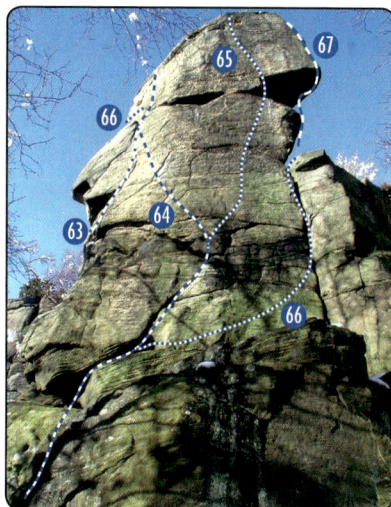

58 **Acid Reign** V5 (E2 6b)
The exciting highball arête reserves its crux for the final move, which will probably be a lunge for something that may or may not be a very sloping top.

59 **Fluff 'n' Stuff** V3 (E1 6a)
For the full mountain experience, a second 'pitch' can be had up the dangerous scooped wall above, going from the right edge of the ledge to a good flat hold.

Rivelin Needle

To the right is the landmark of the edge. All its routes are well worth doing and three of the routes have a common finish – the easily identifiable flake above a ledge called the Notch, situated on The South-West Corner. Treat the flake with respect, it's a little hollow. **Descent:** This is by abseil from a tatty-looking chain down the short back side, giving most climbers a close look at what E6 climbing entails. The first route starts on the platform on the back of the Needle.

60 **The Eye** E2 6a ★   1.4.1961
7m From the right-hand edge of the platform move up to a break. Place gear as far right in the break as you can and climb the black arête to a rounded finish.

61 **Declaration** E5 6c ★   1986
12m A difficult route taking the challenge of the west face head-on. Start down and right of the platform below a thin crack. Climb to the crack and arrange good protection before slapping up the blunt arête to gain the break. Finish direct.

62 **Angst** E3 5c ★★   1984
12m A very good route, with an exciting finish. Climb the groove in the arête to the overhang. Move out left and follow thin cracks to the break and a steep finish up the wall above.

63 **The South-West Corner (Original Route)**
      E2 5c ★★   1935
14m A historic route, and the first to be ascended on the Needle, albeit on a top-rope. Follow Angst to the overhang and move up right with difficult long stretches onto the cracked wall. Finish up this and the flake above. Low in the grade.

64 **Croton Oil** HVS 5a ★★★   1953
20m An excellent route, giving great climbing to a true summit experience. If you only do one route at Rivelin, this is it. Climb a deep, wide crack to a ledge. Balance up the face to a short crack and crucial stretch left for a flake. Follow this to the Notch and a finish up the large fragile flake.

The Needle and the Damage Done

Rivelin Crag was a favourite haunt of Ebenezer Elliot, the Corn Law Rhymer ("Now, what rhymes with Croton Oil?") at the beginning of the nineteenth century. The first climbing nails to scratch the rock were, of course, those of our old friend JW Puttrell who arrived there at the end of the century. More attracted by the fine spire at the centre of the crag then any thoughts poetic, the first thing that Jimmy did, was to rename the 'Rivelin Steeple', as it was then known by locals, to the 'Rivelin Needle', a name which hinted more towards Alpine grandeur than industrial scruffiness. The next thing he did was to spend the afternoon trying to lasso the top of said needle from the edge opposite, but to no avail; the summit was left untrod. He obviously had fun trying, however, and managed to convince his friends Henry Bishop and Dougles Yeomans to pass another afternoon similarly engaged. Again, the needle was more than a match for the rope tricks of these early pioneers.

In 1932 a fresh group of explorers came from Sheffield to visit these fine crags, Eric Byne, Rupert Brookes and their friends, who managed, finally, to get a rope over the top of the Needle. This achieved, they monkeyed up the short side, and the group summited – albeit hardly by fair means. They left their names in a tin box on the summit, and top-roped the line of the South-West Corner. Two years later this feat was repeated, "aided by a top-rope, and another rope encircling the needle as a handrail" by the Doncaster brothers from the Sheffield University Mountaineering Club. The tin box was still on the summit, untouched.

By now the Needle had suffered these various embarrassments, but worse was still to come. In 1935, Byne and Clifford Moyer, having decided that such a challenge as an unled Needle was unacceptable, led the South-West Corner route, but committed the criminal act of placing two pitons to allow their subjugation. Progress? Not really. These pegs, the first pegs ever to be placed in the Peak, were later removed, but the climb was found impossible without them.

The next significant activity was in 1944, when, after lashing ropes around the noble feature to be used as handrails and safety lines (visions of Ahab lashed to Moby Dick), RE Davies free climbed, albeit on top rope, what became known as the Spiral Route, which found reasonable climbing by circumnavigating all four sides of the needle. This was repeated again on top rope in 1949 by Dick Brown, J Renshaw and Donald Wooller, and the following weekend, Wooller did the decent thing and finally did a clean lead of the Rivelin Needle, with his historic lead of the Spiral Route.

However, the sad history of man's assaults on the Needle doesn't end there. Any good karma that Wooller earned for his free ascent of the Spiral Route, he surely lost again when he was joined by Frank Fitzgerald and Dick Brown, and ascended Croton Oil, in the process of which, despite being nowhere near the standard of the day, the team smashed five pegs into the rock to ensure glory. Luckily the Needle breathed a sigh of relief, and had some dignity restored when The Master, Joe Brown, freed the South-West Corner in 1954, using talent instead of pegs, and Pete Crew did the same for Croton Oil in 1963.

As a final desecration of this fine and long suffering obelisk, Roger Greaterick again hammered a peg in on the south east face to produce the poor Alternative Seven. This offending article was duly removed by one Chris Craggs. He noted this in the then Doomsday Book of Peak District climbing, the notorious Stoney Café Routes Book; "Peg Removed from Rivelin Needle. Route now clean." Under this the graffiti had been added – "Six pegs now removed from the washing line. Clothes now dry." John Allen stepped in to do the decent thing in 1988, and in sympathetic mood, renamed his peg-free version of the climb 'Only Human'.

The Needle now has eight routes of many different grades. Having suffered hard over the years in the name of man's need to conquer, it now stands more proud as one of the finest climbing features in the area, and hopefully its days of hurt are finally over.

Niall Grimes

65 **Only Human** E5 6c   1983

18m Desperate wall climbing with scratchy rock and disappointing protection. Climb the centre of the wall with hard moves to reach a break. Continue steeply above this following a faint weakness.

66 **The Spiral Route** VS 4c ★★   1950

22m The first free route on the Needle. Start as for Croton Oil and continue up the next crack to the platform. Belay. From its end, traverse out rightwards along the horizontal break to The Notch and a finish up the flake.

67 **Jumpey Wooller** E6 6b ★★   1998

6m Exciting stuff, with good climbing above a gnarly landing. The small overhang and perched slab directly below the abseil chain are climbed by bold, slappy moves.

The Needle has been girdled in both directions and one is described as it appeared in *Climbs on Gritstone – Further Developments in the Peak District* (1957). 'Biven's Girdle, (Hard) Very Severe. Start from the Platform and traverse left by very hard moves across the face (Croton Oil wall) to the Notch. Reverse the Spiral Route until the platform is reached.'

Face Climb Area: Behind the Needle is a series of shorter walls containing many technical climbs. **Descent** is by a short and fairly tricky (about D) chimney just round left from Face Climb No, 1. ● **Pensioner's Wall**, VS 4c (1999), is a line up the front of the narrow wall just left of the descent gully.

● The dirty chimney and leftwards-trending ramp to the left is **Grandpa's 'tache**, VS 4b (1999). Round to the right of the descent slot is a slabby wall:

68 **Face Climb No. 1** VD ★   1933

7m Follow a line of square-cut holds up the left-hand side of the wall passing a flake and ledge on route. ● **Unbelievable**, VS 5a (1999), climbs the left sidewall just right of the descent.

69 **Face Climb No. 1.5** VS 4b ★   1962

7m VS moves in an E1 setting. From the foot of Face Climb No. 1 step right and follow a line of flat holds trending diagonally rightwards.

70 **I'm Back** E4 6a ★   1985

7m A bold, fingery climb taking the wall just right again. After a very thin start the climbing steadily eases, providing a fine test of nerve and technique. It is worth having a spotter for the initial moves.

71 **Jelly Baby** HVS 5b   1977

7m The slim corner is a tough exercise in finger jamming and laybacking, but the crux is keeping off the next route.

72 **Face Climb No. 2** VS 4c   1933

7m Go straight up the narrow face on big flat holds to a high crux. Use runners in Jelly Baby at HS.

73 **Crack One** S 4a   1950

7m The corner-crack is slabby at first and leads to a steep, reachy finish.

74 Garibaldi Twins E2 6a — 1988
12m Traverse the thin break rightwards from Crack One to finish up the arête.

75 Takes the Biscuit E4 6b ★ — 1999
10m A well-named direct start to Garibaldi Twins up the faint blunt arête, using small flaky holds to the break. ● Highball V5.

76 Oversight VS 4c — 1963
7m The cramped wall just right has a tricky unprotected start and an extending finish.

77 Crack Two HD — 1955

78 Where Bulldykes Daren't V4 (E2 6b)
The reachy boulder problem up the vague rib.

79 Shelf Wall VS 4c ★ — 1950
6m A perfect mantelshelf exercise starting at a large flake.

The Brush Off Area

Moving right and across a gully is an impressive buttress, complete with a bay at its left-hand side.

80 Birth of Venus E2 6b — 1984
5m The left arête of the bay is climbed on its left-hand side to a niche before a horizontal loose flake is negotiated below the top. Desperate reachy climbing, fortunately protected by a high side-runner up and left. The arête on its steep right-hand side awaits a sufficiently brave and talented climber.

81 Easy Picking E2 6b ★★ — 1953/76
9m A superb testpiece. Initial bouldery moves lead to a bumper juggy flake and protection. It is at this point that many would-be ascensionists realise why the route name is the biggest joke on the edge. The upper cracks provide sustained climbing all the way to the top. As time and climbers take their toll on this route, it is worth noting that once-perfect gear now takes a little longer to arrange.

82 Holly Gut VS 4c — 1953
8m The corner is often green, and always tricky.

83 Oliver's Twist VS 4b ★ — 1963
8m On the right are twin cracks. This is the left-hand fist-wide crack. ● The thin crack just right gives a variation, **Short but Thick**, HVS 5a (1981).

84 The Terminator E5 6c ★ — 1985
9m A hard and technical climb. A high side-runner on the left protects the desperate initial moves to gain, and then leave, the obvious sloping pod, trending rightwards towards the centre of the wall. As you get higher, the standard gets more amenable, but from this point the protection will be of little help in the event of a fall; 6b for the tall. ● **I'll be Back**, E5 6b (2003), is a counter-diagonal to Terminator. Start up Grim Fandango until a line of leftward trending sloping holds is reached. Follow these finishing with a long reach right of the crack.

85 Grim Fandango E5 5c ★★ — 1999
10m Somebody has finally 'Don' it. The arête of The Brush Off in its entirety on the left-hand side with poor protection. A superb, steep and surprisingly overlooked line.

86 **The Brush Off** E4 5c ★ ★ ★   1963
10m Simply brilliant – well worth the risk. The arête, climbed on its right, provides a precarious series of balance moves. A classic adrenaline trip and not one for the faint hearted.

87 **Party Animal** E3 5c ★   1985
10m Good climbing requiring an honest approach. Move cautiously up the slab to gain a thin break and welcome small cam protection. Finish directly up the centre of the slab above.

88 **Fringe Benefit** E1 5b ★ ★   1980
9m Memorable, inventive climbing with refreshing exposure. Move delicately right from the foot of Party Animal and pad nicely up the right-hand side of the slab.

89 **Deep Chimney** VD
7m The chimney. ● Stepping left to the steep wall and flake just left is **Ebenezer's Staircase**, VD (1949-50). ● The direct start is 5b.

90 **Fumf** VS 5a ★   1962
5m The arête has a bouldery start and exciting moves above. ● Highball V0+.

91 **Wobbly Wall** HVS 5b ★   1969
5m An elegant, unprotected problem climbing the groove on fingery holds. ● Highball V1. Sweet.

92 **Europe After Rain** E4 6b ★ ★   1984
5m This splendid, elongated problem takes the right side of the wall with a distressing, grasping climax. ● V5, with a high 'buzz' factor.

Plague Buttress: Twenty metres further right past a useful way down, a steep buttress sports an overhang at mid-height, adorned with an old bolt. This marks the route Plague.

93 **Caravaggio** E2 5c   1979
9m Start just left of the arête. Gain the break and climb leftwards through the shelf and overlap to finish direct. E3 6a for all but the tall.

94 **Outsider** E2 5c ★ ★   1976
9m A consummate gritstone offering with an exhilarating run-out above good protection. Climb just left of the arête, gain the break, and swing onto the front face. Superb climbing up the arête remains, which keeps you guessing all the way.

95 **Ring of Roses** HVS 5a ★   1981
14m An interesting and sustained girdle that feels hard for the grade, especially if you can't jam. Start as for Outsider then follow the break quickly rightwards to escape at the top of The Crevice.

96 **Big Al** E7 7a ★   1986/2000
9m Technically one of the hardest routes on the edge, with poor handholds and considerably poorer footholds. Climb the wall passing an undercut flake to gain the easier headwall. Originally climbed by stepping in from the right, and with the bolt on Plague pre-clipped, at E5 6c.

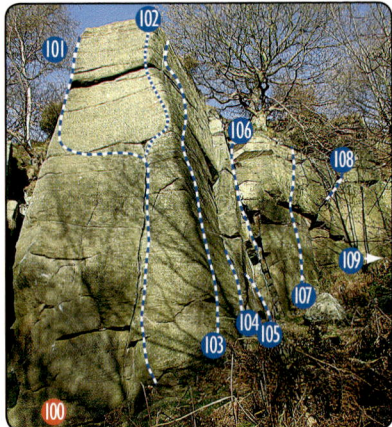

97 Plague E4 6b ★   1976

9m Climb the front face past an ancient bolt. Elongated monsters may pass the bolt direct, but most will skirt it on the right. The bolt is even more of a museum piece than it was in the last guide.

98 The Crevice VD ★   1935-51

8m Bridge the corner to the ledge then climb the wall just right of the arête. The top corner is HVD.

99 Lichen Slab S 4a   1935-51

6m Climb the centre of the slab to the right, avoiding the overhang on the left (direct is HVS). ● The left edge of the slab is, **Moss Side**, VS 4b (1991).

100 Sparks V8 (6c)

A superb and fierce problem up the undercut rib.

101 Palm Charmer E3 5c ★ ★   1985

11m A (slightly) easier alternative to Auto da Fe going left to the arête and climbing it on its right side. At the top end of the grade. The arête can also be reached from the crack at a lower level, 6a.

102 Auto da Fe E4 6a ★ ★ ★   1976

10m A stupendous route, one of the best E4s on grit. Strenuously climb the blind finger-crack in the front face to the break. Arrange protection then climb the bald right arête on its left-hand side to a second break. Finish more easily. A bold pitch and no give-away.

103 Reprieve E3 5c ★   1961

10m A serious line up the wall immediately right of the arête. It requires a cool head, although the section above the break is protected and quite a lot easier than the lower section.

104 Left Holly Pillar Crack S 4a ★ ★   1935-51

6m The left of two cracks in the right wall has good protection and perfect jams; underrated.

105 Right Holly Pillar Crack S 4a   1935-51

6m The deep right-hand crack is a bit of a thrutch and easy to get lost in. Be careful with the chockstones at half-height, one wobbles.

● **Heretic**, VS 4c (1999), girdles this section at two-thirds height.

To the right is a quarried wall.

106 Kellogg Corner VD   1956

6m The flake-choked corner is poor and loose

107 Double Decker E4 6a   1981

6m A difficult wall climb; good, but rarely climbed.

108 Caveman's Caper HS 4b   1951

6m Jam the diagonal crack to a scruffy finish.

109 Boulder Club E3 6c   1985

6m Five metres right of Caveman's Caper is a small, steep slab complete with a thin slot. Climb direct past this but warm up first, as this route is notoriously hard on the fingers.

escape can be made at virtually any point. Not to be confused with the slab further to the right which, according to a very well-respected climber, is impossible. Do we hear the sound of a gauntlet being thrown down?

113 **Mount Krusty** VS 4c   2000
7m   To the right, start at a flake and move up to a wide diagonal crack. Step left and trend leftwards up a scoop to finish over a small overlap.

● To the right, across a blocky gully, that can be used as a descent, is a small arête giving a bold 4b problem. ● To the right the easy-angled narrow rib is **Snell's Rib**, VD (1999), with a step left at the end.

Confusion Slab: Around to the right the edge returns to a natural state at a small overgrown slab. The first routes to be ascended on this slab, Diffusion and Confusion, were poorly described and undergraded at Severe in the last guide. ●**Daylight Arête,** HVS 5a (1995/99), takes the left edge following a groove, the slab above and the overlap with difficulty. ●**Diffusion,** VS 4b (1952-56), ascends direct to a stump in the middle of the wall, steps left to a ledge then uses the arete and holds on the right to gain the break. Move right to a kink and pull over. ●**Who let the Daylight In?** VS 4c (1995) avoids the arete by going direct to the kink. ●**Confusion,** VS 4b (1951), climbs the slab and right arête.

Herbacious Arboriculture Area: ●Another 8m right is a holly tree and behind it is the short corner crack of **Compulsion**, VD (1952), now in the clutches of a holly tree. ● The overgrown crack just to the right is **Herbacious Arboriculture**, VD (1956); ● right again is a cleaner crack with a small sentry-box; **Cartridge Crack**, HS 4b (1952-56), ● the right-hand corner of the recess is **Hole and Corner**, D (1935-51) and leads to a squirming finish behind the chock and finally:

Right-Hand Area

After the Auto da Fe area, the edge becomes less continuous, providing instead, several smaller, individual buttresses. These buttresses are as good as any on the edge, with the last one, Altar Crack Buttress, being one of the finest small outcrops in the Peak. The setting also changes, with close tree cover giving a unique and secluded ambience.

Wilkinson's Wall Area: Twenty metres right is a clean slab. On its left is:

110 **Chimp 'A'** V7 (E2 6c)
The fiercely undercut arête. Other short problems have been climbed here including ●**Bust a Gut**, HS 4b (1999), the dirty corner crack on the left and ●**Tapas,** V0 (5b), starting in the corner and going right to a flake. ●**Ribelin** HVS 5a (1999), is the crack and wall left again.

111 **Wilkinson's Wall** VS 4b ★   1951
8m   A leftwards-rising traverse on polished holds leads to ledges near the arête. Finish direct. ●**Cocaine Place**, HVS 5a (1979), is a variation on the left and up the arête to a bulge with a crack on its right-hand side. Use this and finish up the wall above. ● A squeezed-in line **Bodle's Bulge,** HVS 5a (1999), takes the overhang and wall just left again.

112 **Of Mice and Men** E5 6b   1992
8m   A poor route. The slab, 1m right of the last route, is climbed on small holds with no protection. It has no line, and blinkers are required, as an

114 **Shocking News** E1 5c   1983
6m   Start just right of the tree, which grows out of Hole and Corner. Finger-traverse right along the lower of two horizontal breaks until a hard move gains a ledge on the arête. Follow this on its left-hand side to the top. The direct start is 6a.

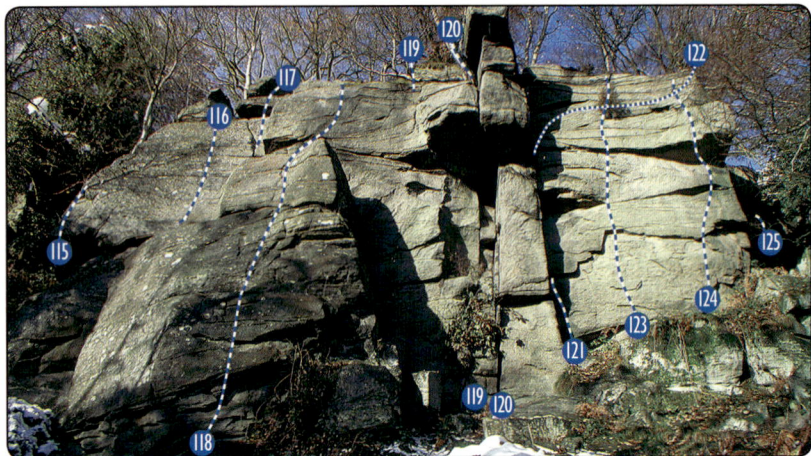

Roof Route Buttress

To the right the crag increases in stature with a large buttress that has a prominent slab leaning against the lower half.

115 Summertime E3 5c   1976
8m   An enjoyable solo up the bulging arête. Difficulties are short-lived.

116 Small Time E2 6b   1985
8m   After placing a high side-runner in Renshaw's Remedy, ascend the centre of the slab. The difficulties are sharp but quick.

117 Renshaw's Remedy VD ★★   1949-50
9m   The corner-crack is a brilliant easy climb.

118 Regular Route HVS 5a   1988
9m   Climb the centre of the leaning slab and finish up the upper wall. This finish is particularly serious and requires some blind faith. At the top of the grade.

119 Groove Route HVS 5b ★   1976
9m   A good climb, strenuous and technical. Ascend Roof Route to the overhang but move left to below a cracked shallow groove and climb this. Possibly 5c.

120 Roof Route HVS 5b ★★   1957-61
9m   Oh dear! This roof crack will have most climbing

wall fans running back to their cars, whereas the true gritstone connoisseur will savour it, bemoaning the fact that it is not another 50 feet longer. Amble up to the roof and enjoy the delights ahead. Many feel the route is E1 but as many again feel it is HVS.

121 Root Route S 4b ★★   1935-51
9m   The clean corner crack is a superb, strenuous challenge. Tough.

122 The Bush Off S 4b ★   2004
15m   Contrived, but good fun. From the ledge of Root Route (or gained from Roof Route at 4a), traverse right to finish up near the arête.

123 Dynasty E4 6a ★   1984
9m   Slightly artificial, but worthwhile. Start up a flake just right of Root Route and climb the wall to a small roof and good but awkward-to-place wires. Pull round this and trend rightwards to undercuts below a small overlap. Finish direct, up the slab above.

124 April Fool E2 5b ★   1976
7m   A route requiring a strong, confident approach. Climb the wall just left of the arête to an overhang and a scary finish.

125 Steph HVS 5a ★   1976
6m   The right side of the arête, with little protection and good bouldery moves. ● Highball V1

Do you climb Very Severe?

The grade of VS used to mean something. It meant Very Severe, and, at one time, stood for the hardest climbs in the country, climbs with the highest levels of exposure and technical difficulty. These days, however, VS ranks, for some, among the lower grades. But VS is still where climbing really kicks in, and, if mastered, a person can really be said to have reached a solid level of performance. Below is a good exam sheet of Very Severe climbs, a list to test the breadth of an aspiring tiger's experience. Have a go, and see if you can really make the grade – but beware – they are all tough tests of that grade.

The File, Higgar – a stern test of one of the most important skills of any gritstoner – the hand jam; **Central Climb**, Dovestones Tor – could this be your first experience of multi-pitch climbing? **Gingerbread**, Lawrencefield – bold technical climbing on polished rock will test footwork to the limit; **Every Man's Misery**, Burbage South – you won't learn how to thrutch at the wall, but by the time you get to the top of this fearsome slot, you will be able to wriggle with the best of them; **Obscenity**, Burbage North – in many ways, this is the definitive Very Severe; **Route 1**, Dovestone Tor – not only is this an exposed and testing climb, but it's also a 40-minute walk to get

there; **Oak Tree Wall**, Agden – introducing the old fashioned skill of using a tree to your advantage; **Scarlett's Crack**, Wharncliffe – a good history lesson in how well people climbed in 1931; **The Ingot**, Ladybower Quarry – an absolutely fearsome corner crack; steep and requiring a bold approach, despite great protection; **Saul**, Burbage South – it's about time you learned how to boulder (and, as it turns out, to be bold); **Skydiver**, Over Owler Tor – a small-looking climb, but a good place to find out if your biceps actually work; **Altar Crack**, Rivelin – the perfect layback. Place some gear from the sacrificial alter, take a deep breath, then GO! Strength dwindles as you get further and further from the gear, but somehow you've got to stop and get some more in.

Below: Steve Knightly and Mike Lee having a very severe time on Altar Crack (next page).
Photo: Nick Smith.

Altar Crack Buttress

The final buttress on the edge is an absolute cracker, with great routes on the finest of Rivelin grit. The first route starts on the left of the arête:

126 Altercation HVS 5a ★   1976
7m Follow a rightwards-trending crack on the left wall to a difficult finish on the arête. ● A more direct start is **Peccavi,** E4 5c (1986), which steps in from the left and follows the arête direct to gain the break at half-height. ● A direct finish utilising an obvious pocket in the headwall is **Deviation**, E2 6a (1985). Contrary to what the old guidebook led people to believe, the arête itself has only been top-roped on its right-hand side, at 6a, but is escapable.

127 Reredos HVS 5a ★   1981
12m An energetic and airy traverse from Altercation to Altar Crack.

The next two routes start off a ledge known as The Altar and both rely on the same protection.

128 New Mediterranean E5 6c ★★   1985
9m Excellent powerful climbing up the blank wall, with side-runners in Moolah. Starting from The Altar climb Moolah to the protection. Descend to The Altar, recompose yourself, then climb the left-hand line on the wall past burly undercut moves and a long stretch to a pocket.

129 Moolah E5 6b ★★   1988
9m A fierce, and relatively safe outing on the right side of the wall. Starting from The Altar climb the flake – committing – and hurriedly place micro-protection in a very thin slot up to the left. Continue direct to the top via some viciously thin pulls on a hold the size of a jigsaw piece.

130 Altar Crack VS 4c ★★★   1949-50
9m A brilliant climb, every bit as good a test of VS as The File on Higgar. Climb the sublime corner-crack by good jams or a thrilling layback to a good resting point near the top. Swing right to finish. ● For for a spot more pump, prolong the enjoyment by reversing Reredos to finish up the left arête, at HVS 5a.

131 Nonsuch HVS 5b ★★   1961-63
9m Gain the crack and follow it on jams and sloping holds. A flawless offering with an abundance of protection, but only if you have the stamina. If you haven't you will complain about the grade.

132 Grimace E5 6c ★   1989
9m Climb the wall with a testing sequence of pulls on pebbles until a strange blobby flake is reached. Take a deep breath and continue, using the arête on the right, to gain a break and welcome gear. Side-runners are used in Nonsuch at this grade and the route needs a direct finish.

133 Gettin' Kinda Squirelly E6 6b ★   1999
8m The right arête is climbed on its left-hand side, joining Grimace at the blobby flake. Scary, but technically fairly straightforward.

134 Vestry Chimney VD   1935-51

135 Too Much E2 6a ★ ★   1976
6m The desperate thin crack is a mini-classic and proves you can't get bored at a crag containing climbs like this. The route is protectable in all the right places, but still sees plenty of the classic British techniques of shaking, swearing and whimpering.

136 Altered V3 (6a)
The thin, final wall.

Important Access Note

Climbers must avoid the edge right of the Altar Crack area and respect its integrity as a nature reserve. Failure to do so will jeopardise all access to the rest of the crag. See access notes at start of section. The following routes are included for completeness.

After a few metres the rocks reappear at a lower level, as a short, slabby wall. **The Orthogonal**, S 4a (1952), is the left arête. **Double Flash**, HVS 5a (1999), is just right. **The Diagonal**, VD (1935-51), is the diagonal crack. **Seth's Slab**, VS 4b (1979), is 2m right; right again is **The Rattler**, VS 4c (1986). **Blue Sky Arête**, E1 5a (1997), is the right arête of the slab. The overgrown crack right again is **Crack-Crack**, VD (1961-63). Two short routes are on the buttress right again. **Towd Crack**, VD (1962), the crack up the front and **Big in Japan**, VS 4c (1985), the leftwards-slanting flake. Twenty metres further right is a buttress. **Lazy Arête**, VS 4c (1976-82), is the arête right of the corner - **Green Corner**, VD (1935-5I). **Pillar Crack**, S (1935-51), is the jamming crack. Ten metres right and at a higher

level, a short scrappy wall is topped by a large tree. **Ash Tree Corner,** S (1935-51), is the right-hand arête. **Ash Tree Flake**, VD (1964-76), starts below the tree and climbs direct to it. Approximately 200m further right is an isolated green wall. **Esoteric Wall**, HVS 5a (1984) is up the centre of the wall. **Smirk**, VS 4c (1985), is the slab to the left. **Pig Bag,** VS 4c (1984), is just right.

David Craig and Terry Gifford on Croton Oil, HVS 5a (page 179), one of the best routes on the fantastic Rivelin Needle, the showpiece of Rivelin Edge. Photo: Ian Smith.

Rivelin Quarry

OS Ref. SK 208849 to SK 288863   altitude 240m

by Paul Harrison

Located on the northern side of the Rivelin Valley and overlooking Rivelin Dam these long-neglected quarries are the western continuation of Rivelin Edge. Situated in pleasant woodland are a number of small buttresses of natural Rivelin Grit amongst numerous quarried rock bays.

freshly exposed and as a consequence occasionally fragile and sandy. The good rock is good, and surprisingly clean considering the lack of traffic. The best time to visit the quarries is during the spring or late autumn. Winter can also be rewarding, the quarried bays receive any available sunlight through the bare trees and provide a welcome haven on windy days. Facing south, it gets a lot of sun.

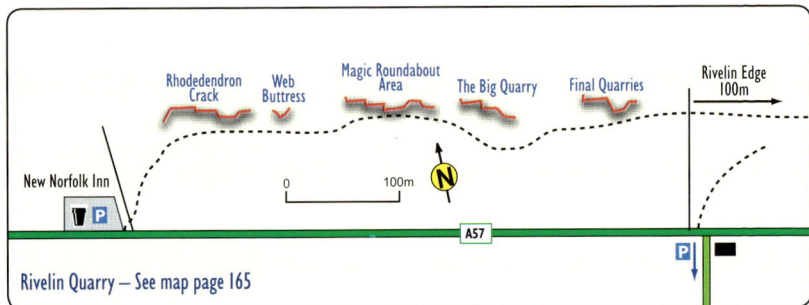

Rivelin Quarry — See map page 165

The Climbing

Smooth slabs and fearsome cracks are standard fare at the quarries, with many routes being sublimely technical rather than strenuous. Good footwork and crisp technique will pay dividends here. The quarry has a reputation for being vegetated. However, such routes that have been are demoted in the text, and ones given full treatment, can reasonably be expected to be climbable. **Routes:** There are about 100 routes, but a good proportion are overgrown. Easier ones have suffered worse, and the crag will be best enjoyed by Extreme leaders. Many of the harder routes have good protection. Belays at the top of the crag can be scarce, please take great care not to damage the farmer's fence or the wall that runs along the cliff-top. **Bouldering:** The Final Quarry has a handful of very good, hard problems, although these are probably best reached from Rivelin Edge.

Conditions and Aspect

The quality of the rock varies from exceptional to the worst imaginable, much of the gritstone being

Parking and Approach

Park behind the New Norfolk Arms pub (and make sure you have a pint when you're done), and follow the old paved quarry track running alongside the car park, then bear right and follow a path below the crag. Alternately, go left from the end of Rivelin Edge, beyond the Birch Buttress area. **Approach:** 5-15 minutes. **By bus:** The First 54 stops at the New Norfolk Arms pub.

Rhododendron Crack Area

In the first bay, there is a prominent wide crack.

❶ Rhododendron Crack El 5a ★   1960-61
18m An ungainly struggle up the unprotected chimney/crack leads to the sanctuary of the rhododendron at mid-height. Fight through this to the easier continuation crack. Solid 5.9 offwidth.
●**Entrapment**, E2 5b (1999), breaks out left to follow a flake and crack to finish leftwards over the overhang.

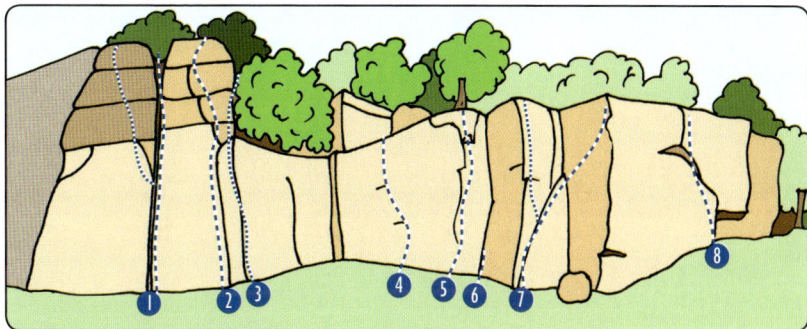

② **Ipecacuanha Groove** HVS 5a ★   1966
18m A worthwhile pitch up the steep corner-crack and left-leaning groove, finishing up the leftward-slanting cracks to the top.

③ **Ipecacuanha Crack** VS 4c   1965-66
12m Beginning at a higher level, follow a rib on the right to a ledge and continue up a wide crack-line exiting rightwards just below the top. ●**Luke Pie Stalker**, E1 5c (1997), is a short slab just right and ●**Digit Groove**, VS 4c (1966-76), the shallow groove right again.

④ **Earthboots** E6 6c ★ ★   1997
9m Superb technical climbing linking two well-spaced slots up the centre of the wall. Begin on the left and stretch or leap for the first slot and small cams, the second slot provides the key to the upper section and more protection from a small nut. Possibly 7a.

⑤ **Jack the Groove** E6 6c ★ ★   1988
9m In the right-hand side of the wall is an enticing smooth scoop, a formidable testpiece. The start is desperate, the overlapping finish just hard and bold.

⑥ **Syrup of Figs** VS 4c   1965-66
9m The sandy corner. ●**Altered Edge**, E2 5c (1997), climbs out rightwards up thin cracks to finish up the arête.

⑦ **Christopher Robin and Winnie the Pooh**
VS 4b   1966-76
11m The rightwards-leaning flake-crack leads to a birch tree in a gully. Cross the gully and step right onto the front of the next buttress to finish. ●**The**

Direct Finish, E1 5b (1980), goes boldly up the left-hand arête above the flake-crack.

⑧ **Honeypot** E2 5c   1980
10m Five metres right a thin crack leads up to an overlap; step left and follow another thin crack to the top. ●**Transit Strap**, S (1966-76), ascends the overgrown corner just right, then cleaner rock on the left. To the right and at a higher level is a series of broken walls and cracks. ●**G'Day**, E1 5a (1997), is the undercut, slabby arête. ●**Black Snow**, S (1997), is a flake above a grassy terrace on the right.

In the next bay to the right lies a clean slab with a fallen tree at its base.

⑨ **Sex Drive** E3 6b ★   1988
6m A short, intense series of moves up the left arête of the slab. The grade presumes a side-runner in the next route; the solo is E4 but watch the landing.

⑩ **Black Slab Arête** E1 6a ★   1980
6m Just right are two slim grooves. The left-hand one has an intricate start but holds on the next route are strictly out of bounds.

⑪ **Black Slab** HVS 5a ★   1965-66
7m The more amenable right-hand groove.

⑫ **The Two Toms** E1 5b ★   1983
7m Good clean fun up the steep slabby wall and leftwards-slanting crack.

⑬ **Piglet** HVS 5b ★   1966-76
7m The clean-cut corner; pleasant and well-protected.

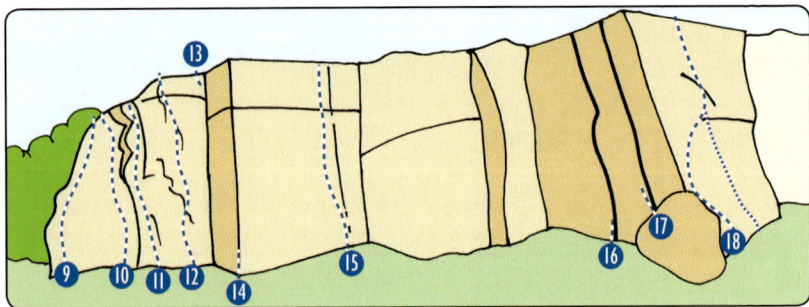

⑭ That's My Lot E8 7a ★ ★ 1999

7m Probably one of the ten purest pieces of grit-stone architecture – barely climbable. The arête is taken initially on its right-hand side culminating in a running layback to gain the obvious sloping hold level with the non-break. An out of control swing round the arête leads to an infinitely easier finish up its left-hand side.

⑮ Luxury Gap E2 5b 1983

7m The thin, dirty crack. ● **Jeremy Bear**, E1 5b (1980), is the appalling corner. The large detached flake to the right shows remnants of a rockfall. ● Two climbs, **Wilson,** VD (1965-66) and **Heath,** VD (1965-66), climb the left and right-hand lines respectively but are best avoided.

⑯ Dirty Dawn E2 5b 1983

11m The left-hand crack features a creaky flake.

⑰ Eutechtoid E2 5b 1980

12m The right-hand crack succumbs to a forceful approach.

⑱ Rabbit Buttress HVS 5a ★ 1966-76

12m Around to the right is a steep slab. From a pedestal up and left take a rightwards line to a flake in the centre of the slab, good holds lead directly to the top; a worthwhile pitch. ● The direct start, **Cup of Tea?** E4 6b (1999), crimps its way up the green slab making the most of the thin 'non-crack' to the right.

● To the right is an overgrown corner, the appropriately titled **Vegetated Corner,** VD (1966). ● Right again is a slightly impending buttress. **Dubious Arête,** VS 4b (1965-66), is the right-hand arête.

Web Buttress

Beyond a small grassy bank and 20m right is a small natural buttress hidden in the trees.

⑲ The Web S 1960-61

7m Start up the slanting crack in the left side of the buttress before swinging right beneath the prominent nose to a ledge. Step left and finish direct. ● **Web Arête** gives a good V2 (5c) on its right-hand side.

⑳ Spiders E2 5b 1999

7m The sharp arête to the right is climbed on its slabby right-hand side with a worrying move to gain the ledge; finish direct. ● The crack-line just right containing a tree gives a VD pitch.

㉑ Black Widow E2 5b 1999

7m From 3m up the VD crack launch rightwards up the steep undercut wall aiming for the prominent flake and then the top; committing. The blocky corner to the right can be climbed at VD but take care.

㉒ Funnel Web HVS 5b 1999

6m The arête right again is slabby at first before steepening to a bulging finish above the break.

Magic Roundabout Area

This is the large quarried bay 60m further right. The left-hand end of the bay is slowly disappearing beneath the undergrowth. At the extreme left is a thin leftwards-slanting crack, ● **Dustbin in Saigon,** HS (1966). ● **Jungle Way**, S (1965-66), is the twin cracks just right. ● **Mr Rusty**, HVS 5a (1966-76), branches right from the last route. ● **Polar Bear**, VS

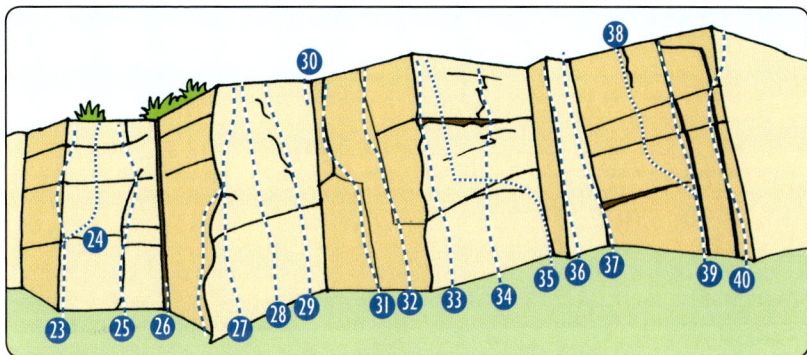

5a (1980), is the slab and wide crack. To the right is a large vegetated corner, ●**Herbaciousness**, VS 4b (1965-66), follows the left-hand line. ●If you thought that was bad, **Paraquat**, VS 4c (1965-66), starts as for Herbaciousness then follows the appalling right-hand line.

23 **And Now For Something Completely Different** E5 6b ★ 1987

11m The arête leads to the wide break and a peg runner up and right. Some insecure moves gain a blind flake on the left-hand side of the arête; launch up this to another break from where easier climbing leads to the top; stake belay.

24 **Snivelin Rivelin** E3 6a ★ 1999

11m Neat, technical slab climbing. Start as for And Now... to the wide break. Step right and begin a series of extending moves directly up the centre of the slab, peg runner, to the top and a stake belay.

25 **Pythonesque** E2 5c 1999

12m Start just right at a large block at the base of the steep slab. Step up and right into a thin crackline and follow it through a small overlap to a wide break. Stretch up the wall above to reach another thin crack and step left to finish; stake belay.

26 **Phallacy** VS 4b 1960-61

12m The vegetated corner. ●**Mr MacHenry**, E1 5b (1965-66), traverses out of the corner and goes left to finish up the arête.

To the right and standing forward is a large steep slab. When clean the routes here give some of the finest climbing in the quarry.

27 **Portnoy's Complaint** E2 5b ★ ★ 1971

13m The left arête of the slab is climbed on its right-hand side and gives excellent bold climbing on positive holds. Decent protection arrives only after the crux has been accomplished; finish rightwards on good holds. A much harder and bolder variation start is possible up the groove around to the left.

28 **Flex** E6 6c ★ ★ ★ 1987

13m An excellent high-standard slab climb to the right of the arête. Crimp desperately up the slab to the security of a peg runner in the thin break. The difficulties continue until a flake is reached allowing an easier, direct finish to be made; stake belay.

29 **The Final Overthrow of The Green Devil** E5 6b ★ 1987

13m The slab just right is only slightly easier thanks to the dubious work of the chisel. Difficulties ease after the peg runner allowing for an enjoyable finish up the leftward-slanting ramp; stake belay.

30 **E.B.M.C. I** VS 4b 1960-61

12m The vegetated corner. ●**Zebedee**, VS 4c (1966-76), escapes left up the ramp of the last route.

31 **Sore Thumb** HVS 5b 1978

14m The thin left-hand crack is followed to a tricky step left to a detached flake and wide crack. Continue up this to a ledge and finish direct.

32 Direct Comeback HVS 5b ★   1971

14m The more strenuous right-hand crack gives a cracking pitch with good protection. ● **Comeback** HVS 5a (1965), steps right beneath the ledge with a difficult mantelshelf onto the upper wall. ● **Go Away**, E3 6a (1987), balances right up the lower scoop to finish on the arête.

33 Stunt Children E4 6b   1987

14m The sharp arête right of Direct Comeback. Boulder out the desperate start to a diagonal break, peg runner up and right. Reach back left to the arête and follow it precariously to the top.

34 Cold School Closure E4 6c ★   1999

13m A direct start and finish to Dougal. Crimp desperately up the centre of the slab using two shallow one-finger pockets to reach the break. Balancey moves lead directly up to a reach for a big flat hold above the upper break. Move slightly left and finish up the crack in the headwall.

35 Dougal E2 6a   1971

14m An extending problem. From 3m up the corner to the right, traverse left along horizontal cracks into the centre of the wall, peg runner. Attempt the 'impossible span' to the thin break up and left and if successful, finish easily up the arête. ● The corner direct is **Menlove**, S (1960-61).

36 Crab Waddy E2 5b ★   1978

13m The clean arête to the right is climbed initially on the right side and finished on the left; great moves but be prepared for that under-protected feel.

37 Florence HVS 5a   1966-76

13m A sustained and worthwhile pitch up the large clean-cut corner containing two trees near the top. Exit with care.

38 Delivered E4 6a ★   2000/2005

13m Good steep climbing. Take the initial crack of Awkward Willy until a line of holds can be used leading diagonally leftwards onto the face. Make long moves up the face passing a peg and a ledge and finish direct up a thin crack. Originally finished right up the left arête of Awkward Willy's final groove, at a similar grade, and called Work in Progress.

39 Awkward Willy E2 5c ★   1978

12m A difficult start is followed by stubborn finger jamming up the left-hand crack. An awkward finish up a small groove completes the route.

40 Tree Surgeon E1 5b   1980

11m Starting from a slightly higher level, climb the awkward right-hand crack to a tree and finish more easily up the right side of the arête. Just right a short wall past a chimney provides two worthwhile problems; ● the central line is **Simmo's Wall**, V3 (6a), ● and the right arête is **Simmo's Arête,** V0+ (5b).

Ten metres right and beyond some broken rocks is a prominent corner capped by a large overhang. To its left is a smaller corner leading to a chimney. ● **Paul**, S (1966-76), gains a small slab to the left and climbs it rightwards to finish up a steep wide crack. ● **Basil**, S (1966-76), continues right and ascend a chimney. A direct start is also possible. ● **Bangkok Highway**, VS 4a (1966), takes a flake in the arête to the right with a potentially terminal finish up the stacked blocks above. ● **Layby**, HVS 4c (1966), is the large corner. ● A worthwhile variation start is possible up the flake in the right wall of the corner; **Hans So Low**, HVS 4c (1997). ● **Headache**, HVS 5a (1978), is the finger-crack in the wall to the right and the wider but looser continuation crack. ● **Biffo the Bear**, HVS 5a (1980), the arête right. ● **Brian**, HVS 5b (1966-76), is the open corner just right. ● **The Magic Roundabout**, E1 5c (1971), is a girdle of the area taking in the best of the vegetation.

Big Quarry

This large quarried bay hosts some of the finest climbs in the quarries. At the left-hand end is a grassy bank giving an easy way down, rising from this is a smooth blunt arête.

41 Feet Neet E5 6c ★★   1988

7m The arête gives a brilliant but quite desperate testpiece. Two pegs offer some encouragement.

42 Super Ted E5 6c ★   1987

10m An extending pitch up the faintest of thin cracks just 2m right of Feet Neet, peg runner.

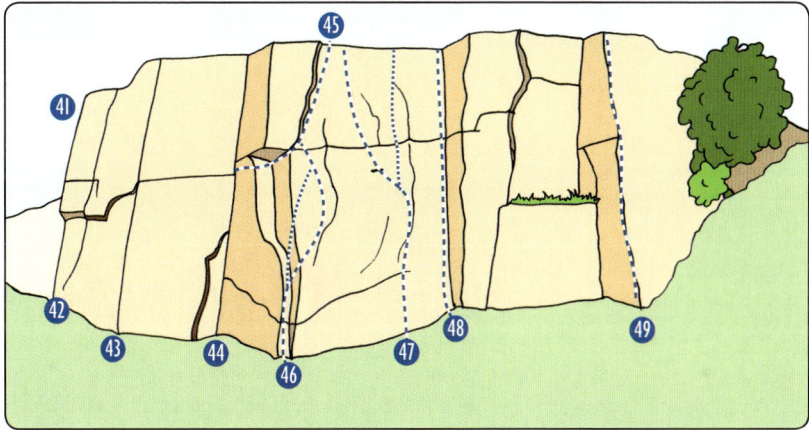

43 Teddy Bears' Picnic E4 6b ★ ★   1982

11m   A high-quality pitch and one of the best routes in the area. The compulsive thin crack-line in the wall right of Super Ted (peg runner) does not let up until the very top.

44 Dextrasol E1 5b ★   1966

11m   The large corner to the right is started on the left and finished on the right. A good sustained exercise and at the upper limit of its grade.

45 Glucose HVS 5a ★   1966-76

11m   Another challenging lead. Start as for Dextrasol and cross the slab on the right to reach a crack splitting an overhang on the right arête. Follow the crack to the top.

46 The Bear Necessities E5 6b ★ ★   1987

11m   An excellent test of nerve and ability up the elegant shallow groove just right. Start at the undercut left arête. Pull up the arête and step right immediately into the groove. Balance precariously up this, peg runner, to join and finish up the crack of Glucose. ● From the start it is also possible to continue up the arête stepping into the groove at the level of the peg, E3 5c.

47 Paddington E4 6a ★ ★   1980

12m   A splendid yet intense excursion up the steep, rippled slab. Follow the ripples up the right-hand side of the slab before trending leftwards to the prominent 'letter-box' and protection. Step up and trend slightly leftwards before climbing direct to the top. ●**Boira Aira**, E4 6a (1990), is an alternative finish taking a direct line from the letterbox.

48 Sucrose HVS 5a   1966

12m   The corner.

●**Jabba the Slut**, E2 5b (1997), is a harrowing experience directly up the blocky arête right of Sucrose, the highlight being a disconcerting à cheval sequence up the detached block at half-height. ●**Fructose**, E1 5a (1971), gains the grass terrace just right and from its left-hand side climbs a steep crack negotiating some detached blocks along the way. ●**Gormenghast**, HVS 4c (1960-61), is the next overgrown corner. Be prepared for some particularly soft moments.

49 Sweeter than Sugar E2 5b   1999

18m   An exciting and direct ascent of the prominent arête right of Gormenghast. Start up the slabby ramp directly beneath the arête and follow the arête initially on its left and then on its right in a fine position to the top. ●**Saccharine**, HVS 5a (1966-76), is the wall just right - anything but sweet. ● To the right and at right angles to the main wall is an orange cracked wall barely defying gravity, **Pervert**, HVS 4c (1960-61), climbs the left-hand crack-line to a dangerously loose finish.

Percy Bishton in action in the Big Quarry, on the first ascent of Jabba the Slut, E2 5b (previous page). The walls behind hold a fine collection of super-tough, though reasonably protected, climbs. Only the technically adept need apply here. Photo: David Simmonite.

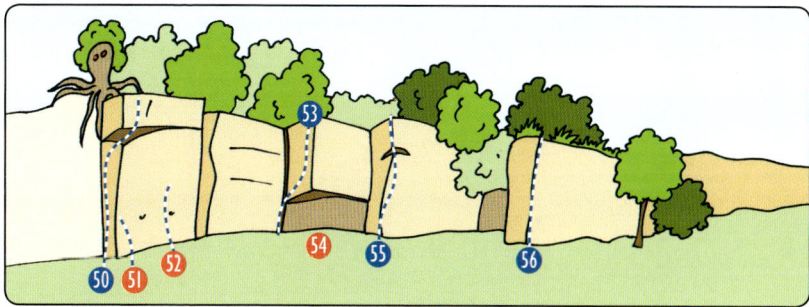

Final Quarries

A further 150m right is another quarried bay. It is worth noting that this bay can easily be reached from the left side of Rivelin Edge, only 150m away. The first routes are impressively dirty. ● **Fond Memories**, E4 6a (1999), is the narrow wall left of the dirty corner, (●**Manque**, HVS 4c 1960-61, the repulsive corner). ● **100 Acre Wood**, HVS 4c (1966-76), is the small corner and wall to the right. ● **The Forest**, VS 4b (1966-76), is the flake-crack to the right. ● **Sewerplumb,** HS (1966-76), surmounts the yellow overhang to the right or the left finishing leftwards or rightwards. Several problems have been done on the tottering walls to the right.

Pass by quickly to where the next route can be found in a small bay 15m right and beneath a large oak tree. ●**Heffalump**, S (1966-76), is the chimney beneath the mighty oak.

50 Jungle Formula E1 5c   1999
7m   Climb the arête on its left-hand side to the break. Step right and pull awkwardly through the overhang at a thin flake.

51 Iain's Arête V7 (6b)
The angular arête on its right, climbed dynamically.

52 Nik's Wall V11 (7a)
After many hours spent with a powerful microscope, you may notice that there are some crimps on this wall. When you learn that this wall has been climbed on these holds, you may well wish to readjust your concept of the possible. ● The right-hand rib/arête of the wall is **Non-Rib**, V6 (6b).

53 Cheeses of Nazareth E2 6a   1997
7m   The undercut arête 5m right is started by bridging out from the left. ● Highball V4. ● Continuing up the corner is **Wol**, HS (1966-76).

54 Happy Campus V8 (6c)
The superb direct start to the undercut arête. ● A sitting start to this is **No Class**, V9 (6c).

● The filthy corner 5m right is **Edward Bear,** VS 4c (1966-76).

55 Woozle Direct VS 4c ★   1997
8m   A neat little pitch up the clean arête to the right of Edward Bear starting on its left-hand side and finishing on its right. ● The large groove to the right is **The Webb**, S (1960-61); beware the 'tree monster'.

56 Gourmet HVS 5b ★   1977
7m   A pleasant aperitif up the blunt arête of the natural buttress just right, via a prominent hole. ● **Kanga**, S (1966-76), takes a wandering line up the four tiers of the broken buttress to the right, starting at a mossy slab up and right of Gourmet.

Private Buttress

OS Ref. SK 267874 altitude 240m

by Graham Sutton

A fairly recent discovery, this isolated and esoteric buttress lies in the trees down from Hallam View Buttress. The access situation is unknown but with the proximity of houses it's likely it would be refused, so keep a low profile. To approach, park as for Hallam View Buttress and walk down the road towards the pub and go into the trees on the left at the end of the crash barrier (stones missing in the wall). The crag is near the top of the hill close to the houses. Four routes exist: ●**Private Line**, S 4b (1999), up the left arête direct, finishing over the nose on the right. ●The central crack and overlap is **Midge It,** HS 4c (2004). ●The crack on the right moving right at the overlap and up is **A Right Crack**, S 4a (2004), ●and the short slab right again is **Slab & Tickle**, S 4a (2004), to the same finish.

Hallam View Buttress

OS Ref. SK 267874 altitude 250m

by David Simmonite

This isolated buttress is formed of good quality Rivelin gritstone in a woodland setting. Unfortunately, due to tree cover and a lack of traffic, the routes are lichenous and would require a brush. A shame really.

See map on page 156. From Rivelin Edge continue past The New Norfolk Arms on the A57 until after an S-shaped bend a small parking bay is seen on the left (about 4 cars). From here a metal gated track leads down into the trees and into the Wyming Brook Nature Reserve. Park here. The buttress is situated 120m back down the road on the opposite side in the trees and close to the road. **Access:** Unfortunately the owner has made it quite clear

that he does not wish people to climb there. The crag is included for completeness, which doesn't imply you have the right to climb there.

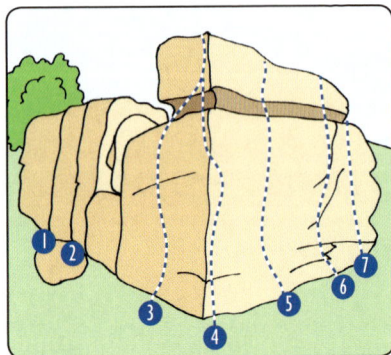

On the left-hand side of the buttress, is a chimney and left again two short wide cracks.

1 Undercover of the Nite S 4a 1999
5m The left-hand crack.

2 Incognito HS 4b 1999
5m The right-hand brother.

3 Flying Start E2 6a 1986
9m Right of the chimney and left of the arête, the green wall is climbed to finish as for the next route.

4 Heaven Can Wait E4 6a ★ 1983
9m A good but bold climb taking the prominent arête. Start on the right and gain a sloping shelf on the arête, step left and back right to a ledge. Compose yourself and finish direct over the overhanging nose. A wire hooked over a pebble protects (or not) the crux.

5 Chocolate Swastika E7 6c ★ ★ 1999
9m An excellent route and the ultimate esoteric gem that somehow climbs the unprotected and blank-looking wall to the right.

6 Wot's in Heaven HS 4a 1985
8m To the right is a curving flake nearly halfway up the buttress. Gain this and finish direct via a recess. Nice climbing when clean.

7 **Kitt** E2 5c   1986

8m   The wall immediately left of the right arête of the buttress is undercut. A quick pull gains a scooped ramp and a finish up the wall. ● The arête to the right is climbed on its right-hand side, **Kat**, HS 4b (1999). The crack immediately right is D. Walk off right at the top of the crack.

Burtinat Rock

OS Ref. SK 266873   **altitude 250m**

by David Simmonite

This obscure outcrop of rock is situated at the western end of Rivelin Dam. According to *Climbs on Gritstone, Further Developments in the Peak District* 1957, there was mention of a buttress towards the bottom of Wyming Brook, in the vicin-ity of the dam. '*Burtinat Rock - Further along the water-works road, towards the Norfolk Arms (on the A57) is a conspicuous face of quarried grit overlooking the river Rivelin. This gives some easy scrambling*'. After further exploration in the area, which did uncover some diminutive outcrops, the only crag that fitted the description is this one. It is likely that the crag was first discovered and climbed upon by the Sheffield University Mountaineering Club sometime in the 1940s and 50s. However, the only routes that were ascended were probably the easier lines on the flanks. These are left unrecorded for the desperate to rediscover. Park as for Hallam View Buttress but follow the metal gated track down into the trees and the nature reserve. After crossing a bridge, continue along the track until after 350m, after a bend, the crag is on the right.

Wyming Brook

OS Ref. SK 272862   **altitude 300m**

by David Simmonite

A scattering of isolated buttresses lying either side of a picturesque pine-scented wooded valley. The rock is rough Rivelin Grit forming everything from steep undercut buttresses to slabby cracks. But bear in mind that the place was 'recommended to enthusiasts of esoterica' in the last guide and in most cases, this still holds true.

Conditions and Aspect
Most of the routes are lichenous and the tree-cover, coupled with other vegetation, keeps many of them wet in all but the driest of weather. Three days or so of fine weather is usually sufficient for most of the routes to dry although some are more open and hence come into condition more quickly. With a little patience, and sometimes a brush, there are good quality routes waiting to be climbed. The valley sides face east/west, but the rocks get little sun.

The Climbing
A scattering of discreet little buttresses containing lots of steep cracks and face climbs from Diff to E6.

Parking and Approach
The road (Redmires Road) linking Sheffield to Redmires Dam descends into a dip at the point it crosses Wyming Brook roughly 1.5km from Lodge Moor (and approximately 1km past The Three Merry Lads public house). From there a dirt track, the waterworks road, leads down the valley to the right and in the direction of Rivelin Dams. Plentiful parking is available close to the road junction and in the summer the area is a busy venue for picnickers down by the brook. **By Bus:** The First 51 bus runs at frequent intervals from Sheffield City centre to a terminus at Lodge Moor, from where the valley may be reached by an easy 20-minute walk along Redmires Road. Occasionally, the bus continues to Wyming Brook, check with the bus company.

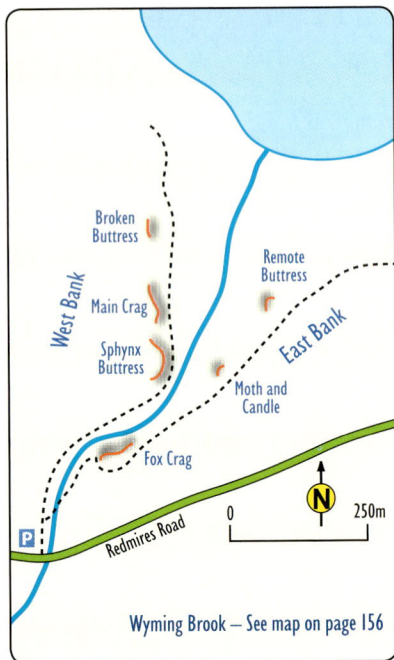

Wyming Brook — See map on page 156

The West Bank

Brook Wall: The first buttress of substance roughly 250m down from the main road. This pocketed wall is 10m or so above and left of the dirt track just past the start of a low gritstone wall running along the right-hand side of the dirt road. ● **Brookside**, HVS 5b is the centre of the wall via small pockets to a slopey finish. ● **Brooklyn Bell**, VS 5a, is the right arête of the wall finishing direct over a small roof (both 1996).

Flake Buttress: This is 40m right, with an obvious chimney splitting its steep face.

① Green Chimney VS 4b   1940s-70s
8m The main chimney. Often wet.

② Hawkline E1 5b   1976
8m To the right; a steep flake leads to difficult moves on the bulging wall above. Good when clean.

Sphynx Buttress: Another 40m right.

③ Sphynx HS 4b ★   1940s-70s
8m The slabby nose of the buttress is climbed from its base before the final overhang is taken on the left. ● **Tish**, HS 4b (1991), goes diagonally left from the start of Sphynx to gain a ledge. Finish up the scoop.

A chimney splits the small and compact buttress to the right.

④ Diff Arête S 4a   1940s-70s
6m Ascend the stepped left arête, beginning on the left. Upgraded and now the name doesn't fit.

⑤ The Green Man and the March of the Dancing Bungalows E2 5c ★   1996
9m Start up the rib to the right, and left of the groove of the following route. Make a tricky pull through a small overlap and continue up to a wide break. Finish directly up the scary slab above.

⑥ The Ent From Kent VS 4c   1983
9m Climb the hanging groove just right to a break. Move leftwards along this, bisecting The Green Man… to an awkward step-up onto the ledge of Diff Arête and the same finish. ● **Diff Chimney**, D (1940s-70s), is a grovel up the chimney to the right. ● **Freedom**, E1 5b (1997), is the arête to the right, using a tiny flake.

Main Crag

To the right and across a wide gully is an impressive steep wall. This wall provides arguably the best routes at the Brook when clean.

⑦ Silent Witness E6 6b ★   2001
8m At the left-hand end of the wall, to the left of Half Man, Half Cake is a roof. Surmount it and finish directly up the arête. Quality when clean.

⑧ Half Man, Half Cake E4 6b ★ ★   1997
8m Excellent pumpy climbing that stays dry in the rain. Levitate up the overhanging face just left of Green Child on small edges to a hard reachy lock for an undercut pocket. Move up to a break and continue, trending leftwards, via a thin flake, to a tree belay on a wide ledge at the top.

He's half man! He's half cake! He's Half Man Half Cake, E4 6b, (opposite page). Photo David Simmonite.

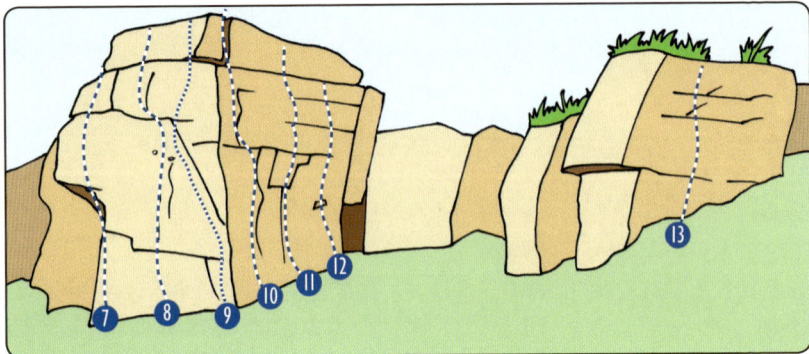

9 Green Child E2 5c ★ 1976
8m Just right, the steep crack is climbed to its end, before a finish can be made up the rounded wall.

10 Seasickness E3 5c ★ 1983
11m Start up the very thin crack around to the right and follow it for 5m. Move left to the base of a second thin crack and climb it to a rounded finish.

11 Altitude Sickness E5 6b ★ 1989
10m Ascend the bold and strenuous overhanging wall to the right of Seasickness.

12 'ere come Fudgie! E4 6b 1997
10m The steep wall just right of Altitude Sickness starts at an obvious jug and continues direct. The name may prove apt for the nervous.

The next buttress has an overhang at 5m and a dirty slabby upper section. ● For **Fragile**, HVS 5b (1976), equip yourself with a spade and climb the overhang followed by the slab masquerading as the Hanging Gardens of Babylon. ● **Wallrush**, HVS 5b (1976), is a better route; to the right again; climb the right wall to a ledge then finish up the arête.

13 Placid House E6 6c ★★ 1997
8m A fine addition and the hardest at the Brook, forges a way up the fingery wall right of Wallrush. A powerful undercut start allows access to the thin scary wall, aiming for the long pocket just below the top. ● **Sleeper**, VS 4b (1984), is the line of flakes at the end of the wall.

Broken Bottle Buttress: This is 70m right.

14 Wet Sunday VD 1940s-70s
9m The left arête of the buttress.

15 Dumbo's Ringpiece E3 6a ★ 1983
9m Climb the steep crack and bulge to the right, with a desperate rounded pull at the finish. A fitting name – just take a look at the finish.

16 The Man in the Woods E4 6a ★ 1983
9m This difficult route takes the right-hand side of the arête on broken flakes to a break and finishes up the wall right of the arête. A good route when clean.

The East Bank

Foxholes: For climbs on the East Bank, a path leaves the car parking area and crosses the brook at stepping-stones. The first rocks, **Fox Crag**, are seen on the left, past the stepping stones, and are reached in a couple of minutes. The rocks are often green and dirty, but a couple of routes stay reasonably clean. From right to left, the routes are: ● **Fungi**, HVS 4c (1999), the right arête; ● **Lost World**, VD (1940s-70s), the corner chimney; ● 5m left again is **Green Crack**, D (1940s-70s), a slabby crack that if clean would be a quality route on any other crag (how many times have I said that?) Unfortunately, it is often dirty and damp but fun anyway. ● For **C.U.R.S.E,** VS 5b (1999), Climb the Undercut Rib, Short and Esoteric. A few metres left and just right of a corner is a dogleg crack. ● **Three Sad Old Men**, HVS 5a (1999), gains the crack directly, steps right

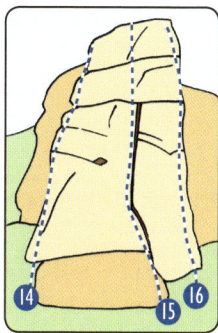

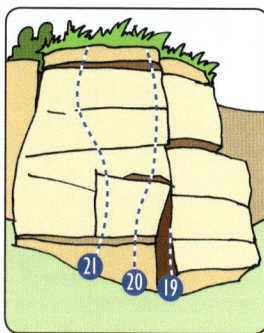

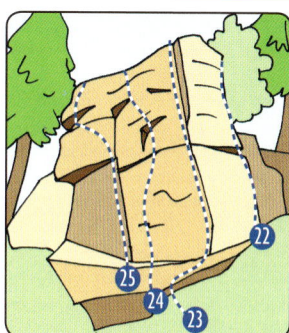

and pulls over the overlap to finish up the rib. ●A good variation start up the blunt arête to the right is **The Fox Mulder Start,** V2 (6a). ●The corner itself is **Fox Hole Corner,** VS 4c (1940s-70s).

Matador Buttress: Gain the clifftop path and continue for 300m. Down right is an overhanging wall. The top of the buttress can also be identified as a large flat, square slab with a pine tree to its right.

17 **Blind Matador** E2 5c   1983
9m   The short crack left of the chimney is climbed to a final pull on bilberry bushes. Alternatively a rope can be left over the top, but why miss out on the fun?

18 **Bidet Wall** E4 6a   1999
9m   Left of Blind Matador, make reachy, unprotected moves (6b for the short) up the lower wall to gear in a break at half height. The finish is easier.

Moth and Candle Buttress: Two hundred metres further along the path, the top of a steep wall can be seen. Descend opposite where a low drystone wall on the right of the path finishes and a fence begins.

19 **Moth and Candle** VS 4b   1983
7m   The right-hand corner crack.

20 **House of Fun** E3 5c   1984
7m   In the centre of the wall is a short crack. Climb the wall right of this to finish up the arête.

21 **Mansion of Invention** E4 6a ★   1983
8m   Climb the short crack then move left to a thin crack, which leads to small holds. Reach right from

these to a slot and the finish. ●The filthy crack on the left is **Death of a Bee,** VS 4b (1983).

Remote Buttress: This is 100m right.

22 **Remote Romance** VS 4c   1984
12m   The upper right-hand arête. ●The wall to the left is **Illuminated,** E3 6a (2005), with unprotected climbing leading to a break at 6m and an easier finish.

23 **Backwater Barracudas** E3 6a ★   1983
12m   The fine arête leads to a well-positioned groove. ●The sloping shelf gives a V2 (5c) traverse.

24 **More Pricks than Kicks** E5 6b   1985
12m   The overhanging wall; committing and strenuous. Start in the centre of the wall, just right of the square-cut overhanging groove, at a small jug. Make hard moves up and right, then go back left to a direct finish through the horrific rounded wilderness.

25 **Samuel Beckett was Right** E4 6a   1983
12m   Follow the blank slab left to a square-cut overhanging groove which in turn leads to a ledge. Finish over the bulge from the left of the ledge.

The Diamond: Another 60m on is an isolated hidden slab. ●**Day-Glo,** E1 5a (1996), takes flakes on the right, finishing with a sprint up the left-hand side of the arête.

26 **Esoteric Slab** E4 6b ★ ★   1984
12m   Climb the centre of the fine slab via an obvious line of small holds to a committing finish. Hard for the short and unprotected for all so don't fall off.

First Ascents

1928-1930 Scarlett's Chimney, Jonathan's Chimney, David's Chimney Harry Scarlett, 'Ginger' Wylie

1933 Ulex Byron Connelly, Bert Smith **Layback Crack** Eric Byne, Jack Macleod **Face Climbs Nos. 1 and 2** Frank Burgess, George Walker

1935 South-West Corner (Original Route) (2 points of aid) Eric Byne, Clifford Moyer *The aid was used on the bulge below The Notch. FFA Joe Brown, 1954.*

1949-50 Ebenezer's Staircase, Altar Crack R A (Dick) Brown, Donald Wooller, Frank Fitzgerald, John Clegg *Altar Crack was impressive for the time.*

1949-50 Renshaw's Remedy J Renshaw

1950s Brown's Unmentionable, The Inverted Arête Dick Brown

1950 Feb Shelf Rib Dick Brown, Peter Wilkinson

1950 Mar The Spiral Route Donald Wooller, Dick Brown, J Renshaw *The first proper lead of The Needle.*

1950 Nov Shelf Wall, Crack One, Crack Two Dick Brown and friends

1951 May 23 Caveman's Caper J Lakey, R Lowrey

1951 Oct 24 Corner Crack D E W White **Confusion** D E W White W Sellars, Dick Brown

1951 Wilkinson's Wall Peter Wilkinson

pre-1951 Birch Buttress, Birch Crack, White House Crack, The President's Crack, Senator's Gully, Rivelin Slab, Angle Crack, Isolation, Temple Crack, Tree Crack, Gardener's Pleasure, Deep Chimney, The Crevice, Lichen Slab, Left Holly Pillar Crack, Right Holly Pillar Crack, Hole and Corner, Root Route, Vestry Chimney, The Diagonal, Green Corner, Pillar Crack, Ash Tree Corner All appeared in the 1951 guidebook.

1942-52 Hyde's Mantelshelf Tony Hyde

1952 Mar 12 Red's Slab Dick Brown, D E W White **Beginner's Buttress** Peter Wilkinson, D E W White, Colin Whittle **Compulsion** D E W White **The Orthogonal** Dick Brown

1952-56 Kremlin Krack, Diffusion, Cartridge Crack

1953 Mar 11 Croton Oil (5 points of aid) Dick Brown, Donald Wooller, Frank Fitzgerald (all led) *Named after a foul tropical purgative. Climbed free in 1963 by Pete Crew and Oliver Woolcock; a magnificent achievement. Crew, who had no driving licence, regularly used to borrow Woolcock's car, and whenever stopped by the police always gave Woolcock's details. Week's later Woolcock would receive summons for offences he knew nothing about.*

1953 Mar 25 Sweet Aloes (Easy Picking) Donald Wooller, Dick Brown, Frank Fitzgerald, D Abbott *'About half of this (in the centre) was found to be unclimbable without aid. Con-*

sequently 8 pitons were used, although it is now ascertained that all of these are not really necessary. The start and finish of the route were climbed clean, and proved to be of hard V.S. standard'. 1955. Led free in 1976.

1953 May All Hallows Dick Brown, Frank Fitzgerald **The Lurcher** Frank Fitzgerald

1953 April Holly Gut Dick Brown, Frank Fitzgerald, Donald Wooller

pre-1953 Early routes on Bell Hagg were first climbed or recorded by members of the Sheffield University Climbing Club, including, T Hyde, J Sargeant, J Renshaw, D Sampson, R A Brown, D Wooler, G Suddaby F Fitzgerald, C Whittle and R Lowry. J W Puttrell, Henry Bishop, C D Yeomans, Harry Scarlett and others, who undoubtedly made ascents here.

1955 May Jonad Rib Glyn Owen *A previous claim by W Sellars on October 24th 1951 was not considered valid. Giving the route Very Difficult didn't help!*

1956 Ray Crack Al Wright, Dave Gregory **Seville Flake, Kellogg Corner, Herbaceous Arboriculture** Al Wright

1957-61 Roof Route Joe Brown

1957-63 Banner's Ridge Hugh Banner **Leo, Church Spire, Steptoe** Len Millson **Hangman's Arête, Denture, Dribble**

1958 Feb 15 Blizzard Ridge Allan Austin *Peter Stone added a direct start in 1998.*

1960-61 Rhododendron Crack, The Web, Phallacy, E.B.M.C.I, Menlove, Gormenghast, Pervert, Manque Barry Webb, Mike Rodgers, Charlie Curtis

1961-63 Rodney's Dilemma Rodney Wilson **Ukase, Pious Flake** Al Wright **Nonsuch** Alan Clarke, Les Gillott

1961-63 Twister, Solitaire, Crack One, Crack Three

1962 Fumf, Towd Crack Jack Soper **Face Climb No. 1.5** Geoff Milburn and friends **The Wigg** Len Millsom

1962-63 Left Edge Pete Crew, Al Wright **Toytuss** Clive Rowland **Rodgers' Arête** Mick Rodgers

1963 May The Brush Off Pete Crew (solo) *For over 20 years the hardest climb on the edge, it was named after an obscure sandstone route. Before its first ascent many people had top-roped it but were unwilling to lead the route. However, news that Paul Nunn had top-roped it easily, spurred Crew into action. Even so, rumour has it a loop of rope preceded him during his solo ascent.*

1963 Oct Oversight Geoff Milburn

1963 Mantelshelf Wall Clive Rowland **The Corner** Paul Nunn **Oliver's Twist** Oliver Woolcock **The Hand Traverse, Griff's Variant** Brian Griffiths **Mantelpiece** Rod Brown

1964 Birch Al Wright, G. Rogan

1965 Comeback Al Parker

1965-66 Ipecacuanha Crack, Jungle Way, Herbaciousness, Paraquat Al Wright **Heath, Dubious Arête** Al Wright, Brian Griffiths **Wilson, Syrup of Figs, Black Slab** Brian

Griffiths, Al Wright **Mr MacHenry** Ted Howard

1968 **Fuhrerbuch, Jan** Al Evans **Varappe** J Goodison *This may be the same as Alkaline.*

1966 **Ipecacuanha Groove** Gerry Rogan, Al Wright **Vegetated Corner, Lay-By, Sucrose** Al Wright, Brian Griffiths **Dustbin in Saigon, Bangkok Highway, Dextrasol** (1 point of aid) Brian Griffiths, Al Wright. *A similar line was claimed, again with aid, as Gladiator Groove by Al Parker, Eddie Thurell in 1967. FFA of Dextrasol by Bob Bradley, 1980.*

1967 **Fructose** Paul Nunn

1969 June **Wobbly Wall** Ed Drummond

1970s **Birch Bark, Left Under** Black and Tans Club *Both lines were claimed again in the 1990s.*

1971 Apr **Portnoy's Complaint** Paul Nunn, Al Parker

1971 **Magic Roundabout** Clive Rowland, Brian Griffiths **Dougal, Direct Comeback** Clive Rowland *Dougal done with some aid. FFA 1982 by Giles Barker.*

1940s to 1970s **Green Chimney, Sphynx, Diff Arête, Diff Chimney, Wet Sunday, Green Crack, Lost World, Fox Hole Corner** *The rocks have been visited occasionally by local climbers, mainly members of the Sheffield University Mountaineering Club probably led by David Sampson, since the 1940s. It is likely that many of the moderate lines were climbed during this period, including the easier cracks on Fox Crag, reclimbed and named for this guide by the author.*

1964-76 **The Flying Pig Variant** Rod Brown **Men Only, Green Gold, Alkaline, Alkali, Ash Tree Flake**

1966-76 **Digit Groove, Christopher Robin and Winnie the Pooh, Piglet, Zebedee, 100 Acre Wood, Sewerplumb, The Forest, Heffalump, Wol, Edward Bear, Wozzle, Rabbit Buttress, Kanga** Al Wright, Brian Griffiths (varied leads) **Transit Strap** Al Wright, Ray Fish, G.Panton **Florence** Al Wright, Ted Howard

1976 Mar 26 **Outsider** Bill Briggs, Andy Parkin **Jade** Andy Parkin, Bill Briggs *Jade was superseded by Exit.*

1976 Mar 28 **Groove Route, Altercation** Bill Briggs, Andy Parkin **April Fool, Too Much** Andy Parkin, Bill Briggs **Steph** Bill Briggs (solo)

1976 Mar 29 **Auto da Fe** Andy Parkin, Bill Briggs *They had top-roped it a few days previously and returned, anxious to get it led. They only had a limited amount of time on the day and so an alarm clock was taken to the crag. It steadily drizzled during the ascent and to cap it all the alarm went off while Parkin was fighting to the top.*

1976 Apr 1 **The Eye** Bill Briggs, Pete O'Donovan

1976 June 18 **Easy Picking** Steve Bancroft, John Allen *FFA of Sweet Aloes.*

1976 Mar **Hawkline, Green Child** Andy Parkin, Bill Briggs

Fragile Dick Swinden (solo) **Wallrush** Dave Morgan (solo)

1976 **Plague** Andy Parkin, Bill Briggs (1 point of aid) *The 'bolt' appeared in the '60s. FFA in 1981 by Johnny Woodward, Ian Maisey, Andrew Woodward. A chipped hold appeared in 1988 and has since been filled in.* **Brigg** Bill Briggs, Andy Parkin **Reprieve** Dave Mithen (solo) **Summertime** Dave Morgan (solo)

1977 **Jelly Baby** Chris Addy, Duncan Munroe **Gourmet** Al Evans

1978 Aug **Sore Thumb, Crab Waddy** Tony Sawbridge, Nigel Halliday **Awkward Willy** Nigel Halliday Chris Parkin **Headache** Chris Parkin, Nigel Halliday

1979 **Caravaggio** Mark Stokes **Cocaine Place** Dave Mirfin, Paul Marsden **Seth's Slab** N Shaw (solo)

1980 **Fringe Benefit** Graham Parkes, Nigel Baker

1980 Apr **Eutechtoid** Bob Bradley, Graham Parkes **Honeypot** Bob Bradley, Mike Browell, Steve Worthington **Jeremy Bear** Mike Browell, Steve Worthington, Bob Bradley **Paddington** Bob Bradley, Mike Browell **Biffo the Bear** Mike Browell, Bob Bradley

1980 May 10 **Polar Bear** Mike Browell, Bob Bradley **Tree Surgeon** Bob Bradley, Jeremy Frost, Geoff Brown, Mike Browell

1981 Sept 23 **Reredos** Johnny Woodward, Ian Maisey

1981 Oct 14 **Double Decker** Johnny Woodward (solo)

1981 **Short but Thick** Chris Plant **Ring of Roses** Chris Craggs, Nigel Baker

1976-82 **Angle Rib, Twin Hole, Lazy Arête**

1982 Sept 7 **Better Late Than Never?** Phil Baker

1982 May 13 **Teddy Bears' Picnic** Bob Berzins, Giles Barker, Graham Hoey

1983 March 12 **Only Human** *Climbed by Roger Greatrick, Andy Kassyk and named Alternative Seven. However, a peg was placed for protection, and the route was dismissed by locals and the peg removed by Chris Craggs. It was led clean by John Allen in 1988, who renamed the route.*

1983 July 28 **The Ent From Kent** Paul Mitchell (solo) **Seasickness** Andy Barker

1983 Aug 8 **Dumbo's Ringpiece** Andy Barker **The Man in the Woods** Paul Mitchell *Originally Mike Browell cleaned Dumbo's Ringpiece ready to do it and gave out an horrendous description in the 1980 guidebook to keep people away, but Barker and Mitchell saw through it.*

1983 Aug 10 **Blind Matador, Moth and Candle, Death of a Bee** Paul Mitchell (solo)

1983 Aug 11 **Mansion of Invention** Andy Barker **Samuel Beckett was Right** Paul Mitchell **Backwater Barracudas** John Allen (solo) *Allen added a direct start in 1986.*

1983 Mar **Exit, Der Komissar** Roger Greatrick, Chris Rowe

1983 Apr **White Out** Bob Bradley, Graham Hoey **The Tempest** Graham Hoey, Nic Hallam **Shocking News** Nigel Slater (solo)

1983 July 28   **The Two Toms**   Mark Bartley, Paul Harrison, Neil Harrison

1983 Aug 4   **Luxury Gap, Dirty Dawn**   Paul Harrison, Neil Harrison

1983 Dec 26   **Trivial Pursuits 2**   Chris Hardy (solo)

1983 Dec 31   **The Final Overthrow of The Green Devil**   Nigel Slater, Alistair Ferguson   *Chipped by some fool at a later date!*

1983   **Heaven Can Wait**   Keith Sharples

1984 Apr   **Angst**   Ian Riddington   **Dynasty**   Keith Sharples, Nigel Slater, Ian Smith

1984 June 7   **Sleeper**   Doug Kerr (solo)   **Remote Romance**   Doug Kerr, Steve Adderly

1984 Sept   **House of Fun, We're Only Here for the Smear**   Paul Harrison, Neil Harrison

1984 Oct 2   **Esoteric Slab**   Paul Harrison (solo)   *Martin Veale may well have made an ascent of Esoteric Slab before this date.*

1984 Nov   **Europe After Rain**   John Allen (solo)   **Esoteric Wall**   Doug Kerr, Paul Harrison

1984 Dec   **Birth of Venus, Crafty Cockney, Long Hot Winter, Parallel Universe**   John Allen, Nick Stokes

1985 Feb   **Small Time**   John Allen   **Big in Japan**   Neil Harrison, Paul Harrison

1985 Mar 5   **The Terminator**   John Allen   **Party Animal**   John Allen, Nick Stokes

1985 Mar 7   **I'm Back**   Nick Stokes (solo)

1985 Mar 12   **New Mediterranean**   John Allen, with Nick Stokes

1985 Apr   **Palm Charmer**   Paul Harrison, Neil Harrison   **Pig Bag**   Paul Harrison (solo)

1985 June 29   **More Pricks than Kicks**   Andy Barker (unseconded)

1985   **Deviation, Smirk**   Doug Kerr   **Wot's in Heaven**   Malc Baxter, Keith Ashton   **Boulder Club**   Greg Griffiths

1986 Mar 27   **The Rattler**   Cliff Mathews, Kath Krzystowski

1986 May 28   **Declaration**   Dave Pegg   *Due to the loss of a pebble or two, this route probably didn't get a second ascent until 1999 by Peter Robins.*

1986 July 1   **Big Al**   Neil Stokes, John Allen   *Despite having hardly climbed for years, Neil produces one of the hardest routes on the edge, albeit with a side-runner. In 2000 Nik Jennings did the deed and straightened out the route with a desperate direct start and without the side-runner. Jennings is not sure that he was the first to do this.*

1986   **Flying Start, Kitt**   John Hesketh

1986 Sept   **Jaded**   Graham Hoey, Nic Hallam   **Peccavi**   Keith Sharples (solo)

1987 Mar 31   **Stealing the Misanthrope's Wallet**   Nick Stokes, John Allen   **The Caress of the Blubbery Hand**   Nick Stokes, Rob Allen, John Allen

1987 Apr   **Interminable Drizzle, Invisible**   John Allen   **The Bear Necessities**   Mike Lea, Nigel Prestidge

1987 June 16   **And Now For Something Completely Different**   Bill Gregory, Paul Guttridge

1988 July 12   **Burglar in My Bedroom**   Paul Mitchell, Paul Evans

1988 Dec 7   **Garibaldi Twins**   Paul Mitchell, John Allen

1988 Mar 17   **Moolah**   John Allen

1988 Mar 18   **Regular Route**   John Allen, Nick Stokes

1987 Sept 30   **Go Away, Stunt Children**   John Allen, Mark Stokes   **Flex**   Mark Stokes

1987 Oct 14   **Moontan**   John Allen, Mark Stokes

1987   **Super Ted**   Paul Pepperday, Dave Candin

1988 Mar   **Feet Neet**   John Allen

1988   **Sex Drive, Jack the Groove**   Mark Stokes

1989   **Altitude Sickness**   John Allen (solo)

1980s   **The Noose**   Dominic Lee

1990 Sep   **Mad as Cows**   Matthew Hill, James Merryman

1990 May   **M and S, No Words to Say**   Toby Spence

1990   **Bora Aira**   Nick Dixon, Andy Meek

1991 Jan 6   **Moss Side**   David Simmonite

1991 Mar 24   **Ausfahrt**   Chris Craggs, Colin Binks, Mike Appleton, Jim Rubery, Dave Gregory

1991 Summer   **Green Thinking**   Paul Mitchell

1991 Dec   **Tish**   David Simmonite, Alex Thackway (both solo)   **Dim 'n' Dismal, Haggled**   David Simmonite (solo)   **Marvin Haggler**   David Simmonite, Roy Bennett

1992 June 6   **Of Mice and Men**   Adrian Berry

1992 Dec   **End of the Road**   David Simmonite, Dave Vincent

1994 June 14   **Don't Birch the Doc**   Graham Hulley, Tony Boreham

1994 Summer   **Birch Branch**   Gordon Mason, Bruce Goodwin   **Silver and White**   Brian Middleton, Gordon Mason

1995 Sept 3   **Daylight Arête, Who let the Daylight in?**   Gordon Mason, Dave Gregory   *A couple of routes climbed on the very confusing Diffusion Slab. The descriptions for the routes on this slab seem to have been totally changed in the last two guidebooks from the original ones. Daylight Arête and Who let the Daylight in? are two straightened out versions of Diffusion. The team here also claimed a well-named route here called Confused? which in fact is Confusion. Confused? The situation is now defused. Daylight Arête was straightened out further with a direct start in 1999 by David Simmonite.*

1996 Summer   **Brooklyn Belle, Day-Glo**   Paul Harrison   **Brookside, The Green Man and the March of the Dancing Bungalows**   Paul Harrison, Neil Harrison

1997 Feb   **Cheeses of Nazareth**   Jon Fullwood (solo)   **Woozle Direct**   Andy Crome (solo)   **Blue Sky Arête**   Peter Goult, John Wilkins

1997 Feb 28   **Earthboots**   Andy Crome

1997 Mar 12   **Altered Edge**   Percy Bishton, Ian Loombe

1997 Mar 21   **Luke Pie Stalker**   Ian Loombe   **So Low, Black**

Snow David Simmonite **Jabba the Slut** Percy Bishton *The routes were followed by either Bishton, Loombe or Simmonite*
1997 Mar 28 **G' Day** David Simmonite (solo)
1997 Apr **Placid House** Andy Crome **'ere come Fudgie!** Jon Fullwood
1997 May 13 **Half Man, Half Cake** Percy Bishton, David Simmonite
1997 June 1 **Freedom** David Simmonite
1998 Feb **Trivial** Percy Bishton, Ian Loombe, David Simmonite **Clinker** Percy Bishton
1998 Nov **Jumpey Wooller** Niall Grimes, Pete Hulley *Also climbed and claimed (Visions in Tan) by Andy Crome two days later, ouch!* **Milena** Andy Healey, Mark Turnbull
1999 Jan 24 **Money for Old Rope** Percy Bishton, Ian Loombe
1999 Feb 11 **Bidet Wall** Percy Bishton, Ian Loombe
1999 Feb **Takes the Biscuit** Peter Robins
1999 Mar **Bodles Bulge** Percy Bishton, Lucy Atkinson or Julia Bodle **Gettin' Kinda Squirelly** Mark Hundleby
1999 Apr 4 **Grim Fandango** David Law, Warren Trippett
1999 April 4 **Entrapment** Paul Harrison, Mike Snell
1999 April 6 **Pythonesque** Paul Harrison, Mike Snell, Mick Carr **Snivelin Rivelin** Paul Harrison, Mike Snell
1999 April 9 **Sweeter than Sugar** Paul Harrison, Mike Snell
1999 May 12 **Jungle Formula**, Paul Harrison, David Simmonite (both led)
1999 May 17 **The Barber** David Simmonite, Paul Harrison
1999 May 21 **Kat, Incognito, Undercover of the Nite, Private Line** David Simmonite
1999 May 26 **Heretic** Dave Gregory, Bruce Goodwin **Pensioner's Bulge, Grandpa's 'tache** Bruce Goodwin, Dave Gregory **Unbelievable** David Simmonite, Mike Snell **Bust a Gut** David Simmonite (solo) **Ribelin** Graham Sutton and friends **Snell's Rib** Mike Snell (solo)
1999 May 28 **Three Sad Old Men** Paul Harrison, David Simmonite, Graham Sutton **C.U.R.S.E** Graham Sutton, David Simmonite, Paul Harrison **The Fox Mulder Start** David Simmonite
1999 June **Double Flash** David Simmonite, Paul Harrison **Muzzled, Byway** Mike Snell
1999 May 20 **Funnel Web, Black Widow** Paul Harrison, David Simmonite
1999 May 24 **Spiders** David Simmonite (solo)
1999 Apr 22 **Fungi** David Simmonite (solo)
1999 Sept 16 **Fond Memories** Nik Jennings
1999 Oct 26 **That's My** Lot Nik Jennings
1999 Nov 4 **Cup of Tea?** Nik Jennings
1999 Dec **Chocolate Swastika** Thomas de Gay **Cold School Closure** Nik Jennings
2000 May 20 **Mount Krusty** Kirsty Raine
2000 June **Work in Progress** David Simmonite, belayed by Ian Smith
2001 Feb 28 **Silent Witness** Dan Honneyman

2003 **I'll be Back** James Ibbertson
2004 **The Bush Off** Sarah Smart, Steve Clark, Nigel Edley *Originally gained from Roof Route.* **Birch Side** Steve Clark
2004 **Midge It, A Right Crack, Slab & Tickle** Graham Sutton, solo, or with Ingrid Crossland **Bewitched** Doug Kerr
2005 July 20 **Illuminated** Paul Harrison, Graham Sutton
2005 Aug 11 **Delivered** David Simmonite *He finally straightens out Work in Progress under the threat of a marauding Harrison. It only took five years!*

Boulder First Ascents

21st Century Fox Dave Parry, 2003
Acid Reign Greg Griffith, 1985
Chimp 'A' John Allen, 1998
Cool Running John Allen, 1984
Faze Action Andy Crome, 1997
Finale Roger Brookes, 1980s
Fluff 'n' Stuff John Allen, 1998
Fox Hagg boulder problems Andy Burgess & Paul Evans, 2002
Friday Club Niall Grimes, 2005
Hanging at the Hagg Graham Sutton, 1999
Happy Campus Paul 'Huffy' Houghoughi
Hot Dog David Simmonite, 1991
Iain's Arête Iain Farrar
Len's Areet Len Millsom, 1968
Lurcher Direct Bill Briggs
Master Kush Ryan Pasquill, 2003
Master's Revenge Roger Brookes, 1980s
The Missing Rib Roger Brookes, 1980s
Nik's Wall Nik Jennings
No Class John Welford, 2003
Nunn's Eliminate Paul Nunn,1963
Phlegm, Sputum, Spasm Dave Price, 1962-63
Savage Dog Roger Brookes, 1980s
Simmo's Wall and Arête David Simmonite, 1999
Sparks Adrian Berry, 1993
Spunky Paul Harrison, 1984
Sputum Dave Price, 1962-63
Tapas Paul Harrison, 1999
Trivial Pursuits 1 John Allen, 1986
Trivial Pursuits 2 Chris Hardy, 1983
Vice Like Grip Paul Harrison, 1999
Where Bulldykes Daren't Andy Pollitt, 1985

4 Derwent to Bamford

"The weather in that winter

of 1900 was severe on the moorlands, and for one particular outing held at Bamford and Derwent edges, only five turned out. A blizzard met them as they ascended the steep slope to Great Tor on Bamford Edge. Conditions were so bad that William Smithard had his left hand severely frostbitten. They retreated to the Yorkshire Bridge Inn where the landlord chipped the icicles off their beards with a knife and swept them down with a brushwood besom before allowing them to thaw out in front of a crackling fire, a somewhat painful experience."

An account of an early Kyndwr Club meet,
from High Peak, by Eric Byne

Mick Carr on Gunpowder Crack, VS 5a (page 256). Photo: David Simmonite.

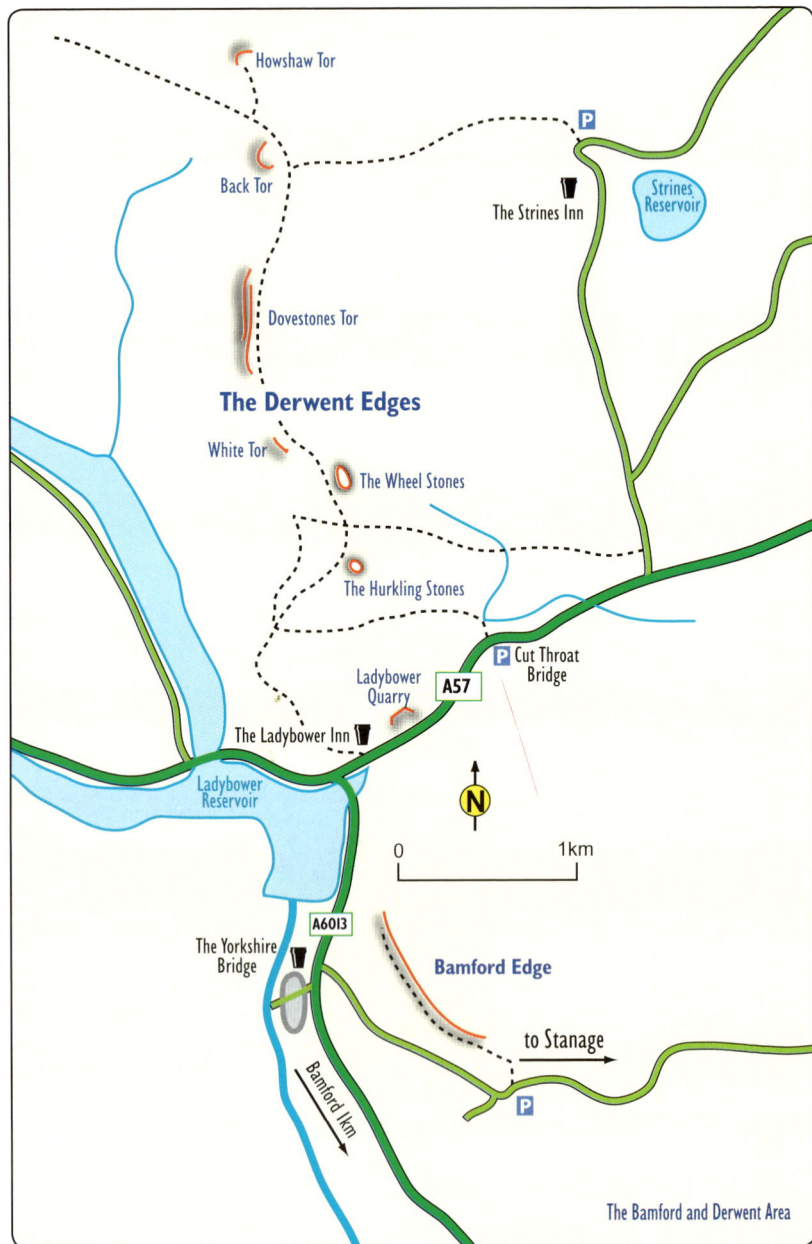

Howshaw Tor

Back Tor

Dovestones Tor

The Derwent Edges

White Tor

The Wheel Stones

The Hurkling Stones

The Strines Inn

Strines
Reservoir

P

Cut Throat
Bridge

P

A57

Ladybower
Quarry

The Ladybower Inn

Ladybower
Reservoir

N

0   1km

A6013

The Yorkshire
Bridge

Bamford Edge

to Stanage

P

Bamford 1km

The Bamford and Derwent Area

The Derwent Edges

OS Ref. SK 202878 to SK 197914   altitude 430 to 520m

The Derwent Edges are a long strung-out collection of tors that overlook the stunningly beautiful Derwent Valley, with its two mighty reservoirs, the Derwent and the Ladybower. There are six of these tors in total, offering everything from powerful bouldering, found in abundance on The Hurkling Stones, The Wheel Stones and Back Tor, to superb challenging routes, found most notably on Dovestones Tor, not to mention obscurity of the highest calibre, tucked away on the edge's final fling, Howshaw Tor.

The wildness of the lonely moorland setting is the great thing that sets the Derwent Edges apart from the other crags in this guide. Couple this with the tremendous variety of the experiences on offer along this lonely ridge, not to mention the chance of a good pint in The Strines after, and you have one of the essential experiences of Peak gritstone climbing.

The Climbing

Each tor has its own individual character and ambience, and gives its own experience. The Hurkling Stones, the first rock reached from Cut Throat Bridge side, offer great bouldering on pebble-dashed slabs, as well as some steeper shorter problems. Next, the Wheel Stones offer classy bouldering, this time of the powerful variety, shunting over roofs and up steep walls on big slopers. Beyond that, the reclusive White Tor offers a few good routes, and is well worth a visit as part of a longer day out. The showpiece of the area, Dovestones Tor, is by far the largest crag of the group, giving loads of sensational, juggy routes which cover mighty ground on great holds, and has an endless supply of classics, as well as shorter, easier routes. It also is a bouldering venue, with its unique hueco-covered boulder. Further again, and nearer the Strines approach, is the beautiful Back Tor. This is an unvisited gem of a crag, giving superb, powerful cranking, as well as a marathon traverse. A few short routes exist there too. Finally, for the advenurer, it is a short stroll over to Howshaw Tor, and a few short climbs overlooking lonely wilderness. **Routes:** The crags together have 175 routes, from the lowest of grades up to easier Extremes, then a small but significant collection of harder climbs. **Bouldering:** There are 75 problems, scattered over all the areas, ranging from V0 to V8, with a good spread at all levels.

Conditions and Aspect

The crags generally face west, getting the sun from the afternoon. With their altitude and their open aspect, they are very exposed to the elements, and catch lots of wind. As such, they make perfect venues to visit in the warmer months when other gritstone crags can feel hot and sweaty, and the wind can also shoo away any midges. A visit in mid to late August will also be rewarded by amazing views of the purple heather stretching out across Bleaklow. The Great Buttress on Dovestones Tor can take a little while to dry early in the season. In winter the crags can feel bitterly cold, and are probably best enjoyed by the arctic hares. The rock is generally very good and sound, although you should be prepared for a slightly scratchy feel on some of the routes.

Parking and Approach

See map opposite. The two main parking areas are at Cut Throat Bridge on the south side of the A57, and parking 300m beyond The Strines Inn, on a sharp bend. For the first of these, park in the large layby 100m uphill from Cut Throat Bridge, walk downhill for 100m and follow a track over a bridge on the right. Follow this as it curves round left and continue until the ridge is reached, and an intersection of paths. Turn sharp right, leading to the main ridge. The Hurkling Stones are 100m right of the path. The Wheel Stones are by it. Another 300m on, White Tor is just below the path. Dovestones Tor is 500m further, identifiable by the large flag stones above it. Another 500m on, and past an easy-to-miss junction for the path leading to the Strines, is Back Tor. Finally, for Howshaw Tor, walk north from Back Tor for 300m across the moor. Approaches: The ridge can be reached in 30 minutes from either parking. From here. the Hurkling Stones and Back Tor are about 35 minutes apart. **By Bus:** The First 54 bus stops at Cut Throat Bridge.

The Hurkling Stones

(AKA Rock Ahoy)

OS Ref. SK 202878   altitude 430m

This is the fine, clean set of boulders found on the right side of the path soon after the approach from Cut Throat Bridge meets the ridge.

1 **Baby Bulge** V0 (4b)

2 **Arête and Seam** V0+ (5a)

3 **Hurkling Towards Earth** V3 (6a)
Go up using the vertical seam in the left hand.

4 **Pothole Slab** V5 (6b)
The very thin slab leads to the sculpted scallop.

5 **The Gurgling Green Streak** V2 (6a)
Pick your way on pebbles, following the vague green streak. Loooooovely.

6 **Little Arête** VI (5c)
On the left of the deep slot.

7 **Other Arête** V3 (6a)
The right side of the slot.

8 **Rock Ahoy** VI (5a)
A beauty up the bold flake-line.

9 **Sick Arête** E6 6c ★★   2003
7m Gain the front of the tall arête from the ledge on the right. Highly technical, as well as just high.

10 **Wall past Flake** V0+ (5a)

11 **All Sloping Arête** V2 (5c)

12 **Captain Ahab** V5 (6b)
Undercut up to a sloping top-out.

13 **Wall above Flake** V3 (6a)

To the right, there is a boulder up on a ledge.

14 **Flake Bulge** V0+ (5b)
The wall above the ledge.

15 **The Arête** V3 (6a)
The arête just on the right.

The Wheel Stones

(AKA Coach and Horses)

OS Ref. SK 203885   altitude 480m

A great scramble of stacked blocks, giving an almost unlimited supply of sloping shelves. Very exposed rock, sometimes a bit scratchy, but all in all a fairly special place, well worth the walk. A great summer venue.

1 Shelf Wall V2 (5c)
The middle of the boxy wall left of the chimney.

2 Puttrell Sitdown V4 (6b)
From a ledge at the back of the block, start at a jug on a lip, and crimp up the well-formed arête.

3 Low Coach V5 (6b)
Climb the arête from a hanging start.

4 Jupiter Collision V7 (6b)
From a low start (heel-toe jam), stretch up the wall past a shoddy sloper.

5 Man Calls Horse V4 (6b)

6 Arête on Right V4 (6b)
Climb up just right of the arête from a sitter.

7 Sidepull Stretch V1 (5b)
The centre of the sidewall.

8 Right Side V0 (5a)
Of the wall, that is.

Lots of other problems can be had on the scattered walls and bulges, as well as the odd scramble to the top of the mountain. All good stuff, you know.

"**A strange array** of stony sentinels are drawn up in a rack along the edge from Hurkling Stones to Back Tor; these are the Cakes of Bread and the Salt Cellar, with many a curious monolith that has no official title in the heraldry of the Ordnance Survey. But the queerest of all to look at is the extraordinary cluster of immense round discs, piled above one another, and nicknamed the 'Wheels Stones'."

Moors, Crags and Caves of the High Peak and the Neighbourhood, 1903

White Tor

OS Ref. SK 199888   **altitude 510m**

by David Simmonite

The tor is a lovely quiet spot with a fine outlook over the Dark Peak and beyond. Whilst there isn't much there, it is a good place to combine with a visit to another area. The rock is very good.

The first feature visible when approaching from Cut Throat Bridge is a buttress containing a large overhang at the southern end of the tor. Just beyond this to the north is a wall facing south and split by a chimney. The gently overhanging wrinkled left-hand side-wall of the buttress is home to the first routes. Ten metres left of this is a small buttress containing problems, the best of which is:

1 **Planet Rock** V4 (6a)
Start under the roof on good holds at the back, just left of a low thin crack and beneath an obvious scoop. Make a long reach over the roof and pull into the scoop. Head for good holds and easier climbing above.

Returning back to the wrinkled wall.

2 **Rafaga** E4 6a ★   1989
8m Almost a highball. Bouldery moves lead to thin breaks. Lunge up for a flat hold and continue on sandy rounded holds to finish in the crease of the capstone. Possibly E4 6b for the short.

3 **The Roger Moore Effect** E1 5b   1989
9m The arête is climbed on its left side. Traverse in via the break from the right, or take the bottom arête direct at 5c. Escapable, so not quite as good as it looks.

Ten metres down on the hillside below this wall is a tilted slab that forms a roof at the bottom. ●**Turkey Trot**, V2 (5c), is a surprisingly worthwhile and pumpy problem taking the rising right-to-left break at the back of the roof from a sit start at the bottom right. Feet must be kept off the slab or it's

about Diff! Step off at the far end or battle round onto the slab at V3 (6a).

4 **Mod** VS 4b ★   1965
9m A tricky and unprotected start from a flat rectangular block is the crux. The arête above is steadier with the help of holds on the wall itself.

5 **Glam Rock** HS 4a   1989
9m The slabby wall 1m right of Mod leads to a rounded finish. Has a squeezed-in feel to it, but is still worthwhile.

6 **Skinhead** HS 4a   1976
8m The arête is pleasant enough. ●**Chimley**, M (traditional), is the chimney.

7 **Rocker** S 4a   1957-71
8m Ascend the right-hand arête of the chimney with the hardest climbing at the start.

8 **Heavy Metal** HVS 5b   1990
6m The centre of the wall to the right provides a pleasant technical route. Pull over the initial roof, bridging helps, to tackle the wall directly above.

Stephen Coughlan on The Roger Moore Effect, E1 5b (opposite), on the rarely visited White Tor. This bijou nubbin is well worth a visit as a warm up if you are making your way towards Dovestones Tor. Photo: David Simmonite.

McVities Buttress: To the right past small blocks is a buttress topped by a big overhang. ● **Harry's Last Stand**, E2 5c (1989), is a somewhat pointless left-to-right traverse of the break beneath the overhang.

⑨ Monks of Monserrat plc E4 6b †   pre-1991
9m From a sloping shelf to the left, climb the roof using the obvious foothold of Wodwo.

⑩ Wodwo E6 6c † ★   1989
9m A fierce route taking the overhang direct, via a long stretch for a hole, to a traverse left at the lip using poor holds and a rounded nose. An obvious foothold enables the top to be reached with great difficulty. A tied-off Friend 1.5 at the lip of the overhang provides the only real protection. Possibly unrepeated, although a line that seems to correspond exactly to this was soloed on-sight by Ben Heason in 2003, at E4.

⑪ McVities VS 4c   1976
8m On the right-hand side of the big overhang, climb the wall below a small overhang and reach over to a small friable ledge. Use this to reach the top. Discontinuous climbing spoilt by the ledge near the bottom.

Dovestones Tor

OS Ref. SK 197898   **altitude 530m**

by Martin Kocsis and David Simmonite, after Chris Craggs

This is the showpiece of the area with a great collection of big, proper routes. It is located just below the point where the paving flags begin, if coming from Cut Throat Bridge, or about 400m south of the point where the Strines path meets the main ridge. The climbs are described starting on the northern, Back Tor, end, where a large jutting roof is situated behind fallen blocks (the Squawk area).

Left of this, low rocks offer bouldering. The low roof next to the flagged path contains two problems. ● The first starts low towards the left of the roof and gains a good hold on the lip before a heave over at V1 (5c) ● and right again a small edge is used to surmount the lip at V3 (6a). ● Moving rightwards round to the front of the edge is a small arched roof, climbed at V0+ (5a) ● and the wall just right is also V0 (5a). ● Right again the next two problems are highball, the first at V0 (5a) takes the roof right of the groove and utilises a chickenhead en route ● and its neighbour over the big roof on the right via an initial flaky wall is V5 (6b).

Across right is a lovely squat roof with perhaps the best problems in this little area. ● The first two problems share a low square hold, Climbing from the hold and out the left side of the roof using brittle flakes is V3 (6a). ● From the same start head out right on a flake to a notch at a quality V2 (5c). ● To the right the widest part of the roof is powerful and reachy, V3 (6a).

The routes now start on the right around a low, projecting roof.

❶ Squawk V4 (6b)
Climb the juggy hanging arête from a low start and make a long reach for the horizontal break.

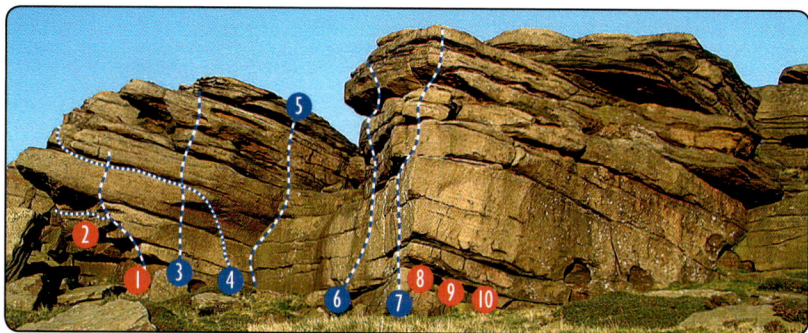

2 Squawk Traverse V5 (6b)

Follow Squawk arête to the roof, then traverse left to finish on the jammed boulder. Good climbing with a disappointing finish. ● A V7 (6c) start is possible left of the arête, crossing the roof with a pinch.

3 Sick as a Parrot HVS 5a   1996

10m The wall on rounded breaks.

4 Sick Bay VS 4b ★   1957

10m A testing exercise in horizontal jamming. Get those fists out!

5 Handy Wall Hole S 4a   1996

8m Climb the groove and wall above.

6 Thunderbirds S 4a   1996

10m From a block, climb onto a higher ledge, through a bulge and leftwards across the finishing wall.

7 Stingray VD ★   1957

8m Good jamming up the major crack leads to ledges and a finish around to the right. ● The thinner crack just left, leading left to a finishing crack, is **Woodentops**, S 4a (1996).

8 Stingray Arête V2 (6a)

The fine arête.

9 Galaxy Dove V6 (6b)

The wall just to the right using a sharp thin hold and a jump for the top.

10 Interstellar Pigeon V7 (6c)

Start from a sitter with the left hand on a layaway to reach an edge and a jump for a sloper and pocket. ● The horizontal and widening seam/break on this wall is **The Cavendish**, V0+ (5b). ● The crimpy wall direct is **Ouch!** V0+ (5b). ● The wall just right provides similarly graded crimpy problems ● and finally the roof on the right using the **Jug of Justice** on the lip is V1 (5b).

Stuart Brooks on Stingray Arête, V2 (this page). Photo: Brooks collection.

Dovestones Boulder

Just below the edge at this point is a fine boulder, with its characteristic huecos.

1 **Perfect Porthole Problem** V2 (5c)
A classic using one hold; simple really!

2 **Huway-Cold** V2 (6a)
Just right, again use a sloper to gain the next hole.

3 **Huway-Day** V1 (5b)
Climb the heucos next to the arête.

4 **Hip Hip Huway** V5 (6b)
Climb the arête on its right-hand side. A spotter is handy.

5 **Play Huway** V1 (5b)
Use the big hueco to climb the steep wall.

6 **The Crack** V0 (4c)

7 **Right Arête** V4 (6b)
Be careful with the landing. The arête to the left is unclimbed.

Below and right is a low roof with a couple of problems. ● The small roof on the left from a sit start is V3 (6a) ● and its right-hand neighbour, using a foot lock in the break is also V3 (6a).

Left: The amazing setting of the Dovestones Boulder, with the lonely wilderness stretching out across Howden Moors. Andy Higginson on Play Huway, V1. Photo: Alex Messenger.

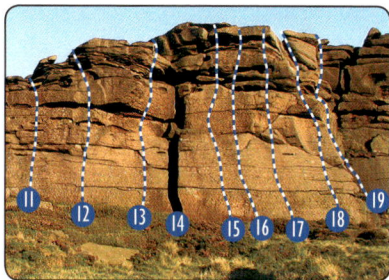

The Jonah Area

Returning back to the edge the bay to the right of Stingray features a narrow chimney and a neat slab containing a plethora of good routes.

11 Windblasted D ★ 1957
9m Fine wall climbing, easy at the grade.

12 Windblown VD ★ 1957
9m A direct line up the juggy wall.

13 Domusnovas E2 5b 2002
9m The slab and hanging groove above.

14 Jonah D ★ 1957
9m Quality. For the full troglodyte experience finish inside the chockstone.

The slab on the right now has four routes rather than the original one. Although close together they are just about independent enough and all worthwhile, due to their fun, juggy nature.

BEWARE! The next two routes pass a loose block just above the bulge.

15 Tight 'uns VS 4c 1996
9m The slab just right of Jonah, and wall above.

16 Titanium VS 4c ★ 1990
9m A slab leads to a bulging wall just left of the blunt rib.

17 Titanic HS 4c ★ ★ 1996
9m Great steep fun. Climb to the diagonal crack and continue steeply up the juggy headwall.

18 Titania HS 4b ★ ★ 1957
9m No longer a sandbag, but still as good as ever. Ascend just left of the right arête and take the leaning wall above on good holds.

19 Iltis VS 4b 1957
9m Ascend the steepening right side of the arête to a tricky exit. Feels a good grade harder if you don't find, or can't reach, a crucial jug. ● **Pocket Rocket,** VS 5b (2002), is the wall just right via a pocket, finishing up the centre of the tower.

The grassy steps to the right can be climbed over (and, amazingly, have been claimed) between VD and VS, including **Foulstone Wall**, VD (1957), taking the pocked wall.

20 Boneyard Buttress VD ★ 1957
9m Disjointed but good climbing. Climb the left side of the clean arête and continue to the crack above.

21 Boneyard Arête V3 (6a)
A very good problem climbing the steep arête on its right side.

22 The Compressor V6 (6b)
Go direct from the slotted block using the sloping pod and some gurning.

23 Black Crimp Problem V2 (6a)
Take the steep wall using the aforementioned crimp.

24 Polecat VS 4b ★ 1957
12m A shallow corner leads to the roof, climbed by means of the obvious flake crack.

Andy Naylor enjoying the well-protected exposure on Lancaster Flyby, HVS 5b (page 225).
Photo: David Simmonite.

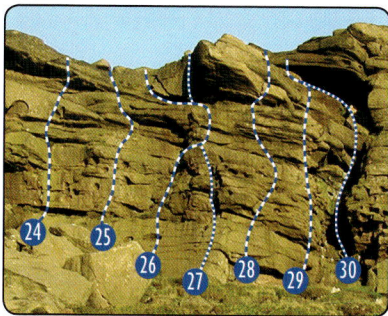

Some **climbs** for the **Beginner**

For climbers taking their first steps onto real rock, here is a series of climbs up to the grade of VD, which are suitable for learning the craft of climbing outdoors. They can be protected with a very basic rack of nuts, extenders and slings, and will give new climbers, and those emerging from climbing walls for the first time, many of the skills needed to advance through the grades.

On **Rivelin**, White House Crack, Solitaire, and the routes in its vicinity, and Renshaw's Remedy, are all good steep crack pitches, and are all quite challenging. On **Carl Wark**, head to Boulder Crack and other routes in the Lookout Area, for a concentration of shorter, easier routes. You could easily tick off half a dozen routes there in an afternoon, with the odd trickier one if you're feeling confident. **Burbage North** is a tremendous venue for beginners, with sound rock and a sunny, friendly aspect. There, try Baseless, Wall Corner and other routes in the Ash Tree area; Bilberry Wall, and other quiet and beautiful routes in the Grotto Area, with its secluded, tree-lined nature; at the far right, head for End Slab and other slabbier journeys. On the mighty **Higgar Tor**, the routes around Greymalkin on the back side of the Leaning Block give an enjoyable trio of short climbs leading to this famous summit. For beginners who also enjoy a good walk in beautiful surroundings, head to **Dovestones Tor** for Stingray, Windblown and Dovestones Wall. **Bamford** is a good place to learn a bit of slab technique; try Leaning Slab, K Buttress Slab and Terrace Trog for starters. Finally on **Wharncliffe**, head for Overhanging Crack for a first lesson in jamming, then to the nearby Great Buttress for Alpha Crack and the Great Chimney.

25 Pole-Axed S 4a ★ 1996
10m The wall just right of the centre of the bay is climbed to a bulge which is surmounted via a flake before moving left up the final slab. A squeezed in line just left is S.

26 Jacobite's Route HD ★ 1949
12m Pleasant enough but a bit dirty. Climb to a grassy corner. Follow this to a step out right onto the edge of the buttress and climb up until bulges dictate moves left to a pleasant flake crack, up which a finish is made. A more direct line of ascent is possible at VD but isn't as good.

27 Slow Cooker S 4b 1996
12m Climb the shallow groove to join the last route, then finish direct up the steep scoop above.

28 Slocum S ★ 1957
12m Start at the foot of the projecting buttress and move up and right to a prominent flake. Continue up to negotiate a steep flake. From the ledge, finish more easily. ● A couple of metres right of Slocum, **First Come**, HVS 5a (1996), climbs the left-hand side of a vague arête.

29 Gruyere VS 4c 1996
12m Another random but enjoyable line going direct up the pocketed wall just right of the vague arête to a nasty finish.

These climbs will give you a good, solid grounding in the skills of real climbing. If you handle all these without too much trouble, then check out the suggestions for some slightly more advanced challenges on page 38.

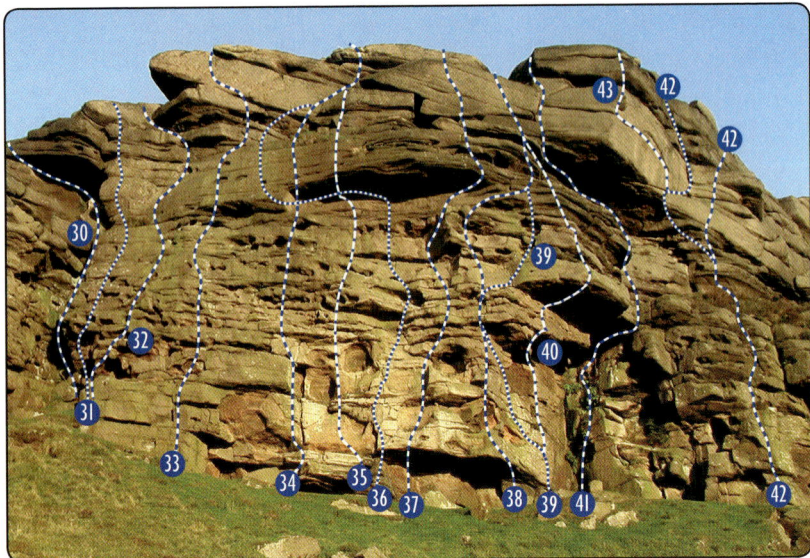

The Great Buttress

It is no surprise that the early pioneers were drawn to produce great deeds on this next section of rock. The Great Buttress is one of the most spectacular pieces of rock in the area, giving long, steep and adventure-filled climbs of the highest quality. The rock is intricate and heavily featured on its bulging lower sections, and rough, hard grit at the top. Combine all this with its isolated setting and amazing views, and it becomes one of gritstone's great venues.

30 Dovestones Gully M   1957

20m The deep chimney has its moments and is better than it looks. Finish leftwards.

31 Dovestones Edge S 4a ★   1996

18m From the bulging start, continue direct up slabby rock.

32 Dovestones Wall VD ★★   1949

20m An excellent, exposed climb and the best of its grade on the crag which unfortunately can be dirty. Climb steep perforated rock to gain a slab. Climb this slightly to the right and then back to the left to finish.

33 A Little Green Eyed God VS 4c ★   1996

20m A fine climb, steep and exposed for its entire length. Climb onto a large jammed block and carry on fairly direct up holey features to finish out on the arête in an exposed position.

34 Barney Rubble VS 4b ★★   1984

20m Excellent sustained climbing on huge holds, full-on VS. Move up into the left-hand sandy cave then climb straight up the steep wall above on big holds until below the flat roof. Pull through the prominent bottomless corner in the roof to gain a slab and an easier finish directly above.

35 Thread Flintstone E1 5b ★★   1996

20m As good as its name. Pull over the low roof, climb between the two caves and continue steeply up on good holds to the capping roof. A big committing yank over this leads to an easy finish.

36 Brown Windsor VS 4b ★   1957

28m A grand route covering adventurous terrain on good holds. Start at an orange weathered thread under the centre of the wall. Trend right to a white block, then go steeply up to the big roof. A long journey left leads to a reasonable pull-over to finish.

37 Mock Turtle EI 5b   1996
20m Cross the hefty roof and carry steeply on past a short corner to the roof. Traverse 3m to the right and pull over the right edge of the large final roof.

38 Great Buttress Eliminate HVS 5a ★ ★   1981
22m A fine steep route. Gain and follow the under-cut rib to a junction with Great Buttress. Continue directly through bulges and until it is possible to traverse right and finish as for Great Buttress.

● A mysterious, indistinct route, **Lament for a Scotsman**, is a direct finish at E2 5b (1993), ● and a mysterious E4 (**Too Long Gone**, 1996) goes through the roof somewhere to the right of Barney Rubble's notch.

39 Great Buttress HVS 5a ★ ★ ★   1957
20m Fantastic! Solid HVS, one of the most thrilling routes of that grade in the Peak. Good holds, good gear and plenty of exposure add to its charm. From near the corner, climb leftwards until just past the arête. Go straight up the steep wall then trend right (quite pushy) through the bulges and just above the lip of the roofs until a final tricky move gives access to the ledge above. You can belay here to reduce rope drag or push on. You now have a choice of finishes. The original took the poorly protected slab on the left at easy E1 5b, whilst a better choice, and more in keeping with the route, is the final section of Central Climb up the undercut corner crack.

40 Sforzando E4 6a ★   1985
17m A steep route crossing the double roofs. The first overhang has a large useful hold which enables the second overhang to be reached. Cross this to easy ground. Wild, and high in the grade.

41 Central Climb VS 4c, 5a ★   1949
An enclosed and atmospheric climb.
1. 13m Climb the corner and trend rightwards to avoid the overhang and reach the corner on its right with difficulty and up to the belay ledge.
2. 12m Move left and make tricky and thuggy moves into an undercut flake up which a finish is made.

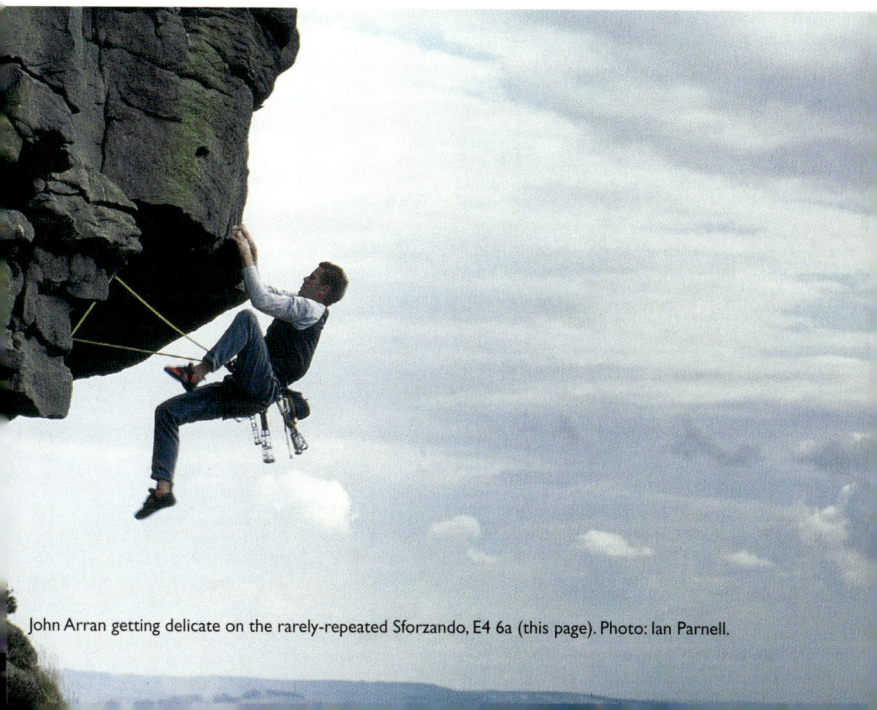

John Arran getting delicate on the rarely-repeated Sforzando, E4 6a (this page). Photo: Ian Parnell.

42 Fennario VS 4b, 5a ★   1957

An indistinct first pitch leads to great rock on the second.

1. 12m Climb the left-slanting crack left of stepped overhangs to a grassy vertical crack and then the terrace stance.

2. 12m Climb straight up the wall to a sloping ledge, generally right of the vague corner. Move up and escape rightwards. A brilliant E1 5b can be had by following the lower roof-crack, then big exposed flakes leading left (the more obvious line).

43 Nippon, Nippoff E3 6a   1983

8m High value exposure. Pull over the roof crack then battle left along the break to finish up the arête.

The next routes start on the grassy terrace up and right. The centre of the upper wall is split by a left slanting crack that provides an awkward descent. Left of this are two routes: ● **Topside**, S 4c (1996), starting at a gravel patch and making tricky moves to the first break then left pleasantly to the top. ● For **Frodsham 3a**, S (1996), climb the centre of the wall to the right of the diagonal break on rounded holds.

Gargoyle Buttress

The first of two fine, compact buttresses lies across the terrace. The gargoyle is actually on the other buttress. The walls to the left have been scrambled on and are pleasant enough (around S).

44 The Diamond V3 (6a)

The triangular wall left of the recess.

45 Gargoyle Traverse S 4b ★   1949

20m Great positions at a reasonable grade. Start on the slab on the left and climb to its top right-hand corner. Traverse right around the buttress, with tricky and exposed moves midway, to finish up a block-filled chimney.

46 Caveman S 4a   1996

13m Climb the recess, then move left below the roof. Move up to climb a rib on the slabby tower above.

47 Dead on a Rival E5 6b † ★   1985

13m A rarely, if ever, repeated testpiece. Boulder up

the square arête with some difficulty. Traverse right into the middle of the wall, then climb directly up this to a ledge and finish through the bulges.

48 Woodhouse's Wandering Way E3 5c   1981

20m Make bouldery moves up the wall, then traverse the break leftwards to the arête. Climb the slab leading to a bulging finish.

49 Stony Faced E1 5b ★   1996

14m Climb the arête on good holds to a slab, then the bulging wall left of the crack to a bold and puzzling final move.

50 Gargoyle Buttress VS 4c ★   1957

15m A fine climb in a good situation. Ascend the corner, then traverse left to attack the bulging crack.

51 Barker's Got a Sweat On HVS 5a   1996

14m Climb to the slanting flake then finish direct. The larger right-slanting flake 2m right is VS.

Buttress I

This is the right-hand twin to Gargoyle Buttress. It is the one with the gargoyle actually on it, and is home to one of the best VS climbs in the Peak.

52 Canker VD   1957

10m Your basic random slab action.

53 Christmas Wrappings HVS 5b   1991

10m Move up, trending slightly rightwards, via a series of horizontal breaks.

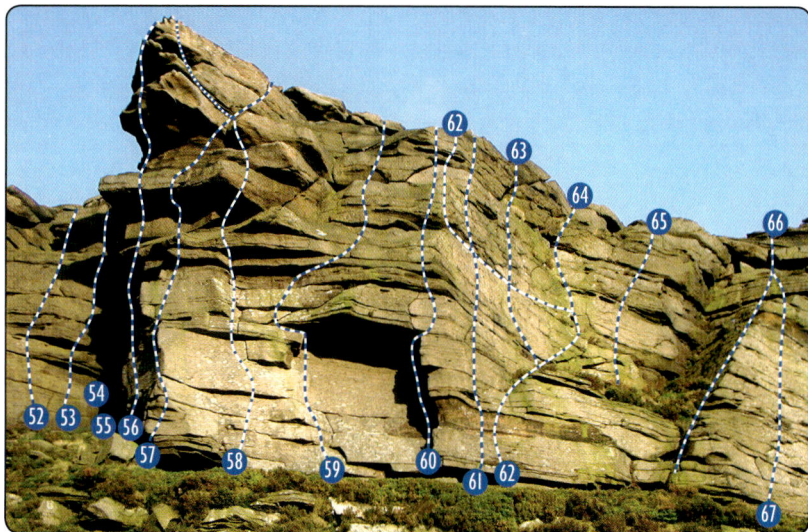

54 Wind Tunnel M   1890s
14m The aptly named deep chimney. Historic.

55 Hurricane VD ★   1957
15m Better than it looks. The square arête on the right of the chimney leads to steeper climbing, trending left up the dark wall.

56 Typhoon HVS 5b   1996
15m The centre of the flat wall left of the main arête leads through bulges to a ledge below the big gargoyle. Cross this steeply.

57 Route I VS 4c ★★★   1949
16m A brilliant, varied route, right at the top of its grade. Follow the square arête, technical and bold, and the first of many cruxes. More steep moves lead to a ledge below an overhang. Difficult moves over this lead to a short, ferocious corner-crack. A good, old-fashioned VS.

● For added exhilaration tackle **The Shylock Finish,** HVS 5a ★★ (1981). From the ledge follow the lowest horizontal break out left and finish in a dramatic situation. An easier alternative is to use the top break for the traverse but this somehow doesn't give the same buzz.

58 Blue Velvet E1 6a ★★   1996
12m A fierce move gains the tiny crack. Continue with the usual ledgey steepness to join the final moves of Route 1.

59 Claw Climb VS 4c ★   1957
14m Steep terrain leads dramatically left under the roof. Get established over this, trend up and right before finishing more easily.

60 Talon VS 4c ★   1957
14m Varied climbing on good rock. Go up the recessed corner until forced out right onto the front face. A couple of quick pulls leads to slabbier rocks.

61 Lancaster Flyby HVS 5b ★★   1996
14m A fine route with steep moves and positive protection, generally taking the wall right of the arête. Escapable in places but with good climbing.

To the right is a grassy ledge 3m up, which can be reached from the start of Lancaster Flyby or more easily from the right. Starting at the back of this are three routes:

62 Route II VS 4b ★   1949
13m From the ledge follow the rising diagonal break

out to the left edge (crossing Lancaster Flyby) and pull around onto a slab in a great position to finish up the arête above.

63 Blue Hare VS 4c   1985
8m Climb the centre of the wall via long reaches and some slightly suspect holds.

64 Grindle Crack HVD ★   1957-71
9m The left-slanting crack is trickier and more worthwhile than it looks.

65 Grinder Wall S   1996

66 A'rete Do S   1996

67 Another Left Wall S   1996
10m A direct line up the blank-looking wall midway between the left arête and the central (grassy) flake-line (which is **Another Flaky Wall**, VD, 1996).

● The wall to the right of this, and left of the grassy corner (the one about 10m right of Route II) is **Another Right Wall**, S. Finish direct. ● The grassy corner is VD, continuing steeply to finish through a 'crevasse'. ● Right 4m is a roof, at 4m. **Left Behind**, HS, climbs around the left side of this roof, then continues to the top up a corner. ● Taking the roof, just left of its centre, is **Frodsham 3c**, VS 5a. ● Right of the roof is a vegetated slab. ● For **Right Ahead**, S, climb the rib on the left of the slab to a ledge. Move right and climb the escapable arête on the right. ● Right, across the slab, and 10m right of the last climb, is a low roof. **Stairway**, D, climbs the slab just left of the roof before moving left to climb a tower. ● **Layby**, VD, laybacks left from under the roof and finishes right. ● **Pock Mark**, S, is a short route passing the right end of the roof. All these routes were claimed and named in 1996, although these rocks have been climbed over for generations.

Caroline Smith on Pole-Axed, S 4a (page 221), giving steep climbing for the grade on continually interesting and varied terrain. Photo: David Simmonite.

The Upper Cliffs

Above and right of the Main Edge is a smaller cliff that, whilst only reaching a height of 8m, presents a series of fine jutting buttresses of excellent quality rock. On the far left is a lovely short slab and right of this are some impressive roofs split by a series of cracks.

68 Barefoot D   1996
5m Tinkle up the slab without any great difficulty.

69 Slab Happy S 4a ★   1996
6m The centre of the slab is pleasantly delicate.

70 Step It Up S 4b ★   1996
6m The slab immediately left of the central groove has a problem start on faint ripples and leads all too soon into a deep crack.

71 Groovy Moves S 4b ★   1996
6m The right-facing groove leading to the jammy bulge.

72 Jam on It HVS 5a   1996
6m The left-hand crack is entered from the left.

73 Squirm HVS 5a   1996
6m The right-hand neighbour is again gained from the left and is a grovel.

74 Hang 'em High VS 5b   1996
5m The short and often green hanging corner to the right is entered with a bizzare and somewhat thrutchy move from a convenient block. Strangely satisfying.

To the left of an easy gully is a projecting beak:

75 Chicken Head E2 5c ★   1991
6m An excellent micro-route but with a gnarly landing and little protection. Gain the prow from the right (better) or left (easier) by a swinging hand traverse and make a couple of delicate moves to easy ground.

To the right is a fine wall with an easy gully on its left and a small triangular ledge at its centre.

76 Pleasant D   1996
6m The arête is climbed from blocks in the gully.

77 Spring Night HVS 5b ★   1982
8m Trend leftwards to climb the left edge of the wall on good breaks and an extended finale.

78 Autumn Day E1 5c ★★   1981
8m Take the centre of the wall past a pull on little holds and a long crux reach for a rounded edge. Excellent, if you can actually do it (aren't they all!).

79 Stretch Marks E1 6a ★   1996
8m More satisfying stretching up the steep wall.

80 Razor Cut VS 4c   1996
8m On the right side of the wall, the straight thin crack is more awkward than it looks and is very escapable in its lower section. A rocking block near the top adds to the tension.

An easy descent gully is to the right and then a projecting buttress with a striking roof and a pillar leaning against its left side.

81 Rocky VD   1996
7m   The front of the pillar. ●The slight corner crack on the right is **Blocky**, HVD, ●and the wall between this and the arête is **Hanging Tree**, HVS 5b (both 1996).

82 Easy Ground HVS 5b ★   1981
8m   The left-hand side of the roof is crossed using a fortuitous hold in its centre.

83 Excel HVS 5b ★★   1976
8m   A good healthy roof thrutch. The centre of the roof is climbed to reach the lip and a tricky move round this to gain the wall above.

84 Swinwood HVS 5b   1981
8m   Another route with a steep start. The over-hanging arête leads to a break, which leads left to the arête. Move left, and finish up the slab.

To the right is a recess with a ledge. In the left wall of the recess is a prominent porthole, two routes pass this feature.

85 Smokin' E1 5c   1996
8m   From the ledge, get the porthole and dilly-dally left with some effort to the arête. Finish up the slab. ●Going directly up past the hole is **Landing Craft**, HVS 5b (1996).

Climbers on Step it Up, S 4a (previous page). Photo: Alex Messenger.

86 **Amen Corner** HS 4b   1996
7m A tricky starting crack accesses the steep left corner

87 **Old Man's Corner** HVD   1996
7m The corner. ● The centre of the wall to the right is **Village Green**, VS 4c (1996).

88 **Iambo** HS 4a ★   1957-71
7m A good little route up the thin crack left of the arête on good holds.

89 **Bertie** E1 5c ★   1996
8m Your basic steep wall/good holds outing. Fun.

90 **Blunt** E1 5b ★   1982
8m The centre of the bulging wall is ascended by means of a blunt nose and a difficult upper wall.

91 **Philby** HVS 5a ★   1984
8m The final steep route on this wall.

To the right is a deep chimney which offers an awkward descent route and beyond this there is an overhanging wall.

92 **Granny Smith** E2 5b ★   1981
8m Make a spirited gallop up the sharply hanging arête.

93 **Cox's Pippin** HVS 5b ★   1957-71
8m Eight muscular metres of overhanging fun. Well-protected.

94 **Ganges** VD   1957-71
7m Swim up the chimney to an awkward finish.

95 **Crackless Bottom** HVS 5b   1996
8m Gain and leave the short overhanging crack.

96 **Soft Top** E1 5a   1996
7m Establish yourself onto the flat wall using the right arête of the cliff and move up to disturbing finish. The wall to the right provides a similar (and scary) problem at 5b.

Back Tor

OS Ref. SK 197910   **altitude 520m**

by Tony & Sarah Whitehouse and Martin Kocsis

A fantastic little boxing glove of a crag, packing a lot of punch into a small amount of rock. The main area is very steep, made of solid rock with a very clean surface, and covered in very interesting holds. Although it is in condition year-round, like most of these crags, it is really a summer venue. It faces northwest, gets the late afternoon sun and would give some shelter from the rain. Although the landing is perfect, a black puddle can spoil some of the bouldering, so you might be best to borrow a friend's bouldering mat. Around the main rock is lots of smaller outcrops, somewhat greener, giving some interesting soloing and bouldering, as well as a very hard project.

Right: Bet you haven't been here before. Stuart Brooks on Back Tor's Slanting Arête, V4 (next page), one of the many obscure gems to be found on this quiet outcrop. Photo: Brooks collection.

The Left End

Sweeping round southwards from the main outcrop is a series of smaller walls, giving some routes and bouldering. This area gets very little sun. The first problems lie on the far left of these rocks, above a pillar of rock.

❶ **Sidewall Scoop** V3 (6a)
A great problem. On the short sidewall that faces Sheffield is a scoop. Enter this.

On the front is a flat wall giving a few V0 problems. Ten metres on is a large pointed finger of rock.

❷ **Slanting Arête** V4 (6a)
The slanting left arête of the finger block, from a sit-start.

❸ **The Blob** V5 (6b)
Just above the overhang 2m right is a blob. Use this to top out. ● The brushed low start to this promises to give a V12 problem. ● The sweet groove right of this is V0− (4b).

❹ **Sharp Rib** VI (5b)
Twelve metres further, past a couple of corners, is a sharp, hanging rib. Climb this. ● The square jutting prow 3m right is V3 (6a).

On the buttress 8m right are 3 routes: ● **Hoc,** VS 5b, is a crack on the left; ● **Haec,** HS 4a, starts on the front face of the buttress up the left side of a faint rib. Climb on to the right-hand end of the ledge. Move up a wall and over an overhang just to the right of a crack; ● **Hic**, HVD, is a crack/chimney on the right-hand side of the buttress, awkward to start and finishing up the cleft (all 1957-71). Further problems and short solos lie further right.

Back Tor Butress

The superb main rock.

❺ **Voice of the Turtle** HVS 5b — 1982
7m Climb the wall left of the arête on rounded holds. ● The wall just left again is **Mertle,** V0+ (5b).

❻ **Brogging Wall** S ★ — 1957-71
8m The fine, slim groove.

❼ **Turtle Rib** HVS 5a ★ — 1957-71
8m Good, and not as easy as it looks.

❽ **Turtle Chimney** S — 1976
8m The narrowing chimney has a choice of exits, but not of climbing style: thrutching and grunting are obligatory.

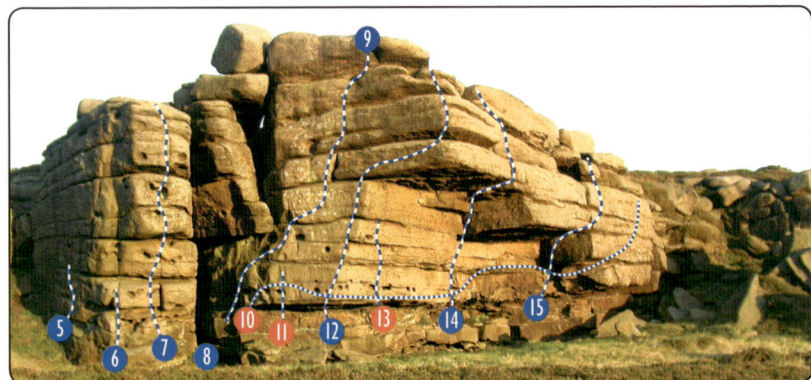

9 **Terrapin** HS 4c   1981
9m Climb the sweet wall on pockets and breaks.

10 **The Bone Cruncher** V8 (6b)
One of the longest and best traverses in the area. From the left, travel all the way across the lip of the buttress on huecos and edges, keeping feet off anything useful. The section crossing the niche is particularly fierce. ●An easier alternative is to get established in the niche below Spartan, thus avoiding the section in the niche, at V6 (6b).

11 **ET** V3 (6a)
Start with hands in the eyes, and climb the bulge.

12 **Hoplite** E3 6b   1993
10m Climb to the wide break and hand-traverse right to a mighty struggle up a blunt nose. Picturesque. ●**Hoplite Start**, V2 (6a), goes from a sit-start, as far as the roof.

13 **Hueco Wall** V6 (6b)
Desperate and fingery. Climb the wall 2m right of the arête from low huecos. ●**Eyes Without a Face** is a similar, and slightly harder problem, which goes from the threadable pockets just right, at V7 (6b).

14 **Spartan** E1 5c ★★   1976
9m A moorland classic. The crack, through the roof at its widest part, makes Cave Crack at Froggatt look like a vicarage tea party: excellent value. ●A fingery traverse goes left beneath the roof using the mid-height break, to the arête; V4 (6b). A fine project crimps across the vertical wall below and right of the roof-crack to rounded breaks to finish.

15 **Tortoise** VS 5a ★   1981
8m The right-hand crack may be climbed elegantly, or more likely, with a desperate struggle. A positive approach pays dividends. ●The wall to the right is **Hare**, HS 4b (traditional), ●and the arête right again, **Grouse Related Nonsense**, is VS 4c (2003).

Miles' Problems

About 100m behind the main area is a small but significant collection of north-facing boulders. The one closest to the main edge often has a dark pool at its base, and will appeal to any deep water boulderers out there. Left of this is a boulder with a pointy roof.

16 **Small but Big** V3 (6a)
Start on crimps under the roof, span out right and overcome the roof. A wild variation on this goes from the crimps directly to the tip of the roof, via a full-body dyno: V7 (6c).

The next block to the left holds:

17 **The B8** V6 (6b)
Start low under the right arête on flat holds then get the sloping nose, and so to the top.

18 **Back to Front** V6 (6b)
A fine problem taking the left arête. Start low and use the left arête to gain the cupped finishing hold.

Howshaw Tor

by Tony & Sarah Whitehouse and Graham Sutton

OS Ref. SK 197914   **altitude 500m**

This small north-facing outcrop can be green, even in summer, and although it attracted some of the area's earliest visitors, it is now strictly for those obsessed with solitude and picturesque esoterica. Its proximity to Back Tor means that it is worth the short stroll across the heather to visit. To approach from Back Tor, head for the rocks visible 200m right of the footpath that heads towards the valley, about 300m away.

The first buttress on the left has an overhung capstone and an overhang at half-height.

1 **Howshaw Tor Eliminate** E2 6a ★   1978
9m Graded for the tall; dynamic and a good grade harder for the rest. Climb the middle of the wall by a long reach over the bulge, to the top overhang which is turned on the right by a flake at the lip. ●The arête to the left is VS 5a. ●The recessed corner on the right is **Threadworm**, HVD (1957-71).

Thirty metres right is a buttress split by a deep square chimney. ● **Insitewe**, VD, is the left side of the chimney, and ● **Rescewe,** S, is the right wall (both 2004). ● **Deep Freeze**, D (1932), crosses the wall right of the chimney from left to right. ● **Phewe**, VS 5a (2004), is a counter-diagonal. ● On the next buttress 6m right, the left arête is D, ● **Flakeaway**, E2 5b (2003), is the flat wall, ● and **Simple Walter**, S (1932), is the shallow corner and short crack 2m right.

Twenty metres right is a buttress with a roof at half-height on its right half.

② **Engram** E5 6b ★   1993
9m The snaking groove above the roof gives a fierce problem. An *in situ* wire used on the first ascent is usually in place.

● **One Ewe Over the Cuckoo's Nest**, VD (2004), is the narrow stepped slab just right of the roof. ● Eight metres right is a blocky overhung niche. **Greensleeves**, VS 5a, is the left corner of the niche

Jams O'Donnell on Rectilinear Wall, HVS 5a (this page). Photo: Graham Sutton.

and ● **Hilly Country Harvest**, HVS 5a, the right corner (both 1978).

③ **100 Not Out** E2 5b ★   2003
9m On the steep prow at the right end of the wall, climb the capped corner, swing left and climb the steep prow finishing on the right. ● **The Gable**, E1 5c (1978), is a direct start up the arête.

④ **Rectineal Wall** HVS 5a ★   1978
9m This lies on the steep, clean sidewall. Start at the right edge of the overhang, pull up into the short hanging corner and work leftwards across the steep wall to finish just right of the arête. Exposed. ● Climbing direct up from the corner is HS 4b, finishing up a short rounded crack.

Upper Derwent Edges

In the upper reaches of the Derwent Valley there are one or two embryonic edges and isolated boulders which provide short routes and an abundance of 'wilderness bouldering'. Many have been explored and are left for those with an adventurous bent, or keen to get away from it all. **The Barrow Stones** (SK135968) and northeast of them is **Howden Edge** (SK145980). The first rocks on the east side of the valley are the **Rocking Stones** and **Crowstones Edge** (SK170970) and **Bull Stones** (SK179961).

Abbey Brook Crags (SK190929) One kilometre up Abbey Brook past the old shooting cabins is a small clough where a stream comes over a line of crags. On the stream's north side in the centre of the crag is a steep wall. ● **P.C.C. One**, S (1949), starts in a shallow overhanging corner in the centre of the face, moves up right to a difficult mantelshelf and finishes on the right.

Abbey Brook Gorgelet (SK201925) More obscurity. ● **Lot's Wife**, HVS 5a (1998), is the obvious crack in the left-hand tower on the crag, starting with a steep pull on jammed chockstones. ● **Pillar of Salt**, HVS 5a (1998), starts up the arête right of Lot's Wife. Move on to the front face of the tower and climb direct on rewarding holds. ● **Remember-ance**, E1 5b ★ ★ (1998), is a fine route up the thin crack up the smooth wall in the centre of the crag. Good gear and hidden holds.

Ladybower Quarry

OS Ref. SK 208867   altitude 350m

by Paul Harrison

The southern end of Derwent Edge tumbles steeply down to the valley and the A57. Lurking behind the trees on the north side of the valley lies a jumble of quarried buttresses and huge blocks protected at their base by a dense carpet of often impenetrable brambles and shrubs. The quarry is a designated nature reserve, amongst the plentiful wildlife the observant may see all manner of birds from Goldcrests to Peregrines.

This is a venue for the lover of the esoteric and the visiting climber should bring an adventurous approach along with a good pair of secateurs. For the good (or bad) of Peak District climbing the majority of the routes had been cleaned and reascended.

Parking and Approach: The entrance to the quarry is tucked away on a dangerous bend in the A57 Sheffield to Manchester road, 200m uphill from the Ladybower Inn. Great care should be taken driving onto and off the drive with oncoming traffic. Alternatively, park in the bays at the reservoir and walk up. **The Climbing:** Despite a poor reputation, there are actually quite a few good routes here. The majority of the routes tend to follow steep, clean-cut cracks, which have a tendency to slant to the left. The rock can be extremely friable in places and demands careful handling particularly on the finishes. **Conditions and Aspect:** The walls are south-facing, quick drying and get sun in the morning. At such times, with the sun's warming rays peering over the hillsides, the seething greenery of the many birch trees, and the life-affirming joy of the birdsong, can there, in reality, be a finer place on earth?

The Upper Tier

The most prominent feature in the quarry is a large projecting buttress left of centre bounded on its left by a steep corner-crack, The Rat. Left of the projecting buttress is a long vegetated terrace at half-height. This is best approached by abseil from the trees above, or by scrambling up just right of the projection, or by a crack in the lower wall. ● **Kleen Crack,** HVS 5a (1967/1988), starts in the centre of the wall just left of a rock step and climbs to a tree belay. Up and left of the terrace is a slanting crack protected by brambles below and with a large oak tree above. ● This is **Blackberry Shuffle,** HVS 5a (1981-82).

On the terrace, 8m left of the corner of The Rat, are two divergent cracks.

① Brer Rabbit VS 5a   1967/1981-82
11m The left-hand crack gives a good climb with a difficult finish where the crack narrows. ● The right slanting crack 5m left is **Reward,** VS 5a (1983).

② Brer Fox HVS 5a   1967/81-82
11m The right-hand crack. Good jams exist above the niche at half-height. ● The dangerously loose groove 3m right is **Tighvor Grooves,** S (1967).

③ The Rat E1 5b ★★   1968
16m The big corner capped by an overhang. A strong line and perhaps the best route in the quarry. Sustained laybacking and jamming leads to a bridging position beneath the roof. Move confidently out on good jams and finish direct. Belay well back.

④ The Rodent HVS 5a   1976
17m On front of the projecting buttress is a steep, exposed flake-crack. Layback the crack and pull carefully round the bulge on hollow blocks to easier ground. Continue up the front face of the buttress to finish.

⑤ Pandora Buttress VS 4b   1966
20m Ascend the twin cracks 4m right of the arête with care.

⑥ Certain Surprise E1 5b   1983
18m Climb a thin flake-crack 5m right of Pandora Buttress.

WOW! It's hard to believe this is Britain, never mind Ladybower Quarry. Paul Harrison on the quarry's stand-out route, The Rat, E1 5b (previous page). Photo: David Simmonite.

7 Giant's Crack HVS 5b   1967

18m Follow the big, slanting crack in the centre of the wall to a large overhang-capped niche. Exit the niche with difficulty. ● **Frilly Bolero,** VS 4b (1983), climbs a slab on the right then traverses left to climb cracks right of Giant's Crack. ● **Hong Kong Garden,** HVS 4c (1983), is a more direct finish past three horizontal breaks.

Meccano Wall: The long orange wall to the right is split by a series of slanting crack-lines.

8 Jemelia E3 5c ★   2003

18m An exciting climb up the tower at the left-hand end of the wall. Start up a thin crack and gain a prominent large sloping ledge with difficulty. Move up to the base of a thin flake and follow it to a break below an overhang. Step right and pull through the overhang on good holds to reach the top. Stake belay well back. ● **Ratchet Crack,** HVS 4c (1981-82), takes the cracks 3m to the right. Dangerous.

9 Clockwork Orange E1 5b   1983

17m A nice technical pitch marred only by some hollow holds at mid-height. Climb the thin crack to a small ledge at half-height. Finish direct up the thin crack in the slim, orange pillar above. Stake belay.

Just right is a large overgrown block, forming a step in the terrace. ● **Onebat,** E1 5b (1986), starts above the step and follows a deep groove to a small overhang and continues up a crackline above to the top. ● Five metres right, just after the step **Malcrack,** HVS 4c (1970), is a prominent leftward-slanting crackline sporting plenty of loose rock.

10 First Coming HVS 5b ★   1983

17m Immediately right is a thin, vertical crack. Fine finger jamming leads to a small ledge just below the top. Step right on good holds and exit with care.

11 The Scoop HS 4b   1961

11m The scoop further right proves more awkward than it looks with a particularly tricky exit.

12 The Black Mini HVS 5b ★   1979

9m In the smooth wall below The Scoop are two cracks 2m apart. Climb the difficult left-hand crack. ● **Eric,** VS 5a (1983), is the easier right-hand crack. ● The obvious slanting break has been climbed; **Checker's Connection,** VS 5b (1987). Finish up or down The Black Mini.

The Smelting Bay: Directly below on a lower level and hidden in the trees is a small, square-cut bay. The left-hand side of the bay is formed by a small, clean slab and round to the left is a shorter wall that provides three short routes. ● **Twenty Feet**..., VS 5a (2001), is a short crack at the left-hand end of the wall. ● **Fatigued,** E1 5c (2003), gives tough technical climbing up the steep slab just right, past two horizontal seams. ● **Scorched Turf**, highball V2 (5c), starts just left of the arête of Anvil and boulders up to reach a jug on the left arête. To the right, in the bay, lies:

13 The Anvil HS 4c   1961

7m The left-hand arête of the clean slab is climbèd on its right-hand side. ● **Furnace Slab,** VS 5a (1961), is the slab on the right ● and the scrappy, corner of the bay on the right is **The Bin,** S (1961).

⑭ Leadsmelter's Crack HVS 4c   1981-82

9m The evil-looking crack-line 4m right guarded by a niche.

⑮ Mad Gadaffi E4 6a ★   1986

10m Just right is a once-pegged, overhanging finger crack. Strenuous and sustained climbing culminates in a difficult landing on the terrace. Peg belay.

⑯ E.N. 24 E1 5b ★   1981

10m Fierce jamming up the overhanging crack right again leads to an awkward finish onto the terrace. Peg belay up and right.

⑰ The Ingot VS 5a ★   1981-82

11m Tough! The imposing corner-crack immediately right packs a lot in for its short length. Peg belay up and right. ● **The Fat Controller,** VS 4c (1991), climbs the leaning corner from the ledge to the right.

⑱ Chocolate Meltdown E2 5b   1987

11m The right-hand arête of the bay.

Septic Area: At a higher level and 50m right of The Smelting Bay is a large corner with a wide cleft in its right wall. ● **Leadbelly's Lament,** HVS 5a (1987), is the sharp arête 10m left of the large corner. ● **Knuckle Knocker's Nightmare,** VS 4c (1981-82), is the sandy corner and crack 3m left of the main corner and above an old tree. ● **End of a Decade,** E1 5b (1989), is a bold but worthwhile proposition up the sharp arête immediately right and above a hole in the ground. ● The corner is **Cartilage Corner,** VS 4c (1981-82). ● **Bone of Contention,** E2 6a (1992), is the short bottomless groove in the wall to the right. Go up the groove with great difficulty to a break and continue up the steep headwall on small but good holds. ● **Septic Cleft,** VS 4c (1981-82), is on the right.

Birch Quarry

OS Ref. SK 210869 Ladybower's poor neighbour (and that is saying something), this small quarry is tucked away in the hillside, 50m up the road from Ladybower Quarry. The approach lies through a narrow hidden path just off the main road. All six routes were probably last cleaned and ascended for the 1981 guidebook, a commendable act, way beyond the thankless task of any writer. This author feels no need and indeed has no desire to repeat this feat.

The first route lies in a shallow bay left of the central arête. ● **Quarrymaster's Crack,** HS (1970), takes a line up the centre of the bay. ● The central arête boasts the cleanest route in the quarry; **The Hairy Ainu,** VD (1961). ● **Ainu's Crack,** VD (1961), is the crack on the right wall to finish on the arête. ● The right-hand wall terminates at a steep corner up a slope and the steep corner direct is **A Little Dilly,** HVS 5a (1970). ● The crag increases in height with **Silviculturist's Dream,** VS 4c (1970), the centre of the wall just right of A Little Dilly to a tree. ● Right again is a leftward-sloping crack **Tighe's Addition,** HS (1970), follows the crack to a grassy ledge. Move up and right to a corner and an undercut slab. Climb a short narrow slab on the right moving left to gain the large slab above and finish direct to a tree belay.

Priddock Woods

OS Ref. SK 206866 At the far northern end of Bamford Edge, on a spur above Priddock Wood, and directly opposite the Ladybower Inn on the A57, is a group of rocks. These rocks are not worth a special visit and none of the routes are longer than 7m. They are also lichenous and have a serious air to them and since the last guide (1989) they have become very overgrown. Because of this the routes haven't been checked and for completeness the descriptions from the previous guide are reproduced. The notes regarding access to Bamford Edge apply to these rocks. The quickest approach is probably to call in the pub (for liquid courage) and then from the car park, cross the water by a concrete pipe and go directly up the hillside, staggering slightly to the left. The highest rock gives some good short problems over overhangs. Directly below this is the largest buttress split in two tiers, the bottom section being scrappy and boasting a mature silver birch. The front of the second tier is climbed by **Woodcracker,** 5a (1960), and takes the overhangs from the right. The steep wall immediately right is **Dogwood,** 5b (1988). Fifteen metres to the left of Woodcracker is **Paul's Wall,** (1988), which goes direct up the centre at 5a. Other problems exist to either side of the buttress.

Bamford Edge

OS Ref. SK 208849 altitude 420m

by David Simmonite

Bamford Edge is truly one of the gems of Peak grit, sat majestically on a wild hillside, with its back turned on the busy popularity of the Eastern Edges, looking instead, longingly, towards the wildness of Kinder and Bleaklow. For this is more where the heart of Bamford Edge lies.

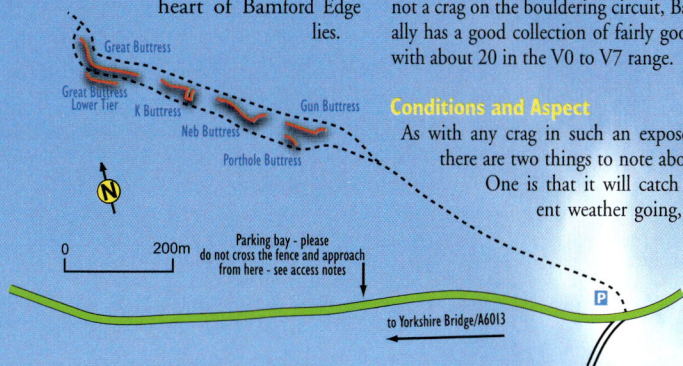

of small buttresses stretching for 800m along the crest of the Derwent Valley. Very solid, with incredible friction. Routes: With 160 routes from D to E7, Bamford has it all. The crag is great for short solos, good stiff cracks and walls in the mid grades, powerful roof climbs for thugs, and the exquisite Salmon Slab for bold technicians. Bouldering: Traditionally not a crag on the bouldering circuit, Bamford actually has a good collection of fairly good problems, with about 20 in the V0 to V7 range.

Conditions and Aspect

As with any crag in such an exposed situation, there are two things to note about Bamford. One is that it will catch any inclement weather going, the other is

Great Buttress

Great Buttress Lower Tier

K Buttress

Gun Buttress

Neb Buttress

Porthole Buttress

N

0   200m

Parking bay - please do not cross the fence and approach from here - see access notes

to Yorkshire Bridge/A6013

P

The Edge has been traditionally seldom visited, although this is now starting to change (due mainly to new access agreements which have removed the ban that kept climbers off for a lot of the year). As such, there was little of the legacy of litter, polish and erosion that other more popular crags have. Instead there was solid rough rock, wildlife and great routes. They're all still there, of course, and while it is now more popular than it has been, it is still a superb place with a great sense of solitude.

that it will dry out in no time. It can be impossible to climb there on a very windy day. The crag faces southwest, and gets sun for most of the day. The views are superb, overlooking Win Hill, the sleepy village of Bamford and the Derwent Reservoirs

Parking and Approach

Read and follow the access notes below. The approach takes a very pleasant 15-25 minutes across gently rising terrain.

The Climbing

Superb climbing on rough, natural grit, with great variety, situated on a number

Important Access Notes

Who owns Bamford Moor?
Bamford Moor is in the private ownership of Mr Jeremy Archdale of Moscar lodge. It is a classic example of a well-maintained grouse moor, and is managed for sporting and wildlife interests. Although the Moor is mapped as open access under the Countryside and Rights of Way (CRoW) Act (2000), this does not preclude the need to respect someone else's property and interest. It is particularly important to avoid damage to walls, fences, and all ground nesting birds and their nest sites.

What are climbers' rights of access to the Edge?
Under CRoW, there is now statutory right of access to the Edge. However, you should use only the agreed access points to gain admission to the moor (see below). Do not attempt to access the Moor or the Edge except by these points. The landowner has a right to close the moor, or any part of it, for up to 28 days in any year (excluding bank holidays, summer weekends or more than four weekend days outside the summer period) for a variety of purposes. Current advice can be checked at the BMC either by phone or at **www.thebmc.co.uk/outdoor/rad/rad.asp** and enter Bamford Edge at the site name prompt.

GO THROUGH THIS GATE ONLY!

There are additional Restrictions at Bamford Edge in respect of dogs because the Moor is a grouse moor. Dogs, whether or not they are on a lead, are banned at all times. The whole of Bamford Moor is part of the Eastern Moors Site of Special Scientific Interest (SSSI), a designation made because of breeding moorland birds. Under the CRoW Act, the Access Authority can close the Moor altogether on the advice of English Nature if the integrity of the SSSI is threatened, for example by a sudden increase in human traffic. Disturbance to wild birds and their nests also constitutes an offence under the Countryside and Wildlife Act (1981). If you trash the place, climbing will be banned.

What are the negotiated access agreements?
While you can reach Bamford across Moscar, from Heatherdene car park, or from Cut Throat Bridge, the only practical access point is from the New Road, which runs from the Yorkshire Bridge Inn to the Dennis Knoll area of Stanage. There is only one access point on this road, at SK 216839 (near the top of Leeside Road/Bamford Clough). When coming from Yorkshire Bridge, after 1km, an iron gate and an old ruin are seen on the left. This has been recommended as an access point in other guidebooks in the past, but DO NOT approach the cliff from here. Instead continue past this, 300m or so up the road, to another lay-by next to an obvious stile and footpath marker post. The Edge is accessed via a sunken trackway, running broadly northwest. It is important not to attempt access from any other point on the New Road. This means that access notes in old guidebooks are now wrong. This access agreement was negotiated by the Access Authority, the landowner and the BMC, and has been endorsed by the Local Access Forum. It was agreed to protect the landscape from vertical erosion and scarring, and in the interests of road safety. It emphatically does not imply any denial of statutory access rights. We do have rights, thanks to CRoW, but we also have responsibilities.

The landowner has also expressed that no dogs are allowed, as the moor is managed for wildlife.

Henry Folkard and Bunny McCullough
BMC Peak Access Team, 2005

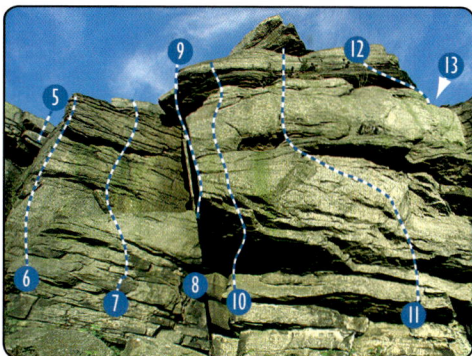

Great Buttress Upper Tier

The proud showpiece of Bamford Edge is the Great Buttress area. Few crags can match the grandeur of its setting, perched high on the bold hillside, guarding the tranquil village of Bamford, looking across onto Win Hill, and of course, along to the dams and reservoirs of the Derwent Valley. Added to this is a great collection of routes in the mid-grades, and you are left with one of the great venues on grit.

Palpitation Buttress: This is the leftmost of the buttresses on the upper tier. ● The deep cleft on the left is **Easy Chimney**, M (1900s). The wall to the left is 4a, first into a cleft and then out left under the overlap. ● The wall left again and via a crack is 4c ● and the leaning crozzled end wall is a good problem; **End Face**, V0+ (5b).

① Palpitation VS 5b   1930
7m Power up the undercut arête with difficulty. Originally given VD? ● Another (and perhaps the original?) way of gaining the arête is by bridging up the corner on the left to good holds and a common finish, **Thumping**, HS 4b (1992).

② Thin On Top E2 5b   1981
8m A bold number rising up the left-hand end of the wall. Go up to a hole and step right to a bald finish up a thin flake. It shares the same low protection as Green and Nasty.

③ Green and Nasty E2 5c   1981
8m Climb a flake and wall trending slightly right

to thought-provoking, reachy moves on sloping breaks. With low protection in the flake, this is not one to fall off.

④ In my Pocket HVS 5b   1999
7m Go direct up the wall passing a prominent pocket. The right arête is 5a.

Kelly Buttress: To the right, across a wide cleft, is the next buttress, with the prominent line of Deep Chimney in its centre.

⑤ Initiation S 4b   pre-1957
6m The short V-corner on the left leads to a layback overhang. A stiff pull leads to the top. The wall left is a 4a problem.

⑥ Beer Matters VS 5a   1997
6m The arête climbed on its right-hand side to a steep finish. The block at the top 'appears' solid enough. ● The slabby left side of the arête and finishing up a cleft is possibly **Introduction**, S 4a (pre-1957), though with a very vague description it has been difficult to locate this route. ● Direct up the green wall just left is HS 4c.

⑦ Fat Cat HVS 5b   1997
6m The short steep wall starting up a leaning flake.

⑧ Deep Chimney M   1900s
10m Chimneys were all the rage then, apparently. Classic stuff.

9 Kelly S 4a   1918

10m Another ancient addition from one of the Peak's great pioneers. Gain the shelf, then take a short crack above and move round right to finish. ● The wall just left passing a loose but seemingly immovable block is **Gene**, HS 4b (2003).

10 Deaf Raspberry Climb E1 5c   1982

10m The undercut arête leads to an easy finish.

11 Astronaut's Wall HVS 5a ★   1963

10m Grunt up to the overhang and go through the weakness before things get easier above. Take care with protection in the hollow rock beneath the overhang.

12 Possibility S 4a ★   1957

12m A fine juggy ramble. On the left wall of Primitive Chimney, go up to below the upper bulge. Move left round the corner in a great situation and a leftwards finish.

13 Primitive Chimney D   1901

10m Another fine Puttrell thrutch. The obvious V-cleft where the huge overhang ends is climbed passing a moving chockstone.

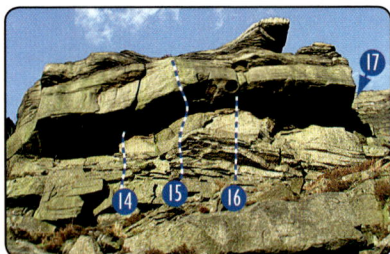

Undercut Buttress: Easily identified by its huge roof. At present this roof is home to two awesome routes, but there used to be another route, A35, and graded E1 5b, with a chequered history. Unfortunately, it lost a large flake and wasn't re-climbed until 1984, at E4 6b, and renamed M35. Since then it has shed any remaining holds and is now deemed 'unclimbable'. Only time and talent will tell. ● **The Overhang Traverse**, M (pre-1957), traverses beneath the roof.

14 Undercut Crack E2 5c ★ ★ ★   1958

10m An unsung classic – thuggery at its best. This is where a gritstone crack climbing apprenticeship will

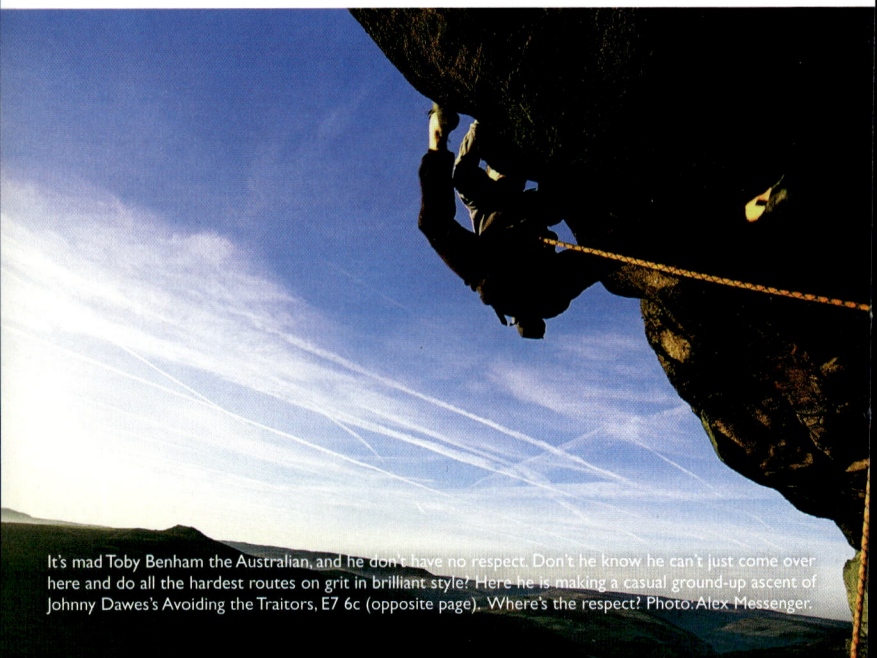

It's mad Toby Benham the Australian, and he don't have no respect. Don't he know he can't just come over here and do all the hardest routes on grit in brilliant style? Here he is making a casual ground-up ascent of Johnny Dawes's Avoiding the Traitors, E7 6c (opposite page). Where's the respect? Photo: Alex Messenger.

pay off; technical wizardry will count for nothing here and only brute force and ignorance pay dividends. And so what if you lose the odd bit of skin, the experience will more than make up for it. Attack the fissure with gusto, passing an old thread.

Just to the right are the remains of M35 whose description from the last guidebook is included for posterity.

15 M35 (was E4 6b)   1958/75

10m This route crossed the roof at a curious series of inverted scallops. Creaking flakes led over the roof to a horrible mantelshelf above. One of the few routes in the world that was harder for the tall. Not only that, but it was first done with a sling for aid, although subsequent ascents found it easier to climb it free. Unclimbed in its current state.

16 Avoiding the Traitors E7 6c ★★   1995

10m Johnny Dawes's fine addition, an elegant and desperate addition to the great roof. The splendid dish and runnels are climbed by powerful, dynamic and bold climbing. With gear at the back of the roof, swing out and launch up the runnel on pinches, slaps and pebbles.

17 Bad Wind HS 4b   traditional

11m This good but scrappy-looking line starts at a crack on the right of the wall. Move up this to a narrowing cleft on the left of a block, overcoming this gives an awkward crux. Finish up a pleasant crack on the left wall or traverse left to the arête at the same grade.

Gargoyle Buttress: The next buttress right has a fine projecting gargoyle pointing towards the valley, and is home to one of grit's finer VSs.

18 Claim to Fame HVS 5a   1981

13m The cracked slab leads to a steeper headwall.

19 Terrace Rib VS 4c   2003

13m A slabby rib gains the steeper arête above.

20 Terrace Trog M ★   1961-63

14m The leftwards-slanting weakness is climbed easily with increasing exposure. ●**Missing ASG,** HVS 5a (1997), takes the bulging wall above the ledge.

21 Terrace Wall VS 4b   1963

13m From Terrace Trog, take a diagonal weakness rising up the steep wall on the right

22 Old Wall HVS 5b   pre-1991

13m Begin below the left side of the overlap formed by the flake of Gargoyle Flake and use flaky holds to climb the wall above.

23 Gargoyle Flake VS 4c ★★★   1963

13m An excellent, photogenic route with reasonable climbing in thrilling positions. Climb the lower arête to a ledge and layback the large flake above to an exhilarating finish over the gargoyles, using the biggest jugs possible. A 5a start on the juggy rib just left of the arête and an inferior finish up the wall left of the gargoyles can be climbed but it just doesn't have the same quality.

It's enough to bring a smile to your face. Few places in the Peak can match Bamford for the grandeur of its setting, and there is no better route to experience this setting than Gargoyle Flake, VS 4c (previous page). Photo: Ian Smith.

● The gully on the right goes at D. ● Four metres right, **Sunset**, HVD (traditional), weaves up to a short offwidth and climbs the juggy wall above.

㉔ Bum Deal E1 5b   1981
10m A thin crack crosses the overhang 6m right of the gulley. Climb it, and the crack above.

㉕ Clean, Squeaky and Scented E1 6b   1985
10m Climb the horrendously difficult bulge 4m right of the crack.

Tinner Buttress: Sat to the right is an isolated buttress, characterised by wrinkles and two flakes. This is the last of the upper buttresses.

㉖ Hard Rain E2 5c   1999
7m Climb the narrow left wall to a break. Stand in this and with help of the left arête, make a hard move to gain another break and soon the top.

㉗ Left Wing S 4a   1961-63
8m The steep broken cracks passing a heathery niche.

㉘ Almost Granite HVS 5a ★   1999
10m Climb the thin crack left of Tinner to an alcove and finish direct up the headwall above. Sparsely protected and at the upper limit of the grade.

㉙ Tinner HVS 5b ★   1958
10m A bold lead, where a steady approach is the key to success. Use the flake to surmount a bulge and continue precariously to a ledge, then the top.

㉚ Right-Hand Twin HVS 5a ★   1958
12m Another good, open voyage. Gain the chunky flake and follow the precarious rightwards-slanting line above. Protection is there but it takes a little finding.

㉛ Private Practice HVS 5b ★   pre-1991
10m A direct line up the buttress gives more of the same quality and boldness.

㉜ Solstice Arête VS 4c   1997
9m Gain the ledge and continue up the lichenous arête to tackle the bulge directly. Escapable.

The Lower Tier

Tucked away under the proud displays of the Great Buttress lies the fabulous lower tier. This contains a good collection of steep cracks, grooves and arêtes. However, sat in the middle of all these is The Salmon Slab, one of the great slabs of grit, and a superb testing ground for the lover of high-end smearing. The tier is gained by scrambling down from below Undercut Buttress or by skirting round beyond Palpitation Buttress.

Salmon Boulders: About 35m left of the start of the routes lie some large blocks. These rarely-visited boulders give some superb problems. The first set of boulders is made up of a large steep block with a couple of smaller ones just left. Twenty metres down and left is a big boulder with an undercut arête.

㉝ Something Silly V5 (E2 6b)
The fierce arête.

㉞ Something Else V0 (VS 4c)
Start up the right arête and traverse the break to finish up the arête.

The next climb is on the left of the next set of boulders.

㉟ Win Hill V0 (5a)
Swing up and left onto a ramp.

㊱ Lose Hill V3 (6a)
Climb the scratchy pillar to the right.

AAARRRRGH! Donie O'Sullivan latches the top hold on Trout, E6 6b (opposite page). Photo: Niall Grimes.

37 **Ping Pong Pocket Rib** V7 (6b)
The classy left arête of the big buttress.

38 **Flaky Fluster** V4 (6b)
Undercut flakes and make a desperate reach for the top.

39 **Wriggly Crack** V0– (4c)
Climb the crack and step left to exit. ● **Snap** climbs the flake just right; V0 (4b).

Moving right, between the upper and lower tier, is a short, smart slab. ● The centre is V0 (5a), ● and the right arête is V0– (4c).

Salmon Slab Area

The quality routes now begin to the right.

40 **Hasta La Vista** HVD   1957
8m A good honest thrutch. Climb the wide crack and step right onto the upper slab. The finish is easier but does feature a short grovel. The shallow corner to the left is VD.

41 **Back Flip** E1 5b ★   1991
11m Follow the left-hand edge of the wall, easily at first, but soon with hard climbing passing the overlaps, to a ledge. Layback the arête above to a capstone, step left and finish directly over the capstone in an airy position.

42 **Benberry Wall** E3 5c ★   1976
10m A harrowing experience. Bold protectionless moves lead up the wall into a leftwards-leaning groove which leads to the top.

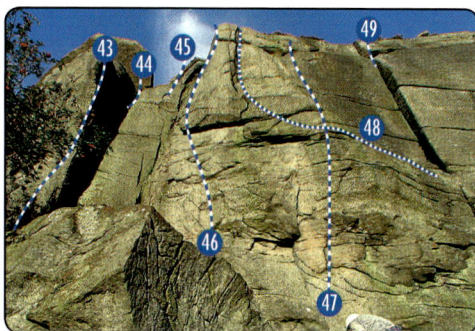

43 The Naked Eye E3 5b ★   1982
10m Start up Benberry Wall but make awkward moves right past loose flakes and a hole to finish up the arête above on its right-hand side.

44 Bilberry Crack VS 5a ★★   1952
10m A little gem. The left-hand corner-crack gives good well-protected climbing with the odd tricky move. 'Bridge it, my son, bridge it!'

45 Recess Crack VD   1952
10m Climb the stiff right-hand corner of the recess.
● The V-groove and wall on the right go at VS 4c.

46 Jive Bunny E4 5c   pre-1991
10m Use a creaking flake to gain the arête and move up to a small ledge. Finish up the blunt rib above mainly on its left-hand side.

47 Nemmes Pas Harry E1 5b ★★   1982
10m A little artificial but still with quality climbing. Follow the disappearing crack over the bulge to gain ledges and finish up the scoop to its right. ● An excellent sustained HVS 5a, **Nemmes Sabe** ★★, can be had by linking the start of Nemmes Pas Harry with the more natural finish of Quien Sabe?

48 Quien Sabe? VS 5a ★★★   1958
14m Guaranteed to brighten your day; safe and technically absorbing. From Brown's Crack, swing up the scoop to a crack in the nose above. The crux is overcoming this and it is certainly no pushover.
● An E3 6a eliminate exists that follows Quien Sabe? to where that route traverses left, and continues up the narrow wall above via pockets.

49 Brown's Crack HS 4b ★★★   1951
12m A tremendous route taking the straight crack that flanks the left-hand side of the slab. It proves tricky to begin and the rest is pure crack-climbing delight.

The Salmon Slab: The stunning slab to the right is home to some of the finest climbs of their type in the country. The routes feature thinner than thin slab climbing, although this all tends to take place above a good break which gives bomber protection. So, while a tumble may be possible, you won't hit the ground. The slab has sprouted lines in abundance and just about every inch of the wall and every combination appear to have been climbed. The most contrived have been ignored.

50 Jetrunner E4 6a ★★   1984
12m A very gentle introduction to the local slab delights, with a couple of tidy runouts. Climb the wall to the mid-height break then finish up the left arête. A start can also be made up the lower arête.

51 Trout (AKA Salmon Left-Hand)
E6 6b ★★★   1995
12m A first-rate route and very onsightable. Climb Jetrunner to the break. Step up and follow pockets until a memorable lunge gains the ledge.

52 Salmon Direct E6 6c ★★★   1998
12m A fine direct companion, without the line of the original, but with great moves and positions nonetheless. From the break, carefully gain the high pocket from the right (left foot in pocket), make a high smear rightwards and up to the top.

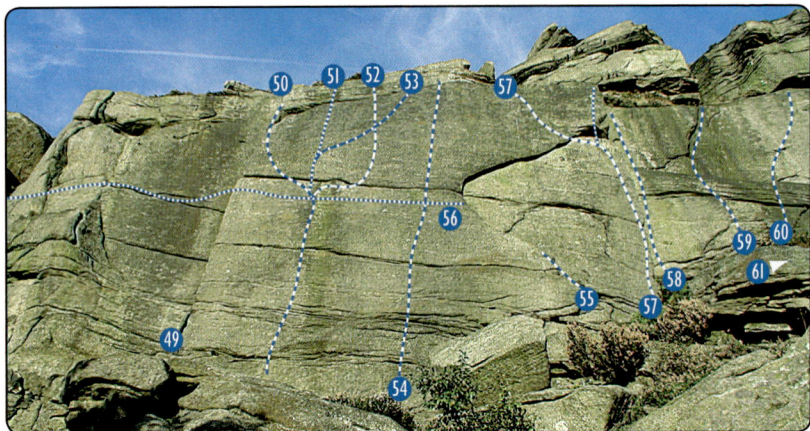

53 The Salmon E7 6c ★★★   1984/95
13m Johnny's original sizzler, updated for the 90s.
The moves in its top half are excellent as is the fall
potential. Gain the break and make a step up into a

Tom Speyer on Jetrunner (previous page) which,
at E4 6a, and easy for the grade, is a good way of
sampling the beautiful, and fairly hardcore Salmon
Slab at a reasonable price. Photo: Dave Parry.

pocket. From here trend rightwards using a combination of poor pebbles and a group of pockets to a
hard finishing move in a committing position.

54 Smoked Salmon E7 7a ★★★   1995
12m Slab climbing at its most tenuous with holds
more imagined than real. Attain the mid-height
break by whichever means you feel necessary (this is
the easy bit) and somehow (using power of thought?)
levitate up the upper slab right of The Salmon. Very
small smears and miniscule pebbles mark the way
up towards a group of small pockets. If you reach
here, via the three consecutive 7a moves, you truly
are a slab master.

55 Curving Crack VS 4c ★   1958
10m Meanwhile, back on planet Earth… Follow
the bold curving feature with great jams and
increasing difficulty to a delicate step into Sandy
Crack and a still interesting finish.

56 Quebec City VS 5a ★   1981
30m An easy drive through stunning scenery. Start
up Curving Crack and keep heading leftwards along
the break to finish up Quien Sabe? or easier, (HS
4b) continue to Recess Crack.

57 Poached Salmon E5 6b ★   1999
10m Make your way up the arête right of Curving
Crack via a series of slaps to the break. Place welcome protection before stepping left and heading

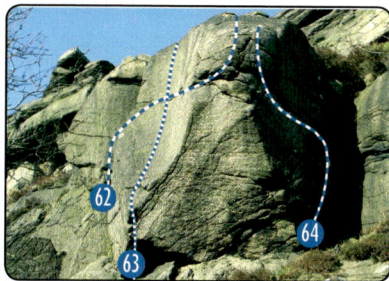

up for a short flake, and a finish on slopers. Reachy at the top. ●A direct finish, **Tartar Sauce**, E5 6b ★ (2003), climbs the arête above the break.

58 Sandy Crack S 4b ★ 1930
8m The corner gives good climbing to a ledge. The offwidth crack above gives an awkward finish.

59 Greydon Boddington VS 5b 1977
7m After the bouldery bottom bulge, the wall and discontinuous thin cracks lead to a grovel to finish.

60 Fizz E1 5c ★ 1980
7m A remarkably joyous little climb, guaranteed to give a buzz. Boulder up to the ledge then climb the wall past two sets of threadable pockets. Reachy.

61 Two Real Doleys Scrounging E3 6b 1990s
7m Gain and climb the scoop in upper part of wall right of Fizz.

Just to the right is the descent path from the Upper Tier. Ten metres right a flake leans against the wall. ●**Flake Buttress Rib**, HS 4b (2003), climbs the centre of the flake and the scoop above. Ten metres right again is a boulder with a fine scoop in it containing the next routes. The crack to its left is VD.

62 The Egg E4 6a ★ 1984
9m Climb up to a crack left of the scoop and using a high pocket, a difficult pull gains entry into the scoop (RPs in the break). Step right and with even more difficulty, make a rightwards exit.

63 High and Dry E6 6b ★ 1986
8m A direct start and finish to The Egg. A hard but well-protected move into the scoop leads to a

harrowing crux exit from it. Take lots of small RPs. For those over six foot tall the route is only E5 6a.

64 The Chicken HVS 5a 1987
7m From the short crack, swing left to gain the rounded arête.

Twenty metres right is a slabby buttress with a prominent wrinkled overlap running right across it. ●**Acid Slab**, VD (2003), is the left edge of the buttress and ●**Assorted Batteries**, HVS 5a (1987), is the centre. ●**Various Undercuts**, HVS 5a (1990), climbs the right-hand side of the slab and ●**Alkaline Arête**, S 4a (2003), is the right arête.

K Buttress Area

The next outcrops are 70m across the bouldery hillside, with a few shorter rocks and a narrow fin sticking out of the hillside on the right, vaguely reminiscent of an Easter Island statue.

On the left are a number of small isolated buttresses, which provide a number of problems. The second buttress leans to the left, while behind and left of this is a square buttress. ●The left arête is **Klever**, VS 5b, ●the rounded arête just right is **Klueless**, HS 5a, ●and the wall on the right is **K'Pow** V0 (5a). ●On the leaning buttress to the right, **Kin 'eck**, S, is the centre of the wall facing Jasmine. ●The arête to the right is VD. ●On the back of the buttress is a 4c hanging crack. ●On the third buttress, with an overhang at its base, **K'kin**, HS 4c, surmounts the overhang and continues up the right side of the arête. ●The wall two metres left is HS 4b (all 1992). To the right is a sprawling slab. ●This can be climbed anywhere at S. Behind this slab is another slab:

65 K Buttress Slab VD ★ 1951-52
8m Pleasantly climb the right-hand edge of the slab. ●The centre of the slab is **K Buttress Slab Direct**, VD (traditional), hardest at the start, while the left edge is also VD.

66 Ko'd V2 (VS 5b)
An ape-man delight. Swing out from the depths on a juggy break to gain and slap up the hanging arête. Feet on ledges on the right at this grade, otherwise it

feels more like V4.

● **K Kole Arête**, V6 (6b), is the sharp, leaning arête direct, starting from a jug at the base.

67 K Buttress Crack S 4a ★★   1951-52
8m A deeply character-building voyage up the spooky dark slanting chimney.

68 Wrong Hand Route E1 5c ★★   1971
10m 'A tough little bastard', but fortunately very safe. A tricky start up the rib leads to the base of the slanting crack. Now stop and think - using the right sequence here will make life easier. An alternative start can be made up the initial wall using a flat hold; 5c if you can reach, otherwise 6a.

69 Skarlati E2 5c ★   1969
10m Good long reaches above distant protection make this a memorable lead. From the right gain a

small ledge on the right arête, then go over the bulge above, trending slightly left.

70 Bracken Crack VD   1963
10m A good climb following the crack, moving out right and over the bulge. ● The vegetated chimney on the left is **Fern Chimney,** D (1961-63).

71 The Bookend V4 (6b)
The end face of the superb fin.

72 Bookend Right V5 (6b)
Climbing the arête on the right is equally fine.

73 Down to Earth E3 6a ★   1985
7m A good but worrying problem up the diminutive arête complete with a scary finish. ● Protectable, although it makes for a brilliant V3 with mats (don't they all?). ● **The Plumber has Landed** is the vague crack/seem just left, V4 (6a). ● The vegetated chimney has been climbed at HVD.

74 Crunchy Nuts VS 5a   pre-1983
6m The square arête. ● V1. ● The arête to the right is **Stoned**, V2 (HVS 5b), ● while **Petered Out** is the crack and arête just right of this, V0 (HS 4c).

The previous problems can be used as a first pitch to the next routes, which start off the ledge above.

75 **Wee Lassie** VS 5a   2000
7m   The bulging wall just left of Special K has good holds and an extending finish.

76 **Special K** HVS 5a   1971
8m   Climb a short crack and bulges above via a very good hold.

77 **Dead Mouse Crack** HS 4c ★   1958
8m   Follow the crack system steeply leftwards. A reach from the top of the crack gains good holds. Can be started and finished direct at a similar grade but is much harder for the short (5b).

78 **Hanging Crack** HS 4b   1958
7m   The undercut crack on the right of the buttress isn't so bad once you get amongst it.

79 **Bamboozer** E3 6a ★   1993
12m   Technical climbing on small holds, and possibly paddable. Climb the wide crack (HVD) then swing boldly right on small holds and finish direct.

80 **Jasmine** E6 6b ★★★   1990
12m   One of Ron Fawcett's last great additions to his beloved grit, and a superb, daring solution to a long-standing problem. The centre of the wall is climbed past poor breaks with no protection. Practice those campus moves!

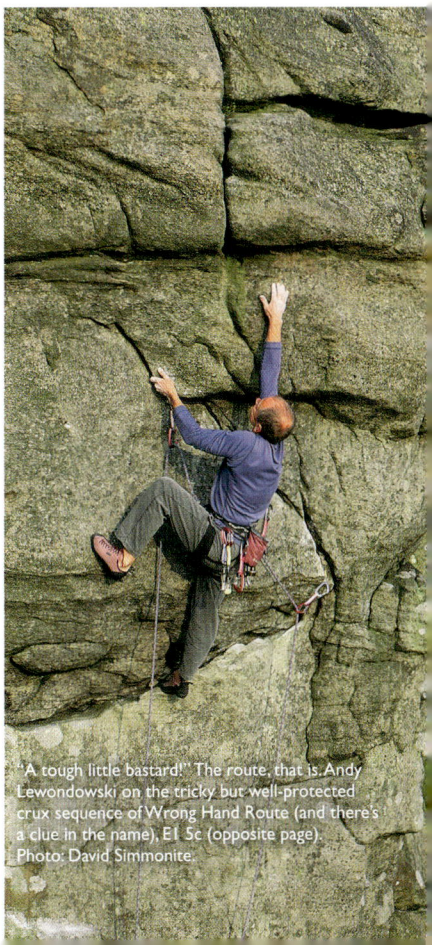

'A tough little bastard!' The route, that is. Andy Lewondowski on the tricky but well-protected crux sequence of Wrong Hand Route (and there's a clue in the name), E1 5c (opposite page). Photo: David Simmonite.

"An absolute must for any VS leader, with solid moves and ever more spaced protection."

Stephen Coughlan on Wrinkled Wall, VS 4c (opposite page). Photo: David Simmonite.

86 **Save Dinnomite** V4 (6a)
The left rib is climbed using the arête and a pocket round left. Good moves, although the crack and ledge on the right are artificially avoided at this grade.

87 **Way Rood** V0 (5a)
Slither into the niche. Fun. The right arête is V1 (5b).

Neb Buttress Area

Twenty metres right sees the beginning of the Neb Buttress area, containing some of the longest and best climbs on Bamford Edge. On the left is a short wall with a horizontal break containing two problems. ●**Twiglet Wall**, V2 (5c), is the blunt rib 2m left of the corner, passing a small twig, with a bold crank for the ledge. ●**Monster Munch** V3 (6a) is the scoop 2m left again, passing a couple of sloping crimps. Both have bad landings.

88 **Cleopatra** VS 4c   1961-63
8m   A burly hanging crack rises from the corner on the left-hand side of the arête.

89 **Samson's Delight** HS 4c ★   1963
8m   An underrated and strenuous route on good, hidden holds. Climb the overhanging arête, then move into a crack and continue to the top.

90 **Dirty Stop Out** E2 5b ★   1981
8m   A fierce little crack leads to delightful moves over the upper bulge.

91 **Delilah** HS 4a   1961-63
8m   The crack has good holds but uncomfortable moves to reach the lip. Very large cams reduce the grade to S and the short will probably quibble no matter what. ●The wall just right has a thin crack that gives a V0+ (5b) problem.

81 **Access Account** E3 6a ★   1985
12m   Hard slapping above a very hard landing are needed to gain the wide break. Step right to finish more easily up the arête.

Wrinkled Wall: The next climbs are on the fine wrinkled wall on the back of the Easter Island feature.

82 **Wrinkled Wall** VS 4c ★ ★   1958
14m   An absolute must for any VS leader, with solid moves and ever more spaced protection. Starting from a short vertical slot, a diagonal line leads leftwards to the arête. An airy finale up this concludes a tremendous route.

83 **The Crease** E1 5a ★ ★   1979
12m   A distinct lack of protection gives the E grade (just) and makes this an exciting but terrific outing. From the start of Wrinkled Wall head straight up to the top using shallow cracks and without recourse to the arête on the right. ●A slightly easier but still bold alternative, is to climb the wall just left of centre. This has recently been dubbed **Old and Wrinkled,** HVS 5a ★ (traditional).

84 **Sinuous Crack** D   pre-1957

The Sugar Cube: Twenty metres right is a large cube of rock sat high on the hillside.

85 **Duff Paddy** V4 (6a)
The right arête of the block using a pocket and a pebble. Bad landing. The left arête is unclimbed.

Twenty metres right, a block sits on top of a small bundle of boulders with a niche in the middle.

> "**I liked it** when it was a **wild crag** and people didn't go. The fairies have been scared away now. Or, rather, the ability to sense them has gone."
>
> **Johnny Dawes**, Climb Magazine

92 **Short Curve** VD   1957-59
7m   Steep, awkward and, of course, good fun.

93 **The Business Boy** V4 (E1 6b)
Follow breaks up the centre of the wall. ●Towards
the right side of the wall, **Snuggazzabug**, HS 4b
(2005), is a fun voyage on unusual holds starting
steeply, then trending left to finish through the
scoop at the top.

94 **N.B. Corner** M   1961-63

95 **Big Ben** VS 4c   1961-63
10m   The side-wall of the buttress contains twin
cracks. The left-hand crack is steep, well-protected,
but technically okay.

96 **Parliament** HVS 5b   1981
12m   The right-hand crack is climbed keeping out
of the left-hand crack. Artificial, but who cares, the
climbing more than makes up for it.

97 **Auricle** E2 5c ★ ★   1971
16m   A tremendous route, with good holds, bomber
gear and, if you have long arms, very gentle for the
grade. Climb the steep and technical face direct,
with reachy moves to pass the mid-height overlap.
Escape right at the top overhang, or try ●**Jumping
Jack Longland**, E3 5c ★ ★ (1979), which continues boldly and acrobatically directly over the roof.

98 **Neb Buttress** HVS 5a ★ ★ ★   1958
20m   A classic and varied climb to rival any on grit.

Climb the thin crack, then traverse left on good
holds to the arête. Step round left to follow the
steep crack to the overhang, then the wall above to
escape strenuously right along the wide crack and
mantel over the nose to finish. Phew! ●Alternatively
try the **Neb Buttress Direct Start**, HVS 5a ★ ★
(traditional), up the delicate left-hand arête of the
buttress.

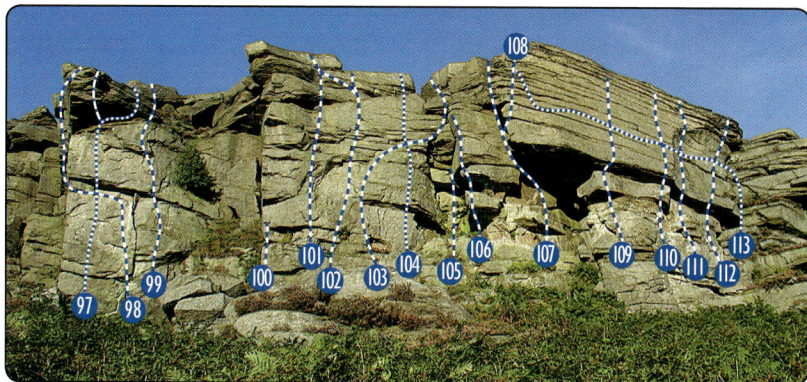

99 Bamford Rib HVS 5a ★ ★   1973

17m A fine companion to Neb Buttress, although this time demanding technique and boldness more than force. Neat moves up the blunt rib lead to a ledge and a prickly rest. Step left and continue up the steeper wall via the obvious lump.

● On the right is **Holly Crack,** VD, ● and the recess on the right is **Bramble Crack,** D (both 1957-59).

100 The Happy Wanderer HVS 5a ★ ★   1967

13m An exquisite and well-protected route – satisfyingly steep on generous holds, although it still requires some commitment. Climb the square arête on jugs to a reachy move below the top overlaps (5b for the short).

101 Reach VS 4c   1981

13m Climb direct 2m right of the arête (and keeping left of Bamford Wall) via a series of long reaches (or awkward mantels) through bulges and niches. Good sustained climbing.

102 Bamford Wall S 4a ★ ★   1960

13m A first-class route and a must for anyone operating at this level. Climb a rightward-slanting flake to the top of a big flake. Move right and go straight up the bulging wall to a finish up the obvious crack. If you wish, from the top ledge you can then move left for an exposed finale.

103 Bamford Buttress HS 4a ★   1958

13m Starting at an obvious yellow hole, climb up

and onto the top of a huge flake at 5m and then slant up and right to finish as for Twin Cracks. Not overly well-protected

104 Busy Day at Bamford VS 5a   1991

12m Climb a blunt rib to an easier pleasant finish up the steep slab above.

105 Twin Cracks VS 4b ★   1960

10m A surprisingly graceful route, considering the terrain. From the cave, climb up to follow the right-hand crack by bridging and jamming.

106 Custard's Last Stand VS 5b   1983

10m The steep arête has some good moves but is artificial.

107 Deep Cleft M ★   pre-1957

12m The chimney is taken in its depths and a tight exit is performed behind the chockstones. If, however, you are a little larger than average it may be necessary to climb on the outside of the chockstones. In which case, the climb is harder (D) and it's time to cut down on the cakes?

108 Oracle VS 4b ★ ★   1971

13m An unsung route with a very traditional feel taking spectacular ground but just meriting the VS tag. From halfway up Deep Cleft, take a deep breath and traverse right above the void using a low break to gain the arête at a small roof. Swing round in a thrilling position and finish up the arête.

Rick Colgreave on The Happy Wanderer, HVS 5a (previous page). Photo: David Simmonite.

109 Sterling Moss E4 6b ★   1984
16m Saunter up to the roof 3m left of Ontos and make a hard crimpy pull over this to easier ground.

110 Ontos E3 6b ★ ★   1966?/74/75
18m A quality route with a definite crux that benefits from colder conditions (i.e. feels easier!) From below the roof, reach round to the obvious jug and somehow use it to attain a standing position in the centre of the wall, then continue more easily with care to the top. One for the shorties!

111 Fatal Inheritance E4 6a   1982
16m Go up to a small roof and after a big stretch over this, take a direct line up the wall right of Ontos via a short curving flake crack.

112 Purgamentum E4 6b   2004
14m The scooped wall. Climb a short corner and make a hard move over the overlap to a break. Climb the overhanging wall trending right using pebbles to breaks and a scary top out. Keep out of the corner!

113 Trouble with Lichen HVS 5b ★   1973
25m A good route crossing memorable territory. From Slanting Slab head leftwards on a narrow ledge to its end where a committing step leaves one stood on the jug of Ontos. An exposed but protectable foot-traverse on the lowest break gains the left arête up which a finish is made.

To the right is a corner crack. ● The slab on the right is **Slanting Slab,** M (pre-1957). ● **Grey Days,** E2 5c (1981), takes the squat roof on the far right-hand side of the wall on the right starting from a hole at the back and with the hard bit at the top. ● Further right, **Three Little Pigs,** HVD 4a (2003), goes straight up from the right side of the ledge via three short awkward walls. Right of this wall is a descent path.

The Little Wings: Right of the descent path are two small blocks separated by a corner crack. ● The left wall is **Mur,** V0+ (5b) ● and the fine wide crack is **Fente** V0− (4c), climbed from a sitter. ● The clean groove in the right-hand block is **Cannalure,** V1 (5b).

Porthole Buttress

About 30m right of Neb Buttress, the rock divides into two tiers. On the lower one there is a buttress, characterised by a painful looking hole on the left.

(114) Slab and Crack D   pre-1957
8m The slab and short layback crack above. ● The left arête is HD.

(115) Moglichkeit VS 4b   1958
8m The overhanging chimney proves to be a little awkward and the fist crack in the overhang is climbed with determination. Large cams useful.

(116) Plimsoll Line HVS 5a   1981
10m Reach the hole from the cave on the left and finish directly up the somewhat bold wall above.

(117) Porthole HVS 5a ★   1961-63
10m A route worth seeking out, offering good but unnerving climbing for the grade. Go easily up narrow overlapping slab to a large hole, the porthole. Move left with difficulty to grasp up the arête.

(118) Leaning Slab VD   pre-1957
10m Climb the slab and the wall above using a small flake. A good route. ● The centre of the slab passing a small hole is V0 (5a). ● The left arête is V0− (4a). ● The left to right ramp formed by the edge of the slab is M.

(119) Trango 2 E3 5c   1987
6m The wall is climbed using a vague flake.

Although small, the crux is at the top and the landing is awful so treat it with respect. ● The left arête of the wall provides a worthwhile HS 4c problem ● and the right arête is HS 4b.

James Pearson on the crux of Ontos, E3 6b (opposite page). Only the strongest of hearts will not sink when climbers feel how poor the sloper is. Photo: David Simmonite

Gun Buttress

This is the tier above Porthole Buttress. Its most obvious feature is the battleship-style gun aiming towards Win Hill. To the left of this, a series of short rocks lead off to the left towards the reservoirs. These contain many diminuitive routes that have been scrambled on for years, giving many problems in the D to HS range. Please, no more claims here.

120 Shadow Wall VS 5a ★   1981
12m   The left-hand sidewall is climbed up its centre before moving right below the gun to finish. Technically intriguing. ● The arête just left, keeping off the large flake is **Jumping the Gun,** HS 4b (2000).

121 Life During Wartime E2 5c ★   1985
13m   Go up to a square roof on the arête, and haul up to climb the arête direct.

122 Randy's Wall HVS 5a ★ ★   1962-63
13m   From the square roof, move up rightwards to runners and a possible rest in the centre of the wall. Finish direct as the first ascensionists did, or, continue along the traverse towards the right edge of the buttress before moving up. Whichever way, it is still quality at the upper end of the technical grade.

123 Magnum Force HVS 5b ★   1981
13m   A slightly harder and more strenuous way up the wall than its randy neighbour. Climb straight over the bulges in the centre of the wall to the mid-height rest on Randy's Wall. Move up and leftwards

almost to the arête before going up. Alternatively, finish as for Randy's Wall at the same grade.

124 Springboard E1 5a   1999
10m   It had to be done. A wild hand traverse of the gun from left-to-right starting on top of the crag. Bicycle clips useful as is a long sling over the nose. It finishes up Randy's Wall but you can keep going if you wish.

125 Gunpowder Crack VS 5b ★   1961
12m   The excellent undercut crack has a hard start and is the scene of some memorable contortions and colouful language. The continuation above is steep, but protection is plentiful.

126 Master Blaster E1 5c ★   1981
11m   On the wall immediately left of Loader's Bay, haul over a small roof and climb direct on not the best of holds. A fine climb and just protectable by small wires (difficult to find).

127 Ammo S 4a   1961-63
8m   Right of the corner, climb the short arête and the wall above. ● The corner is **Loader's Bay,** D (pre-1957).

128 Long John HVS 5b   1961-63
8m   The hugely undercut arête. A gigantic reach, a gnarly leap or a difficult 5b traverse from the corner on the left gains good holds on the lip of the roof. A pile of stones is useful if lacking in inches, ethics or both.

⑫⑨ Three Real Men Dancing E2 6a ★   1982
8m Pull over the overhang left of the chimney and climb the difficult thin wall.

⑬⓪ Green Chimney VD   pre-1957
8m A hard pull starts the constricted chimney, which is easier than it looks.

⑬① Artillery Corner D   pre-1957
8m Green, but straightforward, corner climbing.

⑬② Gangway S 4a   pre-1957
8m The gangway. ● The steep line through this is HS 4c.

⑬③ Green Parrot VI (5b)
A boulder problem over the undercut nose. ● **A Minah Variation**, V3 (6a), is the obvious traverse in from the right. A direct through this would suit someone with a very short left arm and a very long right.

⑬④ Bosun's Slab D   pre-1957
8m Take the slabby wall trending slightly left.

⑬⑤ Concave Slab M   pre-1957
8m A good micro-route up the narrow slab from the block.

⑬⑥ Adjacent Slab D   pre-1957
8m Follow the centre of the pleasant slab. ● A more direct line is VD 4a. ● **Convexed or Perplexed**, VS 5a (1991), is over the nose to the left.

⑬⑦ Hypotenuse M   pre-1957
8m The corner would make a good beginner's route.

⑬⑧ Opposite S 4a   1991
9m Climb straight up the wall on good holds.

⑬⑨ Vertigo HS 4c   1963
10m The left arête of the buttress. A problem 4c start over the initial overhang starting just to the right of the overhang's 'arête' leads to a stretch for a break on the left. Move back right to finish. It's HS 4b if you traverse in above the starting bulge.

⑭⓪ Armed and Dangerous E4 6a ★   1987
10m A powerful little number. From the back extend up to an obvious flake then make hard moves leftwards across the roof. If victorious an easy finish awaits.

⑭① Dynamite Groove E1 5b ★   1981
10m Start on the sloping block below a shallow cracked groove (or from the back of the roof). Make a hard pull into the groove and from its top either step left or continue up shelving rock. The short may find it technically 5c.

⑭② Right Side S 4a   1987
6m Ascend just left of the blunt arête. ● **Sunny Side**, HS 4a (1981), the middle of the wall left again, is slightly harder. ● **Funny Side**, S (1987), takes the left-hand side of the wall.

⑭③ Slopey Side E1 5b   1991
6m Right of a blunt arête and starting beneath a hole.

Bamford Quarry

OS Ref. SK 215843 This esoteric gem is nothing to write home about and contains only one route worth climbing, the rest is very overgrown or the rock poor. Access is via a vague track leaving the road between Bamford Edge and Stanage Edge at a stile (OS Ref. SK 215839), which is the same access point for the main edge. The same points regarding access to Bamford Edge apply here. It contains three notable features, an arête flanked on either side by corners.

❶ Long Times HVS 5a   1986
10m Climb the steep corner-crack left of the arête to finish up the delicate slab above.

❷ The Big Excellent Adventure E5 6b †   1991
10m The obvious central arête, first on the right face then on the left. Pull back on the right at the top using the obvious pocket. The best route here. **No Q**, VS 5a (1966), starts up the grassy corner right of the arête and follows the natural line to the top of the arête.

Up and right are a couple of small friable and dirty walls and bays. These provide short problems, all of which have been climbed from VD to 5b but don't bother, you aren't missing anything!

First Ascents

1890s J W Puttrell and W J Watson paid visits to Derwent Edge and probably ascended the most obvious, easy, lines including Wind Tunnel.

1900s **Deep Chimney, Easy Chimney** Members of the Kyndwr Club including J W Puttrell, Ernest A Baker, H Smithard

1901 **Primitive Chimney** J W Puttrell, H Smithard

1915 Henry Bishop and Douglas Yeomans visited Bamford Edge and climbed easier lines but left no details of their ascents.

1916-20 H M (Harry) Kelly made various visits over four years and climbed various lines of weakness but he also failed to record his endeavors, except the one below.

1918 **Kelly** Harry Kelly

1930 **Palpitation, Sandy Crack** Eric Byne, Clifford Moyer *They also reascended and recorded for the first time the 'obvious lines of weakness' but failed on the lines of Hasta La Vista, Quien Sabe? and Moglichkeit among others.*

1932 **Simple Walter, Deep Freeze** Eric Byne, Clifford Moyer

1940s David Sampson and members of the Sheffield University Mountaineering Club made spasmodic visits to add more routes to Bamford, but unfortunately details were lost.

1949 **P.C.C. I, Gargoyle Traverse, Jacobite's Route, Dovestones Wall** Albert Shutt, Roy Beadham, Ron Ibbotson **Central Climb** Albert Shutt, Roy Beadham (first section), Robert Gratton, Reg Pillinger (second section) **Route I, Route II** Albert Shutt, Peter Rickus, Peter 'Ben Nevis' Todd

1951 **Brown's Crack** R A (Dick) Brown, David Sampson and other members of the S.U.M.C. *'Another interesting piece of exploration about this time (1950), full of portents for the future, was Dick Brown's opening-up of Bamford Edge. Since H M Kelly's visits in 1918 (even though others had been there before) nobody had climbed here apart from Moyer and Byne in 1930, and some S.U.M.C. members led by David Sampson ten years later. The reason for this was the heavy keepering, for the crag is sufficiently obvious from the valley to attract attention. Even in 1950 R A Brown and his Sheffield companions were forced to confine their visitations to midweek. They found various routes, but more perhaps more important still was the actual charting of the rocks, which was to serve as bait to some of the best gritstone climbers a decade later in the tradition of the crag.'* High Peak, 1966. This implies that Brown's Crack, K Buttress Crack, K Buttress Slab, Recess Crack, Bilberry Crack were, in fact, climbed in 1950 but conflicting reports give the dates listed here.*

1951-1952 **K Buttress Crack, K Buttress Slab** Dick Brown, et al

1952 **Recess Crack, Bilberry Crack** Dick Brown and party

pre-1957 **Hypotenuse, Adjacent Slab, Concave Slab, Bosun's Parrot, Gangway, Artillery Corner, Green Chimney, Loader's Bay, Leaning Slab, Slab and Crack, Slanting Slab, Deep Cleft, Sinuous Crack** Details unknown

pre-1957 **Introduction, Initiation, The Overhang Traverse** Probably climbed by the S.U.M.C or as they were affectionately now as the SCUM.

pre-1957 A number of routes were climbed at Priddock Woods prior to 1957 by Frank Fitzgerald and Dr E J (Kangchenjunga) Clegg but no records were kept.

1957 **Gargoyle Buttress** Geoffrey Sutton **The Great Buttress, Brown Windsor** Ted Howard, Barry Pedlar **Claw Climb, Talon** Ted Howard, G B (Tanky) Stokes

1957 **Hurricane, Canker, Fennario, Dovestone Gully, Slocum, Polecat, Boneyard Buttress, Foulstone Wall, Iltis, Titania, Jonah, Windblown, Stingray, Sick-Bay, Windblasted** These were almost certainly climbed by Ted Howard, Barry Pedlar and/or Tanky Stokes, but were named by Oliver Woolcock whilst checking routes for the 1971 Bleaklow Area guidebook.

1957 Publication of Further Developments in the Peak District, Climbs on Gritstone (Volume 4). The first guidebook to Bamford Edge contained some 27 routes and problems of which six; Possibility, Undercut Crack, Terrace Wall, Hasta La Vista, Quien Sabe? and Moglichkeit were recorded as being unclimbed.

1957 Nov **Hasta La Vista** Geoffrey Sutton, Geoff Roberts *Originally named Probability before it was climbed.*

1957 **Possibility** Bob Downes, Harold Drasdo, Philip Gordon *In the book, High Peak by Eric Byne and Geoffrey Sutton, it was written that 'During their spare time (from the White Hall Outdoor Centre which he ran), Sutton and his assistant Bob Downes, Harold Drasdo, Geoff Roberts and Gordon Mansell often explored the crags, caves and rivers of the district for pleasure.' It went on to add that Sutton had done 'several climbs on Bamford and Derwent Edges.' The routes above appear to be the only ones recorded here as well as one on Derwent Edge.*

1958 Jan **Curving Crack** Allan Austin, Brian Evans, Doug Verity

1958 Apr 4 **Moglichkeit, Neb Buttress, Wrinkled Wall, Dead Mouse Crack, Undercut Crack** Allan Austin **Bamford Buttress** Brian Evans **Quien Sabe?** Brian Evans Allan Austin *Austin gave Undercut Crack HVS but what do you expect from a Yorkshireman. Quien Sabe? translated it means Who Knows? and was seen as a big breakthrough at the time. The route had been top-roped on a rainy day in November 1957 by Geoffrey Sutton.*

1958 Aug **Hanging Crack, Right-Hand Twin, Tinner** Allan Austin, Brian Evans

1958 Nov **A35** Joe Brown, Joe (Morty) Smith (1 point of aid) *The first ascent description graciously stated; 'A sling can be used on the second flake.' Free-climbed in 1975 by Jim Reading or John Allen, and most thought it was easier without the sling. The flake broke and was reclimbed at a significantly harder grade by Steve Allen in 1984. Since then, more has broken off and it has not been reclimbed.*

1957-59 **Direct start to Neb Buttress, Bramble Crack, Holly Crack, Short Curve** Details unknown

1960 **Twin Cracks, Bamford Wall** Hugh Banner **Woodcracker** Malc Baxter, Jim Heys

1961 Winter **Gunpowder Crack** Hugh Banner

1961 **The Scoop, The Bin, The Hairy Ainu, The Anvil** Malc Baxter, with Graham West or Jim Heys **Furnace Slab** Graham West, Malc Baxter **Ainu's Crack** Jim Heys, Malc Baxter

1962-1963 **Randy's Wall** John Robson

1961-63 **Long John, Ammo, Porthole, Big Ben, N.B. Corner, Cleopatra, Fern Chimney, Delilah, Left Wing, Terrace Trog** Details unknown

1963 **Vertigo, Samson's Delight, Bracken Crack, Gargoyle Flake, Terrace Wall, Astronaut's Wall** M P (Pete) Hatton, John Robson

1965 Apr **Mod** Paul Nunn (solo)

1966 Jan 1 **Ontos** D J Clegg, P T Clegg *This claim was largely discounted as nobody had heard of the first ascensionists. The likely first ascent was made in 1974 by John Yates, Richard*

McHardy with 1 nut for aid and named Virgin Wall. FFA 1975 by John Allen.

1966 Sept **Pandora Buttress** Brian Griffiths, Rod Brown, Jackie Griffiths

1966 **Long Times** Malcolm Baxter, Trevor Tighe

1967 May **The Happy Wanderer** Geoff Morgan

1967 **Tighvor Grooves, Giant's Crack, Patleen Cracks** Malc Baxter, Trevor Tighe *One point of aid was used on Patleen Cracks. FFA 1988 and renamed Kleen Crack. The second pitch started up what is now Brer Fox and finished up Brer Rabbit.*

1968 **The Rat** Keith Myhill, Al Thewliss (1 point of aid) FFA unknown, 1970s

1969 **Skarlati** Martin Boysen

1970 **Quarrymaster's Crack, Little Dilly, Silviculturist's Dream, Tighe's Addition, Malcrack** Malc Baxter, Trevor Tighe

1957-71 **Rocker, Ganges, Cox's Pippin, Iambo, Grindle Crack, Brogging Wall, Turtle Rib, Hic, Haec, Hoc, Threadworm** These were all probably climbed by Oliver Woolcock whilst working on the 1971 guidebook.

1971 May **Oracle** Paul Nunn, Ken Jones

1971 Nov 13 **Wrong Hand Route** John Gosling

1971 **Auricle** John Gosling, Arthur Robinson, B Cardus **Special K** Arthur Robinson, Bill Birch

1973 **Bamford Rib, Trouble with Lichen** John Allen, Neil Stokes

1976 May 8 **Skinhead** Con Carey (solo)

1976 Aug **McVities, Spartan** Con Carey **Turtle Chimney** John Tout, Con Carey

1976 Sept 7 **Excel** Con Carey, Brian Cropper (both solo)

1976 **Benberry Wall** John Allen, Nick Stokes, Steve Bancroft **The Rodent** Peter Brayshaw, Al Wildman

1977 Oct 23 **Greydon Boddington** Martin Veale, Dave Mirfin

1978 June 18 **Rectineal Wall** Nick Colton, Con Carey **The Gable** Nick Colton (solo) **Hilly Country Harvest** Nick Colton, Loris Doyle **Greensleeves** Loris Doyle (solo) **Howshaw Tor Eliminate** Nick Colton, Dave Banks

1979 **Jumping Jack Longland** Steve Bancroft, Bernard Newman **The Crease** Mark Davies **The Black Mini** Paul Mitchell (solo)

1980 **Fizz** Martin Veale, 'Irish' Mick

1981 Jan **Dynamite Groove** Martin Veale, Chris Craggs **Master Blaster, Magnum Force** Chris Craggs, with Martin Veale or Colin Binks **Plimsoll Line** Colin Binks, Chris Craggs **Sunny Side, Shadow Wall** Chris Craggs (solo)

1981 Mar 28 **Grey Days, Thin On Top** Colin Binks, Chris Craggs **Green and Nasty** Chris Craggs, Colin Binks

1981 Apr **Quebec City, Reach, Parliament** Chris Craggs,

Derwent to Bamford > First Ascents

Graham Parkes **Bum Deal** Chris Craggs, Dave Spencer **Claim to Fame** Dave Spencer, Chris Craggs

1981 May **Dirty Stop Out** Chris Lawson, Trevor Pilling

1981 Aug 16 **Nemmes Pas Harry** Gary Gibson, Phil Gibson

1981 Nov 8 **E.N. 24** Mike Browell, Jeremy Frost

1981 Sept **Granny Smith, Easy Ground, Autumn Day** Graham Hoey (solo) **Woodhouse's Wandering Way, Terrapin, Tortoise** Stuart Gascoyne (solo)

1981 **Great Buttress Eliminate, The Shylock Finish** Stuart Gascoyne **Swinwood** Dick Swinden

1982 **Deaf Raspberry Climb** Andy Barker **Three Real Men Dancing** Martin Veale, Simon Horrox, Mark Stokes **Fatal Inheritance, The Naked Eye** Gary Gibson

1982 **Blunt, Spring Night, Voice of the Turtle** Chris Craggs

1981-82 **Blackberry Shuffle, Brer Fox, Ratchet Crack, Leadsmelter's Crack, The Ingot, Cartilage Corner** Barry Platts, Alan Wilson **Brer Rabbit, Knuckle Knocker's Nightmare, Septic Cleft** Alan Wilson, Barry Platts

pre-1983 **Crunchy Nuts** Details unknown

1983 Aug **First Coming, Clockwork Orange, Certain Surprise, Reward** Doug Kerr, Jon Handley **Hong Kong Garden** Doug Kerr, Pete Moulam **Frilly Bolero, Eric** Jon Handley, Doug Kerr **Nippon, Nippoff** Andy Bailey

1983 **Custard's Last Stand** Paul Evans (solo)

1984 **Jetrunner** Andy Bailey **Sterling Moss** Johnny Dawes, Tony Ryan *Maybe a reference to Dawes driving style.* **The Egg** Johnny Dawes, John Dunne *Dawes claimed to have soloed the route but it came to light recently that he was seconded by Dunne. It was the first and last time they climbed together. Originally named Noel Coward, a more direct line (High and Dry) was added by Dunne in 1986.*

1984 **The Salmon** Johnny Dawes *An amazing route. Dawes swore that the fall from the final moves was possibly even better than the route. Re-ascended in 1995 by Dawes after the loss of a crucial pebble.*

1984 Sept **Barney Rubble, Philby** Paul and Neil Harrison

1985 Apr 17 **Clean, Squeeky and Scented** Mark Stokes, John Allen

1985 Sept **Access Account** Al Rouse, Simon Wells **Down to Earth** Al Rouse (solo)

1985 Nov 17 **Life During Wartime** Keith Ashton

1985 **Sforzando** Alan Monks *A similar line was climbed, but never claimed, by Andy Parkin a few years earlier.* **Blue Hare** Trevor Pilling, Sarah Kew **Dead on a Rival** Nick White, Steve Yates

1986 Mar 12 **Mad Gadaffi** Paul Harrison, Doug Kerr

1986 May 18 **High and Dry** John Dunne, Dean Eastham *The Yorkshire raider leaves a very underrated route.*

1986 July 27 **Onebat** Brian Davison, Andy Smith

1986 Sept **No Q** Malcolm Baxter, Adrian Hughes.

1987 Apr 26 **Armed and Dangerous** Mark Stokes, Steve Bancroft

1987 May 6 **Trango 2** Martin Boysen, Martin Veale

1987 Sept 14 **Right Side, Funny Side** Keith Ashton, Malc Baxter, Paul Durkin (all solo)

1987 Nov 12 **The Chicken** Con Carey **Assorted Batteries** Malc Baxter, Con Carey

1987 Nov **Leadbelly's Lament, Chocolate Meltdown, Checker's Connection** Malc Baxter, Keith Ashton

1988 Jan 16 **Kleen Crack** Malc Baxter, Keith Ashton, Chris Hardy

1988 Oct **Dogwood** Malc Baxter **Paul's Wall** Paul Dawson, Malc Baxter

1989 Dec 31 **End of a Decade** David Simmonite *"Unseconded as Roy Bennett had froze whilst belaying, it was bloody cold."*

1989 May 29 **Rafaga** Andy Barker

1989 June 3 **Wodwo, Harry's Last Stand** Andy Barker (unseconded) **Glam Rock** Mike Guy, Andy Barker **The Roger Moore Effect** Andy Barker, Mike Guy *Ben Heason soloed a line corresponding to Wodwo, on sight, in 2003, at E4 6a*

1990 Apr 21 **Various Undercuts** Keith Ashton, Malc Baxter

1990 Apr **Jasmine** Ron Fawcett (solo) *Ron's last major addition to gritstone. Named after his daughter.*

1990 **Titanium** Steve Burns **Heavy Metal** David Simmonite

pre-1991 **Monks of Monserrat plc** John Allen **Private Practice, Old Wall** John Allen, Mark Stokes **Jive Bunny** Steve Bancroft *The whereabouts of this E3 were a mystery for a while after being reported as left of Benberry Wall, which is where Black Flip goes at E1. Hopefully, it is now in its right place.*

1991 Apr 27 **The Big Excellent Adventure** Stuart Bolton, Seb Grieve, Derek Touallen

1991 June 23 **Chickenhead** Paul Mitchell

1991 Oct **Opposite, Convexed or Perplexed** Chris Craggs (solo) **Busy Day at Bamford** Chris Craggs, Jim Rubery **Slopey Side** Colin Binks (solo) **Back Flip** Gwyn Arnold, Andrew Wragg

1991 Nov 10 **The Fat Controller** David Simmonite, Roy Bennett

1991 Dec 25 **Christmas Wrappings** David Simmonite. Roy Bennett *Egg mayo sandwiches, carrot cake and a wee dram for lunch, exquisite. The route initially finished on the left. Chris Craggs (1996) climbed a short finishing slab to straighten out the line.*

1992 Mar 24 **Thumping, K'kin, Klueless, Kin 'eck, Klever** David Simmonite (solo)

1992 Sept 25 **Bone of Contention** Malc Baxter, Keith Ashton

1993 Summer **Hoplite** Simon Lovely, Rob Morrison **Lament for a Scotsman** Dave Hassell, Chris Rhodes, Anthony Addis **Engram** Paul Mitchell

1993 **Bamboozer** Andy Popp

1994 May 1 **Hare** Doug Kerr

1995 April 27 **Smoked Salmon** Johnny Dawes *Unbelievably climbed in one day, an excellent achievement. And if that wasn't* *enough Dawes also reclimbed The Salmon on the same day, after it lost a crucial pebble. Nick Dixon repeated Smoked Salmon after six days of trying. The route lost a pebble on an ascent by James Pearson but the grade remained the same.*

1995 June 20 **Avoiding the Traitors** Johnny Dawes *Another good effort from Dawes and top-roped only once prior to the lead. Climbed ground-up with two falls by Toby Benham in 2004.*

1995 **Trout** Nick Dixon *Easy for the grade, and commonly on-sighted.* **Tight 'uns** Chris Craggs

1996 **Groovy Moves, Step It Up, Slab Happy, Rocky, Pleasant, Village Green, Razor Cut, Squirm, Old Man's Corner, Blocky, Handy Wall Hole, Thunderbirds, Woodentops, Another Right Wall, Another Left Wall, A'rete Do, Barefoot, Another Flaky Wall, Pock Mark, Grinder Wall, Stairway, Right Ahead, Left Behind, Layby, Titanic, Gruyere, Dovestones Edge, Pole-Axed, Slow Cooker, 'Frodsham 3a', 'Frodsham 3c', Topside, Tevas, Caveman** Many routes claimed as 'First Recorded Ascents' by combinations of Chris Craggs, Dave Gregory, Martin Veale, Jim Rubery, Mike Appleton and Dave Spencer *It is certain that most of these routes, particularly the easier ones, had been climbed in the preceding years. As 'Sandy' Sanderson of Kettleshulme remembers 'the good old days' when it was only acceptable to record new routes that were considered 'ground breaking'. Anything considered less than that was just climbed, enjoyed and left for others to rediscover. According to his memories of climbing up here in the '60s, all the above routes would have been done by both himself and his contemporaries. "After the ascents of Great Buttress, Central Climb and Route 1, anything else was just left, we didn't write in to anyone about them because we'd have been laughed out of the pub! Good little routes though, all of them."*

1996 June **Blue Velvet, Lancaster Flyby, Hanging Tree, Jam On It, Stretch Marks, A Little Green Eyed God, Sick as a Parrot, Crackless Bottom** Chris Craggs, with combinations of Dave Gregory, Martin Veale, Dave Spencer, Jim Rubery **Hang 'em High** Dave Gregory, Chris Craggs **Bertie, Landing Craft, Soft Top** Martin Veale, Chris Craggs, Dave Gregory **Smokin'** Dave Spencer, Martin Veale, Dave Gregory, Chris Craggs

1996 July 14 **First Come** Chris Craggs, Dave Gregory

1996 July 21 **Typhoon, Stony Faced, Mock Turtle, Thread Flintstone** Mike Appleton, with either Dave Gregory, Chris Craggs, Martin Veale **Barker's Got a Sweat On** Martin Veale (solo) *See comments above about new route claims. These routes were more than likely first ascents.*

1996 Summer **Too Long Gone** Malcolm Taylor, Alison Taylor

1997 Feb 24 **Missing ASG** David Simmonite (solo)

1997 Mar 22 **Fat Cat, Beer Matters** Paul Harrison

1997 Dec 21 **Solstice Arête** Peter Stone *Peter Stone and friends claimed numerous routes on the scrappy, short walls left of*

Gun Buttress. Many had been done before and have been left for climbers to rediscover.

1998 Dec **Salmon Direct** Jon Read *Climbed in mistake for The Salmon*

1998 Nov 10 **Remembrance, Lot's Wife** Jon Wilson, Jez Portman **Pillar of Salt** Jez Portman, Jon Wilson

1999 **Poached Salmon** Jon Read

1999 Oct 10 **Hard Rain** David Simmonite (self-protected solo)

1999 Nov 6 **Springboard** Peter Robins (solo) **In my Pocket** Paul Harrison (solo) **Almost Granite** Paul Harrison, Mick Carr, David Simmonite

1980s/90s **Two Real Doleys Scrounging** Details unknown

2000 Mar 31 **Wee Lassie, Jumping the Gun** David Simmonite

2001 **Twenty Feet** Tony Sawbridge, David Simmonite

2002 Apr 24 **Domusnovas, Pocket Rocket** *Paul Harrison* **Grouse Related Nonsense** Kate Cox, Martin Kocsis

2003 **Sick Arête** Miles Gibson *Ben Heason made a swift second ascent 15 minutes after the first ascent.*

2003 Sept 16/17 **Flakeaway** Sarah Whitehouse, Tony Whitehouse **100 Not Out** Tony Whitehouse, Sarah Whitehouse

2003 **Tartar Sauce** James Ibbertson **Gene, End Face** David Simmonite **Three Little Pigs** Steve Clark, Simon Triger

2003 **Bad Wind, Terrace Rib, Flake Buttress Rib, Acid Slab, Alkili Arête** Steve Clarke

2003 May 25 **Jemelia** Paul Harrison, Tony Sawbridge, Graham Sutton

2003 June 23 **Fatigued** Graham Sutton, David Simmonite

2004 Apr 13 **Purgamentum** James Pearson, David Simmonite

2004 Summer **Insitewe, Rescewe, Phewe, One Ewe over the Cuckoo's Nest** Graham Sutton *For a few magical summer days, Sutton found meaningful experiences in the cold sunless solitude of Howshaw Tor.*

2005 **Snuggazabug** Niall Grimes

Boulder First Ascents

The Business Boy Martin Veale, Andy Cave, 1987
The Cavendish Simon Crossley, 2003
Galaxy Dove Jason Myers, 1990s
Green Parrot Martin Veale, Chris Craggs, 1981
Interstellar Pigeon Jason Myers, 1990s
Jupiter Collision Jason Myers, 1990s
K'Pow David Simmonite, 1992
Ko'd Paul Harrison
The Pope, Duff Paddy, Save Dinnomite, Way Rood Niall Grimes, 2005
Something Else, Something Silly Adrian Berry, 1990s
Scorched Turf David Simmonite, 1998
The Plumber has Landed David Simmonite, 1992

Stephen Coughlan makes the dramatic moves into the finishing crack, high on Grammarian's Progress, VS 4b, in the fabulous Long John's Stride area of Wharncliffe (page 286). Photo: David Simmonite.

The **Wharncliffe**
Area

5

'The aim of this is not to convey that in Don Valley there exists a rival to Wastdale Head. Climbers know the limitations of their playground as well as they know its advantages. It is true, in an article that appeared in an enterprising halfpenny journal, it was suggested that in course Sheffield might become an English Zermatt; this was an astonishing flight of imagination of a kind which only an enterprising halfpenny morning journalist is capable in these days.'

C F Cameron, 1902

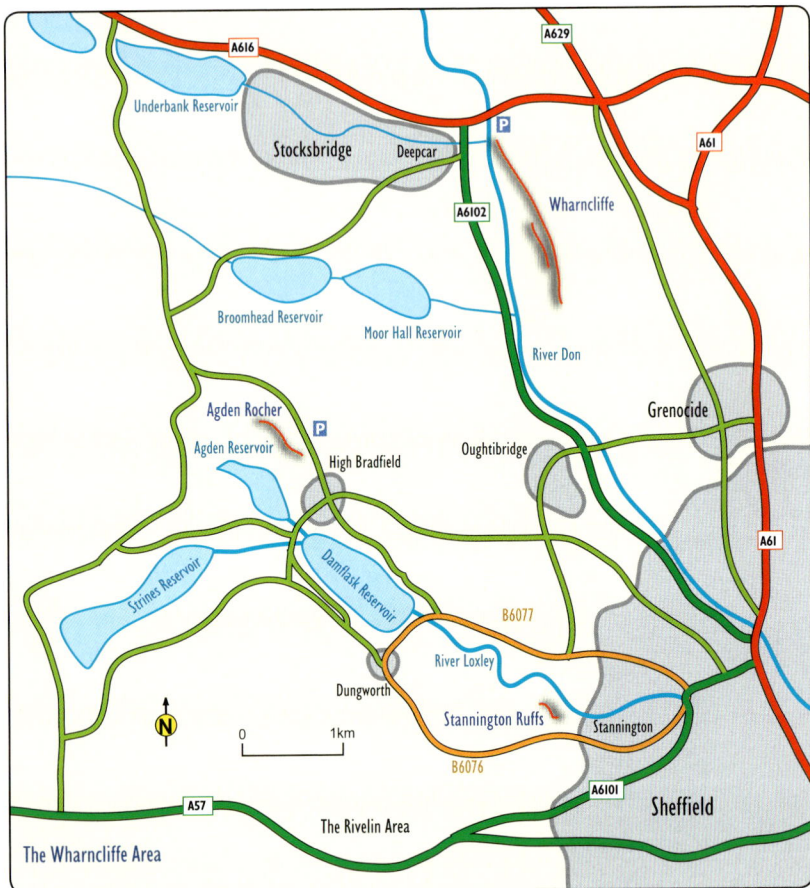

A616
A629
A61
Underbank Reservoir
Stocksbridge
Deepcar
P
A6102
Wharncliffe
Broomhead Reservoir
Moor Hall Reservoir
River Don
Grenocide
Agden Rocher
P
Oughtibridge
Agden Reservoir
High Bradfield
A61
Strines Reservoir
Damflask Reservoir
B6077
River Loxley
N
Dungworth
Stannington Ruffs
Stannington
0   1km
B6076
A6101
A57
Sheffield
The Rivelin Area
The Wharncliffe Area

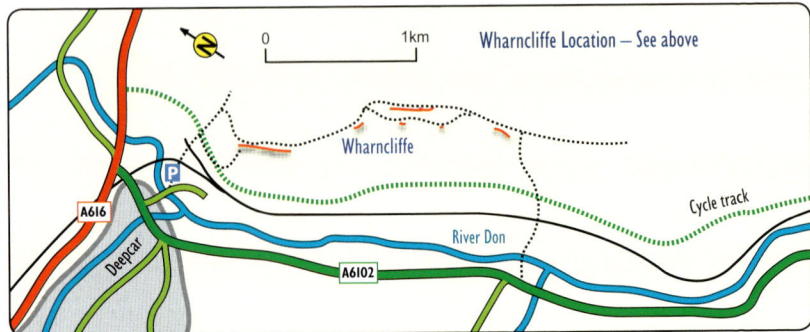

N
0   1km
Wharncliffe Location — See above
P
Wharncliffe
Cycle track
A616
Deepcar
River Don
A6102

Wharncliffe Edge

OS Ref. SK 296977 to SK 303970   altitude 250m

by Frank Horsman and David Simmonite

This is the great edge on the northwest of Sheffield, with a huge collection of dark buttresses strung out along 2½km, overlooking trees, reservoirs, pylons and steelworks. The edge is fairly continuous for about 500m from the northern end but then the buttresses become more isolated. However, the outlook becomes increasingly picturesque as one moves south, a view of steelworks and pylons being replaced by the moors, woods and reservoirs of Ewden Valley.

The Climbing

The rock is of a much finer texture than a true grit and is actually a Coal Measure Sandstone of fairly coarse grain. This results in a greater abundance of incut holds, and in a rippled surface which rewards precise footwork especially on the harder routes. Wharncliffe has traditionally been the home of many sandbags and in the last three guides many of the easier routes have been upgraded to bring them into line with other Peak crags. In this guide the process is, where necessary, continued. In particular the protection on some of the more recent shorter climbs would be unlikely to prevent a ground-fall and these have been upgraded to take account of this, especially in view of the lethal landings lurking below some of the routes.

The nature of the climbing is such that good balance and a good head are more likely to be advantageous than brute strength. Vertical cracks are not as common as on conventional gritstone and, therefore, the ability to run it out from gear could well be useful, even on a few of the easier climbs. On some routes reach is critical and climbers a bit low on the old ape index may find a few grades a touch on the mean side; try Gavel Neese for example. But don't let this put you off – there's plenty for everyone. **Routes:** Almost 350 routes with an even spread across all grades from D to E7. **Bouldering:** About 40 problems, V1 to V9, spread out all along the edge, with a few more concentrated circuits. Some

have dangerous landings. Quite a lot of exploration still to be done.

Conditions & Aspect

The crag faces west and gets lots of sun in the afternoon and evening. It is very quick drying, and takes little seepage. The rock is generally very clean, although some of the buttresses in the trees, e.g. Bass Rock and Long John's Stride, remain green in winter. Its altitude is less than that of most grit crags (around 250m), and it is very sheltered. A good winter venue.

Parking & Approach

For the north (Deepcar) end go down the A6102, Vaughton Hill, from the Deepcar traffic lights, turn right along Station Road immediately after the bridge. Cars may be parked just beyond The Lowood Working Men's Club. Take a footpath left, steeply upwards, from the road just over the bridge.

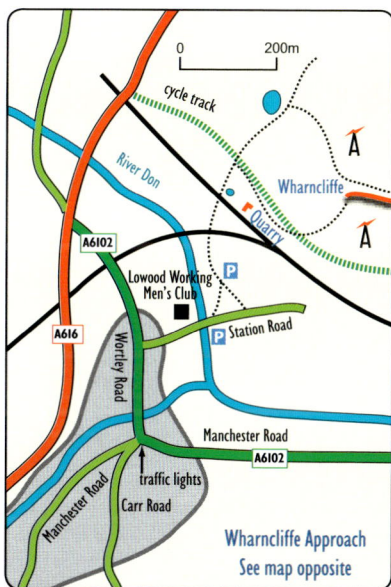

Wharncliffe Approach
See map opposite

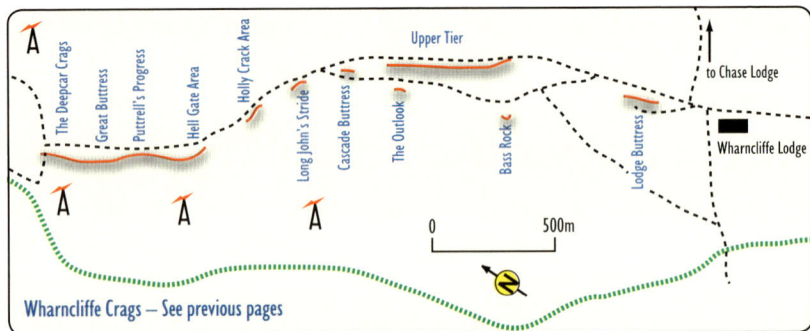

Labels on map: The Deepcar Crags, Great Buttress, Puttrell's Progress, Hell Gate Area, Holly Crack Area, Long John's Stride, Cascade Buttress, The Outlook, Bass Rock, Lodge Buttress, Upper Tier, to Chase Lodge, Wharncliffe Lodge, 0 500m, N, Wharncliffe Crags — See previous pages

This joins a well-worn track, which leads under two bridges. Continue upwards past a small pool on the right and just past this the path forks at some small boulders. Take the right fork to join the well-made Plank Gate forestry track about 500m from the road. Turn right along this and take a path to the left (difficult to see) through the trees immediately before the huge pylon. On emerging from the trees the blocky Gallipoli Rock, with a prominent widening crack on its left side, will be seen in front and towards the right.

Other approaches can be made from the Woodhead Road from Grenoside, to Long John's Stride from a lay-by at SK 311975 via bridleway, woods and footpaths; to Lodge Buttress from Chase Lodge (park at SK 312971) or to the latter buttress steeply from More Hall Bridge on the Oughtibridge - Deepcar Road.

Public Transport
Barnsley and District/Yorkshire Traction buses 23, 23a, 24 and 24a from Barnsley and Penistone go through Deepcar and 25 goes down Finkle St Lane. From Sheffield the First Mainline services 57, 57a, 58, 66, 67 and 67a all reach Deepcar via More Hall Bridge. There - you've no excuse - instead of squeezing into that indoor wall with all the other sardines go and boulder on Lodge Buttress.

Orientation
The climbs are described from the Deepcar (north) end. In order to facilitate the finding of the best locations and more southerly isolated buttresses, which have a much more amenable environment

and, in general, better climbing, the distance of various points along the crag top path from the north end has been measured. To find one buttress from another, subtract the appropriate distances and pace it out along the top.

Access
The crags are the property of Wharncliffe Estates and there have been no known access problems in recent years.

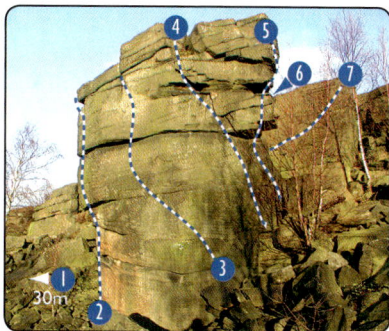

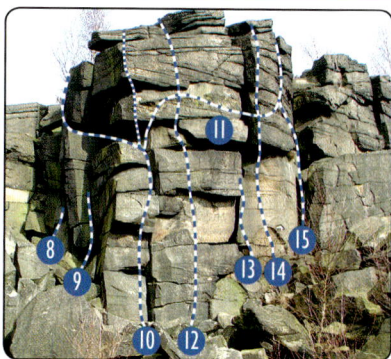

The Deepcar Crags

The largest concentration of climbs on the edge lie in the northernmost end, where a constant procession of small tidy buttresses stretch out over the next 500m. The first of these lies about 100m from the pylon encountered upon leaving the trees.

Gallipoli Rock: The first squat blocky buttress to be seen with a widening crack on its left-hand side.

1 Gallipoli Rock VS 4c ★   1965
6m   Go over the cutaway on the left of the buttress before moving left onto the arête to finish. ● **Tailor's Crack,** VD (traditional), is the offwidth to the left, and ● **Face Climb**, VS 4b (1965), is the right side of the face. ● A squeezed-in central eliminate is **Insurrection,** HVS 5b (1987).

Prow Rock: The next routes are 30m to the right on a pillar. Descent from the top of which is by either a spectacular, but unforgiving, leap to the main edge or more sensibly by reversing Inside Route.

2 The Moire E5 6b ★   1978
9m   Ascend the arête of The Prow, moving left at the top. ● Highball V6 to the big break. ● The face on the left is **Steeltown**, E5 6b ★ (1989).

3 Querp E3 6b   1989
9m   The enticing scoop in the upper of wall.

4 Outside Route HS 4b ★   1885-1910
8m   Move up and traverse diagonally leftwards, via a crack and niche, to the top.

5 The Nose VS 4c ★   1933
6m   Use mostly big holds to tackle the right-hand arête direct.

6 Inside Route D ★   1885
8m   Climb the centre of the inside face to the crack, preferably with hemp rope and wearing a Norfolk jacket. Reverse the route or leap off the top singing praises to Mr Puttrell. ● The faint rib just left is **The Tip Test**, E3 6b ★ (1994). ● The arête to the right is **Inside Edge**, HVS 5b (1994), climbed first on its right and then the left.

The next routes lie on the crag sidewall facing The Prow. The short chimneys on the left are D, the prow between them S.

7 Exonian's Return HVS 5b   1961-63
8m   A somewhat artificial traverse across the wall. Start in the chimney on the left and traverse right on small holds and up the obvious gangway. ● A direct start to the gangway is a tough 5b. A spotter is recommended. ● The left arête is **Green Arête**, VS 4c (1998), ● and the spidery crack with a direct start is **Proud,** E1 5c (1990), ● and the slabby right arête S.

Hamlet's Wall: The next climbs are on the large buttress immediately right. It used to have a concrete pylon base at the top, back from the edge, but all that is left now is a stump.

8 Pylon Crack D   1885-1910
8m   The leftmost crack, left of a wedged pillar.

Paul Harrison on Requiem for Hamlet's Ghost, E1 5b (opposite page). Photo: David Simmonite.

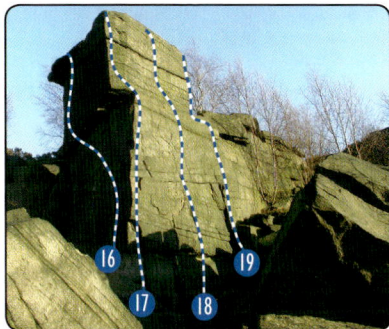

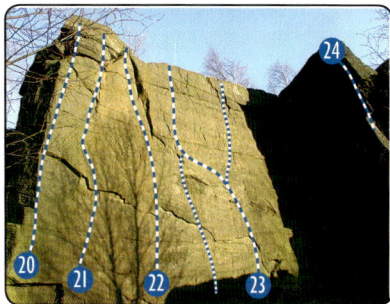

9 Quern Crack S   1885-1910
8m The crack right of the pillar.

10 Hamlet's Climb VD ★   1885-1910
12m Climb a thin crack to the gash where a traverse left leads to Pylon Crack. The direct finish is VS 4c, as is the arête in its entirety.

11 Hamlet's Traverse VS 4b   1949-50
17m An exciting alternative finish to the last climb, traversing above the overhang to finish up Chockstone Climb.

12 Requiem of Hamlet's Ghost E1 5b ★   1976
9m A direct line up the buttress. The crux is a poorly protected (with runners behind a 'shipwreck of a flake') and worrying blind move above a horrible landing.

13 The Crack of Doom S 4a ★   1885-1910
8m The steep, dark crack; a deeply traditional route.

14 Despair E2 5c   1982
9m Climb the right-hand arête of Crack of Doom to finish over an overhang and up the pillar above.

15 Chockstone Climb D   1885-1910
7m The chimney-cum-groove leads to a step left, on good holds, to gain a crack with a chockstone.

Ten metres to the right is a pillar.

16 Earth Blues E5 6b   1985
9m Trend leftwards to the horizontal break. Follow this until you are nearly back on the ground and layback precariously to the top. A somewhat contrived way to risk your neck.

17 Scarlett's Wall Arête VS 4c ★   1965
9m A good little route following the bold arête

18 Scarlett's Climb HS 4a ★   1931
8m Another bold route straight up the front face of the pillar to a ledge from where a long reach or a tricky move (possibly 4c for the short) gains the top.

19 Scarlett's Edge HS 4b   traditional
8m The arête to the right. ● The chimney right again is **Scarlett's Chimney**, D (traditional).

Tensile Test Area: A further 15m brings one to a smooth wall. This has long been a bouldering wall, in fact with the use of bouldering mats it could be argued that these are merely highball problems. Over the years many problems and infinite variations have been climbed here and every hold has been caressed at some time or other.

20 Suspense VS 5b   1957-60
6m The enjoyable left-hand arête proves hard to start and then... ● Highball V1.

21 Mellicious E1 5c   2000
6m The crimpy wall. ● Highball V2.

22 Tensile Test E1 5c ★   1977
6m The faint groove gives good technical climbing with the crux in the lower half and is the best route on the wall. ● Highball V2.

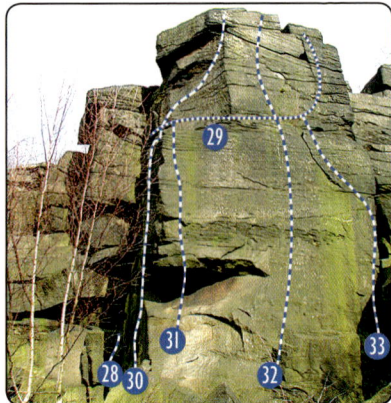

23 Elastic Limit E1 5c   1977

6m   Climb the centre of the slab to a break, and step left to finish. ● Highball V1. A direct start is V2 (6a), ● and a thin direct finish is V4 (6a). ● The wall just left of the gully is **Forget-me-Not,** S 4a (1957-60), ● and a traverse of the top break, from the gully, is **Abair,** E1 5b (1978).

24 Handover Arête HVS 4c ★   1955

8m   Climb the arête to the right, to a crux overhang, which is attacked from the left-hand side. Only just merits HVS. ● **Patricia's Wall,** E1 5b (1991), takes the wall to the right to the right-hand side of a cutaway. Leave this rightwards, and climb up the centre of the wall. VS 4c if the arête is used.

● The wall to the right again provides numerous easy problems, the best being the flake crack in the arête at VD ● and the wall to the left at S 4a. ● Just right again is the chimney of **Monolith Crack,** VD (1885-1910). ● The right edge of the chimney is **Mignon,** VS 4c (1969), climbed by laying away to the right to gain a recess and a pull over the block at the top. Unfortunately escapable at the top but not where it matters on the unprotectable lower section.

Immediately right is a detached pillar.

25 Mantelshelf Pillar HVS 5a   1957-60

7m   The left edge of the pillar.

26 The Mantelshelf HS 4b ★   1885-1910

6m   Via... yes, an awkward mantelshelf.

27 Back and Foot VD   1885-1910

6m   The deep square-cut cleft on the right can be done in its original manner of back and footing. However it is more logical to use the corner crack.

Letter-Box Buttress: Another clean buttress lies immediately right. ● **More Fool You,** HVS 5b (2001), is just left of Rook Chimney, taking a steep direct line to finish over the capping roof. ● The original line on this wall, **Quicksilver,** VS 5a (1969), ascends easy blocks just left to the ledge and steps right on to the wall. This is climbed via a long reach to a final pull over the overhang.

28 Rook Chimney D   1885-1910

8m   The corner-chimney is steep and exposed. Hidden inside the midway cave are all sorts of delightful explorations for troglodytes.

29 Letter-Box Buttress VD   1885-1910

9m   An exciting finish to the last climb going right to finish up a short crack on the front of the buttress.

30 Post Horn VS 4c ★   1961-63

9m   Climb the wall just to the right of Rook Chimney to a ledge and a finish up a blunt rib and capping block above.

31 Tears Before Bedtime E4 6a ★   1987

9m   The arête is climbed on its right-hand side above a nasty landing. Previously graded E1 5b – but only for adrenalin injected spider monkeys. The left-hand side of the arête does go at E2 5b.

32 Reveille E4 6a   1979

9m   The hard fingery wall leads somehow to a ledge. From the ledge go straight up the wall above.

33 **Curved Balls** VS 4c   2001
8m   Climb the flake, gained from the right. ●The pleasant right arête can be climbed mainly on its left side; **Letter-Box Arête,** VD (traditional). ●**The Girdle Traverse,** S 4a (1880s), goes from Handover Arête to Letter-Box Buttress.

The rocks to the right become shorter and more broken. All have been climbed upon at some stage over the years and give problems between moderate and severe standard.

Rocking Block Slab Area: Thirty five metres further on is a slab with a large block on top, which is reputed to rock in stiff breezes (easier to see once you have walked past it and looked back). Ten metres or so before the slab is a partially recessed gully.

34 **Mystery Route** VD   1996
8m   Climb the crack in the right-hand side of the aforementioned partially recessed gully. ●The left-hand crack is D and ●the little slab on the left is **Mantelshelf Slab Right,** HS 4b (2002). **Addy's Addition**, HVS 5b (1961-63) is the wall right of Mystery Route to the cutaway, and rib above. **Parrafin Jack**, E1 5c (1996), heads left at mid-height to climb the left arête.

35 **Slab and Corner** HS 4a ★   1933
8m   Start in the centre of the slab and move diagonally leftwards to a slabby groove/niche on the arête. An awkward mantelshelf leads to the top. ●The direst start up the arête is **The Corner,** VS 4c (1955).

36 **Photo Finish** E1 5b ★   1979
9m   From the niche, go onto the middle of the wall via a flake and up to a ledge. Above, surmount the rocking block using two slots or, with trepidation, up the rib just right to a tricky sloping exit.

37 **Dead Heat** E5 6a ★★   1985
8m   No gear and a hideous landing make for an unforgettable experience but the climbing is excellent. Climb the thin slab 3m left of the edge of the slab to a small overlap. Undercut this and make a thin pull over the overlap before committing to the reach for the break.

38 **Renrock** E1 5a ★   1957-60
6m   Only just E1, but still a bold proposition up the technical blunt right-hand edge of the slab.

Cheese Block Area: Fifty metres further on, passing short rocks that again have been climbed, is a compact buttress which provides some good easier routes. This is 165m from the north end and directly opposite the first pylon. Some misguided soul has also painted a (fading) yellow number 34 on a block at the top of the crag.

39 **Black Wall** S   1961-63
8m   The left wall by a series of tricky mantelshelves.

40 **Hard Cheese** E1 5b ★   2000
8m   Climb the centre of the wall and pull over the small roof to finish up the right-hand side of the arête.

41 **Cheese Cut** D ★   1885-1910
8m   The chimney-crack in the back of the corner.

42 **Cheese Cut Crack** D   1885-1910
8m   The crack is steep but has good holds.

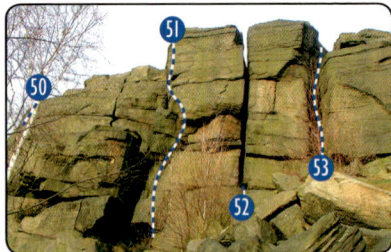

43 Cheese Block VS 4b   1961-63
7m Pull over the cutaway on its right-hand side and continue up the arête above. A bold route (HS with side-runners). The flaky cleft round to the right is **Not Cheese Cut Flake**, M (1885-1910).

44 Cheese Cut Flake VD   1885-1910
8m Layback the flake-to-hand crack.

Thirty-five metres past a small buttress is a prominent small face set high up;

45 Bilberry Face S   1885-1910
6m Start in the centre, step up and move left to finish up the left edge. ● Continuing direct from the start and up the centre of the wall gives a HS 4b problem. ● The narrow sidewall to the left is HS 4b.

Fifteen metres further on at a lower level, is a rounded buttress. The left wall of which has three possible lines at a similar grade, the best being:

46 Owen's Dilemma VS 4c   1957-60
6m Climb a central line up the left wall.

47 Imaginary Boulder Climb HS 4c ★   1885-1910
8m A Puttrell sandbag from the 1900s. On the front face is a steep crack. Climb this ignoring the adjacent boulder and continue up the wall above.

48 Authentic Boulder Climb VS 4c   traditional
6m A central line starting from a good flat hold on the right that pretends to be a tiny ledge before trending slightly left.

The small buttress 15m to the right and across a 'bay' has a steep left wall above a shallow pit and a slabby right-hand side with a wide crack .

49 Zigzag Climb S 4a   2002
7m Hand-traverse right along the obvious narrow break to finish left up the slab's left arête. Pleasant. ● The slab can be climbed in its entirety on its right at M, while ● **Ocumen,** HVS 5a (1969), is the steep wall above the traverse.

Cumberland Buttress: This is 15m right.

50 Railway Wall VS 4b   1933
8m Follow the wide crack then move onto the arête, which provides the crux. The easy rocks to the right have all been climbed.

51 Pinnacle Arête E1 5b   1957-60
9m Start up the wall to the right of the deep corner-chimney and move onto the small pillar on the left-hand arête. Delicate and thought provoking climbing remains up the arête.

52 Cumberland Crack HVD   1885-1910
9m The steep fissure to the right offers arduous climbing. The buttress has been traversed. ● The minuscule wall right is **Subterranean Blues**, HVS 5a (1991).

53 V-Groove VD   1885-1910
9m The cute groove. ● **Wheelspin Wall**, VS 5a (1991), starts just to the right of V-Groove and climbs the centre of the wall just to the right. ● The wall immediately right is VS 5b.

> ## "The **finest land prospect**
> ## I ever saw — except for Wharncliffe."
> Lady Mary Wortley Montagu, of a view near Avignon, 1745

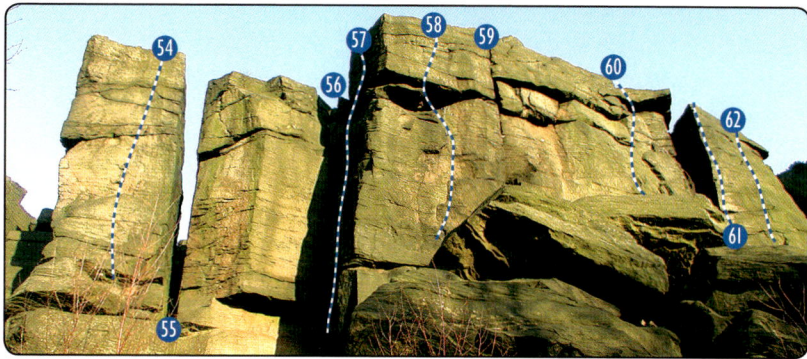

Pete's Sake Area: To the right, past a scree slope/gully, is a buttress made up of five blocks. ● The poor groove on the back is **Gully Side**, VS 5b (1994) ● The blocky arête to the right is **North Side Route**, HVS 5a (1965), finishing left from the ledge. ● The direct finish, up the left arête is **Baal**, E2 5c (1981).

54 Pete's Sake HVS 5b ★   1961-63
12m An impressive outing. Climb the centre of the face to gain the obvious break where a strenuous move up and right leads to better holds on the right edge.

55 Leftover Chimney D   traditional
9m Climb up to and continue up the narrowing chimney, staying near the outside for maximum enjoyment. The arête on the right is unclimbed.

56 Overhanging Chimney HVD   1885-1910
9m Enjoyable climbing for the chimney freak.

57 Ma'son E2 5b ★   1971
8m The steep, narrow face just to the right again provides a sustained, serious challenge.

58 Drums and Kicks E1 5b   1981
6m The groove 1m left of Overhanging Crack is easier when you know what to go for.

59 Overhanging Crack VD ★   1885-1910
6m A worthwhile route demanding good jamming technique. ● For **The By-Pass**, VS 4c (1931-33), traverse rightwards from 2m up Overhanging Crack to the upper part of Split Chimney.

60 Pass By E1 5c   1978
6m The blind flakes near the arête above an awkward landing. ● The wall just left is 6b (**En Passant**, 1987), ● and the open groove left again is 6c (**Passerine**, 1989). ● The chimney on the right is **Split Chimney**, D (1885-1910).

61 Splitter E1 5b ★   2001
6m The arête immediately right of Split Chimney is climbed on its right-hand side and once committed is far from escapable.

62 Split Chimney Wall HVS 5b ★   1968-76
6m The centre of the wall to the right is climbed direct. ● The dirty wall across the gully on the right is **Delta,** HS 4a (1969). Other routes have been climbed hereabouts and are left to rediscover.

Great Buttress Area

Just right is another area of clean, high-quality buttresses, containing one of the best routes on the crag. ● The deep cleft on the left of the buttress is D, and the clean rib just left is **Omega Rib** VS 5a (2001).

63 Alpha Crack M ★   1885-1910
9m Climb up via flakes to the platform, from where a variety of finishes can be taken.

64 Beta Crack S ★ ★   1885-1910
9m The well-marked flake crack provides a fine, well-protected route at the grade. ● For **Trapeze**, HS 4a ★ (1957-60), swing rightwards into the top of The Great Chimney. Fun.

Stephen Coughlan getting a right old buzz from soloing Black Slab Right. D (page 277).
Photo: David Simmonite.

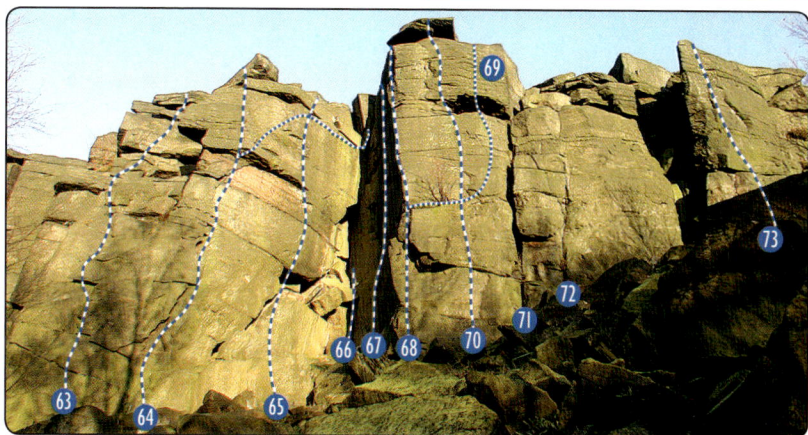

65 Trapezium El 5c — 1978
9m The steep wall.

66 The Great Chimney HD ★ — 1885-1902
9m The cleft. A route can also be climbed at D. ●The crack on the right is **Great Chimney Crack,** S 4a (1885-1910). Often dirty.

67 Thrown Away E2 5c — 1981
12m An escapable line offering good climbing, that starts up the thin crack left of Great Buttress Arête. Finish up the wall above and left via long stretches between positive holds.

68 Great Buttress Arête El 5b ★★★ — 1961-63
12m A superb exposed route blazing a way up the arête on the right, past a somewhat dodgy spike runner. Reasonably well protected by small and medium wires but with a bold upper section and at the top end of the grade. Mind the final rocking block.

69 Great Buttress VS 4c ★ — 1933
14m Ascend the arête as for the previous route, but traverse right after 4m and climb the wall to a cave (runner in Romulus at this grade; HVS without).

70 Just a Minute El 5b ★ — 2000
12m Climb without deviation, hesitation (except to place good small cams) or repetition in a straight line up the centre of the buttress until under the middle of the rocking block. Climb over this to finish.

71 Romulus VD — 1895-1910
8m The left-hand crack.

72 Remus S 4a — 1885-1910
8m The right-hand crack. ●The wall just right is **Fly Wall,** HS 4a (1955).

●For **Central Traverse,** HS 4b (1880s/pre-1951), start at Fly Wall, and traverse 150 feet left.

73 Leaf Buttress VS 4c ★ — 1957-60
6m Climb the centre of the main detached buttress just to the right, trending leftwards and finishing just right of the left-hand arête. ●The arête direct is **Gold Leaf,** HVS 5b ★ (1990).

Twenty metres further on is an easy-angled slab left of which, and on its side-wall, are two chimneys. ●**Chimney and Crack,** HS 4b (1972), is the left-hand chimney and short crack up right; ●**The Warp,** VS 4b (1969), is the right-hand chimney and same finishing crack. A rightward finish is also possible.

The slab contains three well worn lines of ascent. It is good for beginners and hence is likely to be swarming with kids in floppy trainers.

74 Black Slab Left VD ★ — 1885

75 Black Slab Centre HD ★ — 1885

Ingrid Crossland making sensational moves on the steep and exposed Puttrell's Progress, S 4a (opposite page). Photo: David Simmonite.

"The great climb in this group, however, is the hand-traverse across the rock face above the cavern's mouth. I am told it is bad form to name climbs after individuals; but I am unwilling to relinquish the title 'Puttrell's Progress' that has been bestowed on this particular piece of work. Mr. J. W. Puttrell, as every reader of this journal knows, is a capable and daring cragsman. This hand-traverse is at present, his monopoly, and is one of the most sensational climbs to be found at the Crags."

CF Cameron, 1902

76 Black Slab Right D ★   1885

Puttrell's Progress Area: Past a boulder-filled gully there is an obvious square buttress with 'Puttrell's Cave' at its base (the back fell out in 1968).

77 Black Finger E2 5c ★   1973
9m Follow thin cracks leftwards above the cut-away, to reach and finish up the left-hand arête. Good climbing and at the upper limit of the grade.

78 Diamond White E3 5c ★   1992
9m Climb Black Finger to the top of the thin cracks and continue up the thin wall above trending slightly rightwards to the arête/rib, which is used near the top.

79 Anzio Breakout/Pilgrimage E4 6b ★ 1987/78
12m A combination of 2 routes gives a desperate eliminate. Climb the short pillar left of the cave and lean out rightwards on a line of fingerholds until it is possible to cut loose and swing round onto the front face. A hard lock-off enables upward progress (Anzio Breakout, E3 6a). Now, go diagonally rightwards and finish directly above, and over the centre of the overhang, with difficulty (Pilgrimage, E4 6b).

80 Puttrell's Progress S 4a ★★   1885-1902
12m A classic route, covering impressive ground considering its age. Climb the right-hand side of the buttress to an awkward entry into the sentry-box. Make committing moves left above the void to reach a finishing crack.

81 The Flue D ★   1885-1910
12m Ascend to the sentry-box and venture inwards to the bowels of the earth. Straddle the depths to a final squeeze out onto terra firma. A speleological experience and worth a star for the fun of it.

82 Helping Hand E1 5c ★   1973
9m Climb the rib right of the sentry-box to the ledge. The blunt arête at the right-hand end of the overhang, climbed mainly on its left side, needs commitment.

The deep fissure of Monolith Cleft is on the immediate right. Its right wall has two routes: ●**As You Like It,** VD, the left-hand crack, and ●**Black Crack,** VD, the right-hand crack (both 1885-1910). ●**Beyond the Pale,** HVS 5b (1985), is the stepped arête right of Black Crack. ●The left-hand side of the arête direct is **Black Cap,** E1 5c (1985). The rock to the right has all been climbed.

Pillar Area: Twenty two metres further on are twin square pillars. On Left Twin Pillar lies:

83 Little Fellow E2 5b   pre-1976/99
6m The short left arête is difficult to start, precarious and above a very nasty landing. The meat of the route was originally climbed by Twin Pillar Left, with additional excitement provided by a traverse right onto Bolster from 'a high handhold on the arête', and was graded S. However, a grade similar to Little Fellow is felt to be more appropriate.

84 Bolster E1 5b ★   1982
8m A route worth seeking out. Climb the centre of the face directly to the overhang. Make bold moves leftwards over it and continue more easily to the top. ●**First Pillar Route I,** HVS 5a (1965), went right under the overhang and rejoins Bolster.

85 **First Pillar Route 2** E1 5a 1965

8m A good route requiring a steady lead (or side-runners, HVS). Step off a boulder and climb to the ledge. Balance leftwards just above the overhang using thin holds to join and finish up Bolster. ● For **Summer Lightning**, E1 5b (1985), gain the ledge, but continue confidently up the left-hand side of the arête above. The crimpy lower wall just right is 6a.

86 **Flake Climb** VS 4c ★ 1957-60

8m Climb the steep flakes on the front of the right pillar until the left-hand arête can be gained. Finish up this with difficulty.

87 **Schard** E2 5b ★ 1976

8m To the right is a groove above half-height. Gain this directly up a technically demanding wall; bold. ● The next groove on the right has a dangerously loose block towards the top; **The Elf**, HVS 5a (1969); not recommended.

Defile Buttress: Twenty seven metres to the right is a large face split by the wide crack of The Blue Defile; ● 10m up and left of this buttress is a short arête taken by Dilemma, VS 4c (1969), starting on the left and finishing on the right. Other problems can be found here; ● of note is the roof left of **Dilemma** at V0+ (5b). ● Five metres right of Dilemma beyond a block-filled chimney (M) are twin cracks; **Crista's Twin** HD (1994). Meanwhile back at Defile Buttress:

88 **Defile Left** S 4b 1968-76

8m Climb the friable wall, moving left onto the arête at the break.

89 **Brand New Nothing** E4 6a 2001

8m Continue directly up the faint flake-line just left of Blue Defile.

90 **The Blue Defile** VS 4b ★ 1933

9m Climb the wide crack, exiting left at the capstone.

91 **Blasphemy** E4 6b 1981

9m The steep wall provides a hard, unprotected start followed by an easier finish up the arête above.

92 **Duplicate** E1 5b ★ 1978

6m Climb the front of the pillar 3m to the right at an obvious chimney weakness, moving left to finish on the left edge. ● The crack and groove on the right is **Groovy**, HVD (2002).

Himmelswillen Area

The next buttress marks the start of the most continuous section of the Deepcar end of the crag, and probably the crag's most popular area. It has superb climbs that rank along the best the Peak has to offer.

93 **Sidewinder** HS 4a 1964-76

7m Start on a boulder up on the left side of the buttress and take the easiest leftwards trending and reachy line above. ● The centre of the wall up and right is **Frigging Saw**, E3 6a † (1983), a variation from Sidewinder into Himmelswillen.

94 **Himmelswillen** VS 4c ★ ★ ★ 1933

15m A classic route with good open climbing and possibly the most sought after tick on the edge. You may even have to queue. Ascend the left-hand arête

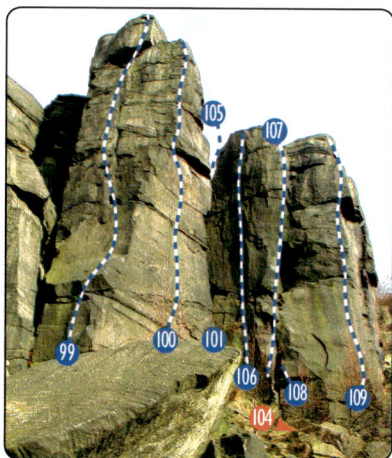

of the front face and move right under the overhang to gain the flake. Climb this, stepping left onto a ledge. Reach the top directly. Even more satisfying is to gain the flake from directly below, move left to the final crack and hand-traverse right and mantelshelf over the top with a final flourish.

95 Serrated Edge E1 5b ★   1981
15m The right-hand arête.

96 Teufelsweg D ★   1936
15m Climb the deep chimney. ● The crack out of the right-hand side is **Y.M.C.A. Crack,** VD (1970).

97 Dragon's Hoard E6 6b ★★   1993
11m An excellent technical route, climbing the sinuous crack-line near the centre of the wall to a challenging and committing direct finish; very fingery and difficult to protect. ● The original route on this section of wall is **Cardinal's Treasure,** E4 6b ★★ (1984), well worth doing in its own right. It climbs the sinuous crack before moving right to finish up Banana Wall.

The thin, narrow wall to the left of the crack was claimed as **Wango Tango,** E6 6c (1987) †. However, there is doubt over the authenticity of the original claim.

98 Banana Wall E3 6a ★★   1977
12m Climb the flake to an undercut move to gain the ledge above. Fingery and with mediocre protection to help concentrate the mind. Technically low in the grade, arguments have raged about whether it is 5c or 6a, however, for those lacking in stature the route is probably E4 6a, just.

Hell Gate Gully Area

Easily found when walking along the cliff top path due to the well-worn top of the crag and a stone wall ahead and left of the path. It is also at the summit of the rising cliff top path from the north end.

99 Tower Face HS 4a ★★★   1933
12m A justifiably popular route with plenty of exposure. Start on the right wall at the base of a cleft and climb up gingerly into a steep scoop. Follow the line of a thin crack on good small holds up the centre of the face. ● A pleasant if disjointed route, **Two Tier Climb,** S 4a (2002), starts up the rib left of Tower Face and steps right to climb the left arête of that route.

100 Down to Earth E4 5c   1985
13m The wall and left arête of the front face provide an airy, if contrived, lead with no protection til above the crux.

101 On the Air E5 6a ★★   1978
12m A committing climb requiring technique and balance. The right arête of the front face is climbed direct, initially on the right-hand side. An alternative start takes the left-hand side of the arête from a slightly lower point and a more satisfying finish is had by moving left onto Down to Earth above the overhang.

One of the finest and most celebrated climbs at Wharncliffe is Himmelswillen, VS 4c (previous page), giving reasonable, but steep and exciting climbing up the impending flakeline. Thea Williams climbing. Photo: Nick Smith.

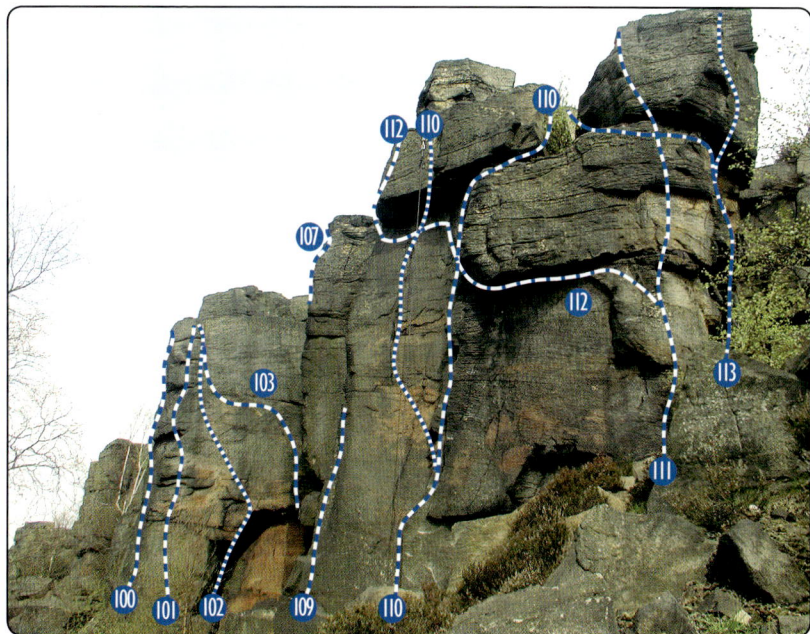

102 Journey into Freedom E7 6b ★   1993

12m The wall to the right of On the Air provides the most demanding route on the edge. Start by bridging out of the cleft, then move leftwards off a large flat undercut to slap up the arête for a couple of moves. Move rightwards to gain thin edges and reach the large ledge. Finish up On the Air.

103 Seconds Out E5 6b   1978

12m Another terrifying pitch. Start 3m left of the cleft by mantelshelving onto the jutting block. Ascend the steep wall above to gain a fingery traverse leftwards to the ledge on the previous route. Finish up this or move back right to the obvious flake above the start.

104 Pointy Block Problem V5 (6b)

Below the edge at this point is a pointed boulder with an overhanging rippled face. Climb this from a sit start. Easier variations are possible.

105 Hell Gate Gully M   1885-1902

12m The major gully.

106 News at Zen E3 5c ★   1993

11m Climb the wall to the left of Desolation Angel via a black pocket.

107 Desolation Angel E6 6b ★ ★ ★   1978

12m The majestic, leaning, right-hand arête gives an outstanding route that ranks amongst the finest anywhere on gritstone. Climb the arête to reach the break, where a final awkward move brings the top.

108 Hell Gate VD ★   1885-1902

15m Varied climbing up the corner to the right. Stuff yourself in the crack or bridge wide according to taste – awkward at the start for the short. The final moves of Gavel Neese provide an airy finish at the same grade.

"The Wharncliffe Grit
is exceptionally angular, and the corners that
are so handy to clutch deprive us, as we go,
of a good deal of cuticle."

EA Baker

⑩⑨ Gavel Neese E2 5b ★   1961-63
14m Climb the arête with a little faith and friction (and no protection) to a ledge. Carry on up the upper arête with interest. Very, *very*, reach dependant.

⑪⓪ Hell Gate Crack HS 4b ★   1934-51
12m The prominent scarred crack to the right is climbed passing an awkward bulge to gain a recess on the right below the top. Sadly now polished. ● A stiff variation is **Lucifer,** E3 6a ★ (1984), stepping left at the bulge to climb the crack to the roof. Hard climbing into and up the scoop above leads to the top.

⑪⑪ Joie-de-Vivre E1 5c ★   1957-60
8m Ascend the rib to the break at 6m then make a dynamic move directly for the top with good protection, et trop joie. Prenez plaisir au mouvement.

⑪⑫ Primal Void VS 5a ★   1998
16m Climb to the first break on Joie-de-Vivre at 3m and traverse delicately left into Hell Gate Crack, which is climbed to just beneath the overhang. Make a long step down left and continue to the arête of Gavel Neese, which provides the finish.

⑪⑬ Ce ne Fait Rien HVS 5b   1961-63
9m Start in a chimney round to the right and hand-traverse left below the overhang to finish in the recess of Hell Gate Crack. ● The direct finish is: **Well Now it Is,** E2 6a (1991). Use a pinch on the arête above the chimney and take a flying leap for the top. ● An easier finish goes right then back left to a short crack, **Wheelbrace,** VS 4c (1961-63).

Behind and right is a shorter wall. ● The prominent groove is **Green Groove,** D (1933). The short rocks to the left can also be climbed; **Footloose,** VS 5a (2000). ● The arête to the right of the groove is **Pleasantry,** HVD (2002). ● The crack just right is **Obscenity,** HS 4b (1957-60). ● The wall on the right gives a VS 5b problem, **Falkway** (1978). Other lines are possible.

To the right is a low wall, split by two chimneys, which are short and about Moderate standard. The walls around the chimneys contain many problems, all of which have been climbed and are left for you to explore as has been the tradition. Of note, however, is **Problem Wall**, the largest and cleanest wall

with some excellent problems the best of which are the left-hand line at 5a and the right-hand line at 4c.

Belle Vue Buttress: Thirty five metres after the low rocks a buttress is reached. This is roughly 500m from the north end and 20m beyond the stone wall which you pass on the left side of the crag-top footpath. It has a terraced 'Belle Vue' at two-thirds height, which can be gained by either a Moderate chimney on the right or by the rather inaptly named Central Route. From the terrace the top can be reached by any line.

⑪⑭ Amnesaic HS 4c   2003
10m Climb the crack on the far left of Belle Vue Buttress to a beefy traverse right, on spaced jugs under the top overlaps, round to the ledge. ● A HVS 5b direct finish (onto the sloping top above the triangular hole) can be climbed.

⑪⑮ Central Route VS 4c ★   1961-63
9m A good route that takes a wandering line up the left-hand side of the front face. Climb up to and surmount the initial small overhang at 3m. Move back left to the first protection and finish on good holds. ● Climbing direct from the left-hand end of the overhang is harder, E1 5c.

⑪⑯ Bay Wall E2 5b   1978
9m Gain a precarious position on the central ledge and climb the overlapped wall above to finish up a short crack. Not at all well-protected.

⑪⑰ Ganto's Axe E2 5c ★   1999
9m Start from the lowest point, just left of the blocky chimney. Hard moves up the wall enable one to gain the right-hand end of the central ledge. Move slightly right, to finish up a slab and crack. ● **Problem Bulge,** E1 5b (2003), is the bulge right of the chimney.

Holly Crack Area

Two hundred and twenty five metres beyond Belle Vue Buttress on the right-hand side of the crag-top path, a lone, sturdy birch tree grows through a split boulder on the crag edge in a clearing in between a collection of stunted oak. Below is a continuous section of shorter rock, starting some 25m left of the routes proper. Many short routes and quality

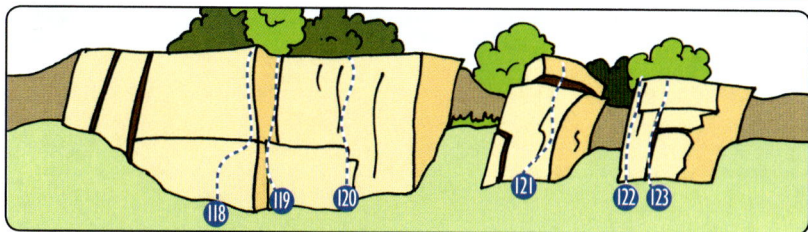

boulder problems can be had in this section. The first taller rock lies right. An obvious corner crack has an old tree-stump at its base (Holly Crack).

118 Hollyoaks VS 4b ★   2001
8m Pleasant climbing up the slabby arête left of Holly Crack, started on the left. ● A direct start to the arête is 5b. ● The slab can also be climbed direct at HVS 5b without using the arête. The crack to the left is VD.

119 Holly Crack VD ★   1885-1910
8m Climb the corner-crack after a tricky start.

120 Holly Scoop E2 5c ★   1981
8m Start 2m to the right and ascend a crack to a ledge. Make hard, difficult to protect, moves up the fine cracked wall above. ● The right arête is **The Thorn,** E1 5a (1984), a short but reachy and unprotected affair.

121 Upwardly Mobile E1 5a ★   1984
8m A few metres to the right is a buttress with a scooped right arête. Balance awkwardly up the scoop and finish up on the wall above. ● The short crack itself is the pleasant though short-lived **Unnamed Crack,** S 4b (traditional). ● The right arête on its right is **Unnamed Crank,** V4 (6a).

To the right is a clean face partially hidden behind trees, with an obvious jamming crack in its lower half.

122 Wienie Roast HVS 5a   2001
7m Climb a thin crack just left of a jamming crack to a tricky finish up the left edge of the wall.

123 Hanging Rock HVS 5a ★   1980
8m Climb the jamming crack and extend up the fine wall above. ● The groove to the right is **Picnic,** HS 4a (1980).

Three Cracks Wall: Forty five metres right of Hanging Rock, and just beyond a large holly tree is a short wall with cracks on its right-hand side and an old tree stump up to its left. ● **Missed Me!,** VS 4b, is the centre of the wall passing a ledge. In the wall to the right are three cracks; ● **Crack One,** D, is the wide left-hand crack; ● **Second Crack,** VD, the slight central crack and ● **Crack Three,** VD, the right-hand of the trio (all 2003). ● The short wall to the right gives a smart V0 (5a) problem.

124 Mad as a Mad Thing VS 4c   2001
7m Fifteen metres right again is a fine looking wall with a short corner on its left side. Ascend the corner with an awkward move on to a ledge. Step right on to the wall and head up to a tricky finish. ● **A Moment of Madness,** E1 5a (2004), is the blunt arête to the right.

Two Tree Wall: Fifteen metres right again is a substantial wall with a holly tree growing out of the crag at its centre and a weird charred stump on the left. ● **Charred** VD, is the wide crack-line containing the charred stump. ● **Two Tree Trip,** S 4a, is the tree-choked central crack. ● **Footin Mouth,** HVS 5a, is the clean rib just right. ● **Too Wide for Some,** S, is the heather-choked crack on the right (all 2003). ● **Bring Back the Birch,** HVS 5a (2004), climbs the thin crack in the small wall 5m right.

Notice Board Buttress: The next routes lie on a collection of short buttresses 60m to the right. The terrain below the crag is tortuous so better to return to the cliff top path. A convenient landmark on the path is a nature notice board. This is also the arrival point of an approach path from the east.

Below the notice board are three small buttresses.
● The left-hand buttress can be climbed at VS 4c,
● whilst the central buttress offers a clean slabby
arête, **Notice Board Slab,** HS 4a (both traditional).
● The right-hand buttress is more substantial and
has a large overhang at the top. **Lundy Calling,** E1
5b (2004), takes a line up the centre of the buttress
via a very thin flake to the overhang. Step left and
pull over to a sloping finish.

Twenty metres right again is a short steep slab;
climbed centrally it gives a nice VS 4b with an
awkward finish. A further 50m right (80m from the
notice board) is a clean arête rising from the trees.

125 Just Commit E1 5a ★   2004
12m Climb the arête on its left-hand side with a
delightful but unprotected high step to reach easier
ground.

Nardil Buttress: This clean tower-like buttress has
an open aspect and is situated 20m right of Just
Commit and 100m from the notice board. A useful
landmark is a boulder of curiously contorted strata
on the left of the cliff top path. On the rock below, there is a chimney near the left. ● This gives
Pentovis, D (1981), where the exit is constricting so
stay on the outside for maximum enjoyment. ● **Rib
Tickler,** HS 4a, (2001), is the rib to the left. The
wall to the right is:

126 Paper Birch E1 5b ★   1999
9m Ascend the fine wall, using the arête as necessary. ● **Nardil,** E3 6a (1981), is the flake on the right
to the ledge. Bold fingery moves lead up the wall
above.

*The edge again dwindles to give sporadic boulders.
One hundred metres further on (roughly 1km
from the north end), and under some large pine
trees, is:*

Long John's Stride

This excellent buttress is composed of four tower-
like pillars, which contain some of the best climbing on the edge, surrounding a rather grubby inner
cove. There is some bouldering on a slab on the
leftmost tower.

127 October Arête E2 5c ★ ★   1955
12m A climb of considerable character. The arête is
taken direct with hard initial moves to a small ledge.
Above, the moves are still bold but easier. ● The
ledge can be gained from the left and the arête
climbed at HVS 5a ★. ● The low corner and wall
on the left give **October Climb,** S 4a (1955).

128 Autumn Wall E4 6a ★ ★ ★   1978
12m The steep wall right of the arête provides an
outstanding route that would make a good introduction into the E4 grade. After a committing start
continue direct via numerous breaks, some good,
some not so good. Possibly the best hard route on
the edge.

129 Deepcar Named Desire E5 6b ★ †   1999
12m A squeezed-in but demanding line up the wall
to the right of the last route. Side-runners protect
the initial moves.

130 Equinox E3 5c ★   1978, 1988
14m Climb the right-hand arête of the wall direct.
Good climbing but unfortunately escapable.

The Cove: The following routes are in the cove itself
and can be green and dirty. ● **Chockstone Chimney,** VD (1885-1902), the block-filled cleft on the
left of the cove entrance, a typical climb of the era.
● **Tiered Pillar,** HVS 5a (1999), is the pillar just
right climbed by either the front or the right arête.
● **V-Chimney,** D (1885-1902), climbs the V-shaped
chimney to the right, and is a good bridging

The Long John's Stride area of Wharncliffe combines stunning architecture, superb routes and a rich history to give one of the finest climbing locations on the whole edge. Here, Dan Cheetham enjoys the final moves on Grammarian's Face, E2 5b (overleaf). Photo: David Simmonite.

problem that is over too soon. ● To the right is a narrow wall with a small capping roof. **V for Victory,** E1 5a (1994), climbs the left rib of the wall and finishes over the left-hand end of the roof. ● **Waxing Lyrical,** VS 4b (1994), is the narrow pillar left of the next route without deviation. At the back of the cove is a sort of inverted V-shaped chimney. ● For **The Candle Snuffer,** HVD (1885-1902), climb this mainly on good holds on the right wall until ejected out rightwards. ● On the pinnacle itself, **Long John's Ordinary,** S 4a (1957-60), climbs the blunt rib right of The Candle Snuffer to a notch in the top left-hand side of the pinnacle. This gives an uncomfortable finish. ● **Spider Cracks,** VS 5b (1957-60), are the thin cracks to the right, leading leftwards to a final hanging crack. ● A slightly more direct ascent up the right-hand crack is **Vapona,** E2 5c (1976), finishing to the right, but is usually very green and greasy. Starting just inside the cove entrance on the right is:

The Long John's Stride

The next routes all finish on the summit of the detached pinnacle. The easiest descent is by striding across the gap at the back of the pinnacle. Otherwise, Long John's Stride can be performed above the cove entrance between the two towers and contains a health warning. The trick is apparently to drop across the gulf at full stretch on to the hands, bring one foot over to a small hold and then do a sort of mantelshelf on to the other side! Only those who are a cam short of a full rack need apply.

131 Grammarian's Progress VS 4b ★★ 1944
12m A quality outing and well worth the walk. Climb the left-hand side of the arête, passing the hole at its right-hand end. Reach the huge angular hold higher on the arête and boldly gain a standing position on it before traversing right on the break across the exposed face to a finishing crack. An odd alternative is to bridge all the way up between the two pinnacles at a similar grade.

132 Gwyn E2 5c ★ 1957-64
12m Climb directly up the centre of the intricate technical face crossed by Grammarian's Progress. *'The first 20 feet to the mantelshelf are perhaps the hardest series of continuous moves on the crag.' 1960.*

133 Grammarian's Face E2 5b ★ 1957-60
12m The right-hand arête. ● Stepping left onto Gwyn at 6m gives an easier variant at E1 5a.

134 Long John's Eliminate E2 5b ★★ 1961-63
15m Superb open climbing but with sparse protection. From 4m up the arête, teeter across the face to a groove on the right arête. Ascend this with difficulty to a ledge leading leftwards to a crack to finish. ● A direct start to the groove can also be made from the left-hand side of the piercing hole: **Cannae,** E2 5b (1982).

135 Long John's Super Direct E2 5b ★ 1999
13m To the right of Long John's Eliminate is a flake. Climb this, step left into the scoop above and follow this directly to the headwall. Traverse right to finish up the arête. ● To the right is a short chimney, VD.

136 Impish V5 (E1 6b)
The short bulging arête is a scary problem. ● The wall on its right is V3 (6a).

137 Long Chimney D ★ 1885-1902
9m To the right again is another narrowing chimney. ● **Long Chimney Variation,** VD ★ (2003), steps left to climb the centre of the wall.

138 Inclusion HVS 5b 1980
9m The right-hand arête of the chimney.

139 Richard's Revenge VS 4c ★★ 1949-50

9m A good exercise in jamming, particularly the upper section. The thin crack is climbed past a niche to a roof and a stiff pull over this on solid jams.

140 Face Dance E4 6a 1980

9m Follow Lincoln Crack to the first break where a step left leads to a desperate rock-over to gain the next break. Finish more easily up the centre of the face. ● A line has been claimed between Richard's Revenge and Face Dance; **Lord of the Dance**, E3 5c (1999).

141 Lincoln Crack HVD ★★ 1949-50

8m Exciting stuff. The layback crack on the right leads to a swing rightwards into a chimney crack above.

142 Long John's Arête V4 (6a)

The short but fine hanging arête.

143 Big Bird HS 4b 2001

6m Climb the centre of the wall around to the right again passing a crescent shaped crack *en route*.

The Central Section (Upper Tier)

The path on top of the edge continues south for 50m from the south end of Long John's Stride then forks. The right-hand fork descends into the woods across a stream towards Cascade Buttress and The Bass Rock which are described later. The left-hand branch keeps to the cliff top.

Puttrell and Watson's Buttress: Following the path south through trees, across three small streams it eventually follows a wall and starts to rise again. About 200m from a blocked-up gateway (i.e. 420m from the path junction and almost in line with a pylon and radio transmitter to the left) and directly below two large stones built into the wall to form a stile, is a vague path to the bottom of the crag where there is a small buttress with a wide crack at its left-hand side.

144 Harrison's Half Hour VS 5b 2001

8m To the left of the wide crack, and on the left-hand side of the arête is a thin crack. Climb this to a technical exit onto the sloping ledge and finish

directly. Gaining the ledge from the blind flakes on the left would give a desperate problem.

145 Puttrell and Watson's Route S 4b ★ 1889

9m The aforementioned crack can be either lay-backed or jammed to its end before taking the obvious line rightwards then up to the top. A real museum piece – the layback is believed to be the first done in the Peak.

146 Greenwood Side VS 5a 2001

9m To the right, climb the arête starting on its right-hand side to a break and follow the narrow pillar above. Pleasant. ● The broken rock on the right can all be climbed at around 4a.

147 Little Wing E4 6a ★ 1985

8m Up the bank to the right is a flying arête. Starting on the right make initial difficult moves to gain the arête and follow it direct.

Holly Route Area

Ninety metres further right is a continuous section of rock characterized by a holly tree in a V-shaped groove on the left and a large wall topped by a long overhang to the right. Left of the V-shaped groove is a wall with a wide break at half-height.

'A good deal of diversion was caused by a non-climbing visitor. Bond and Baker had struggled with much ado up a difficult cleft when this gentleman, after watching them compassionately called out 'But why don't you chaps do it this way?' and straight away ran up the cliff after the fashion of a cat storming a wall, quite heedless of the fact that he ought to have nails on his boots. This gentleman must be kept out of the Climbers' Club at all hazards, for climbing will cease to be an art if our pet scrambles are massacred in this way.'

Climbers' Club Journal Volume 3, September 1900

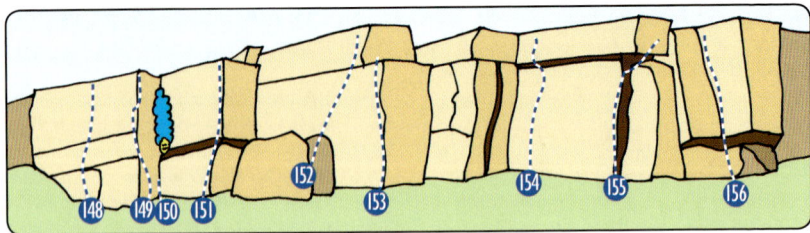

148 Changeling E2 6a ★   1982
8m At the left-hand end of the wall is this thin crack protected by small wires and with the crux at the top.

149 Mark E2 5b ★   1981
9m Go up the left arête of the V-shaped holly-clad groove, to a ledge. Finish straight up the small arête above. ● An alternative way up similar ground is **S.M.O.** E2 5c (1982), which climbs the wall just left of the arête using it in places and moving slightly left to finish on the ledge.

150 Holly Route D   1949-50
8m The corner with, guess what? Who needs rock?

151 Emma E1 5c   1979
8m Climb the arête right of Holly Route, with protection from the tree branch or half a dozen good spotters. ● The chimney just right is **Chimney and Crack,** VD (1949-50).

152 Spanish Caravan E1 5c   1982
8m Across to the right, step off a boulder to cross the slanting overlap with caution, moving slightly right to finish. ● **La Mancha**, E2 6a (1989), is the wall to the left via a short left-facing groove.

153 Contemporary HVS 5a ★   1979
9m Move right to follow the arête with some delicacy. Stiff at the grade. ● Climbing the wall 1m left is the same grade (**Same Rain**, 1982), while the arête on its right is more like E2 5c: **Antique**, (1986).

● **Traditional,** D (1885-1910), is the wide corner on the right. ● **Hanging Chimney,** S (1885-1910), is the wall and flake 2m right. ● **Gone for a Burton,** VD (1999), is the cracked arête to the right.

Round the corner lies a large open face. It has an overhang along its entire length at 9m. The wall on its left is split by two cracks. ● **Bill,** D, is the left-hand crack, complete with a chockstone. ● **Ben,** D, is the right-hand crack. ● **Big Corner,** VD, is the corner. Bridging makes the climb much better (all 1885-1910).

154 Mr Mojo Risin' E5 6a ★★   1982
12m An excellent route up the sandy wall 2m right of the corner. Bold and technical climbing leads to runners in the break. The roof and headwall above prove a little less intimidating.

155 Easy Gully D
8m The block-filled gully. For those needing a check-up from the neck up, an exciting hand-traverse along the top of the edge and above the long roof can be done. Usually climbed from right-to-eft the start is best reached from Easy Gully. **Ridge Climb,** HS 4b (traditional), is the ridge right of the rift.

● Around to the right, **Just a Little Bit,** E2 5b (2001), ascends the shallow corner crack and pulls over the roof to a wide cleft. Make a difficult step up and finish up the centre of the slab. Bold.

156 Rainbow Crack D   1949-50
6m A good exercise in jamming up the corner crack just right. Move left at the pointed block.

Fifteen metres right is a buttress with a corner on its left-hand side and a wall on the right with a short wide crack at its base. ● **Corner Climb,** VD, is the dirty corner behind the tree. ● **Crack and Wall,** S, is the wide crack and the wall on the right. ● **Trouser Browser,** HS 4a (2001), uses two pockets right of the wide crack and ascends the wall and arête to a ledge. Take the arête above. ● The short wall to the right starting from the ledge is **Fizz,** VS 4b (2001). Further on is the last buttress of note, which is well worth seeking out.

Even Chance Buttress: The front face has three grooves leading to an overhang. ● **Even Chance**, HVS 5b (1980), climbs the left-hand groove and moves out to the lip to finish up a short crack. ● **Long Odds**, E5 6b (1980), climbs as for the previous route to the lip and uninspiring runners. Swing wildly rightwards and make a desperate move up to easy climbing. Short but very sharp, like the landing.

⓳ **Toss Up** E5 6a ★ 1980

9m Three metres right is a short layback crack leading to a double overhang. Layback up and go over the first overlap to gain holds on the lip of the second overlap. Pull up, moving slightly left to reach hidden holds on the slab above; runner on left. A final hard move brings the top. A sustained and committing route.

The Wharncliffe Adventurer

Many climbers start at the Deepcar end and get no further than Great Buttress, thus missing the longest and best quality climbs and the delightful situations of the middle and southern end of the crags. With this in mind the distance to key locations has been accurately paced out along the crag top path to save the visitor the time-consuming, shin-snapping expedition along the bottom. Rather than endure the visual and chemical pollution of power lines and other abominations, on first acquaintance try walking along the top to the Hell Gate area, which has climbs of all grades to compare favourably with the best at Stanage. Other highly recommended locations are Long John's Stride, Lodge Buttress and, when dry, Bass Rock and Cascade Buttress. You can find solitude in some of these places on a fine Sunday afternoon when Stanage and Froggatt are like Blackpool Prom.

⓲ **Chancer** VS 4c 2001

6m Five metres right, climb the sharp arête. ● The wall just left provides a pleasant S 4a, ● whilst the crack right of the arête is D ● and the wall just right again provides a good 5b problem.

From here, the edge gets smaller and more broken. However, the next 150m offer a great supply of boulder problems and highballs, many of which may still be unclimbed. They often take good lines on clean rock, mainly in the V3-V6 range.

The Lower Rocks

Returning back north to the fork in the path, some 40m from the south end of Long John's Stride, the right-hand fork descends into the woods and across a stream and gives access to several isolated buttresses.

Cascade Buttress: Following the path one arrives in 100m at a collection of buttresses on the left. These are characterised by a prominent triangular slab, The Sliding Stone, on the left of the path (water-worn and proof that the stream crossed earlier used to flow directly over the buttress, hence the name), and an ominous, central V-shaped cleft.

⓳ **Cascade Climb** VS 5b 1955

12m The short problem arête left of the V-shaped cleft is ascended to a horizontal gash. Hand-traverse, stomach-traverse or use any other part of your body you feel is appropriate, to move leftwards to a ledge and finish up the wall above.

⓴ **Flying Angel** E1 5b 1961-63

9m Character building. Climb the V-shaped cleft moving out left at the overhang to gain the upper crack above the void with difficulty. ● The wall immediately left is **Fountain of Youth,** E2 5b (1981), climbed using small holds and plenty of adrenalin.

㉑ **Watson's Crack** HS 4b ★ 1885-1902

8m A fine museum piece. The wide fissure leads over an awkward overhang. Impressive for its day. ● The sharp arête just left is taken by **Spring Tide,** E2 6b (1988), which then continues over the hanging nose above (side-runners).

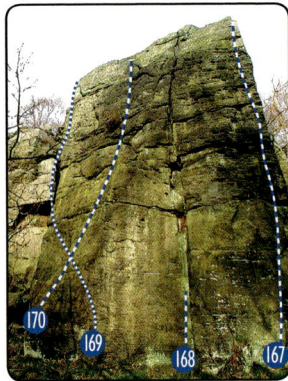

162 Bedrock E5 6b ★   1987
8m Climb the exciting and technically absorbing arête above the start of Watson's Crack on its right-hand side. E6 without the side-runners in Watson's Crack.

163 Puttrell's Crack VD ★   1885-1902
8m One of the first routes climbed on the edge. To the right the broken corner/chimney is climbed all the way on the outside, with a daunting but well-protected finish.

164 Pocket Buttress VS 4b ★ ★   1955
9m Start in the centre of the wall on the right and climb to twin pockets. Move right to the arête and go up over the nose on the left side to gain the top.

165 Pocket Buttress Direct E5 6a ★ ★   1984
9m Climb direct past the twin pockets on Pocket Buttress and gain a standing position with difficulty. Wave goodbye to your gear and make a long move left to a final steep pull.

● Round to the right of the buttress is the traditional pleasures of **Deep Chimney**, VD (1885-1910).

166 Cadence E1 5b ★   1980
9m Climb Deep Chimney, and swing left to reach a groove, which is followed to the top.

● **Penis Town,** E1 5c (2001), follows Cadence to the base of the groove. Make a hard pull right to the arête and climb it, with difficulty, on its left-hand side. The rocks immediately to the right of Deep Chimney provide a few short routes and problems. The most worthwhile is the first clean arête at HS 4b.

Fifty metres further right of Cascade Buttress is a steep buttress with a prominent overlap. ● **Envy**, S 4a (2002), climbs the green left side of the left arête. ● **The George Formby Appreciation Society,** E2 5c ★ (2001), climbs up to a prominent undercut and make a long reach up the wall above to a precarious finish.

The Outlook

The path from Cascade Buttress descends into the wood and 250m from the junction, or 150m from Cascade Buttress, is a prominent flat-topped boulder projecting out into the valley. This is home to some good bouldering. See topo on opposite page.

The Bass Rock

This elusive obelisk sits somewhat hidden among the trees some 200m beyond The Outlook, on the downhill side of the path. It consists of a detached pinnacle with a crack up its long face overlooking the valley. Access is easiest down to the left looking out before skirting round rightwards to the front face. Alternatively take the descent gully down rightwards behind the pinnacle.

For a change these climbs are described from right-to-left, the way that they are best approached.

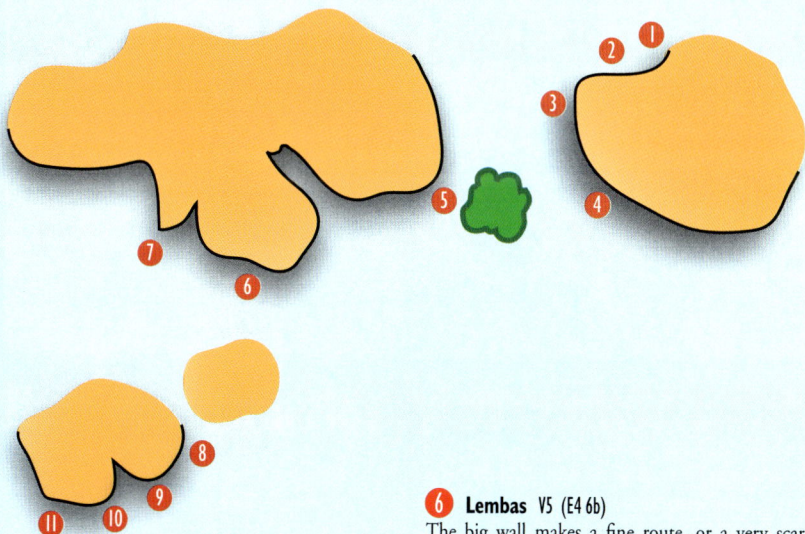

◀ Cascade Buttress 150m   Bass Rock 330m ▶

6 Lembas V5 (E4 6b)
The big wall makes a fine route, or a very scary boulder problem.

7 Pixie's Arête V0– (VS 4c)
The overhanging arête is easier than it looks. Good moves.

8 Pockets V3 (6b)
A sitting start is possible at V6.

9 V3 (6a)
A problem to the left is of similar difficulty.

10 V3 (6a)
From a low start make slappy moves up steep ground.

11 V7 (6b)
From a sitting start climb the bulging face with the aid of the right arête. Hard to start.

1 Outlook Lip V3 (6a)
Traverse the lip from left to right into a rockover on problem 3.

2 The Gruelling Mantel V4 (6b)

3 V2 (6a)
From the low break, work out through the roof to rock over on the left - good eliminates possible.

4 Pete's Route V2 (HVS 6a)
Climb out through the roof via the horn.

5 Kim Span V6 (6b)
Climb the small leaning wall from a sitting start, then make a ridiculous span to the crozzly edge near the arête of the roof, use it to gain the top.

On the left of the left-hand descent path, and approximately 15m from Bass Rock, is a series of small walls that give a number of short routes and problems, many of which may have been climbed in the past. The first wall seen has an obvious arête topped by a perched block with a slabby groove at its right-hand side. ● This is **Top Heavy**, VS 4c (2001), which climbs easily up the arête on its left-hand side to an awkward step up onto a ledge. Make an intimidating pull rightwards into the slabby groove, which is followed to its end. Strangely satisfying.

● On The Bass Rock itself is **Southern Route,** S 4a (1955), situated up and round to the right of the front face. Gain the top of a block via a crack on its right side and finish up the cracked groove to the summit. ● **Dorenuts,** E1 5a (2001), is down and left of the block, using a flake-crack to gain the top of the block. Make a step left and climb the bold wall above. 5b for the short.

(167) Brooks' Route HVS 5a ★   1933
12m Returning back to the front face, climb the right-hand arête in its entirety. Low in the grade but the finish is delicate and requires steadiness. ● An eliminate direct up the wall to the left via pockets with a mantelshelf start is **Bass Relief,** HVS 5b (2001).

(168) Scarlett's Crack VS 5a ★★   1931
12m Boulder out the hard, tricky start up the often green V-cleft to gain the central crack that proves to be very enjoyable and well-protected.

(169) Rossiter's Route HVS 5b ★   2000
12m Start via a boulder problem start just right of Byne's Route and move left to climb the arête direct on its right-hand side.

(170) Byne's Route S 4a ★★   1933
12m This starts off a boulder at the base of the left arête before moving right and up the centre of the face just to the left of Scarlett's Crack.

(171) Norwand HVS 5b   1961-63
9m Climb the steep left wall on small holds trending right to an awkward finish on the arête.

Descent: From the Rock is made via the short crag side or by the '**Monkey Jump'** (1890-1900). This is made from the northeast corner to land on the main edge below a flat overhanging rock on a small ledge. This requires a turn in mid-air along with strong legs, a lot of nerve and no brain cells.

● Across the gully to the left is **Split Decision**, E1 5b (1984). Climb the undercut groove just left of the gully moving right to finish. ● An alternative finish moves left onto the front face of the small buttress at 5c. For **Mind Game,** E1 5a (1984), follow the slab and scoop 2m left to finish direct on rounded holds. ● The right arête of the buttress to the left is **Harvey,** S 4a (2001), reached via a short dirty wall and is climbed to a ledge. Finish over the capping block above. ● Unfortunately a bit close to **Andrew**, HVS 5a (1982), which climbs the centre of the buttress just left with blinkers and keeping right of the detached flake in the gully.

● **This Year's Model**, E5 6a (1985), is the slab and flying arête 3m left of Andrew. Spotters could be essential since the arête is probably not the only thing that may be flying.

● Sixteen metres further left is a detached pinnacle containing **Sleight of Hand**, HVS 5b (1984). Make strenuous moves to gain a standing position on the undercut right arête and continue direct. ● Finally, **Confidence Trick**, E1 5b (1984), moves from the prominent boulder to make a committing pull leftwards over the abyss to gain the front face of the pinnacle. Continue on good holds to the top.

Lodge Buttress Area

From The Bass Rock the path climbs the hillside to meet up with the path from The Central Section. The trees increase in size and number. Eventually Wharncliffe Lodge is reached, and beginning roughly 200m before it are a number of pleasantly situated buttresses providing some good routes worth seeking out.

Dragon's Den Bouldering: At the left end of this section lies a collection of short rocks which give the best bouldering on the edge.

Lodge Buttress 30m ▶

172 **Fishboy** V6 (6b)
Starting on goodish holds toward the back of a cave, tricky bridging moves lead out to a kneebar rest at the cave entrance, from here mammoth thrutching may attains the top.

173 **Jellyeyes** V8 (6c)
Use a good edge in the break and poor holds above to gain the top. A big rockover dyno. No undercutting break. V6 using undercut sequence, but not half as satisfying. ● The groove on the right is V1 (5b), ● and the left arête is V2 (6a).

174 **The Arête** V3 (6a)

175 **The Bear Pit** V8 (6c)
Starting on the left side of the crack in the pit, cross the roof on pockets to gain edges over lip, hang the swing and finish up the wall.

176 **Dragon Slayer** V7 (6c)
Climb the prow of the flake from a low start, avoiding the right wall.

177 **The Dragon's Den** V3 (6a)
Undercut the flake, span round and yard up the wall above.

178 **The Big Flake** V0– (4b)

179 **Jorge** V8 (6c)
Climb the rib, eliminating the sloping hold and pocket on the wall to the right. Brilliant.

180 **Crouching Tiger** V7 (6c)
Dyno from the break to the sloping hold.

181 **Blunted** V7 (6b)
Start low on an edge and climb to the big break. Continue up the blunt rib above on it's left-hand side. ● The section above the break makes a good V4 in itself.

182 **Sweet Release** V9 (6c)
Start up Blunted, cross the thin break leftward to its end from where a hard span gains the flake, and a finish up The Dragon's Den.

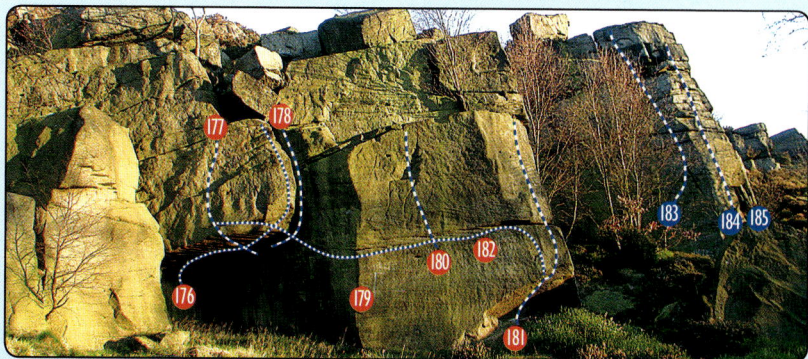

J W PUTTRELL

In climbing terms J W Puttrell was a man operating way ahead of his time. Towards the latter part of the 19th century he began exploring the Derbyshire moors and edges and, in between dodging irate gamekeepers, made the first recorded ascents on many of today's popular cliffs. In an age where the only means of transport was by foot the net was cast incredibly wide: Stanage, Froggatt, Bamford, Cratcliffe, Kinder and Black Rocks to name just a few all fell to this gifted yet unassuming Sheffield man.

It was, however, on his local crag, Wharncliffe that Puttrell excelled. As early as 1885 Wharncliffe became the birthplace of gritstone climbing, often climbing alone and sometimes with his great friend W J Watson, Puttrell's appetite for unclimbed rock was insatiable. After dispensing with the traditional lines of weakness Puttrell began to scrutinise the faces in between them and recorded some remarkable first ascents for the age. The Wharncliffe 'circuit' became legendary and Puttrell would take great delight in showing visiting climbers around the many problems and gymnastic feats.

Typical amongst these was the 'Monkey Jump' on The Bass Rock, this daring feat involved a jump to a small overhung ledge on the main edge with a turn in mid air. Amongst the many fine rock climbs recorded during this period, Puttrells Progress stands out as one of the best. After an inital sentry-box groove an impasse is reached, here the route breaks out left across a steep undercut wall to reach an awkward finishing crack. Technically tricky and incredibly exposed the route is a real 'tour de force' for its age.

So here it was on Wharncliffe's finely textured rock that the gritstone art was played out for the very first time. For all of us who have wedged and udged, jammed and bridged, crimped and balanced our way up those gritstone precipices this really is where it all began.

Paul Harrison

Paul Harrison on Ewden Wall VS 4b (opposite page). Photo: David Simmonite.

Lodge Buttress: The slabby wall to the right contains a few easier problems. On the right side of the cleft, is Lodge Buttress. This contains a myriad of variations including long established routes. The following seem to give the most logical lines at the respective grades. On the left wall is a crack. This is:

183 Ogilvie's Corner HVS 5a ★ 1961-63/78
9m Start up the bank, 3m left of the thin crack on the left-hand side of the arête and traverse into the crack using the obvious line of finger-pockets. Continue up the crack to finish over bulging blocks. The direct start up the crack is 6a. ● **Famine Cracks**, HS 4a (1956), are the wall and cracks to the left.

● A hybrid covering little new ground but with good climbing up a logical line is **Middle Way**, E1 6a ★★ (1997). Climb the direct start to Ogilvie's Corner for 3m then ascend diagonally right to gain a ledge on the very front. Finish direct, as for Nightjar.

184 Nightjar E3 5c ★ 1991
9m The blunt arête to the right of Ogilvie's Corner gives a surprisingly independent route. Gain the arête from the right-hand side by a short delicate traverse from a boulder. Progress by some intriguing moves and the occasional small pocket. ● **Angus** (1978), originally graded HVS 5a, appears to take a similar but higher line, traversing in from Lodge Buttress Direct, and is not much easier than Nightjar.

185 Lodge Buttress Direct VS 4c ★ 1955
9m On the front of the buttress, climb flakes in a scoop to the overlap, then swing left and ascend the top wall on good holds. Beware loose rock! ● For **Opportunist**, E2 5c (1984), follow the Direct to the overhang, but swing right and pull over the centre of the overhang with difficulty.

Ewden Buttress: The buttress 15m right.

186 Windfall E2 5c ★ 1978
8m Begin on the left and, using a crack, pull through the overhang into the niche. Undercut up for small edges just left of the arête and a final fingery heave to the top. ● The escapable arête to the left is **Clean Hands Mick**, E1 5c (2002). A powerful start over the initial bulge (V1) gains a break and an easier but bold finish up the arête.

187 Ewden Edge VS 4c ★ 2002
9m Round on the front of the buttress, climb the left arête to a break, step left above the overhang and finish up the left-hand edge of the wall.

188 Ewden Wall VS 4b ★ 1961-63
9m The right side of the long wall.

Crazy Legs Block: The undercut boulder 20m right.

189 Crazy Legs Crane V4 (6b)
The left wall is climbed leftwards from the slot to an exciting topout

190 The Parson's Finch V8 (6c)
The rounded prow direct. Starting at the lip, launch for slopers and technical topout moves.

Other Bits around Wharncliffe

A few other bits and bobs exist in the Wharncliffe Area. There is a quarry which has been climbed on over the years, and is marked on the Wharncliffe map. **Mesolithic Arête** VS 5a (5000BC), is on a scrappy outcrop 100m along the river path opposite the Lowood Working Men's Club. **Tor Quarry (SK 250912)** has good potential for dirty wet lines. **Hay Crook Common (SK293996)** has a cutaway with two VDs, Central Line and Hay Crook Corner on the right (2004), both admirably loose. **Hay Crook Common (SK 294997)** has more pointless, loose, dirty overgrown climbs. To get here, Park at Wortley Top Forge, and walk to the forth quarry. ● **Kide Kodoke**, S, is a broken line of cracks 3m left of the gully. ● **I Must stop thinking about Suspenders**, VS 4c, climbs the wall 1m right passing through the small overlap. ● **What about Child Care**, HS 4a, is the wall just left of the gully and ● **Hubble Bubble Toil on Rubble**, HS 4b, is the arête and wall right of the gully (all 1993). **Langsett Bank Quarry (SK207003)** has a VD on the right of the entrance, along with plenty of overgrown walls. Cool! **Wind Hill Farm Outcrop (SK243985)** has a steep cave that has been climbed on for years. Other old quarries along the A6102 have been climbed on in the past, but recorded nothing. They are all now overgrown. Of course, there is also the fabled Loxley Valley Ice Falls (clue! be sure to check in the loft).

Agden Rocher (Harecliffe)

OS Ref. SK 264934   **altitude 340m**

by Paul Harrison

A long and seldom visited crag, set amid beautiful pastoral scenery above Agden Reservoir. A crag for the rural adventurer.

The Climbing
One hundred and forty climbs, mainly from VS to E4, generally steep. The unstable nature of the cliff has given Agden a poor reputation and indeed those who like their rock predictable (and the holds polished) would be wise to stick to Stanage. Despite this reputation, many of the climbs are perfectly solid, and those that aren't are obvious. Belays at the top are scarce and in some places non-existent, a number of iron stakes are in place above the popular routes but please take great care not to damage the stone wall above the cliff top.

Situation and Aspect
Situated some 10km northwest of Sheffield and 1km north of the village of High Bradfield, this extensive edge holds a commanding view over the Agden Reservoir and surrounding countryside. The rock comprises of the lower band of Chatsworth Grit, fine-grained and much less resistant to weathering than the upper band, which forms edges such as Stanage. In the Great Wall Area the crag attains a respectable height of almost 30m. Although the holds are square-cut the rock is of variable quality and rockfall is not uncommon. All said, the crag does have its attractions. Its southwesterly aspect attracts plenty of sunshine and consequently the rock dries quickly after rain. Its position and outlook, above mature oak woodland is unrivalled in the Peak. There are a number of pubs in the villages of High and Low Bradfield but the warmest welcome and finest ale is to be found at The Royal Hotel (SK 280898) in the nearby village of Dungworth.

Parking and Approach
The village of Low Bradfield is easily accessible by car from either the A57 via Strines or the A6102 to the north and from Sheffield by the B6077 or B6076 via Stannington. Drive up the hill to High Bradfield and a T-junction at the Old Horns pub. Turn left and after 1km a gated green drive with a stile will be found on the left-hand side of the road

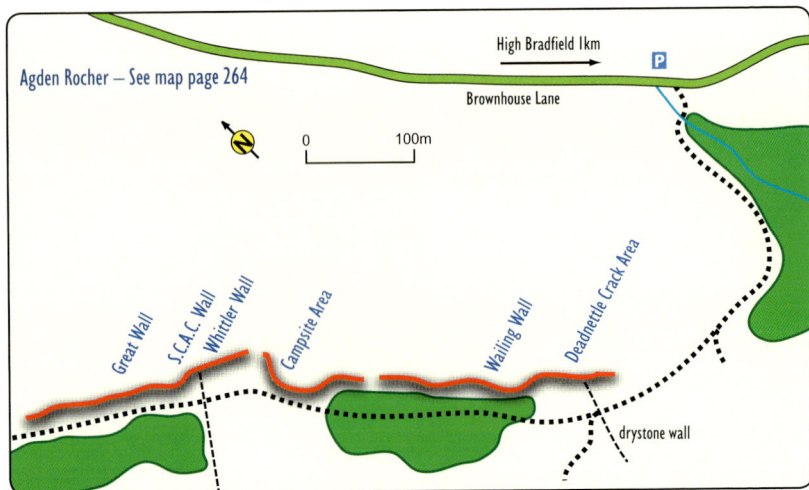

Agden Rocher — See map page 264

High Bradfield 1km

Brownhouse Lane

0   100m

Great Wall

S.C.A.C. Wall

Whittler Wall

Campsite Area

Wailing Wall

Deadnettle Crack Area

drystone wall

(SK 266934). Park here. A pleasant five-minute walk down the drive leads beneath the right-hand end of the crag. **By Bus:** The First 61 goes from Hillsborough Interchange to Lower Bradfield. From here, walk to Higher Bradfield and follow the approach above.

Access

This crag is thought to be in private ownership, but no problems with access have been reported in recent times. Climbers should look out for local signage during the nesting season, when voluntary restrictions on access may be agreed. Any restrictions will be regularly reviewed and lifted once the birds have fledged, at which time the signs will be removed. Contact the BMC office or visit the Regional Access Database on the BMC website (www.thebmc.co.uk).

The climbs are described as one approaches the crag, from right-to-left.

Deadnettle Crack Area

A large yew tree signals the start of the cliff. ● **Hypotenuse Wall,** VD (1966), is the cracked wall immediately right of the tree. ● **Square Chimney,** VD (c. 1914), is the chimney on its left. ● **Arachnid Cracks,** HS 4a (1963), are the twin cracks in the left wall of Square Chimney via a small bulge. ● **Tarantula,** VS 4b (1963), climbs directly up the clean-cut groove just left of Square Chimney past a small overhang to the top. ● **The New Foggy Dew,** S (1952), starts just left of Tarantula beneath a hanging block. Move up to the block and step quickly right. Climb diagonally right until it is possible to step back left and up to a ledge. Exit rightwards to finish.

❶ The Bits With Hairs On HVS 5b ★ 1996
15m The slim groove has a technical entry. Follow a left-slanting crack through the overhang to finish. ● The line to the right is **Demolition**, VS 4a (1963); beware, the demolition is still in progress

❷ Sandyman E2 5c 1999
15m Climb the large sandy groove to the overhang and swing left to a ledge. Step back right and make a difficult pull through the overhangs into a tree. Finish direct.

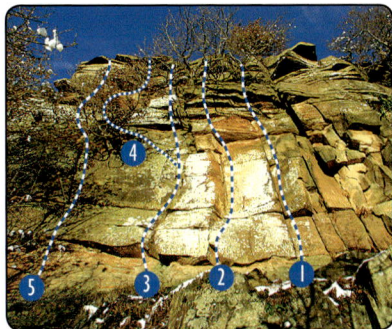

❸ Deadnettle Crack VD 1953
16m Climb the wide crack past an oak tree to a ledge. Finish up the wall above.

❹ Protozoan HS 4a 1953
18m A wandering line but with some good climbing. Follow Deadnettle Crack to the oak tree, traverse left above another tree to a prominent nose and gain a ledge above. Move up the wall and traverse right for 5m to finish by the obvious weakness.

❺ Pyrology VS 4b 1966
18m Climb the crack steeply to a tree, step left and finish direct through the capping roofs. ● The thin crack just right is **Catherine**, VS 4c (1980).

❻ Tartan Slab VS 4c ★ 1952
18m A good pitch with an exciting finale. Start beneath a V-groove 3m left of Pyrology. Climb the groove for 6m to a small overlap, swing rightwards and cross the slab to finish up a crack splitting the overhang above.

The routes in the next 30m are quite poor. ● **Agden Arête**, HS 4a (1952), is the blocky arête directly above the start of Tartan Slab and right of a dirty gully. ● **Boadicea's Wall**, VD (1952), follows this for 5m before crossing the gully on the left and finishing up the wall to its left. ● **Iceni**, VS 4c (1966), starts 2m left of the gully and climb a thin crack to a niche at 5m. Continue up a wider crack moving left to a ledge and a short wall to finish. Slowly engulfing the wall to the left is a large patch of ivy. ● **Judas**, VS 4c (1952), pulls round the overhang just right of the ivy and climbs a tricky groove, past a tree, to the top. ● **Hey Jude,** E2 5b (1968), is under the ivy. ● **Fourth Apostle,** VS 4b (1952), is a crumbly corner 4m left. ● **Savoury Crunch,** HVS 5a (1996), is the arête left, finishing up the right-hand side of the arête in a fine position. ● **Hagg,** HS (1955), is a dangerous proposition up the big blocky corner to the left.

Wailing Wall

The quality now improves as the walls get bigger, steeper, and less broken.

7 **Narrow Minded** E1 5c ⬤ 1996

14m The narrow slab just left of Hagg, past a ledge, and avoiding adjacent routes.

8 **Double De-Clutch** VS 4c ★ 1963

14m The fine clean arête is climbed direct, the left wall proving more useful than the right. ● To the left is a dirty gully; **Disappointment,** VD (1955).

9 **Aberration** HVS 5a ★ 1966

15m A good climb taking a direct line up the centre of the wall. From the ledge finish up the tricky thin crack.

10 **Death-Throes in the Hedgerows** E1 5c 1996

15m Follow the left edge of the wall to the ledge just left of the tree. A runner in the tree protects a couple of difficult moves up the continuation arête. ● The chimney to the left is **Funeral Crack,** S (1952).

11 **Grey Wall** VS 4b 1952

17m Climb the centre of the small wall moving left to gain a ledge and tree. The wall and bulge above lead to a steep exit corner.

12 **Bradfield Arête** S 1952

16m Climb cracks on the left of the arête until an airy move can be made onto the arête and an exposed finish. ● The arête to the left is **Q.E.D.,** S (1967).

13 **Then Jericho** E1 5b 1996

12m Start at a vegetated flake. Climb straight up to a ledge and a sandy scoop and finish direct using a suspect jug.

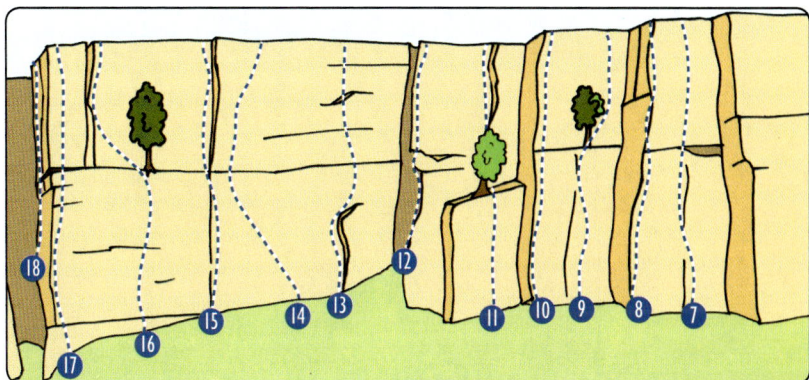

14 Fall of Jericho E2 5b   2005
15m The wall just left leads to grassy ledges. Trend left and climb the wall direct, finishing at a flake.

15 Jericho Wall VS 4b   1955
17m The crack that becomes a corner.

16 Scarred Climb HS 4a ★   1952
17m Climb the rugosity-covered wall to a tree. The twin cracks to the left provide a pleasant finish.

17 Aaron VS 4c   1980
16m The sharp arête climbed on its right-hand side. An interesting pitch if easier options are ignored.

18 Baker Street VS 4c ★   1979
12m The fine steep crack in the side-wall is climbed direct.

19 Lemon Entry VS 4c   2005
12m Follow the right-hand edge of the block and from its top climb the thin crack above the leaning block and finish rightwards.

20 Leaning Block Wall VS 4c   1952
18m Follow the last climb to the top of the block and climb the wall above leftwards to a steep, loose finishing corner.

21 Painter's Climb S   1955
16m The prominent flake crack just left of the leaning block is climbed to a tree belay. Take the corner above to the top. Beware of some unstable ground.

22 Numenorean HVS 4c   c. 1975
17m The arête right of the wide crack of White Rose Flake is gained directly from that route via the orange overhang. Move right to finish up the crack.

23 White Rose Flake VS 4c ★   1952
17m A good, varied pitch up the wide crack and steep flakes on the right-hand side of the slab.

24 Martini VS 4b ★   1952
18m Start on the right-hand block. Step awkwardly up onto the slab and continue to a tree. Traverse left to a thin crack almost on the arête and climb it in a fine position.

"Gritstone is as **solid** and as **firm as granite**, and inferior only to the gabbro of Skye as an instrument of torture if you happen to get your hand between the rope and the rock."

EA Baker, 1903

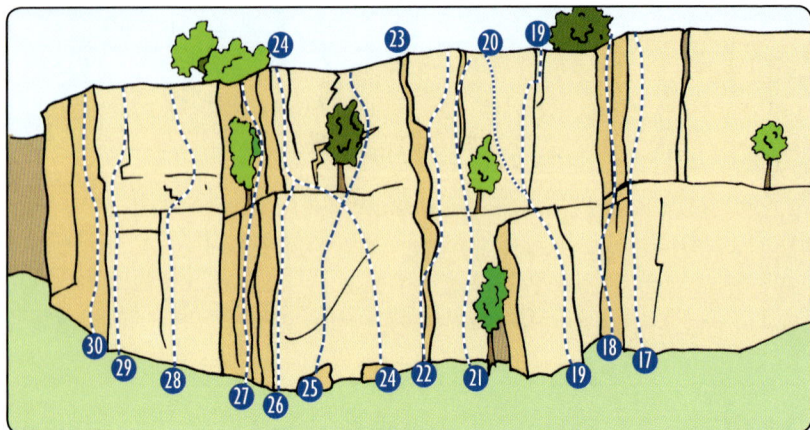

25 Martini Crack VS 4b   1952
17m Step off the left-hand block and climb diagonally right towards the tree. The wide flake crack above is dangerously loose.

26 Bianco VS 4b ★   1962
17m Elegant climbing up the left arête of the slab, finishing up Martini.

27 Filth S   1952
14m The twin cracks in the wall to the left leads to a ledge. Finish up twin cracks on the left. ● A poor route **Derision,** S (1952), takes the large corner direct.

28 Extra Tasty E4 6a ★★   1996
18m An excellent and challenging pitch. Climb the crack in the centre of the wall to the second horizontal break and traverse right to a small niche. Stretch up the wall above, and finish slightly leftwards on small holds.

29 The Resurrection E2 5b ★   1980
17m Climb the left arête of the wall on its right-hand side to the second of two scoops, step right and climb boldly up the faint weakness. Alternatively, finish up the arête on its right-hand side.

30 Koh-i-Noor HVS 5b ★   1999
15m The arête is climbed in its entirety on its left from its lowest point. The crack on the left can be reached from the last climb at HVS. **Taurus** (1968).

Oak Tree Wall Area: To the left is a short corner and left again a wall with two small trees at half-height.

31 Scarecliffe E3 5c   1997
12m The wall 3m left of the corner has a bold feel as far as the horizontal break; finish direct. ● The wall left again is **Hanging Garden Wall,** S (1952), finishing up the crack behind the tree.

32 E.N. 24 VS 5a ★   1968
16m A tough, well-protected crux. Climb directly to a bulge 15m left of Scarecliffe. Surmount this via a thin crack, peg runner, and continue up a short, finishing corner.

33 Oak Tree Walk VS 4b ★★   1944
18m A cracking pitch, one of the finest on the edge. Start 5m right of the edge of the wall at a straight crack. Climb the crack to the tree. Using the tree as carefully as possible, gain the wall above and finish rightwards.

34 Flamingo Wall HVS 5a ★   1968
16m Start 1m left of Oak Tree Walk. Climb the wall via a thin flake to the bulge. Pull through between the oak trees and climb the scooped crack, finishing direct with a long reach. ● **Flaming 'ard,** E1 5b (1996), is another reachy proposition this time up the left-hand side of the arête left of Flamingo Wall.

The edge now falls back. The wall bounding the arête just to the left at this point has two cracks. ● **Jackdaw Crack,** VD (1952), is the right-hand one and ● **Straight Crack,** D (1953), the left. ● The wall between the two is taken by the groundbreaking **Hard Men Don't Spot Lines Like This,** VD (1980). ● Another 75m left is a small buttress split by a wide crack, **Rowan Tree Crack** VD (1952). ● **Bogey's Beacon** S (1982) is a poor eliminate up the wall and bulge just to the left.

The edge is now broken and rather scrappy, after 100m a level area of grass is reached, beneath a large open-book corner. This is known as:

The Campsite Area

This is a good open area, with some short, technical problems, and some long, challenging expeditions.

At the right-hand end of The Campsite Area lies a dirty corner with a short arête to its right and a yew tree at half-height. ● **Gimli,** HVS 5a (c. 1975), gains the arête by an awkward move and climbs it, finishing carefully over broken ground above. ● **Crumbler,** E1 5a (c. 1975), is a direct and harrowing experience up the crack and overhangs to the left. ● A poor route, **Bostonian,** S (1974), climbs the crack of Crumbler to the ledge then walks left to climb a short wall and vegetation above an oak tree. ● **Bostonian Direct,** HS (1974), follows Crumbler to the yew tree, exiting right beneath the overhang to a platform and finishing up a short wall.

After this the climbing improves considerably. To the left is the prominent square-cut arête of Artifax Arête. The next two climbs lie on the slab to its right.

35 **Dreams by the Sea** E2 5c ★ 1984

10m Neat, technical face climbing. Start up a faint crack in the slab right of Artifax Arête, step left at the break, peg runner, stand up and finish slightly rightwards to the tree; abseil descent.

36 **Are We There Yet** E4 6a ★ 1999

10m Take a direct line to the peg on Dreams by the Sea and crimp straight up to finish left of the tree.

37 **Artifax Arête** E3 5b ★ 1968

10m The left arête of the wall is climbed initially on its left-hand side with a final worrying move on its right. Abseil from the tree. Grossly undergraded in the past.

38 Man of God HS 4a — 1952
10m An honest, well-protected pitch up the clean-cut corner crack just left. Abseil from the tree or scramble carefully to the top.

39 Libra HVS 4c — 1968
15m Follow Man of God until level with a large pocket in its left wall. An exposed traverse left gains the arête, which leads to a ledge. The vegetated slab above is taken to the top.

40 Armstrong's Eliminate E4 5c — c. 1975
15m A mysterious and scary proposition directly up the wall bisecting Libra's traverse. Gain the large pocket direct and make committing moves, slightly leftwards, to a ledge.

41 Scouting For Boys E3 5c ★ — 1997
20m An exciting pitch up the right arête. Climb the initial arête and jam the roof crack above to a ledge. A sandy corner leads to a break, swing right onto the arête and make difficult moves up its right-hand side to the top.

42 Campsite Crack S ★★ — 1952
20m A classic; a varied and sustained pitch at the grade. Climb the corner, moving right after 10m to a large ledge and possible belay. Continue up the corner for an exposed finish.

Variations around Campsite Crack are: ● the arête to the right is **Paul's Arête Start,** (now the start to Scouting for Boys) E1 5b (1963), joining Campsite Crack on the large ledge; ● **David's Other Start,** E2 5c (1999), climbs the same arête on its right-hand side going direct over the overhang; ● **Indirect Start,** HS 4a (1952), climbs the short, undercut crack right again, before moving left to join Campsite Crack. ● For the **Indirect Finish,** E1 5b (c. 1975), move right from the upper section of the corner and climb a roof-crack in the final overhang.

43 Gemini VS 4c — 1968
18m A thin crack in the slab 4m left of Campsite Crack leads to a grassy ledge. Move right to twin sandy cracks and jam and layback steeply to the top.

44 Mike's Route HVS 5a — 1999
18m Climb a short slab just left of Gemini and continue over broken ledges to the base of a flake crack in the arête. Follow this, in a fine position, to the top.

Two short pitches have been ascended to the left of Campsite Crack. ● **Begum Behar,** VS 5a (1999), climbs a slab and arête just left to finish at a tree, and ● **Jalfrezee Jug Fest,** S 4a (1999), follows a series of flat ledges around the corner to the left.

The edge now recedes giving an easy way down an open gully. Left again is an isolated buttress with a yew tree at its base. ● **The Gatepost,** VD (1952), climbs a crack and wall to the right of the tree. ● **Min-Arête,** E1 5b (1996), is the undercut arête and thin crack above the tree, whilst ● **Nill,** VS (1967), is a suicidal proposition up the crack and groove left of the tree. ● To the left again is a broken gully and another 10m left is a crack with a tree at its base, **Harlequinade,** VD (1952).

Whittler Wall

Further left is a clean-cut wall, home to some of the finest routes at Agden. ● **Cock o' the North,** S (1952), climbs thin parallel cracks in the right edge of the wall finishing up a chimney.

45 Spring Lamb Dopiazza VS 4c — 1999
16m Climb the wall to the left of chimney to an overlap. Step right into the chimney for a move or two and then back left along a narrow ledge; finish direct.

46 The Avenue E2 5c — 1996
17m A good, if green, eliminate line just right of the crack of Briggs' and Titterton's. Climb the wall direct on small holds to a large horizontal break. Traverse left and pull up into a small groove and a junction with Briggs' and Titterton's. Finish up this.

47 Briggs' and Titterton's HVS 5b ★★ — 1952
17m This fine route follows the line of the straight thin crack making good use of holds on its left to the tree. Finish up the wide crack above and right. ● **Lemon Squeezy,** HVS 5b (1996), is a tight but worthwhile eliminate pulling through the overlap to the left and taking a direct line up the wall above via twin, thin cracks.

John Arran on Pollux, E1 5b (next page), a fearsome crack pitch to rival anything in the Millstone area. Photo: Ian Parnell.

48 **The Whittler** VS 4c ★ 1952
18m A good climb, delicate and nicely exposed. Start at a small cutaway just right of an oak tree. Pull over the overhang and climb up and leftwards to reach a grassy ledge and a tree. Finish up the layback crack left of the tree. ● **The Tittler,** HVS 4c (1978), pulls awkwardly through the overlap left of The Whittler and takes a bold and wandering line up the large vegetated slab to its left.

49 **Castor** E1 5c ★ 1969
19m Behind an oak tree is the first of two peg-scarred cracks. Climb the wall in the line of the crack and fight past a holly to an easier upper section.

50 **Wheat Thin** E4 6a ★★ 1984
19m An absorbing pitch up the wall between Castor and Pollux; the small holds may need a brush prior to an ascent. Pull through the overlap 3m left of Castor and step up to a peg. Step right and move up and left, crux, to reach a small flake and better holds above. Easier climbing leads directly to the top.

51 **Pollux** E1 5b ★★ 1969
19m The left-hand crack is an excellent pitch, nicely sustained and well-protected with small wires. Follow the crack to a difficult sequence through the overlap, peg runner, to reach an oak tree. Finish up the arête to the left.

To the left, a fence with a stile comes right up to the crag. Left again is a clean, easy angled slab. ● **Three Pitch Climb,** S (1952), follows the right-hand edge

of the slab to a ledge and yew tree. Finish up the loose corner on the right. ● **Double Shuffle,** HS 4a (1953), is the centre of the slab. ● **Twentyman's Terror,** HS 4a (1953), is the left edge. Move left, to finish up a crack in the back wall. Left again and set further back is a steeper slab. ● **The Flying Dutchman,** VS 4a (1952), goes from the lowest point of the slab to a grassy ledge. Shuffle right and climb up and left via a small recess and a creaking flake. Exceptionally loose. ● **Scratching Around,** E2 5c (1997), follows the last route to the ledge. Step left and climb the steep slab above on small holds directly to the top. ● **Schizont,** VS 4c (1963), is the left-hand end of the grassy ledge past a small stump. Escape from the ledge by the awkward left-hand corner.

Immediately left is a steeper wall of sounder rock and with a gully to its left. The gully provides a convenient descent. ● **Lundy High,** E1 5b (1997), is the right arête of the wall gained via a thin crack and a steep pull; worthwhile. ● **Chains,** HVS 5b (1970-73), is the central line. Gain the horizontal break by a slight groove and stretch through the overhang at the obvious weakness. Continue more easily to the top. ● **Chicken Wall,** VS 4c (1963), climbs up, just left of Chains to the break, steps left and surmounts the overlap on good holds and so to the top. ● For **Chicken Run,** VS 5a (1999), ascend the short arête just left of Chicken Wall in its entirety, after a stiff pull around the initial overhang.

S.C.A.C. Wall

To the left is a wall, which stands further forward with the ground dropping away steeply below it. ● The right-hand retaining wall, beginning with a steep crack is **The Wall End** VS 4c (1952). ● **Mollie's Climb,** S (1952), climbs into the square-cut niche on the right side of the wall, then exits left and goes to the top. The direct finish, via a crack, is VS 4b. ● Traversing above the lip to finish up the arête is **Little John,** S (1974). ● **Bull Crack,** VS 4b (1952), gains the circular cave just right of the centre of the wall, which is left by means of an awkward jamming crack. ● The unpleasant pillar and wall right (side-runners) are **Chicken Silly Hot** HVS 5b (1999). ● **Hollow Victory,** E1 5a (1996), is the wall 3m to the left, climbed by a thin crack and a series of dangerously loose flakes. ● **Decep-**

tive Crack, S (1952), is the thick crack to the left. ● To the left, **Tiptoe**, VS 4b (1969), is a direct and pleasant line up the wrinkled wall. ● **Still Life**, HS 4a (1963), climbs the steep offwidth crack just left again. ● The blunt arête to its left is **Artist's Arête**, S (1952). ● **Minsk**, HS (1952), climbs the left-facing corner left of Artist's Arête, which leads into a steep crack. ● Going left to finish up a crack in the retaining wall is **Hedony**, HS (1952). ● Finally, **Chauv's Last Stand**, VS 4b (1982), is quite a good little route up the arête and bulge left of Minsk.

Great Wall

To the left of S.C.A.C. Wall is the showpiece of the crag. ● Bounding the wall to its right is a steep, grassy gully. **May Climb**, S (1952), is a scrappy climb from halfway up the gully. ● **Harry the Dog Tosser**, E1 5b (1999), goes from a short way up the gully to an obvious pocket and flat ledge. Make a difficult mantel and continue direct to the top to finish right of an oak tree.

52 **Ocydroma**   E3 5b   1999
15m   Start as for Ignis Fatuus and at the overlap move slightly right and follow the vertical crease on small holds, moving right near the top to finish right of the oak tree.

53 **Ignis Fatuus**   E3 5c ★   1983
22m   Requires a confident approach. Move up to an overlap and turn it via a thin crack. Step left and climb the wall above direct. ● The ivy-cloaked groove to the left hides **Limbus Fatuorum**, HVS 5a (1968).

54 **Conjunctus Viribus**   E1 5b ★ ★   1967
28m   An excellent pitch, sustained but with good protection. Climb directly into a groove and follow it to an overlap. Step right and storm the steep headwall via twin cracks to an easier finish.

55 **Asteris**   E1 5c ★ ★   1953
29m   A fine climb, tackling the impressive crack in the centre of the wall. The initial crack leads to a standing position atop a large detached block. A difficult and fingery section protected by a peg runner gains easier cracks leading to the top.

56 **Monster Munch**   E4 6a ★ ★   1996
29m   A big pitch – downright intimidating. From 3m up Asteris step left, peg runner, and move left again to an undercut ledge. Difficult climbing on small rugosities, peg runner, leads to the overlap where exciting moves up and left gain a good horizontal break. Step right, peg runner, and take a direct line up the centre of the headwall to the top.

Paul Harrison enjoying the beautiful end-of-day light on Ignis Fatuus. E3 5c (previous page).
Photo: David Simmonite.

57 Speak Easy E3 5c   1971
29m A wandering line with some anxious moments.
Start beneath a rightward-slanting ramp in the left
edge of the wall. Climb the wall below the ramp and
move up and left to the sanctuary of a large tree.
Traverse right for 3m and climb the left edge of the
headwall to the top.

58 S.O.S. VS 4b ★   1952
29m A route with some worthwhile climbing and
plenty of character. At the left edge of Great Wall is
a small undercut corner. Climb the corner and move
right to a shelf, continue easily to the large tree and a
possible belay. Move up above the tree and traverse
left to the base of a steep corner, climb this exiting
right at the top.

59 The Great Wall Traverse VS 4b, 4c   1952
45m Pull up into the initial corner of S.O.S. and
traverse right above the cutaway to a belay on
Asteris. Move around the large block and continue
rightwards to a finish up May Climb.

*To the left a stacked pile of blocks lean precariously
against the base of the cliff.*

60 Hit and Run Driver E3 5c ★   1983
20m Climb the wall 3m right of the blocks to a
small ledge just left of a tree. Move rightwards up
the wall above, peg runner, to a poor flake, then
back left for a direct finish through the overlap on
good holds.

61 Ardua E1 5b ★   1963
19m Just right of the stacked blocks is a thin crack.
Ascend the crack to a grassy ledge and a tree. The
fine continuation crack, peg runner, is followed to
the top.

● **Yewberry Groove**, HS (1953), climbs the pile
of blocks, then makes a long traverse left to an oak
tree. Move back right and follow a groove to the
top. ● **Terrace Traverse,** S (1952), follows this to
the tree then continues the traverse left to a crack
to finish.

62 Jaffa E1 5b ★   1999
19m Start immediately left of the stacked blocks
and climb the wall stepping right to a tree atop the

blocks. The wall above is taken direct on good but
not always obvious holds, peg runner, to the top.

63 The Snip E1 5b ★   1998
19m Start just left of Jaffa. Good holds lead directly
to the base of a short corner. Step right and follow
the left edge of the wall with the help of a thin crack
to the top.

Saint's Wall: Left again and at a higher level a
grassy terrace splits the crag. The upper tier has a
prominent black corner and the lower tier becomes
a steep wall with a narrow ledge along its base.
● **Black Wall,** VS 4b (1952), follows the right side
of the wall to an overhang, turns this on the right
and move up past an oak tree to the terrace. Move
left and layback the flake, then go left again to a
finishing crack. From the terrace one can also move
right to climb the right wall of the black corner.
● **St. Oliver,** HS 4a (1963), climbs to a tree just left
of the black corner then goes rightwards to the terrace and a tree. Utilising the tree, ascend the wall
above and move left to a short finishing corner.
To the left a dislodged oak tree attempts to grow
downwards. ● **St. George,** S (1954), climbs a short
corner 6m right of the tree to an overhang, moves
left and climbs a crack until a step right can be made
onto a 'rocking stone'. Trend left to the terrace and
a holly tree and finish up the short wall on the left.
● **St. Peter,** S (1952), starts up a short bottomless
rib above the oak tree and climbs diagonally right to
the terrace and the finish of St. George. ● **St. John,**
VS 4b (1952), starts just left of St. Peter and climbs
an awkward wall to a hawthorn on the left. Continue up the narrow slab and wall above. The
edge continues for some distance but becomes very
broken before disappearing into the hillside.

Finally just when you thought it was safe...

64 Little X VS 4b   1967
160m A girdle of the eastern section. Start up Hypotenuse Wall and traverse left at the level of Tartan
Slab, before crossing Hagg high or at mid-height
(equally dangerous). Leaning Block Wall is crossed
at the level of the top of the block and the route continues across Martini and Taurus to a rarely achieved
finishing goal on Hanging Garden Wall. The
alternative finish is far better…. the pub.

Stannington Ruffs

OS Ref. SK 311893 to SK 303892   **altitude 210m**

by Mike Snell

The Ruffs, as they are known, lie on the south side of the Loxley Valley overlooking the river and the village of Loxley some 8km north of Sheffield. The crag is an exposure of sandstone caused by landslip, is as yet unweathered and tends to be angular, loose and friable. Cracks predominate, but so does vegetation. A plethora of trees above and below the edge and a northerly aspect, make for a pioneering climbing experience. It is likely that many of the routes have had no more than one or at best a few ascents. Care is, therefore, necessary with all subsequent forays. Furthermore the path beneath the main edge is poor, at best, and is in places, non-existent. This is esoteria with knobs on and an edge for those with sufficiently masochistic tendencies - wonderful!

Parking and Approach: The easiest access is from the Robin Hood public house at Little Matlock. Approach from Malin Bridge via the A6101 and the B6076. Turn right into Wood Lane, right again into Myers Grove Lane (in front of The Anvil public house) and then right again onto Greaves Lane, which leads to The Robin Hood at the road end. There are two separate areas, each with its own access. The Robin Hood area lies below the

> "The **face** has **been left**
> by a large landslip. The rock is as yet
> unweathered, and the holds tend to be angular
> and there is much loose rock. All the rock tends
> to be friable but there are extensive friable
> sections. The crag faces north, and is masked by
> trees above and below the crag and vegetation
> on the face. The rock tends to be lichenous. A
> new housing estate is being built on the top of
> the crag and further detritus may result from
> this"
>
> Dave Gregory, **1976 guidebook**

road only 50m before the pub. One can scramble or abseil from sturdy trees at road level, although it is perhaps easier to follow the path down from the right side of the pub. At the bottom the buttress is just visible through the trees on the right.

The Ruffs main edge is approached from the byway (continuation of Greaves Lane) to the left of the pub. Bear right through a stile by a gate, 25m past the pub buildings. Follow the footpath for 150m, take a left fork on a fainter, slightly uphill path, from whence the crag can be seen, vegetation permitting. The first rocks are on the left, but keep going for 70m more, where path meets rock at the start of the East Buttress.

The climbs are generally described from left-to-right.

Robin Hood Buttress

Routes here are described from right to left. The right side of the buttress is very broken and has no routes. ● To the left the buttress is between 8m and 12m in length and roughly in the centre of the buttress is the obvious corner crack of **Little John,** VS 4c. ● The wall 2m left to a flake and the huge oak tree above is **Will Scarlet,** S. ● **Robin Hood,** VS, climbs the V-groove 3m further left, moving left round the overhang to finish right up the wall above. ● The next groove has an exit left round the overhang to a tree finish, **Sherwood Forest,** HVD (all 1968). ● Twenty five metres left, just beyond an unclimbed overhang, is another groove of **Ode to a Footrot Woolly,** S (pre-1970), which leads to a roof and a drystone wall. The wall can be climbed but is best avoided by a traverse off. Other easy lines can be made hereabouts at no more than VD, all avoid the drystone wall. Two more routes have been climbed around here, on a small outcrop 70m right of Robin Hood Buttress. They are: ● **Zero Drift**, S, the overhanging right wall of a small amphitheatre at the start of the buttress' and ● **Transducer**, S, a wall 20m right to a flake and right up the arête (both pre-1970). It is best to return to the pub, should you wish to climb on the main edge.

The Main Edge

The path from the pub (see approach), meets the main edge below Grotty Groove, which can be clearly identified by a painted number '2' at its foot. A few other lines are similarly identified. Numbers do not correspond with the present numbering system. Routes here are listed from left-to-right, beginning 6m left of Grotty Groove and just right of an arête. This is East Buttress.

❶ Bovril S · 1968

9m Climb the groove right of the left arête, 25m left of Grotty Groove. Step left to finish. ●**Lesark,** S (1968), is the crack to the right, just left of the centre of the wall, leading to a ledge and tree. Continue via a bulge and flake.

❷ Marmite S · 1968

9m Go up the next crack and the wall above, to a dirty finish (blue 1). ● The crack and corner behind the tree is **Sycamore Saunter,** D: give it a miss. ● Ten metres right, **Enna**, S, pulls over a small overhang, just left of ●**Dihedral**, VD, which continues up the wall from the dirty ledge (all 1969-76).

❸ Grotty Groove D · 1968

9m The chimney-groove left of another overhang (blue 2), whilst ●**Taurus,** VS 4c (1968), scoots up the wall, goes over the overhang and on to the top (blue 3).

❹ Oxo S · 1965

8m Follow the crack right of Taurus to a step left into a wider crack (blue 4). ● The crack just left over a bulge is **Vegimite**, VS 5a (2005). ● The left side of the arête on the right is **The Editor's Cracked**, VS 5a (2005). ●**Oxo Arête**, S (1968), is the right side of the arête using the wall. ●**Cobweb Crack**, S (1968), is the corner (blue 5).

❺ Dextrous HS · 1968

8m The V-groove right again. Pull into the sentry box, exit on left and follow the crack.

❻ Ruff Crack S 4a · 1969-76

8m A decent line up the next crack. ●**Derision**, D (1968), is at the right end of the wall and climbs to and up the V-groove.

After a gap of 25m there is a square arête with a block overhang. This is:

❼ Apeman's Arête S · 1968

9m Use the tree to pass the overhang. ● Alternatively, traverse to the right arête after the tree; **Rover's Return**, VS 4c (1968).

❽ Splurp VD · 1968

6m Climb the corner crack right of the arête. ●**Nebula,** VS 5a (1968), fires up the crack 3m right, goes over the roof and finishes slightly left. ●**The Bogie**, VS (1969-76), is the roof to the right. Finish up earthy ledges. ●**Tarzan**, D (pre-1970), is the chimney-groove 2m right. Struggle onto a ledge and easier ground.

1847 Area

A number of easy, but scruffy lines are possible on the next stretch of rock, mainly around a groove, containing a sycamore tree. The 1847 Area is 25m on, notable for a bay capped by a large yellow roof.

These routes run from right-to-left.

❾ The Ghoul HVS 5a · pre-1970

11m Attack the large overhang at its obvious point of weakness. A short wall ends it all.

❿ 1847 HS 4b · 1968

14m Tiptoe delicately up the crack on the left edge of the bay. Move left round the arête to a tree stump; go up to a ledge and trend left to finish on Galvo Groove. ●**The Direct Finish** VS 4c (1969-76), tackles the overhang, moves left from the face above to a ledge and heads over the overhang up and right.

⓫ Off My Rocker VS 4b · 2000

11m Start on the right wall of Galvo Groove and head straight to and beyond the tree of 1847. ●**Galvo Groove**, D (1968), is the wide groove on the left, and ●**Gold Rush**, HS 4b (1968), is the wall left.

"Stannington's Rough!" — Anon.

The V-groove to the left is **Chisel,** HD (1969-76). ● **Hammer,** VD (1968), is the corner to the left leading to a chimney-groove in the right wall. Finish via its capstone. ● **Birth of Liquid Desires**, VD (1969-76), is the crack in the shattered wall to the left.

The Pinnacle: To reach the pinnacle 50m further on requires resilience and often a fight with the vegetation. To the left is a small overhanging buttress, capped by a large oak. Left of this is a prominent arête and wall. Left again a big groove starts part way up the crag. ● This is **Drippy**, VD, going from the centre of the wall and stepping left from the first ledge. Scale the wall then the groove to exit between overhangs. ● **Dognut**, S, begins as for Drippy, but climbs the crack, direct to the overhang. Traverse right to the arête to finish (both 1968). ● **Dognut Direct**, HS (1969-76) takes the crack all the way. ● **Erosion Groove,** HVD (1969), is the wide unpleasant crack right of the arête. The next two routes are on the pinnacle. ● **Trapeze**, S (1968), is the V-groove on the left side of the outer face, climbed to a ledge on the left. Swing right and up, with or without the aid of a tree, to finish to the left. ● **Pinnacle Face**, VD (1965), is direct up the wall 3m right. Fifteen metres beyond The Pinnacle, a tree grows out of the face. To the left is a large detached flake. ● **Birthday Flake**, D, scrambles up the flake taking the overhang on the left. ● **Trinity Cracks**, HVS 5a, jams up the fine crack to the ledge and steps right to finish over the overlap (both 1968). ● The right side of the arete on the right is **A Bit of Ruff**, E1 5c (2005). ● **Stannington's Rough**, S (2003), gains the right arête of the wall on the right, followed by earth with some rock in it.

The Cascade Area: The ever-flowing waterfall is a dank and forbidding feature. Just left of the black staircase, is the only route of the Cascade Wall. ● **Cascade Crack**, HVS 5b, takes the straight thin crack to a vegetated ledge, whence a variety of escapes are available. ● Another route paddles up the succulent ledges, **Merman's Meander**, M (both 1968). Prior inoculation is strongly recommended. Nine metres right are three grooves: ● **Egroeg**, HS 4a, climbs the left one by its left wall to a tree belay. ● The middle groove is **Sevad**, S, and ● **Big D**, D, is the right-hand groove, keeping left of the rib and

overhang at the top. ● The corner right of the rib is **Little D**, S (all 1969-76). ● The next route sits all alone 25m beyond Little D. Look for a yellow wall, with a triangular niche and a prominent pulpit above and right. ● **Gollyberry**, HVD (1969-76), ascends to and across the pulpit, from just right of the niche, via a steep crack and ledge. Continue traversing under an overhang to reach and climb a groove to the top.

Gromlech Buttress Area: The going gets more difficult hereabouts as the path disappears under vicious vegetation. Approximately 50m beyond the end of the Cascade Area is the next set of routes.

The large V-groove of Sennapod Corner with the stump of four trees from a common bole at its base, should identify the area. Also look for another group of trees from a common bole, beneath the chimney of Sabre Cut. The first route is 10m left of Sennapod Corner.

⑫ **Entanglement** VD   1968
15m Go up the groove, avoiding the top overhang on the left.

⑬ **Barnsley Bitter** HVD   1968
15m This is the groove 8m right of Entanglement. Avoid the overhang on the left and then go right up to a tree and finish direct. ● **Sennapod Corner**, HS (1965), is the big corner-groove. Exit left at the overhang. The right exit is VS 4c. ● The crack in the right wall of Sennapod Corner leads to the arête and a belay: **Cemetery Grapes**, HS (1965).

⑭ **Excursion** HS   1967
14m Meander up the front of the buttress just right by a crack and then traverse right to a short corner. Go up this, passing one ledge to another on a pedestal, then finish left and up the wall. ● The deep chimney on the right is **Sabre Cut**, S (1969-76). ● **Deceptio Visus**, S (1967), starts on a flake left of Sabre Cut to move up then left to Excursion's pedestal. Go right on another flake, to cross Sabre Cut and reach a crack on the right wall to finish.

West Wall: Jungle bash for another 40m to reach the next section. This area has yet another massive, but decaying, multi-trunked tree with an exposed root system. There are also a couple of ancient names and dates carved in the rock. ● The first line is 10m left of the tree up the crack; **Eureka,** HVD. ● Seven metres right is **Quicksilver,** HS, up the left-hand of two grooves. ● **Diplopia,** VD, is the right-hand groove to a ledge followed by a blocky wall and another groove and a tree stump belay. ● The corner right of the multi-trunked tree is **Hanging Rib Groove,** VD. Exit to the left (all 1968). ● **Brass Bees,** S, begins on the rib right of Hanging Rib Groove. Go up to the overhang and over it to a groove on the right. Climb this and the looser one above. This almost certainly supersedes the old aid route **Coward's Way,** HVD A1 (pre-1970). This was described as 6m right of Hanging Rib Groove and used three pegs to climb the overhang between two grooves.

Old Man's Stairs may be a convenient descent hereabouts. It begins 6m right of the top of Quicksilver. Fifteen metres right of the foot of the descent, about 25m right of Hanging Rib Groove, is a buttress with three grooves.

⑮ **Apprenticeship** VD   1969-76
11m The middle groove of the three passes the overhang on either side. ● **Chaika,** S (1969-76), is the right-hand groove, moving left to a ledge and continuation groove.

⑯ **Angelique** HS   1969-76
12m Start at a niche in the middle of the wall 3m right of Chaika. Climb up to the oak tree then step right to finish.

⑰ **Christmas Climb** HVD   1969-76
12m Some 7m right gain the holly groove via a small overhang and an oak.

⑱ **Roat** VD   1969-76
12m Yet another groove 3m right, leads to another oak and a right trending ridge to the top.

Two routes, **Slippy,** D (pre-1970), an arête, and **Bird's Nest Crack,** S (1967), a crack are described in the interim guide to The Ruffs as being about 90m beyond Hanging Rib groove. They are, apparently, left of and above a good bivouac site. They have been impossible to locate accurately. In con-

trast, the following lines can be located, but are un-reachable without extreme gardening.

The crag steps out, after 75m or so, of 'less worth-while' rock beyond Roat. It then forms a shallow left-facing corner. To his eternal shame, 'Richard J Bramhall 6.9.72' is carved on the rock. ● **Patience,** S (1969-76), is the wide crack on the right wall of the corner leading to an overhang and a swing right into the upper crack. Twenty metres right is another left-facing corner. There is a minor corner 5m left; ● **Confused,** HD (1969-76). ● The cracks 3m right of the main corner are **The Grayling,** VD (1969-76). An ivy-covered buttress 20m right is reputed to have two grooves running up it, but only one route. Close inspection, however, is not recom-mended without serious protection. ● **Hedera,** VD (1969-76). Follow the left-hand groove and cracked wall above and left.

The rock now swings round to meet a path that climbs up and out of the woods, leading to Acorn Drive, another possible approach . On the way up it passes the final bit of rock, some 50m beyond Hedera.

Dead End Buttress: This has a right-angled left arête with a short, steep tapering wall on the right. ● **Dead End Buttress Direct,** S (1969), takes the crack just left of the angled arête. ● Whilst the final route on the edge is **Why Am I Here?** S 4b (2000), is a wide crack right of the arête.

Wharncliffe Area First Ascents

1880s   **The Girdle Traverse, Cumberland Traverse, Central Traverse** J W Puttrell *The Girdle Traverse was one of the first routes on the crags. The first ascents of the Cumberland and Central girdle traverses are a bit of a mystery, but they were probably climbed around the same period by Puttrell.*

1885   **Inside Route, Black Slab** J W Puttrell (solo)

1885-1902   **The Great Chimney, Puttrell's Progress, Hell Gate Gully, Hell Gate, Chockstone Chimney, V-Chimney, The Candle Snuffer, Long Chimney, Puttrell's Crack** J W Puttrell, W J Watson

1885-1902   **Watson's Crack** W J Watson, J W Puttrell

1889	**Puttrell and Watson's Route** JW Puttrell, WJ Watson
1885-1910	**Outside Route, Pylon Crack, Quern Crack, Hamlet's Climb, The Crack of Doom, The Mantelshelf, Back-and-foot, Rook Chimney, Letter-box Buttress, Cheese Cut, Cheese Cut Crack, Cheese Cut Flake, Bilberry Face, Imaginary Boulder Climb, Cumberland Crack, V-groove, Skylight Climb, Overhanging Chimney, Split Chimney, Alpha, Beta Crack, Great Chimney Crack, Romulus, Remus, The Flue, As You Like It, Black Crack, Holly Crack, Deep Chimney, Traditional, Hanging Chimney, Bill, Ben, Big Corner** J W Puttrell, W J Watson, Henry Bishop, Douglas Yeomans with occasional help from Dr G A Dawes, G F R Freeman, Archer, William Smithard, C F Cameron, Dr E A Baker *The majority of the above routes were unnamed when first done and have been identified from brief descriptions given in Henry Bishop's article in the Climbers' Club Journal Volume III, 1910, which contained some 110 climbs.*
c. 1914	**Square Chimney** Henry Bishop
1931	**Scarlett's Climb, Scarlett's Crack** Harry Scarlett *Led in rubbers, the latter route was 'a last great problem'.*
1933	**The Nose, Slab and Corner, Railway Wall, The By-Pass, Great Buttress, Green Groove?** Fred Jones and members of the Sheffield University Mountaineering Club and Sheffield Climbing Club *The original description to Railway Wall was unclear and the line described in the guidebook is that climbed by Pete Crew 30 years later. It was also claimed in 1987 as The Mourning After by Roger Brook and Roger Doherty and included in the 1989 guidebook as a separate route. Further investigation identified it be the same as Railway Wall.*
1933	**The Blue Defile, Himmelswillen** Tom Stobart (solo) *Asked what the former route was like after he had just done it Stobart answered Bloody Vile, hence the name. The second route translates as 'Good Heavens'!*
1933	**Tower Face, Byne's Route** Eric Byne, Frank Burgess *The latter route was only top roped. Probably led sometime between 1949 and 1951.*
1936 Spring	**Teufelsweg** Hans Teufel, Heine Sedlmayr and others *This pair caused controversy by bashing a peg into British rock during the same visit (Munich Climb on the East Face of Tryfan). They obviously not only upset the climbers, as Teufel died shortly afterwards, ironically when an ice peg failed, whilst he was descending from the North Face of the Schneehorn!*
1930s	Eric Byne visits Stannington, but strangely, records no routes.
1944	**Oak Tree Walk** Albert Heath, L S Thomas, R E Davies, R D Woolhouse
1944	**Grammarian's Progress** R A (Dick) Brown
1949-1950	**Hamlet's Traverse, Richard's Revenge, Lincoln Crack, Holly Route, Chimney and Crack, Rainbow Crack** Dick Brown *It was reputedly Reg Addey who defiled the*

start of Richard's Revenge with a peg. Lincoln Crack may have been climbed in the 1900s.

1934-1951	**Hell Gate Crack** Details unknown
1952 Feb	**Man of God** Dick Brown and party
1952 May 10	**Three Pitch Climb** Terry Lee, Pete Titterton **Leaning Block Wall, Terrace Traverse** John Gordon
1952 May 11	**Scarred Climb** Roy Briggs, John Gordon **Agden Arête** Terry Lee, Pete Titterton **Painters' Climb** Terry Lee **Campsite Crack** Eric Byne, Charles Ashbury *The Indirect Start had been climbed the previous day by John Gordon.*
1952 May 17	**Harlequinade** Pete Titterton **Cock o' the North, Deceptive Crack** John Gordon, Pete Titterton **Grey Wall** Roy Briggs, Pete Titterton
1952 May 18	**Mollie's Climb** Terry Lee, Roy Briggs **Gordon's Climb** John Gordon **Martini** Roy Briggs, John Gordon, Pete Titterton
1952 May 21	**The Flying Dutchman** Eric Byne, Charles Ashbury
1952 May 25	**The Foggy Dew** Pete Titterton, Roy Briggs **Tartan Slab** John Gordon, Roy Briggs, Pete Titterton **Judas** John Gordon, John Gordon, Roy Briggs, Pete Titterton **Fourth Apostle** Terry Lee, Roy Briggs, John Gordon, Pete Titterton **Bradfield Arête** John Gordon, Roy Briggs **S.O.S.** Roy Briggs, Pete Titterton **Boadicea's Wall, Rescue Route** John Gordon *The latter took a poor line just left of S. O. S.*
1952 May 29	**Funeral Crack** Eric Byne
1952 May	**Jackdaw Crack** Eric Byne, Charles Ashbury **May Climb** Pete Titterton **Bull Crack** John Gordon, Roy Briggs, Pete Titterton **The Gate-Post** Terry Lee or John Gordon **Rowan Tree Crack** Pete Titterton, Roy Briggs **The Wall End** Pete Titterton, John Gordon, Roy Briggs *Also known as S.C.A.C. Wall End* **Briggs' and Titterton's** Roy Briggs, Pete Titterton *It originally finished up Gordon's Climb. The present finish was added by John Gordon in the same month.*
1952 June 1	**Martini Crack** (Pitch 1) Pete Titterton, Roy Briggs, John Gordon (Pitch 2) John Gordon **White Rose Flake** John Gordon
1952 June 3	**St. John** John Gordon, Pete Titterton **St. Peter** Pete Titterton, John Gordon
1952	**Hanging Garden Wall** Pete Titterton, Roy Briggs **The Great Wall Traverse** John Gordon, Roy Briggs
1952 Aug	**Filth, Derision, Minsk, Hedony** Dick Brown
1952 Sept 23	**Black Wall** E J (John) Clegg, Dick Brown *Two routes, Black Corner and Flake, and Black Corner Right Wall, were originally climbed but these have since been combined.*
1952 Oct 15	**The Whittler** C B (Colin) Whittle, Dick Brown, Frank Fitzgerald, Donald Wooler *At the time this was the most difficult climb on the edge, a suitable climax to a frenetic year.*
1953 April 16	**Protozoan** E (Ernie) Marshall, Pete Titterton
1953 May 31	**Double Shuffle** Donald Wooller, Frank Fitzgerald **Twentyman's Terror** Frank Fitzgerald, Donald Wooller, M E (Maurice) Twentyman, Eric Byne

1953 July 11   **Straight Crack**   G H (George) Kitchin

1953 Aug 9   **Yewberry Groove**   G W S Piggott, Arthur Birtwistle

1953 Sept   **Demolition**   G H (George) Kitchin   **Asteris**   J N (Neil) Mather, Arthur Birtwistle   *"A piton is inserted to surmount the overhang, further aid may be necessary above". FFA 1969.*

1954 July 11   **St. George**   George Kitchin, Reg Pillinger

1954   **Brooks' Route**   John Henry Fearon   *Top-roped by Rupert Brooks, Jack Macleod in 1933.*

1955 Sept   **Jericho Wall**   Peter Biven, Trevor Peck

1955 Oct 9   **Hagg**   J R (Nat) Allen, D Godlington, F Howell, N Gregory   *Hagg takes its name from the pioneer's initials who were probably responsible for Disappointment on the same day.*

1955 Summer   **Handover Arête, Fly Wall**   Frank Fitzgerald (solo)   **The Corner**   John Henry Fearon   **October Arête, October Climb, Cascade Climb, Pocket Buttress, Southern Route, Lodge Buttress Direct**   John Henry Fearon, Dave Gregory (both solo)   *They were accompanied occasionally by Harry Shillam, Reg Pillinger, Alan Wright and Bernard Wilson. October Arête was started on the left. The direct start was climbed by Pete Crew sometime between 1961 and 1963.*

1956   **Oak Tree Saunter**   *Most probably climbed by George Kitchin during work for the 1957 guidebook*

1956 Summer   **Famine Cracks**   Alan Wright, Dave Gregory   *So-named because the climbers had cycled over from work and had had no tea.*

1958 Aug 9   **Deadnettle Crack**   Geoffrey Pigott, Arthur Birtwistle

1957-1960   **Suspense, Leaf Buttress**   Probably Pete Crew   **Mantelshelf Pillar, Spider Cracks**   John Henry Fearon (solo)   **Renrock, Grammarian's Face**   Rodney Wilson   *Grammarian's Face originally stepped left onto Grammarian's Progress. The direct finish was added in 1982 by Gary Gibson*   **Owen's Dilemma**   Mick Owen (solo)   **Pinnacle Arête, Joie de Vivre**   Pete Crew, John Henry Fearon   **Flake Climb**   Jack Soper

1957-1960   **Forget-me-not, Long John's Ordinary, Leaf Buttress**   Details unknown

1950s   R A Brown makes the same mistake that Eric Byne made in the 1930s by visiting Stannington. Again, no routes were recorded.

1962   **Bianco**   Bob Hassel   **St. Oliver**   Oliver Woolcock

1961-1963   **Exonian's Return, Addey's Addition, Gavel Neese?, The Left Wall, Post Horn, Gwyn**   Reg Addey (solo)   *Addey was a talented young climber who made himself somewhat unpopular by marking his lines of ascent with virtually indelible yellow paint and by using pegs on some of the climbs. Gavel Neese may have been climbed previously by Pete Crew or Jack Soper. It was named by John Henry Fearon after the ridge close to another Hell Gate, that on Great Gable. The Left Wall originally used a peg but was led without before the guidebook of 1964 and was superseded by Lucifer in 1984.*

1961-1963   **Pete's Sake, Great Buttress Arête, Ce ne Fait**

Rien, Long John's Eliminate   Pete Crew, John Henry Fearon   **Wheelbrace**   George Kitchin   **Central Route, Norwand**   Pete Crew (solo)   **Flying Angel**   Hugh Banner, Rodney Wilson   **Ogilvie's Corner**   Alan Clarke, John Henry Fearon   *The direct start was added in 1978.*

1961-1963   **Black Wall, Ewden Wall**   Details unknown

1963   **Arachnid Cracks, Tarantula, Schizont, Chicken Wall, Still Life**   Michael McMahon and members of the Sheffield University Mountaineering Club   **Double De-Clutch**   David Price, Michael McMahon   **Ardua** (5 points of aid)   Mike (Nigger) White   *White was 'six-foot-seven-inches high with short arms and long pockets' Ten pounds for a month in the Alps was typical. FFA 1969.*

1957-1964   **Castor, Pollux** (both with aid)   Details unknown

1965 April   **Gallipoli Rock, Face Climb, Scarlett's Wall Arête, North Side Route, First Pillar Routes 1 and 2**   Reg Addey

1965   **Oxo, Sennapod Corner**   Pete Scott, unseconded, or with Al Evans   **Cobweb Crack, Cemetery Grapes, Pinnacle Face**   Al Evans, unseconded, or with Pete Scott.

1966 July 9   **Llareggub** (1 point of aid)   Pete Scott   *The name is the reverse of the comment made when asked what there was to stand on. There's even less now - it fell down in 1971.*   **Pyrology, Iceni**   Pete Scott, Al Evans

1966 Sept   **Aberration**   Al Evans   *"I fell the whole length of the climb due to a dirty finish, completely ripping my jeans, which was embarrassing as I had to travel home on the bus. I then cleaned the top and soloed it." Eric Byne climbed the lower section in 1952 as an alternative start to Wailing Wall.*

1966   **Hypotenuse Wall**   Al Evans, Brian Chisholm

1967 July   **Q.E.D.**   Al Evans   **Conjunctus Viribus, Nill**   Al Evans, Joe Goodison

1967 Oct 30   **Little X**   Al Evans, Brian Chisholm   *Much of the route had been previously climbed by Ernie Marshall.*

1967   **Excursion**   Al Evans, Joe Goodison   **Birds Nest Crack**   A N Burgin, R Weatherley   **Deceptio Visus**   Pete Scott, Al Evans

1968 Aug   **Libra**   Al Evans   **Taurus, E.N. 24**   Al Evans, David Lloyd   *One point of aid was used on E.N. 24. This was eliminated by Evans on the second ascent. Taurus may have been climbed by Pete Biven and Trevor Peck in Sept 1952. "A few feet left of Derision a climb was made directly up the wall."*

1968 Sept 5   **Gemini**   Keith Myhill, Al Evans (alternate leads)

1968   **Limbus Fatuorum**   Al Evans, Dennis Orwin   **Artifax Arête**   Dennis Orwin   *Artifax Arête originally known as Bald Patch and graded VS.*

1968 March   **Trapeze**   Al Evans   **Grotty Groove**   Keith Myhill, Steve Chadwick   **Taurus**   Keith Myhill, Steve Chadwick, Al Evans

1968 March 27   **Bovril**   Al Evans, Denis Orwin   **Will Scarlet, Robin Hood, Sherwood Forest**   Steve Chadwick, Al Evans   **Marmite**   Keith Myhill, Al Evans   **Derision**   Al Evans, Steve Chadwick

1968 March 28 **Oxo Arête** Keith Myhill, Steve Chadwick **Dextrous** Steve Chadwick, Keith Myhill **Birthday Flake** Al Evans and friends **Trinity Crack** Steve Chadwick, Al Evans

1968 March 30 **Little John** Al Evans, Phil Ideson **Apeman's Arête** Al Evans, Pete Scott **Splurp** Phil Ideson, Al Evans **Rover's Return** Al Evans, Phil Ideson

1968 April **Cascade Crack** Keith Myhill **Galvo Groove** Al Evans.

1968 June **Nebula** Brian Chisholm, R Haslam, Al Evans **Dognut** R Haslam, Brian Chisholm.

1968 October **Quicksilver, Diplopia** A N Burgin, G Laurie **Gold Rush** Al Evans, Phil Ideson **Hanging Rib Groove** G Laurie, A N Burgin, R Weatherley

1968 November **Entanglement** P Garner, G Laurie **Barnsley Bitter** M Hoyle, P Garner, G Laurie, R Weatherley **Drippy** G Laurie, A N Burgin **Eureka** R Senior, P Pearson **1847** Brian G (Tanky) Stokes, Albert Hattersley

1968 **Hammer** G Laurie, R Weatherley **Merman's Meander** Al Evans

1969 April 25 **Hey Jude** Keith Myhill, Al Evans **Flamingo Wall** Al Evans, Keith Myhill

1969 May **Green Wall, Delta, The Warp, The Elf** Barry Clarke

1969 June 10 **Castor** (FFA) Keith Myhill, Al Evans **Pollux** (FFA) Al Evans, Keith Myhill

1969 June **Asteris** (FFA), **Ardua** (FFA) Keith Myhill, Al Evans (alternate leads) **Tiptoe** J Stanger, R Sanderson

1969 June **Mignon, Quicksilver, Ocumen, Dilemma** Barry Clarke

1969 **Erosion Groove, Dead End Buttress Direct** Bill Briggs, Martin Laycock

1970 **Y.M.C.A. Crack** Members of the Barnsley Y.M.C.A.

pre-1970 **Ode to A Footrot, Woolly, Zero Drift, Transducer, Ruff Crack, Tarzan, The Ghoul, Cowards Way, Old Man's Stairs, Slippy** Details unknown

1971 Apr 17 **Ma'son** Robert Taylor, Barry Needle, G Rhodes

1971 **Speak Easy** Ron Fawcett, Al Evans *Evans had led the upper section in 1968.*

1970-1973 **Chains** Keith Myhill (solo)

1972 **Chimney and Crack** Details unknown

1973 **Black Finger, Helping Hand** John Allen, Neil Stokes

1974 June 8 **Bostonian** Barry Needle and members of the Stocksbridge & District Mountain Rescue Team. *The direct was climbed by the same team on Aug 4 1974.*

1964-1976 **Sidewinder** Details unknown

1968-1976 **Split Chimney Wall, Defile Left** Robert Taylor

1969-1976 **Lesark, Sycamore Saunter, Dihedral, Enna, The Bogie, Birth Of Liquid Desire, Chisel, Dognut Direct,** **Egroeg, Sevad, Big D, Little D, Gollyberry, Sabre Cut, Brass Bees, Apprenticeship, Chaika, Angelique, Christmas Climb, Roat. Patience, Confused, Grayling, Hedera** Details unknown

1975-1976 **Indirect Finish to Campsite Crack** Terry King

1975-1976 **Numenorean, Gimli, Crumbler, Armstrong's Eliminate** Details unknown

1976 Aug **Requiem of Hamlet's Ghost, Schard** Terry Hirst (solo)

1976 **Vapona** Alan Blakeman

1977 Mar 11 **Tensile Test** Terry Hirst (solo)

1977 Mar **Elastic Limit** Michael Anderson (solo)

1977 **Banana Wall** Don Barr, Paul Hallos

1978 Feb **Pass By** Don Barr (solo)

1978 Aug **Seconds Out** Don Barr, Paul Hallos

1978 Sept 11 **On the Air, Desolation Angel** Terry Hirst *Desolation Angel was soloed in 1992, eliminating the side-runner, by Simon Jones. Incredibly Pete Robins on-sight soloed it on a warm day in 2001.*

1978 Sept 25 **Autumn Wall, Equinox, Windfall, Angus, Duplicate, Direct start to Ogilvie's Corner** Terry Hirst (solo) *Equinox originally traversed left at 6m to finish up Autumn Wall. A direct finish was added in 1988 by John Hesketh.*

1978 **The Moire, Abair, Trapezium, Falkway, Bay Wall, Pilgrimage** Don Barr, Paul Hallos

1978 **The Tittler** D Mollson, R Egan

1979 Mar 31 **Contemporary** Terry Hirst (solo)

1979 Apr **Photo Finish, Emma** Terry Hirst, Ian Hirst

1979 **Baker Street** Paul Baker, Ted Ellis

1980 May **Inclusion** Terry Hirst, Ian Hirst **Face Dance, Long Odds** Terry Hirst (unseconded) **Even Chance, Toss Up, Cadence** Terry Hirst (solo)

1980 May **Insurrection** Mike Hunt, Phil Neame, Dave Glover **The Resurrection**, Mike Hunt, Phil Neame, Gill Haddon, Dave Glover, Robin Sermon

1980 June **Picnic, Hanging Rock** Terry Hirst (solo)

1980 **Aaron** Mike Hunt, Robin Sermon **Hard Men Don't Spot Lines Like This, Catherine** Robin Sermon, Mike Hunt, Cath Bates

1981 Feb 15 **Thrown Away, Serrated Edge** Gary and Hazel Gibson

1981 May **Baal** Gary Gibson, Hazel Gibson, Elaine Wroe

1981 May 11 **Drums and Kicks** Gary Gibson (solo)

1981Aug **Blasphemy** Ian Hirst (solo) **Holly Scoop** Ian Hirst, Dave Limb

1981 Oct 16 **Pentovis, Nardil, Fountain of Youth** Terry Hirst, Ian Hirst

1981 Oct **Mark** Terry Hirst (solo)

1982 Feb 22 **Cannae** Gary Gibson (solo)

1982 June **Bolster** Terry Hirst (solo)

1982   **Despair, On The Edge**   Nick White, Mark White

1982   **Changeling, S.M.O., Spanish Caravan, Same Rain, Mr Mojo Risin'**   Don Barr, Paul Hallos, Chris Farnsworth *These were Don's last additions to the edge; he was tragically killed in the Verdon Gorge in France.*

1982 Nov 30   **Bogey's Beacon**   Bob Gookey, Mike Hunt   **Chauvi's Last Stand**   Mike Hunt, Bob Gookey

1983   **Frigging Saw**   Nick MacFarlane, Kevin Howard

1983 Oct 23   **Ignis Fatuus**   Roger Brookes, Andy Lewandowski

1983 Nov 6   **Hit and Run Driver**   Andy Lewandowski, Roger Brookes

1984 Sept 8   **Pocket Buttress Direct, Lucifer**   Terry Hirst *Lucifer supersedes The Left Wall, which originally went left below the roof to finish in Hell Gate. It appeared in the 1983 guidebook even though it hadn't actually been climbed at the time!*

1984 Sept 10   **Split Decision, Mind Game, Sleight-of-hand, Confidence Trick**   Terry Hirst (solo)

1984 Sept   **The Thorn, Upwardly Mobile**   Terry Hirst (solo) **Andrew**   Tony Hirst, Tom Valentine   **Opportunist**   Tony Hirst, Ian Hirst

1984 Nov 25   **Dreams by the Sea**   Doug Kerr, Paul Harrison

1984 Dec 7   **Wheat Thin**   Paul Harrison, Neil Harrison   *It originally stepped into Castor for protection. Straightened out by Paul Harrison in Oct 1997.*

1984 Dec 16   **Cardinal's Treasure**   John Allen, Mark Stokes, Pete Lowe

1985 Feb 27   **Down to Earth**   Roger Doherty, Roger Brook

1985 Mar 13   **Summer Lightning**   Roger Doherty (solo)

1985 Apr 13   **Hobo, Mescalin, Black Cap, Beyond the Pale, Kipke**   Roger Doherty (solo)   *Hobo and Mescalin aren't described in the text as no one can find them.*

1985 May2   **Little Wing**   John Hesketh (solo)

1985 Oct   **This Year's Model**   Terry Hirst (solo)

1985 Nov   **Earth Blues**   Roger Doherty (solo)

1985   **Dead Heat**   Nick White, Steve Yates   *A side-runner in Photo Finish was used. Soloed on-sight without in the same year by Roger Doherty.*

1986 Oct4   **Antique**   Nick White

1987 April 26   **Bedrock**   John Hesketh (solo)

1987 July 25   **En Passant**   Jon Darwin (solo)

1987 Sept 23   **Insurrection, Tears Before Bedtime, Anzio Breakout**   Jon Darwin (solo)

1987 Dec 5   **Whisky Breath**   Roger Doherty, Roger Brook *Doherty also claimed Wango Tango on September 26th of this year but in view of attempts to climb this line major doubts have been expressed and in fact, it is now widely believed the line hasn't been climbed.*

1988 Apr 9   **Spring Tide**   John Hesketh (solo)

1988 June   **Passerine, La Mancha, Steeltown, Querp**   Howie Darwin

1991 June 1   **Well it is Now!**   Andy Barker

1991 July 25   **Nightjar**   Howie Darwin (solo)

1991 Aug 11   **Patricia's Wall**   David Simmonite (solo)   **Subterranean Blues**   Michael Piggot, Richard Evans   **Wheelspin Wall**   Richard Evans, Michael Piggot

1992 Mar 23   **Gold Leaf**   David Simmonite (solo)

1992 Oct   **Diamond White**   David Simmonite belayed by Patricia Evans after TR practice

1993 Mar 11   **Dragon's Hoard**   Simon Jones, Roger Brook   *A great answer to a challenge set down in the last guidebook*

1993 Mar 15   **News at Zen**   Simon Jones, John Stanger, Barry Clarke

1993 July12   **Journey into Freedom**   Simon Jones (solo)   *Inspirational and very serious climbing and still unrepeated. Jones commented that it was "tasty". The relatively unknown Barnsley bred climber leaves his mark with a series of bold ascents and in the process climbs two of Wharncliffe's last great problems.*

1993 Summer   **Kide Kodoke, Hubble Bubble Toil on Rubble, What About Child Care?, I Must Stop Thinking About Suspenders**   Combinations of Roy Bennett, David Simmonite, R Grimes   *Routes on the only (just) climbable rock at Hay Crook Common ranging from S to VS 4c. Nothing to write home about.*

1994 Apr 11   **Crista's Twin**   Crista Hollingworth, Dave Gregory

1994 June 5   **V for Victory, Waxing Lyrical**   David Simmonite

1994 July 23   **The Tip Test**   Simon Jones, David Simmonite   **Inside Edge**   David Simmonite, Simon Jones

1994 Nov 11   **Gully Side**   David Simmonite (solo)

1996 Mar 16   **Paraffin Jack**   Tim Green   **Mystery Route**   Andy Woodhouse

1996 Apr   **Then Jericho, Flaming 'ard, Hollow Victory**   John Painter, Gerald Lee   **Narrow Minded**   John Painter

1996 July 15   **Lemon Squeezy**   Paul Harrison, Neil Harrison, 'Black' Mike Snell

1996 July 22   **Extra Tasty**   Paul Harrison, Neil Harrison   *The initial, on-sight ended with a spectacular plummet into the tree.*

1996 July 25   **Death-Throes in the Hedgerows, The Avenue**   Neil and Paul Harrison   **Savoury Crunch**   Paul and Neil Harrison

1996 July 27   **Monster Munch, The Bits With Hairs On**   Paul Harrison, Neil Harrison   **Min-arête**   Neil Harrison, Paul Harrison

1997 Apr   **Middle Way**   Frank Horsman, Phil Bartlett

1997 July 14   **Scarecliffe, Scratching Around**   Frank Horsman (solo)

1997 Sept 12   **Scouting For Boys**   Paul Harrison, Graham Sutton

1997 Oct 26   **Lundy High**   Paul Harrison, Sandy Wilkie, Mike Snell

1998 June   **Primal Void**   Frank Horsman (solo)

1998 June   **Koh-I-Noor**   David Law, Warren Trippett (both led)

1998 Sep 24   **Green Arête**   Peter Stone, Ian Woodyatt

1998 Nov 17   **The Snip**   Paul Harrison, Graham Sutton

1999 May   **Ganto's Axe**   Frank Horsman

1999 Summer   **Long John's Super Direct, Paper Birch,**

Another view of Wharncliffe's outstanding VS climb. Paul Harrison on *Himmelswillen* (page 278).
Photo: David Simmonite.

Tiered Pillar, Lord of the Dance Bill Birch, Roger Birch, Richard Hyde

1999 Sept **Deepcar Named Desire** Bill Birch, Roger Birch **Gone for a Burton** Nick Taylor (solo)

1999 Oct 9 **Little Fellow** Nick Taylor, Duncan Frisch (both solo) *Takes in the majority of Twin Pillar Left from pre-1976*

1999 Jan 22 **Jaffa** Paul Harrison, Graham Sutton, Mike Snell, David Simmonite **Mike's Route** Mike Snell, David Simmonite **Chicken Run** David Simmonite (solo)

1999 Jan 31 **Sandyman** Paul Harrison, Graham Sutton

1999 Apr **Begum Behar, Jalfrezee Jug Fest, David's Other Start, Chicken Silly Hot** David Law, Warren Trippett **Spring Lamb Dopiazza** Warren Trippett, David Law **Harry the Dog Tosser, Ocydroma** David Law (solo) **Are We There Yet** Warren Trippett, Simon Royston, M Robinson (all led)

2000 Apr 24 **Hard Cheese** David Simmonite (unseconded, belayed by Ian Smith)

2000 Summer **Footloose** Dave Millar, Frank Horsman; **Rossiter's Route** Brian Rossiter **Mellicious** John Camateras

2000 Oct 8 **Just a Minute** Frank Horsman, Bill Phillips

2000 Feb 23 **Off My Rocker** Mike Snell, Tony Sawbridge **Why Am I Here?** Tony Sawbridge, Mike Snell

2001 Apr 1 **Curved Balls** David Simmonite, Paul Harrison, Graham Sutton **More Fool You** Paul Harrison, David Simmonite, Graham Sutton **Big Bird** Graham Sutton, David Simmonite

2001 Apr 8 **Trouser Browser** Jim Dalley, Richard Swindon, David Simmonite, et al **Just a Little Bit** David Simmonite (solo) **Chancer** Paul Harrison, Mike Snell (both solo) **Greenwood Side** David Simmonite, Paul Harrison, Mike Snell (all solo) **Harrison's Half Hour, Fizz** Paul Harrison (solo) **Harvey** Paul Harrison, David Simmonite, Mike Snell (all solo) **Top Heavy** Paul Harrison, Mike Snell, David Simmonite **Dorenuts** Paul Harrison, David Simmonite, Mike Snell *A productive day. News had got around that the Foot & Mouth ban had been lifted at Wharncliffe and the edge was awash with climber and more akin to Stanage. The team went to the far end of the crag for solitude and found it.*

2001 Apr 10 **Weinie Roast, Hollyoaks, Charred, Two Tree Trip, Footin Mouth** Paul Harrison (solo) *A variation on Hollyoaks, Pylon King Slab was claimed 10 days later by Mark Stephen Davies but had already been climbed by Harrison*

2001 Apr 11 **Penis Town** Paul Harrison, Mike Snell, David Simmonite

2001 Apr 16 **Rib Tickler, Mad as a Mad Thing** David Simmonite, Paul Harrison (solo) **Easter Mellody** John Camateras *Basically the same as Diamond White* **Long John's Arête** John ? *The editor lost the piece of paper with John's full name on it. Sorry!*

2001 Apr 27 **Omega Rib** Paul Harrison (solo) **The George Formby Appreciation Society** Paul Harrison, Mike Snell, Jez

Portman *Named after a regular gathering of the Society at the Wortley Arms pub in the nearby village of Wortley*

2001 Apr 29 **Splitter** Paul Harrison, Steve Coughlan, David Simmonite

2001 May 2 **Leftover Chimney** Steve Clark, Simon Trigger (both solo) **Just the Chimney** Dave Gregory, John Street

2001 May 4 **Brand New Nothing** Paul Harrison, David Simmonite

2001 May **Bass Relief** Rick Gibbon, Bill Birch

2002 Feb 17 **Ewden Edge** David Simmonite, Mick Carr **Clean Hands Mick** Mick Carr, David Simmonite

2002 **Foot and Back, Zigzag Climb** Steve Clark (solo) **Chockstone Climb** Lynn Robinson, Steve Clark (both solo) **Two Tier Climb, Pleasantry, Groovy** Steve Clark, Gareth Wood (both solo) *Steve Clarke, Lynn Robinson and friends claimed many short routes, the majority of which had been climbed before but left unrecorded and will remain so.*

2003 May **Problem Bulge** David Simmonite, David Trelawny Ross

2003 June **Amnesaic** Steve Clark, Iain Mount *A direct finish was added the same day (pre-practiced once) by the Iain Mount, Steve Clark*

2003 **Long Chimney Variation** Steve Clark

2003 Nov 16 **Missed Me, Crack One, Second Crack, Crack Three, Too Wide for Some** David Simmonite (solo)

2003 Mar 6 **Stannington's Rough** Tony Sawbridge, Mike Snell

2004 July **A Moment of Madness, Bring Back the Birch, Lundy Calling, Just Commit** Paul Harrison (solo)

2005 May 18 **A Bit of Ruff** Paul Harrison, Tony Sawbridge, Mike Snell

2005 July 20 **Vegimite** Tony Sawbridge, Mike Snell, David Simmonite **The Editor's Cracked** David Simmonite, Mike Snell, Tony Sawbridge *A call above and beyond the duty for the editor.*

2005 **Fall of Jericho** Paul Harrison, Tony Sawbridge, Mike Snell **Lemon Entry** Tony Sawbridge, Paul Harrison, Mike Snell

Boulder First Ascents

Wharncliffe Bouldering Dragon's Den, Lodge Buttress and The Outlook developed and recorded by Jon Fullwood, Kim Thompson, Iain Farrar, although John Allen also climbed extensively on these boulders in the 1970s.

Routes Graded List

E10
Equilibrium

E9
Parthian Shot

E8
Captain Invincible
Fagus Sylvatica
Superstition
Simba's Pride
That's My Lot
French Kiss
Elm Street

E7
Smoked Salmon
Living in Oxford
Messiah
The Braille Trail
The Bad and the Beautiful
Drifter
Avoiding the Traitors
The Notorious BLG
Toploader
The Salmon
Balance It Is
Three Blind Mice
Chocolate Swastika
Monopoly
Scritto's Republic
Master's Edge
Shadows on the Wall
Masters of the Universe

E6
Jack the Groove
Earthboots
Linkline
Desolation Angel

Flex
Dragon's Hoard
Sick Arête
Jumpey Wooller
Adam Smith's...
Perplexity
Gazebo Watusi
Block and Tackle
Mother's Pride
Lost World
Gettin' Kinda Squirelly
Placid House
Silent Witness
Milena
Nefertiti
The Psycho Path
Jasmine
Winter's Grip
Pulsar Direct
Salmon Left-Hand
Nosferatu
High and Dry
Life Assurance

E5
Feet Neet
London Wall
Super Ted
Adios Amigo
Green Death
The Simpering Savage
Big Bad Wolf
Coventry Street
Declaration
Edge Lane
New Mediterranean
Jermyn Street
On the Air
Moolah
Bat out of Hell

Mr Mojo Risin'
White Wall
London Pride
Pebble Mill
Goliath
Pocket Buttress Direct
And Now For Some-
  thing...
Offspring
Crikey
Great Arête
Black Choir
The Snivelling Shit
The Rack
Dead Heat
Pool Wall
Poached Salmon

E4
Block Wall
Teddy Bears' Picnic
Heaven Can Wait
Flute of Hope
The Knock
Mad Gadaffi
Arnold Schwarzenegger...
Sforzando
Blind Bat
Rock Around the Block
Plague
Silent Spring
Above and Beyond...
The Tempest
Esoteric Slab
The Rasp Direct
Wheat Thin
High Street
Tea for Two
Auto da Fe
Delivered

Extra Tasty
Rafaga
The Little Rascal
High Plains' Drifter
Monster Munch
Jaded
Hell For Leather
Xanadu
Half Man, Half Cake
Europe After Rain
Freight Train
The Brush Off
Paddington
Autumn Wall
We're Only Here for the
  Smear
I'm Back
Jetrunner

E3
Ontos
Saville Street
Sex Drive
'ere come Fudgie
Twikker
Boulevard
The Searing
The Arctic Mammal
Scouting For Boys
Backwater Barracudas
Conan The Librarian
News at Zen
March Hare
Jemelia
Down to Earth
Benberry Wall
Angst
Exit
Hit and Run Driver
Dumbo's Ringpiece

Nightjar
Time for Tea
Ignis Fatuus
Scoop Connection
Dextrous Hare
Cauldron Crack
Boggart Left-Hand
Artifax Arête
Gates of Mordor
Party Animal
Snivelin Rivelin

E2

Howshaw Tor Eliminate
Nick Knack Paddywack
Undercut Crack
Billy Whiz
Windrête
The Boggart
The Rasp
Easy Picking
Too Much
Awkward Willy
The Resurrection
Zeus
Great West Road
Long John's Eliminate
The Mighty Atom
Midge
Green Child
October Arête
Dreams by the Sea
Grammarian's Face
Suspense
Skarlati
Regent Street
Mark
Granny Smith
April Fool
Knightsbridge
Stretcher Case
Street Legal
Commix

Sorb
Erb
The Sentinel
Watling Street
Portnoy's Complaint
Ausfahrt
Auricle
Outsider
The South-West Corner

E1

Frustration
The Fin
Brimstone
The Gnat
E.N. 24
Great Peter
The Knack
Black Slab Arête
Great Buttress Arête
Dextrasol
Billingsgate
Lotto
Only Just
Embankment Route 3
The Irrepressible Urge
Dynamite Groove
All Stars' Goal
The Rat
Wrong Hand Route
Autumn Day
Aeroflot
Thread Flintstone
Pollux
Fizz
Blue Velvet
Asteris
Rhododendron Crack
Millwheel Wall
Castor
Long Tall Sally
Nemmes Pas Harry
Windjammer

Embankment Route 4
Jaffa
Evening Wall
Dexterity
Your Round
Banner's Ridge
Better Late Than Never?
The Crease

Hard Very Severe

Surform
Roof Route
Groove Route
Blizzard Ridge
Nonsuch
The Grogan
Great Buttress
Magnum Force
The Riffler
Delectable Direct
Trouble with Lichen
Plexity
Tower Crack
Lancaster Flyby
All of a Quiver
Great North Road
Tinner
Kremlin Krack
No Zag
Croton Oil
Great Portland Street
Brooks' Crack
Ring of Roses
Petticoat Lane
Crew Cut
Great Buttress Eliminate
Glucose
Briggs' and Titterton's
Ogilvie's Corner
Astronaut's Wall
Beach Tea One
The Happy Wanderer
Pete's Sake

Private Practice
Excel
Rectineal Wall
Randy's Wall
Bond Street
Whitehall
Flamingo Wall
Wobbly Wall
First Coming
Neb Buttress
Tower Wall
Lyon's Corner House
Limmock
Bamford Rib
Shylock Finish
Aberration
Turtle Rib
April Arête
Shaftesbury Avenue
Brown's Unmentionable
David
Estremo
Philby
Hyde's Mantelshelf
Pebble Crack
Leo
Gable Route
The Knight's Move

Very Severe

The Ingot
Route 1
Great Harry
Fumf
Skydiver
The Rat's Tail
Gingerbread
Altar Crack
Gunpowder Crack
Keep Crack
Barney Rubble
Dowel Crack
Fricka's Crack

319

Graded List > Routes

The File
Double De-Clutch
Tartan Slab
Pocket Buttress
Billberry Crack
Quien Sabe?
Hathersage Climb
Obscenity
Delectable Variation
Orange Juice Wall
Roof Route
The Mall
Red's Slab Variations
Dowel Crack
The Spiral Route
Gargoyle Buttress
Gimcrack
Byne's Crack
Wrinkled Wall
The Blue Defile
Every Man's Misery
Dunkley's Eliminate
Gallipoli Rock
Excalibur
Lodge Buttress Direct
Embankment Route 2
Face Climb No. 1.5
Little White Jug
Scarlett's Crack
Richard's Revenge
Oriel
Oak Tree Walk
White Rose Flake
Hollyash Crack
S.O.S.
Grammarian's Progress
Curving Crack
Covent Garden
Skywalk
Pulcherine
Limpopo Groove
Tortoise
Furherbuch

Mod
Oracle
Sick Bay
Fox House Flake
Griff's Variant
Gargoyle Flake

Hard Severe

Scarred Climb
Scarlett's Chimney
Three Tree Climb
Mutiny Crack
Titanic
Scarlett's Climb
The Drainpipe
Eartha
Dead Mouse Crack
Watson's Crack
Tower Face
Amazon Crack
Cordite Crack
Brown's Crack
Balloon
Outside Route
Samson's Delight
Hell Gate Crack
Brook's Layback
Jonathan's Chimney
The Great Slab
Jambo
Titania
Wazzock
Hell's Bells
Route 1
Summer Climb
Chiming Cracks
The Staircase

Severe

Root Route
Byne's Route
Campsite Crack
Leaning Crack

Pole-Axed
Loki's Way
Left Holly Pillar Crack
Puttrell and Watson's
   Route
Beta Crack
K Buttress Crack
Rodney's Dilemma
Twenty-Foot Crack
Possibility
Brogging Wall
Puttrell's Progress
Cioch Corner
Rocker
The Bush Off
Tower Crack
Bamford Wall
Carl's Buttress
Greymalkin
Ash Tree Wall
Birch Buttress
Amen Corner Right
Step It Up
Slab Happy

Hard Very Difficult

Wall Chimney
Grindle Crack
Route 2
Lincoln Crack
Ring Climb
Snail Crack
Twin Chimney's Layback
Broken Buttress
Close Shave
Paddock
Wall Corner

Very Difficult

Pulpit Groove
Dovestones Wall
Renshaw's Remedy
Triangle Buttress Arête

Hamlet's Climb
Hurricane
Lime Juice Chimney
Falstaff's Chimney
Stingray
Brixton Road
Holly Crack
Ash Tree Crack
Windblown
Face Climb No. 1
K Buttress Slab

Hard Difficult

Black Slab Centre
Ingle Nook
Cranberry Crack
Jacobite's Route
Boulder Crack
Billberry Wall
Birch Crack

Difficult

The Belle
Ender
The Flue
The Great Flake Route
The Scoop
Sinuous Crack
Inside Route
Windblasted
Jonah
Cheese Cut

Moderate

Breaststoker
Deep Cleft
Wind Tunnel
Overhang Buttress Arête
Alpha Crack
End Slab
Rivelin Slab
Terrace Trog

Bouldering Graded List

V11
Nik's Wall
Westworld
Blazing 48s
Intense
Blind Drunk
Bohemian Grove

V10
Striker
Master Kush
Zorev Sit Start
Darkstar
Western Eyes
Zippatricks
The Terrace
Submergence

V9
Blind Fig
Zorev
No Class
Left-Hand Man
Shit
Little Pig
Zaff's Problem
Sweet Release
Talk to me Martin
Once Upon a Time
Rollerwall
Zaff Skoczylas
West Side Story
Dick Williams
Guplets Sit Start

V8
Blind Date
Happy Campus
The Rib

Giza
Sparks
Jellyeyes
Jorge
Mother's Pride
David
Master Chef
Desparête
Fireball
Keyhole Cave Traverse
Piss
Green Death Superdirect
The Famous Grouse
The Parson's Finch
Little Gem
The Bone Cruncher
True Git

V7
Purple Haze
Jupiter Collision
Pets Win Prizes
Interstellar Pigeon
The Sphinx
Iain's Arête
Green Flag
Pebble Mill Traverse
Blunted
Velvet Crab
Electrical Storm
Moontan
The Flying Arête
Faze Action
Pet Cemetery
Violence
Pistol Pinch
Eyes Without a Face
Ron Side Force-It
Ping Pong Pocket Rib

V6
Trellis
Galaxy Dove
Nick Knack Start
Mermaid
The Compressor
The Alliance
Fishboy
Friday Club
Beach Ball
Back to Front
Small is Beautiful
The Nose
Kim Span
Broddle's Baby
Eating Out
Hueco Wall
The Grazer
The Attitude Inspector

V5
Something Silly
Squawk Traverse
The Sheep
Acid Reign
7 Ball
Pothole Slab
Bad Attitude
Pepper Mill
Sputum Traverse
Beach Bum
Lurcher Direct
Life in a Radioactive
   Dustbin
Hip Hip Huway
Spider Crack
Lembas
Definitive 5.12
Technical Master Left-Hand

Proper Grit
The Blob
Breakfast
Combine Harvester
J-Warkin
Low Coach
Little Brown Thug

V4
The Business Boy
Conan The Librarian
The Bookend
Nicotine Stain
Squawk
Planet Rock
Twentieth Century Fox
Flying Arête Left
Banana Finger Direct
Safe Bet
The Blue Whale
The Barrel Slap Problem
Golden Arête
The Hanging Rib
Not Westworld
Remergence
Seventies Style Wall
Secret Garden Traverse
Man Calls Horse
Technical Master
Caley Slab
Save Dinnomite
The Duck
Crazy Legs Crane
Tiger
Puttrell Sitdown
The Harvester
Duff Paddy
Sailing
Sitting Duck

V3

Cool Running
Sidewall Scoop
Lose Hill
Sick
Hurkling Towards Earth
Cool Rib
Altered
ET
Ladder Rib
Boneyard Arête
All Quiet on the Eastern
  Front
Son of a Birch
The Diamond
Nunn's Eliminate
Wafery Flake
Little Limmock
Moby
Go West
The Celtic Cross
Minah Variation
Banana Finger
North Roof

V2

Velvet Roof
Ahab
Topless Crack
The Gurgling Green Streak
Stingray Arête
Lurcher's Nose Front
Not Zaff's
Black Crimp Problem
Perfect Porthole Problem
The Housebrick
Tree Stump Traverse
Sidepull Arch
Banana Arête

V1

Green Parrot
Cleo's Edge
Play Huway
West End Girls
Rock Ahoy
Monk's Bulge
Beach Crack
Len's Areet
Lurcher's Nose
Rod Stewart
Chockstone Crack
Huway-Day
Foxy
First Bulge
Jawbone
The Shearing
Foxy Loxley
Guppy Left
Sharp Rib

V0+

Friend Slot Wall
Buoux Style Pockets
Tiptoe
Bridge Wall
Fingersplitter
Beached Whale Crack
Hot Dog
The Careful Trotter

V0

Something Else
Really Exciting Flake
Flake 'n' Blob
Sputum
Gog Arête
Alleluia
Win Hill
Lil' Arête

Left Tower
Jigsaw Puzzle
Baby Bear Wall

V0-

Pixie's Arête
Cherry's Crack

Flake Arête
Dominican
Ink Cap
Crow Man Groove
Friar's Wall
Wriggly Crack
Daddy Wall

Paul Houghoughi on Zorev, V9 (page 51).
Photo: John Coefield

Answers to Boulders: Know your Holds!

Answers? Life's not about answers.

Index

Index

Index

Index

Index

Index

Index

Index

Leon Zablocki experiencing the foreboding atmosphere of The Burbage Quarries, where dark rock, howling winds and steep routes all make for a challenging experience. Seen here on the first ascent of Fox House Fake HVS 5a (page 52). Photo: Alex Ekins.

Neil Mawson soloing The Boggart, E2 6a (page 41) on Burbage South Edge.
Don't worry, by the way – it's not as steep as it looks.
Photo: Pete O'Donovan.

Dave Turnbull fighting hard on Saville Street, E3 6a, on the North Bay area of Millstone (page 96).
Photo: Niall Grimes.

Ben Moon on his recent addition to the Burbage Valley, Voyager. This new problem just about sums up all that's best about grit – great features, amazing rock, fabulous moves, and all at that perfect height.

This desperate problem weighs in at a mighty V13 – by far the hardest problem in the area – and was climbed in late November, 2005 – a little too late to make it into the main text. It is to be found on the Sphinx block (page 17). Begin by swinging onto the holds by his foot and follow the prow direct.
Photo: Jerry Moffatt

US	Aust.	UIAA	German
5.2	10	I	I
5.3	11	II	II
5.4	12	III	III
5.5	13	IV	IV
5.6	14	IV+	V
5.7	15	V−	VI
5.8	16	V	
		V+	
5.9	17	VI−	VIIa
5.10	18	VI	VIIb
5.10+	19	VI+	VIIc
5.10++	20	VII−	VIIIa
5.11a	21	VII	VIIIb
5.11b	22	VII+	VIIIc
5.11c	23	VIII−	IXa
5.11d		VIII	IXb
5.12a	24	VIII+	IXc
5.12b	25	IX−	Xa
5.12c	26	IX	Xb
5.12d	27		
5.13a	28	IX+	Xc
5.13b	29	X−	XIa
5.13c	30	X	XIb
5.13d	31		
5.14a	32	X+	XIc
5.14b	33	XI−	XIIa
5.14c	34	XI	XIIb
5.14d	35		

Dave Parry on Mermaid, V6, at Burbage Bridge (page 83). Photo: John Coefield.

Dave Musgrove on Sentinel. E2 5b, Burbage North (page 20). Photo: Niall Grimes

UK adj.	UK tech.	Frenc
M		Fl/2
D		Fl
VD	3c	F2
S	4a	F3
HS	4b	F4
VS	4c	F4+
HVS	5a	F5
		F5+
	5b	F6a
E1		F6a+
E2	5c	F6b
E3		F6b+
		F6c
E4	6a	F6c+
		F7a
E5		F7a+
	6b	F7b
E6		F7b+
		F7c
E7	6c	F7c+
		F8a
E8		F8a+
		F8b
E9		F8b+
		F8c
	7a	F8c+
E999		F9a

Dave Parry on Mermaid, V6, at Burbage Bridge (page 83). Photo: John Coefield.

UK adj.	UK tech.	French	US	Aust.	UIAA	German
M		FI/2	5.2	10	I	I
D		FI	5.3	11	II	II
VD	3c	F2	5.4	12	III	III
S	4a	F3	5.5	13	IV	IV
HS	4b	F4	5.6	14	IV+	V
VS	4c	F4+	5.7	15	V−	VI
	5a	F5	5.8	16	V	
HVS		F5+	5.9	17	V+	VIIa
	5b	F6a	5.10	18	VI−	VIIb
E1		F6a+	5.10+	19	VI	VIIc
E2	5c	F6b	5.10++	20	VI+	VIIIa
		F6b+	5.11a	21	VII−	VIIIb
E3		F6c	5.11b	22	VII	VIIIc
E4	6a	F6c+	5.11c	23	VII+	IXa
		F7a	5.11d		VIII−	IXb
E5	6b	F7a+	5.12a	24	VIII	IXc
		F7b	5.12b	25	VIII+	Xa
E6		F7b+	5.12c	26	IX−	Xb
		F7c	5.12d	27	IX	
E7	6c	F7c+	5.13a	28	IX+	Xc
		F8a	5.13b	29	X−	XIa
E8		F8a+	5.13c	30	X	XIb
		F8b	5.13d	31		
E9		F8b+	5.14a	32	X+	XIc
		F8c	5.14b	33	XI−	XIIa
	7a	F8c+	5.14c	34	XI	XIIb
E999		F9a	5.14d	35		